The Making *of* Environmental Law

The Making *of*

RICHARD J. LAZARUS

Environmental Law

The University of Chicago Press   CHICAGO AND LONDON

RICHARD J. LAZARUS is professor at the Georgetown University
Law Center and director of the Georgetown University Supreme
Court Institute. He served as assistant to the solicitor general of the
United States and has served on the U.S. Environmental Protection
Agency's first national environmental justice advisory committee,
the litigation review committee of the Environmental Defense
Fund, and the national council of the World Wildlife Fund. He has
represented federal, state, and local governments, environmental
organizations, and individuals in thirty-seven cases before the U.S.
Supreme Court. In the early 1980s, he litigated on behalf of the
federal government in *United States v. Chem-Dyne,* which first
established the liability standard under Superfund.

The University of Chicago Press, Chicago 60637
The University of Chicago Press, Ltd., London
© 2004 by The University of Chicago
All rights reserved. Published 2004
Printed in the United States of America

13 12 11 10 09 08 07 06 05 04   1 2 3 4 5

ISBN: 0-226-47037-7 (cloth)

Library of Congress Cataloging-in-Publication Data

Lazarus, Richard J.
    The making of environmental law / Richard J. Lazarus.
        p.   cm.
    Includes bibliographical references and index.
    ISBN 0-226-47037-7 (cloth : alk. paper)
    1. Environmental law—United States.   2. Environmental
law—United States—History.   3. Environmental protection—
United States.   4. Environmental protection—United States—
History.   I. Title.

    KF3775.L398 2004
    344.7304'6—dc22   2004002971

TO M&M, D&D, JEANNIE, SAM & JESSE

Contents

Acknowledgments

This book is the result of years of thinking about environmental law. The book's content necessarily reflects discussions that I have enjoyed and immensely benefited from in different stages of my career, including those with law school classmates and faculty at Harvard in the 1970s, with colleagues at the Department of Justice in both the Environment and Natural Resources Division and the Solicitor General's Office in the 1980s, and with faculty and students at Indiana University, Washington University, and Georgetown University for more than two decades. The book also harmonizes, modifies, and builds on some ideas expressed in a variety of discrete areas of environmental law in several of my prior publications, including "The Tragedy of Distrust in the Implementation of Federal Environmental Law," 54 *Law & Contemp. Probs.* 311 (1991); "Pursuing 'Environmental Justice': The Distributional Effects of Environmental Protection," 87 *Nw. U. L. Rev.* 787 (1993); "Shifting Paradigms of Tort and Property in the Transformation of Natural Resources Law," in *Trends in Natural Resources Law and Policy* (L. MacDonnell & S. Bates eds., 1993); "Meeting the Demands of Integration in the Evolution of Environmental Law: Reforming Environmental Criminal Law," 83 *Geo. L.J.* 2407 (1995); " 'Environmental Racism! That's What It Is,' " 2000 *U. Ill. L. Rev.* 255; "Restoring What's Environmental about Environmental Law in the Supreme Court," 47 *UCLA L. Rev.* 703 (2000); "The Greening of America and the Graying of Environmental Law: Reflections on Environmental Law's First Three Decades in the United States," 20 *Va. Envtl. L.J.* 75 (2001); "A Different Kind of 'Republican Moment' in Environmental Law," 97 *Minn. L. Rev.* 999 (2003).

I am especially indebted to those giants in the legal academy whose early environmental law scholarship played a significant role in shaping modern environmental law in the United States. Three such scholars, Joe Sax,

ix

Bill Rodgers, and Dan Tarlock, were kind enough to comment on a draft manuscript and to offer significant ideas for its improvement. As is well known by many at both the Department of Justice and the Department of the Interior, no wiser environmental advisor exists than Anne Shields, who also generously provided extensive comments on an early draft. Chris Schroeder, an environmental law scholar of enormous intellectual breadth, similarly provided comments that made me rethink portions of the draft, all to its betterment. I was also fortunate that two representatives of what I expect to be the next generation of outstanding environmental law scholars, Sean Donahue and Amanda Cohen Leiter, read early drafts and offered insightful critiques. The final product is far better as a result of all these reviews as it is from workshop presentations at the law schools at Georgetown University, Harvard University, Stanford University, University of Georgia, Tulane University, and Widener University.

Georgetown University Law Center Dean Judith Areen generously provided me with summer research support for this project, and my faculty colleagues, especially Mark Tushnet, Peter Byrne, Hope Babcock, Lisa Heinzerling, Lois Schiffer, Mike Seidman, and Dan Ernst offered me wise counsel when I first commenced the project. The Woodrow Wilson Center for International Scholars, where I served as a Fellow, provided me with an academic year away from law teaching that allowed me to conduct the necessary preliminary research in a collegial environment surrounded by gifted scholars from a variety of academic disciplines and nations. Numerous law students at Georgetown contributed invaluable research assistance for this book, including Michael Doherty, Carrie Jenks, Kate Mayer, Kelly Moser, Dan Eisenberg, and Ramy Sivasubramanian. Mike Doherty, in particular, performed yeoman's work in preparing the graphs of congressional voting reproduced in chapter 7. Georgetown law student and in-house editor John Showalter repeatedly lent his extraordinary talents to the drafting process. I am grateful to John Tryneski of the University of Chicago Press for his early and consistent support for the project, for securing outstanding anonymous peer reviews of drafts, which immensely improved the book's quality, and for bringing such skilled individuals as Leslie Keros and Ashley Cave of the Press to the final stages of the manuscript's preparation and production. David Bemelmans performed a masterly and thoughtful edit of the final product and Martin White skillfully assisted in the preparation of the index.

Finally, my own family played no small role in the book's production. My two sons, Sam and Jesse; my wife, Jeannie Austin; my brother, Billy; and my sisters, Barby and Twiggy, served as a constant source of inspiration. Jeannie, who is also an outstanding lawyer, a gifted writer, and a former EPA economist, was an invaluable sounding board from the very beginning. A kind, supportive, and patient reader, her substantive contributions are present throughout the final product.

Introduction

In the fall of 1975, I worked evenings as a bartender while completing my senior year at the University of Illinois at Urbana-Champaign. I was pursuing degrees in chemistry and economics in anticipation of enrolling in law school the following year, with the ultimate aim of becoming an environmental lawyer. I well remember a conversation I had one evening with a customer who turned out to be a high-ranking corporate officer for the only major private manufacturing facility in the community. Upon learning of my plans to become an environmental lawyer, he gamely responded that environmental law was a mere "fad"—a "flash in the pan" that offered no meaningful future career opportunities. At the time, I silently labeled him a fool: a businessman clearly lacking any appreciation of the compelling nature of the environmental threats and resulting political forces then driving the emergence and spread of environmental law. Now, with the benefit of more than twenty-five years of hindsight, I realize that there was far more force to his intuition than my own youthful self-assuredness allowed me to perceive.

I understood the events of those years—such as the inauguration of Earth Day in April 1970; the creation of legal institutions such as the President's Council on Environment Quality and the U.S. Environmental Protection Agency (EPA) also in 1970; and the passage of federal statutes such as the National Environmental Policy Act of 1969, the Clean Air Act of 1970, and the Federal Water Pollution Control Act Amendments of 1972—to be the inevitable product of irreversible social and political forces emanating from the environmental protest movements of the 1960s. As a twenty-one-year-old, I was not surprisingly unappreciative of the relative youth of events, institutions, and laws then in existence for fewer than five years. I also lacked any comprehension of how extraordinary it was for such laws to have been enacted in light of their enormously radical redistributive thrust and the inherently and deliberately conservative nature of the nation's lawmaking institutions. Nor could I predict the strength and tenacity of the efforts that would attack the redistributive impact of new environmental protection laws.

But what is even more remarkable than my youthful impertinence was that my intuition, notwithstanding its thin basis, turned out to be correct. Environmental law in the United States has been surprisingly persistent—almost stubbornly so. It has not proved to be a "flash in the pan." In fact, the opposite has occurred.

Environmental law's obituary in the United States has been written repeatedly during the past three decades in response to a series of powerful, seemingly overwhelming efforts to reverse course. Not long after initially embracing environmentalism, establishing the EPA, and promoting early environmental legislation, President Richard Nixon became one of environmental protection law's sharpest critics. Nixon, like his successors Presidents Ford and Carter, saw the energy crisis of the mid-1970s as reason for significant retreat from the overly ambitious environmental laws enacted earlier in the decade, which had made more costly the extraction and combustion of domestic coal. Nixon advised his cabinet to "Get off the environmental kick."[1] In 1980, presidential candidate Ronald Reagan campaigned successfully on a platform openly hostile to federal environmental protection regulations, and upon taking office he immediately sought to reduce substantially their scope and reach. In its final year, the George H. W. Bush administration similarly took specific aim at environmental protection, with the Vice President's Competitiveness Council singling out environmental laws as a target for its regulatory reform efforts.

A few years later, in 1995, the Contract with America promoted by Speaker of the House of Representatives Newt Gingrich and the 104th Congress was deliberately designed to cut back on environmental laws by reducing federal budgets used for their implementation, by relaxing requirements that states implement environmental controls, by permitting industry to emit higher levels of pollution, and by compensating property owners for reductions in property value resulting from environmental restrictions. The administration of George W. Bush has, as of this writing, been marked by a series of efforts to reduce the scope and intensity of federal environmental regulations. Indeed, the first few weeks of his presidency witnessed the abandonment by the United States of the Kyoto Protocol to the United Nations Framework Convention on Climate Change, the initial revocation of stricter regulations regulating arsenic in drinking water, the staying of new Clean Water Act standards, and the announcement of a new energy initiative that seemed to contemplate a relaxation of environmental protection and resource conservation requirements. The administration has since reversed many of the major environmental protection and resource conservation regulatory initiatives promulgated by the EPA and by the Departments of the Interior and Agriculture during the Clinton administration.

While it is plainly too soon to know how these most recent reform efforts will ultimately be received, if the past is any guide they are unlikely to succeed and may well unleash a backlash of even more demanding environmental requirements. Environmental protection law in the United States has not only surmounted each major past challenge, but paradoxically it seems to have rebounded and thrived as a result of those challenges. The premature predictions of its demise in the mid-1970s were followed within that same decade by congressional enactment of even more ambitious laws relating to clean air, clean water, and the disposal of hazardous chemicals and wastes. The early efforts of the Reagan administration in the 1980s to reduce the federal role in environmental protection ultimately yielded the adoption of stricter federal environmental controls. The Contract with America was likewise repudiated in the 1990s and seemed to prompt the Clinton administration to embrace a series of new tough regulatory initiatives regarding air and water pollution, mining, and forest lands. Finally, in 2001, partly in response to the Bush administration's environmental policies, Senator James Jeffords of Vermont stunned the Republican Party by becoming an independent aligned with the Democratic Party. Jeffords's switch allowed the Democrats to obtain majority status in the Senate and Jeffords to chair the Senate Committee on the Environment and Public Works.

A snapshot comparison of our nation's environmental laws in January 1970 with those today starkly reveals a dramatically changed legal landscape. In 1970, there were only a smattering of emerging state environmental laws and even fewer at the federal level, which lacked any pollution control agency. Today, there are comprehensive and stringent pollution control and natural resource management laws, and corresponding agencies responsible for their implementation and enforcement, in the federal government, all fifty state governments, and an increasing number of tribal authorities.

In 1970, a few national environmental public interest groups were emerging. Now, membership in those organizations has swelled to millions and the organizations have been joined by literally thousands of grassroots efforts around the country. Environmental education has become a standard part of the curriculum in many schools and there is a $190 billion pollution control industry in the United States that employs more than 1.4 million workers.[2]

The significance of environmental law is not confined, however, to the environmental protection laws themselves or to their most obvious regulating institutions, such as the EPA. Those laws and legal institutions are just the most recognizable expression of the legal transformation. Environmental law's emergence during the past three decades has triggered a broader evolutionary process, as the teachings and values of environmentalism have infused one intersecting category of legal rules after another, transforming the nation's laws in response to the public's demand for environmental protection. Areas of the law as diverse as administrative, bankruptcy, civil rights, corporate, criminal, free speech, insurance, property, securities, tax, and tort law each underwent (and is still undergoing) a significant process of transformation in response to the public's desire to have laws that better reflect the public's environmental protection goals.

The results of this extraordinary transformation of our nation's laws are both palpable and positive. Few would dispute the contention that our air, water, and land are far cleaner today than they would have been absent such legal reform. In many respects, the quality of the natural environment in the United States is better on an absolute scale than it was over three decades ago, notwithstanding the tremendous increases in economic activity during the same period. The air we breathe in many urban areas is far healthier than before. According to a recent EPA report, aggregate emissions of the six principal air pollutants monitored since 1970 have decreased by 25 percent, while energy consumption has increased by 43 percent, vehicular miles traveled by 149 percent, and gross domestic product by 160 percent. Waterways that were no better than open sewers once again support healthy aquatic ecosystems suitable for recreation. Two-thirds of the nation's surveyed waters are currently safe for fishing and swimming, compared to half that number in the early 1970s. Waste disposal, especially the disposal of hazardous wastes, is closely regulated, and the inactive and abandoned waste dumps that serve as the legacy of past inattention are being cleaned up.[3]

No doubt the significant gaps in the coverage, implementation, and enforcement of existing laws leave much work undone and some resources misdirected and unduly fragmented in their focus. More than 121 million Americans still live in areas where pollution levels exceed national ambient air quality standards; nitrogen oxide emissions have increased during the past twenty years; and, because of largely unregulated sources of water pollution, much of the nation's waterways and drinking water fail to meet water quality standards. Yet the far worse environmental catastrophes experienced by many other industrialized nations offer compelling testimony to what environmental law has spared the United States. As a former EPA administrator boasted, there is "no more significant success

story in the realm of public policy" in recent history than U.S. environmental regulation.[4]

How environmental law first emerged, why it has since evolved in the way that it has, and what challenges it presently faces make for a fascinating and revealing story, which this book seeks to tell. In telling that story I show how the effort to fashion pollution control laws confronts special problems both because of the nature of pollution itself and the known means of pollution control and because of our nation's varied processes for lawmaking and the ways those processes relate to important cultural norms. Many of these challenges relate to the varied, complex, and uncertain spatial and temporal dimensions of pollution itself, factors that resist simple redress.

The purpose of this book is to describe these challenges, relate them to actual events that occurred during the past three decades, and discuss what lessons can be gleaned from those decades to meet those same challenges today and in the future. The book is, accordingly, divided into three parts.

Part 1, consisting of three chapters, provides a theoretical overview of the challenges presented by environmental protection for lawmaking. The first two chapters describe the relevant physical features of the natural environment and its transformation by humankind, with emphasis on their spatial and temporal dimensions that especially challenge the fashioning of legal rules. The third chapter analyzes in greater detail how these features relate to the structure of U.S. lawmaking institutions in federal, state, and tribal sovereign authorities and within all three branches of government.

Part 2 is more explanatory in nature. It relates the more theoretical analytic framework regarding the nature of environmental lawmaking developed in part 1 to the actual events surrounding modern environmental law's evolution. The first chapter in part 2 describes in detail why environmental law emerged in the manner and form that it did in the 1970s. The next three chapters of part 2 describe and analyze events and public attitudes in the 1970s, 1980s, and 1990s. For each decade, there is a discussion of both the laws enacted and the major controversies, all expressly linked to the theoretical discussion set out in part 1.

Finally, part 3 is more critical and speculative than the chapters that precede it. The first chapter of part 3 considers the current state of environmental law, including both how environmental protection law has evolved during the past three decades and how those evolutionary trends reflect the features of the ecological problems environmental law seeks to address. The second chapter in part 3 considers the ways in which environmental law is likely to continue to be challenged in the future, especially by ever-changing conceptions of time and space. The final chapter of part 3 considers the potential historical significance of current times given the unprecedented ascendancy to dominant positions in both the federal legislative and executive branches of government officials who favor major reforms of existing environmental laws.

By reviewing the first several decades of modern environmental protection law in the United States, I hope we find not a description of this law's life cycle, but rather a useful history of what will naturally become over time environmental law's early years. It remains for future lawyers and scholars to carry forward the stewardship of environmental law in response to the world they find and to tell their own story in due course.

PART I

Making Environmental Law

Law is inherently contextual, and its content invariably depends on its subject matter. Legal substance must be responsive to the character of the conduct or activity it purports to govern. The focus of some areas of law is itself a legal construction. This is so, for example, with civil procedure, evidence, federal courts, legislation, and both administrative and corporate law. These are all areas of the law largely internal to the legal system. Many other areas of law, however, must be primarily responsive to fixed factors, wholly external to the law itself, that determine the character of the problems and associated human activity that the law seeks to govern. Family law must, for example, respond to certain biological and sociological facts. Telecommunications law must similarly reflect the principles of physics implicated by the electromagnetic spectrum and by various telecommunications technologies.

Environmental law falls largely into the latter, external, category. Its touchstone is ecological injury caused by human activity. Broadly stated, environmental law regulates human activity in order to limit ecological impacts that threaten public health and biodiversity. Its premise is not that any human transformation of the ecosystem should be *per se* unlawful. Environmental law's objective is far more nuanced. It accepts, in light of the laws of thermodynamics, that ecological transformation is both unavoidable and very often desirable, yet seeks to influence the kind, degree, and pace of those transformations resulting from human activity.

Environmental protection law is, however, intrinsically difficult to make in the first instance and can be just as difficult to maintain over time. The source of these difficulties is the relationship between the two most basic ingredients in any effort to develop such laws: (1) the features of the ecological injuries that environmental protection law is designed to prevent, reduce, and redress, and (2) the structure and character of lawmaking institutions in the United States. The special challenges faced by drafters and practitioners of environmental law are derived from some basic incompatibilities between these two ingredients.

Several dominant characteristics of the problems presented by ecological injury are systematically problematic for the ways in which law is made in this nation. As a result of this mismatch, it is exceedingly difficult to enact, implement, and enforce needed environmental laws. Moreover, over the longer term, these laws invariably become sources of great controversy and resistance, generating a destructive cycle of public distrust of law and of lawmaking institutions. Most revealing of this mismatch are the contrasting natures of the spatial and temporal dimensions of ecological injury and of lawmaking institutions. The temporal and spatial dimensions of the former are ill-suited for redress by those of the latter. Indeed, the chasm between the two explains much about the peculiar way in which environmental law has evolved during the past three decades.

The notion that environmental lawmaking presents unique institutional and social challenges, especially for Western legal traditions and lawmaking processes, is not new. Based on just such generalized concerns, many commentators prophesied thirty years ago that environmentalism would inevitably lead to enormous political upheaval in the United States. Some predicted that only a fascist state could meet the challenges of effectively regulating environmental pollution. According to William Ophuls in the initial edition of his darkly foreboding *Ecology and the Politics of Scarcity,* published in 1977, "[t]he golden age of individualism, liberty and democracy is all but over." Garrett Hardin, author of the widely influential essay *The Tragedy of the Commons,* in 1968, similarly contended that what was needed was a "world government that is sovereign in reproduction matters" and went on to claim that "injustice is preferable to total ruin." Still others, while less pessimistic about democracy's capacity to embrace the necessary legal regime, were confident that such revolutionary strides could occur only with the rise of a "Green Party" championing such a cause.[1]

None of these now seemingly extreme prophecies, of course, has been realized, but that is not because their shared assertions concerning the substantial difficulties associated with environmental lawmaking were invalid. They are instead instructive of the capacity of the U.S. legal system for law reform and legal evolution.

This part of the book has three chapters. The first two separately discuss the two basic components of environmental law: (1) the features of the ecological injuries that environmental protection law seeks to address, and (2) the implications of these features for environmental protection law. The final chapter of this part analyzes the inherent mismatch between these characteristics and U.S. lawmaking institutions, and describes the resulting challenges to adopting, implementing, and enforcing environmental law.

CHAPTER ONE

Time, Space, and Ecological Injury

Environmental law must necessarily be responsive to the types of problems it seeks to address, including the physical causes and effects of environmental degradation. Although concerns regarding humankind's impact on the natural environment have only recently intensified sufficiently to prompt the development of a comprehensive legal regime for environmental protection, scientific concerns by the end of the eighteenth century were sufficient to trigger meaningful, focused research. Precipitated in part by observations of the fragility of ecosystems on various islands used by trading companies in the eighteenth and nineteenth centuries, scientists began to study the potential for irreversible environmental damage to such ecosystems. An especially prescient contribution was a paper written in 1859 by the British scientist J. Spottswood Wilson on what he described as "The General and Gradual Desiccation of the Earth and Atmosphere" by, *inter alia,* "changing proportions of oxygen and carbonic acid in the atmosphere."[1]

Without question, however, George Perkins Marsh's classic work *Man and Nature: Or Physical Geography as Modified by Human Action,* published in 1864, is the earliest known comprehensive scientific examination of human activity degrading the earth's ecosystems. His explicit purpose was "to point out the dangers of imprudence and the necessity of caution in all operations which, on a large scale, interfere with the spontaneous arrangements of the organic or the inorganic world." That thesis, which succinctly declares the importance of objective scientific information, the propriety of adhering to a precautionary principle, and the potentially exponential nature of large-scale ecological threats, is as relevant to questions of environmental law in contemporary times as it was to the scientific debate in Marsh's day.[2]

5

While environmental law's overarching rationale may be both simply stated and capable of perseverance, its precise terms necessarily possess neither of those attributes. Its terms are complex and dynamic, susceptible to constant change. The reason, though, is clear. Environmental law cannot be a simple matter because the objects of its concern, the ecosystem and the human activities causing its degradation, are themselves not simple. Environmental law is necessarily almost as complex and dynamic as the ecosystem it seeks to protect.

The Earth's Ecosystem: Complex and Dynamic

Ecologists typically describe the Earth's ecosystem as having two fundamental features. The first is its sheer *complexity;* the second is its *dynamic* nature. For that reason, it should not be surprising that the Earth's ecosystem defies a precise unitary or static description. For some purposes, the global ecosystem is often conceptualized as being divided into the atmosphere, the biosphere, the hydrosphere (aquatic systems), and the lithosphere (the solid portion of the Earth including the outer surface and the solid interior of the planet). For others, the more traditional classification has been to distinguish between air, water, land, plants, and animals. A mixed approach contends that there are seven different types of ecological systems: vegetation cover, animal populations, soil, waters, geomorphology (creation of land forms), atmosphere, and climate.[3]

A sharply contrasting and more accurate image, however, is revealed by focusing on the critically important chemical cycles that interlock, and resist any notion of meaningful boundaries between, various aspects of the ecosystem. Whether basic chemical elements (such as carbon, hydrogen, sulfur, and nitrogen) or chemical compounds essential for life on Earth (such as water), constitutive components of life on Earth are perpetually cycled through virtually all ecological systems in exceedingly complex and dynamic combinations of interrelationships. These geochemical cycles bind the entire global ecosystem together over time and space and are the root cause of the spatial and temporal spillover effects of activities at one place and time on other places and other times.

Chemical cycles in the ecosystem involving elements such as carbon or compounds such as water are likely the cycles best known by members of the public,[4] but they are just two of the many systems essential to ecological sustainability. Sulfur, for example, is found in the atmosphere, hydrosphere, lithosphere, and biosphere, but sulfur's predominant chemical compound differs considerably in each place. The vast majority of Earth's sulfur exists as inorganic metal sulfides and sulfates in rocks in the lithosphere, which consists of a solid shell of soil and rocks at the Earth's surface extending to a depth of fifty kilometers. Sulfur in the soil layer immediately at the Earth's surface, known as the pedosphere, is generally in organic compounds, as is atmospheric sulfur, predominately as carbonyl sulfide.[5]

Sulfur flows between the Earth's crust, atmosphere, and oceans, mobilized by both natural and human causes. The former includes volcanic emissions, biological decay, sea spray, and the weathering of rocks and soils. Human influences in the flow of sulfur include fossil fuel combustion, metal smelting, sulfur mining, and agricultural activities. Both the natural and human sources of sulfur flow are, accordingly, nonuniform in terms of both their spatial and temporal dimensions. They depend on events that predominate in only some parts of the planet and only at certain times.[6]

Soil illustrates how a chemical cycle like sulfur's results in an exceedingly complex and dynamic ecosystem, with heightened potential for spillover effects. Seemingly static to most people, soil is understood by those expert in its science to be an exceedingly dynamic system over both time and space. Soil represents a "zone of interaction at the elusive boundary of the biosphere and geosphere." The various gaseous, liquid, and solid chemical compounds found within any given soil system at any one moment in time, as well as its particular micro-, meso-, and macrobiota, reflect the unique blending of continuous atmospheric, hydrospheric, biologic, and geologic processes occurring there.[7]

The soil system serves several varied essential ecological functions. It not only supports life, both plant and animal, but also provides the physical locus for necessary interactions of the carbon, nitrogen, sulfur, and oxygen cycles. The soil system further serves a primary function in regulating the chemical composition of the atmosphere and hydrosphere. Soil, through its respiration, engages in a constant exchange of gases, including methane, ammonia, hydrogen sulfide, and nitrogen oxides, with the lower atmosphere. Finally, soil serves as an important repository for the accumulation of organic matter, allowing for the natural recovery and recycling of the energy and valuable minerals contained within dead plants and animals.[8]

The Earth's climate is another, and perhaps the most obvious, example of how chemical cycles interact to establish exceedingly complex and dynamic ecosystems. Climate is the product of five interwoven ecological subsystems: the atmosphere, oceans, cryosphere (consisting of ice and snow), vegetation, and land. The interactions of these subsystems are exceedingly complex; for example, changes in one part of the climatic system at a given time can affect other parts of the system at a later time. Again, such effects may be far removed both spatially and temporally, or they may be quite localized—immediate both in both time and space. Little clarity exists in identifying the precise cause and effect of climatic changes.[9] As noted by one prominent academic expert on predicting long-term climate behavior,

"If you were going to pick a planet to model, this is the last planet you would choose."[10]

As with the sulfur cycle, there are both natural and human sources of climatic change. Natural sources are either external or internal. An example of an external source is a change in solar output or a change in the tilt of Earth's axis, either one of which may significantly affect the amount of radioactive energy in the atmosphere. Internal sources of climatic change include naturally occurring feedback loops between different parts of the system, such as between the atmosphere and the polar ice caps, in which a change in one can prompt a responsive shift in the other with potentially countervailing climatic impacts. Human influences on climatic change include industrial emissions of carbon dioxide and other chemical compounds that promote atmospheric warming through the so-called greenhouse effect, deforestation that reduces consumption of carbon dioxide, and use of aerosols that may affect the balance of solar radiation in the atmosphere.[11]

This picture of the natural environment and its complex array of interlocking ecological systems sharply contrasts with the once-dominant but now-antiquated notion of nature as dependent on the maintenance of a static equilibrium. Nature is not at all static, but is constantly changing. As aptly described by one ecologist, nature "is only a shimmer of populations in space and time."[12] Hence, transformation or change cannot itself be dubbed either "natural" or "nonnatural," or for that matter always be labeled "good" or "bad." The absence of such a fixed natural baseline, of course, renders far more difficult any possible sorting out of human versus natural sources of ecological change, let alone determining which transformations should, as a matter of policy, be allowed, restricted, or even promoted. Aldo Leopold's famous maxim that "[a] thing is right when it tends to preserve the integrity, stability, and beauty of the biotic community" and "wrong when it tends otherwise" is wonderfully evocative but, as Leopold himself understood, inapposite as a touchstone for the formation of ecosystem management. Ecosystems are dynamic in space and time and effective ecosystem management must, accordingly, constantly reconcile nature's spatial and temporal scales with those of humankind, including the latter's often far more limited planning horizons.[13]

The Transformation of Earth

Environmental law's challenge is to regulate, where possible, the process of ecological transformation. This includes regulating the *extent* of transformation, its geographic *location,* and, at least as important, its *pace.* While much disagreement persists about each, it seems quite plain that the spatial and temporal scales of ecological transformation have increased from the local and regional to the global. We have traveled far beyond merely scratching the surface of the planet's ecosystem. Today, we are "altering the fundamental flows of chemicals and energy that sustain life," and "no ecosystem on earth's surface is free of pervasive human influence." The twentieth century witnessed a dramatic escalation of humankind's impact on the natural environment in virtually every aspect of the planet's ecosystem: atmosphere, hydrosphere and biosphere.[14]

On a global scale, humankind has transformed 40 percent of the land surface, increased carbon dioxide levels by 20 percent, and used 50 percent of the fresh water supplies currently available. Ten to fifteen percent of land is now given over to agricultural, urban, or industrial uses. In 1995, 22 percent of recognized marine fisheries were being overfished and 44 percent were already being fully exploited. In the United States, 40 percent of the nation's fisheries were classified as overutilized and 43 percent were fully utilized. Worldwide, an estimated 15 percent of all plant species are currently threatened with extinction.[15]

Here again, the effects of human activity on the soil, the sulfur cycle, and the climate illustrate what is a widespread ecological phenomenon. Human activities have resulted in significant soil losses due to irrigation, desertification, agriculture, and settlement and road construction. Estimated total "losses of organic carbon from the humusphere of the earth, just within the history of agricultural civilization, is 268 million tons or 15.8% of the original stock."[16]

The dust bowl storm of May 1934 is nothing more than an extreme example of the norm. Tough economic times in the aftermath of the Great Depression resulted in too-rapid cultivation of farmlands in the Great Plains. The exposed soil combined with an especially dry, hot year to produce an ecological disaster: a massive storm that spread approximately 300 million tons of dirt over fifteen hundred miles, all the way to the northeastern United States. A contemporary example of the same effect is the airborne dust resulting from the desertification of thousands of square miles in China and western Africa. Immense clouds of dust (sometimes binding with toxic industrial pollutants) from China now regularly cause schools to be closed, flights to be canceled, and local health clinics to be filled in South Korea. Plumes of dust from both China and Africa travel thousands of miles through the jet stream and reach the western United States. Worldwide, approximately 430 million hectares (seven times the size of Texas) have been irreversibly destroyed by erosion. Within our own borders, the United States currently loses 1.7 billion tons of topsoil a year to

erosion and during the entire twentieth century lost an amount of topsoil
that had taken a thousand years to be produced.[17]

Human activity has similarly affected the sulfur cycle. Consumption of
fossil fuel, metal smelting, and other activities have been so pervasive that
"global fluxes of sulfur induced by humans and those from nature are of
comparable magnitude." Because, moreover, many of those human activities are concentrated in certain heavily industrialized locations, the local
contribution of sulfur flow from human activities can substantially exceed
the level generated by nature.[18]

Finally, while considerable scientific controversy continues to surround
theories of climatic change, the "modern increase in [carbon dioxide] presents the clearest and best documented significant human alteration of the
Earth system." A consensus now exists within the "climate research community that carbon dioxide levels from human activity probably already
affects climate detectably and will drive substantial climate change in the
[twenty-first] century." What remains far less certain is precisely what will
be the myriad and multiplying impacts of climate change on human health
and biodiversity.[19]

The spatial expansion of the effect of human activities on the natural
environment is not, however, exclusively global. Environmental impacts
can also result in localized problems. Extremely low concentrations of
trace pollutants in the biosphere, between one part per billion and one part
per million, present serious environmental threats in discrete geographic
locations. This pollution is the result of trace metals deposited by many
industrial processes, including mining, waste incineration, and fuel combustion. The worldwide increases in the amounts of lead, arsenic, cadmium, and mercury in the biosphere resulting from human activity are
now several times greater than the levels of these elements attributable to
natural releases. Trace pollutants are likewise the by-product of the vast organic chemical industry, which both creates and incidentally releases into
the environment new, often quite persistent, chemical compounds. There
are many localized "hot spots" where these contaminants persist and accumulate. And, at least as unsettling, there is virtually no place on the globe,
from the most seemingly remote polar icecap to the bottom of the oceans,
where evidence of such contamination cannot be found.[20]

Whether global or local in nature, discerning the cause and effect of
ecological transformation is often impossible, or at a minimum daunting. The underlying interactions can elude ready observation because they
occur either over huge spatial dimensions or, conversely, only microscop-
ically. Further, a single phenomenon often has multiple, diffuse causes
from a variety of environmental media with unanticipated and undetected
synergistic results. For this reason, sometimes even the best-intentioned

curative efforts go tragically awry. Such was the result of the classic intervention in Borneo in the 1960s when public health workers sought to control mosquito-borne malaria by spraying village huts with the insecticide DDT. The resulting chain of events unwittingly caused even worse consequences for all. The local lizard population was decimated after eating DDT-contaminated food, leading to decreases in the local cat population that was dependent on lizards as a dietary mainstay. The scarcity of cats led to a population explosion of caterpillars and rats that the cats had previously kept in check, with the caterpillars destroying the thatched roofs and the rats causing increases in disease within the village.[21]

But it is not simply the scope or complexity of ecological transformation that challenges the implementation of effective environmental law, but also its temporal dimension, including the pace of the transformative process. Life forms can adapt to ecological change, at least to some extent—that, after all, is the evolutionary process. But time is required for adaptation, and the accelerating pace of ecological transformation increasingly precludes that possibility for plant and animal species, as well as for the microbiota underpinning all life on Earth.

Irreversible effects are one obvious result of the increased pace of change. Such effects may take the form of the extinction of a species, the depletion of a fossil fuel resource, or the destruction of a unique land formation. Even "flow" resources, which are theoretically renewable to the extent that their supplies may be replenished by natural processes, can become irretrievably lost when the pace of their consumption outstrips the potential for their replenishment.

The now-looming threatening cataclysmic collapses within various aquatic ecosystems suffering from overexploitation are emblematic of the problem. Technological advances in commercial fishing techniques have decimated fishing grounds that not long ago were considered too enormously abundant to be threatened. The rapid destruction of wetlands risks destroying an essential ecological link between land and water ecosystems, both as a place of interaction and redistribution and as an important buffer protecting one system from the excesses of the other. The Black Sea, once the source of abundant supplies of sturgeon, mackerel, and anchovies, and boasting of popular beach resorts, is suffering from an ecological collapse caused by pollution originating from at least six different nations. As described by one Russian biologist, "Even if we stopped all the pollution as if by magic, it would be impossible to go back to the 1950s. Nature has its own laws."[22]

Another feature of the temporal dimension of ecological injury is its inherently threshold character. One cannot safely assume a predictable linear correspondence between cause and effect. Just a little more pollution or a little more natural resource extraction does not necessarily lead to just a little more environmental harm or a little less available resource. A catastrophic consequence may instead result.[23] The reasons for this unpredictability are deeply ingrained and largely unavoidable. They are an expression of the ecosystem's sheer complexity, within which there exist cliffs and abrupt thresholds. At concentrations below a certain level, an agent might show no discernible effect. But at concentrations slightly above that level, the ecological effects of the agent can be widespread, irreversible, and perhaps even unforeseen. In a chemistry lab, the chemical reaction sought may not occur unless the two chemicals to be mixed are in the requisite physical states and concentrations. The same dependencies exist in the natural world. While there is much linearity in ecological cause and effect, there are also some instances of "all or nothing." Coral reefs, for instance, can suffer just such threshold ecological collapses in response to incremental changes in temperature or in the concentrations of toxic contaminants. An increase in the usual maximum temperature as small as one to two degrees centigrade can be fatal to life within the reefs.[24]

The roles of human population and technology also promote a tendency toward exponential impacts. Increases in human population are themselves exponential and place proportionate pressures on the ecosystem. Technological innovation, while creating opportunities for increased resource efficiencies, also creates the potential for even greater resource exploitation and further "advances" in human health and welfare, and thus, increased population. The resulting increases in the scale of human interaction with the ecosystem place the sustainability of the latter at greater risk absent self-imposed limits.

The impact of even a level rate of consumption may, at least for a non-renewable resource, become exponential over time as the proportion of the resource remaining unexploited shrinks. A decrease of two units is only 2 percent when there is a starting level of one hundred units. When, however, there are only ten units to start with, that same two units now represents 20 percent of the available resource. So too, even seemingly small increases in rates of consumption or pollution may in relatively short order reach extraordinarily high levels. An increase of merely 3.5 percent a year, whether in the ability to exploit a resource or in the demand for its production, leads to a doubling of consumption every twenty years. The early effects of such an exponential trend are thereby naturally disguised for the first several iterations. No matter how small the starting point, however, it does not take long before a simple function of doubling produces overwhelming consequences.[25]

Actual human transformation of the Earth's ecosystem suggests just such trends. World human population did not reach its first billion until about 195 years ago, but to reach the next succeeding billions required only 115, 35, 15, and 11 years respectively. A comparable pattern is revealed by examining the various rates of ecological transformation occurring in the period beginning ten thousand years ago through 1985. Taking that total transformation as 100 percent and then estimating the dates for reaching the first, second, third, and fourth quartiles of transformation for several indicators, the pace of change is starkly suggested. Water withdrawals reached those quartile percentage stages in 1925, 1955, 1975, and 1985; carbon releases did so in 1815, 1920, 1960, and 1985; and deforestation did so in 1700, 1850, 1915, and 1985.[26]

The projections for the extinction of plant and animal species reflect similar exponential trends. Ecologist Thomas Lovejoy predicted that as many as 20 percent of all species would become extinct by the close of the twentieth century, and the extinction rates for the tropics, where there are as many as ten times the number of species than in temperate zones, were predicted to be even higher for that century. Lovejoy further claimed that "projections on into the twenty-first century, given continuing deforestation, are that 66% of plant species and 69% of Amazon birds will be lost." Habitat destruction is the primary cause of this mass extinction, but focusing on habitat masks what is often a far more complicated chain of events. "[B]ecause of the intricately interlocking nature of ecosystems, direct anthropogenic perturbations cause more subtle secondary effects through . . . 'cascades' of species interaction."[27]

One recent comprehensive examination of the biochemical flows of the biosphere published in 1990 concluded that "[o]nly a few of the components of the biosphere examined . . . attained 50% of their current level of change before the twentieth century, and probably the majority attained this level around or after the midpoint of this century." A similar survey published in 1997 concluded "[t]he rates, scales, kinds, and combinations of changes occurring now are fundamentally different from those at any other time in history; we are changing Earth more rapidly than we are understanding it." Finally, the National Academy of Sciences published in 2002 an article that purported to assess the relationship between human demands and the biosphere's regenerative capacity, concluding that "humanity's load corresponded to 70% of the capacity of the global biosphere in 1961, and grew to 120% in 1999."[28]

The temporal dimension of human transformation of the ecosystem has other consequences as well. Some pollutants simply persist in the natural environment over long periods of time. Radioactivity, lasting thousands of year, is an obvious example, but not an isolated one. Many modern chemicals, ranging from DDT to polychlorinated biphenyls (PCBs), resist ready breakdown. Just as numerous sources of environmental degradation may be spatially diffused, complicating their control at any one moment in time, so too may sources be temporally diffused. Thus, trace pollutants that persist within the natural environment may accumulate over time and, while remaining at nonthreatening levels for years, might suddenly cross a threshold. Moreover, because some environmental systems such as those in certain population systems and river systems have threshold points at which huge jumps in impact occur, unexpectedly crossing such a threshold can lead over time to catastrophic results. For instance, increases in water temperature in areas of the Atlantic Ocean apparently have no discernible effect on the development of hurricanes until a threshold temperature of 26 degrees Celsius is crossed; but once crossed, there is a nonlinear increase in the spawning of hurricanes. Global warming may well already be destined to have such a devastating impact.[29]

Finally, the temporal rates of exposure frequently determine the consequences. For instance, human health may not be adversely affected by exposure to low levels of pollutants over a relatively short period of time, yet health may be significantly harmed by exposure to an even lower level of pollution over a much longer time. Similarly, exposure to certain pollutants at extremely high levels may cause harm even if the time of exposure is exceedingly short.

Seasonal variations in climatic conditions often add a further related temporal element. Wind, precipitation, and temperature all vary by season, and each is likely to affect the environmental impact of pollution in air, land, or water. They may exacerbate the potential harm or substantially mitigate it, even eliminating the need for controls. Water flows are generally greater in the spring and, consequently, a water body is then better able to assimilate pollutants than it can at times of low water flows. The hole in the ozone layer varies seasonably because of differences in atmospheric temperature. Accordingly, whether designed to safeguard human health or some particular aspect of the ecosystem, effective pollution controls necessarily possess distinct temporal and sometimes seasonal dimensions. There may need to be one set of controls to avoid high exposure rates over short period of time (e.g., eight hours), a distinct set of controls for yet another exposure period (e.g., twenty-four hours), and perhaps even another for a longer time period (e.g., one year). An even more precise finetuning would then account for possible seasonal variations.

No matter the setting, environmental law cannot dispel the dynamic and complex nature of the Earth's ecosystem. Nor can it ignore the closely related spatial and temporal features of ecologic injury. These factors are controlling throughout the establishment of environmental protection standards, including setting pollution control levels for ambient air or water, establishing the best management practices aimed at reducing environmental harms caused by soil erosion, curbing fossil fuel combustion in order to restore balance to sulfur flows, or imposing restrictions on deforestation because of its impact on global climate change. As the defining characteristic of the cause and effect underlying ecological injury, the ecosystem's dynamic complexity supplies the context for any regime of law that seeks to govern human activity that transforms the natural environment. As discussed in the next chapter, the implications of this complexity for lawmaking institutions are considerable.

CHAPTER TWO

The Implications of Ecological Injury for Environmental Protection Law

The varied features of ecological injury have many direct implications for making environmental protection laws, providing opportunities for innovative lawmaking, presenting peculiar challenges, and restricting some choices. As succinctly described by one recent commentator, environmental law has difficulty developing legal rules because "nature refuses to cooperate."[1] This chapter discusses the dominant characteristics of environmental protection laws and how they are largely unavoidable reflections of the nature of the problem of ecological injury that they seek to address. These characteristics include *complexity, scientific uncertainty, dynamism, precaution,* and *controversy.*

Complexity

For those who study, teach, or practice environmental law, its complexity is virtually a mantra. Complexity is "[t]he catchword for the study of environmental law" and "the price of escape from awkward universality."[2] Although there are ultimately any number of interrelated reasons for environmental law's complexity, the dominant causes are twofold: first, the complexities within the workings of the ecosystem itself, and second, the complexities of a highly industrialized economy, the activities of which are the primary object for environmental regulation. Lawmakers cannot avoid those complexities; instead, they must ultimately subsume them within a regulatory scheme.

An effective legal regime for environmental protection must consider these complexities when deciding what level of ecological transformation is permissible and then in deciding how best to achieve that objective. If a particular ecological threat has multiple spatial and temporal pathways, the law must take each of them into account in fashioning a program for legal governance. Otherwise, it risks both underregulation and overregulation. For instance, industrial dischargers of water pollutants often complain that the federal Clean Water Act disproportionately targets their discharges for control, especially in light of the increasingly high percentage of water quality problems caused by contaminated runoff from agricultural activities, which are much less regulated.

The amount of complex scientific information—from physics, chemistry, geology, and biology—underlying any effective pollution control standard is simply extraordinary. The fashioning of any such standard requires assessment of the multiple pathways that a particular pollutant has into, for example, ambient air or water. The standard must consider the impact of seasonal, geographic, and climatic variations, and that inquiry should examine possible synergistic reactions between different chemical constituents within the atmosphere or the aquatic system under different ecological conditions. The environmental standards must also take into account the often enormously varying susceptibilities of different aspects of the natural environment, including species and subspecies of animal and plant life, to a broad temporal range of exposures to each of the molecules in the chemical pollutant's degradation pathway. Wide variations exist not only between species but also within them, so that a pollution standard that is protective of most individual organisms may nonetheless present a very serious health threat to an especially vulnerable subpopulation.

National ambient air quality standards for particulate matter under the federal Clean Air Act, for instance, have to take into account not just one source of particulate matter, but all possible sources, both regulated and unregulated, natural and manmade. There are many types of pollutants that contribute to the presence of particulate matter in the atmosphere, and their respective contributions are highly dependent on the occurrence of chemical reactions between various chemical compounds in the atmosphere. Wind, temperature, and atmospheric pressure are accordingly relevant. Moreover, the adverse impact of particulate matter on human health depends on the size of the particle and the duration of the exposure. That impact, of course, varies considerably among persons with different susceptibilities rooted in personal physical and biologic differences, as well as lifestyle differences. The challenge for a government agency responsible for promulgating a national ambient air quality standard for particulate matter is to choose a legal standard that sensibly accounts for all these variables without being overwhelmed by the associated scientific complexity.[3]

Similar, and even greater, scientific complexities are repeated and magnified through efforts to fashion environmental law. The law must draw distinctions depending on levels of ecological concern and susceptibility to redress. Because those distinctions depend on an extraordinarily complex array of ecological interrelationships, environmental law necessarily incorporates those complexities into controlling legal tests. That is why any legal definition for what waste is "hazardous" is inevitably so technically complex. A chemical compound such as sulfuric acid may pose huge adverse risks in one setting, present none in another, and provide possible benefits as a useful consumer product in yet another. The component elements and chemical structure of a compound are not the exclusive basis of its potential hazardousness. The presence of other chemicals, an agent's potential mobility (enhanced by water or air), and prevailing temperature and atmospheric pressure are all determinative of the nature and degree of hazards presented. So long as the hazardousness of a particular chemical compound is so context dependent, the legal test for hazardousness must incorporate all those contextual intricacies if it is to avoid being either too broad or too narrow.[4]

That is likewise why the legal definition for what constitutes a "wetland" for the purpose of water pollution control law is necessarily so cumbersome, technically inaccessible, and potentially controversial. A lawmaker can conclude that "wetlands" should be protected, but then must look to the scientist for guidance in defining that legal construct in a way that addresses the environmental concerns underlying the desire for a wetlands protection law. Under existing federal law, whether a particular property is a wetland turns on the presence of certain saturation levels of water and the existence of certain vegetation types on the property at a specific time of year. These are not physical characteristics plainly visible to the untrained eye and, therefore, often disrupt private expectations and generate opposition when landowners are informed of the legal restrictions imposed on their properties. But so long as the ecological importance of that portion of an ecological system in fact turns on its ability to serve several complex functions in nature, the legal test for what constitutes a wetland must reflect an inquiry of similar complexity. Here, too, the price of ignoring these complexities would be to fail to impose necessary restrictions without which potentially serious environmental consequences may ensue. The Supreme Court, in explicit recognition of the "inherent difficulties of defining the precise bounds" between land and waters, has stressed the corresponding propriety of judicial deference to the "ecological judgment" of expert agencies charged by Congress with making that definition.[5]

Yet a further reason for the complexity of environmental law is the complex nature of the various human activities it must govern. A system of laws that seeks to dictate maximum pollutant emissions levels based on the degree of pollutant reduction technically achievable must reflect the complexities inherent in knowing both the current state of pollutant reduction technology and what it could be in the future. Furthermore, there

are different technologies available for different sizes and kinds of manufacturing processes. Moreover, the available technology also depends very
much on timing, including whether a particular facility is new or existing.
An existing facility has less flexibility in its ability to adapt to new technology than does a proposed facility that can be constructed accordingly.
Environmental protection law inevitably reflects all such complex and intricate distinctions.

The economic feasibility of measures to reduce pollution only further
increases the complexities faced by lawmakers. A system of laws that seeks
to dictate emissions levels based on what is economically feasible must respond to the complexities of forces in a modern economy. Economic feasibility depends on the costs of existing and future technologies, a question
that turns, as before, on myriad factors, such as the kind of industrial process, its size, and its age. Indeed, economic feasibility as the legal standard
can be further complicated by requiring that the extent of pollution control
required be based on economic profitability and/or viability, a touchstone
dependent on ever-shifting forces within the economy that are likely just
as intricate as the interlocking relationships within some ecosystems.

Of course, a system of laws could ignore all of these scientific and economic complexities and simply set forth a set of bright line rules based on a
fictionalized schema of how the natural environment and the human economy operate. The most likely result, however, would be environmental
laws that were unduly burdensome in many significant respects and unduly relaxed in many others, achieving the worst of both worlds. Serious
environmental degradation would not be prevented because critical aspects
of problems would go unaddressed. And valued human activities would be
curtailed for no good reason, at least in terms of achieving environmental
protection goals, while other, damaging, activities would go unhindered.

Neither the complexities of nature nor those of our modern market
economy are incidental factors in fashioning a legal regime for environmental protection. They are central, necessary features that not only must
be addressed by environmental protection law, but must also be closely reflected in the many legal distinctions contained therein.

Scientific Uncertainty

Scientific uncertainty is another inevitable feature of any system of laws
for environmental protection. The most obvious source of this uncertainty
is the same as the source of environmental law's complexity: the elaborate
intricacies of the workings of the natural environment and, therefore, the
causal mechanisms underlying its transformation. The sheer complexity
of the global ecosystem defies our ready understanding. We often do not

know exactly what will happen if certain environmental restrictions are imposed, and we are sometimes just as blind as to what will happen if they are not.

The spatial dimensions of ecological injury suggest part of the explanation for this unavoidable uncertainty. The scope of change is simultaneously too small and too big. Much of the critical causal mechanics of the process of ecological transformation occurs at microscopic and subatomic levels where scientific observation is limited. Even sophisticated theories regarding quantum mechanical forces at the subatomic level defy accurate measurement, as the observation process is itself inherently disruptive of the measurements being taken.

On the other hand, the extremely large spatial dimensions associated with other types of ecological injury likewise generate tremendous uncertainties. The larger the spatial dimension, the greater the likelihood that there will be an increase in the number of potentially contributing sources and other variables complicating the sorting out of cause and effect. When the use of aerosol cans in North America and the introduction of different chemicals from a host of other human activities elsewhere on the globe are all somehow contributing to the destruction of the ozone layer through a series of chemical reactions, the scientific challenge of determining the "cause" of the problem is daunting.

The temporal dimensions of ecological injury create uncertainty in an analogous fashion. Ecological injuries can occur over very long periods of time, even crossing generations. The longer the time period, the greater the number of intervening activities, and thus the greater the difficulty of unraveling cause and effect. Negative response mechanisms within the ecosystem can exacerbate the problem. For example, deforestation can increase the "greenhouse effect" and thereby promote global warming, but the resulting lack of vegetation on the land leads to greater reflection of solar radiation and thus a cooling tendency. Also, although increases in carbon dioxide in the atmosphere cause global warming through the greenhouse effect, such a warming can cause a rise in the oceans from the melting of polar icecaps, which in turn reduces the amount of carbon dioxide in the atmosphere once absorbed by the oceans.[6]

Even apart from the tendency of longer periods of time to complicate matters, the passage of time leads to more uncertainty simply due to the natural tendency of information and memory to dissipate. It is difficult to predict far into the future, but it is also difficult to recall precise circumstances of the past. Legal rules that purport to assign responsibilities for harms or threats of harm now occurring but resulting from conduct that occurred far in the past face considerable informational obstacles. Somewhat paradoxically, the very immediacy of other ecological injuries generate its own scientific uncertainties. When a proposed course of conduct must be regulated in the face of exponentially increasing ecological threats, there is little time for meaningful scientific inquiry. The upshot is that decisions have to be hastily made before much of the relevant information is known.

A third source of the scientific uncertainty surrounding environmental law derives from the law's goal of protecting human health from harms caused by environmental contamination. Determining what types, levels, and periods of exposure to contaminants cause harm to human health is plainly difficult even under the best regime of scientific examination and testing. The workings of the human body are far from perfectly understood. But what makes the degree of uncertainty especially pronounced for environmental law is the impossibility of using the scientific approaches that would, at least in theory, most readily provide the needed information regarding human health. A quite direct way, for instance, of determining the impact of different levels of chemical compounds on human health would be to expose different groups of individuals to varying concentrations of the compounds in a controlled laboratory setting while holding other factors constant. By exposing human subjects to a variety of environmental media containing different combinations of potentially harmful chemicals, scientists could determine the levels at which the agents became harmful or lethal. For obvious reasons, such human experimentation is forbidden, as it should be. The result, nonetheless, is that lawmakers are required to make determinations regarding environmental cause and effect based on information, including epidemiological studies, that are necessarily fraught with uncertainties.

The problem of scientific uncertainty is so endemic to environmental law that it has prompted some scientists to refer to the science of environmental protection law by different names—"trans-science" or "science policy"—reflecting an awkward melding of public policy and pure science. When scientists are compelled to give scientific "answers" within time constraints under which no such answer based in science is possible, they are no longer strictly acting purely as scientists—or at least they are not acting consistently with the norms of their scientific disciplines. Instead, they are being invited to fill in the substantial gaps left open from scientific inquiry with more subjective personal judgment and, unavoidably, with value judgments and biases not drawn from their scientific expertise.[7]

Dynamism

Environmental law is also naturally dynamic. Because of the complexity and scientific uncertainty surrounding ecological injury, much of environmental law, particularly the environmental standards themselves, are based on "scientifically informed value judgments."[8] Because so much of the scientific information underlying environmental law is tentative and uncertain, and thereby subject to frequent revision, the momentum towards legal evolution is constant. "[E]very solution seems provisional and subject to reevaluation as new information appears and old solutions are tested against experience."[9]

New scientific information regarding the causes and the effects of environmental pollution and other ecological threats is constantly coming to light. Such information can lead to either the tightening or relaxing of standards. New data can prompt wholesale shifts in regulatory focus from one set of possible causes to another. It is not at all unusual in the environmental field to have the benign recast as the malignant or (less frequently) the malignant as the benign.

The chemical dioxin, which is a shorthand reference to many related chemical compounds, provides a good example. During the early 1980s, concerns about dioxin prompted widespread, costly environmental cleanups and the imposition of stringent nationwide regulation of emissions into air and water. Entire towns were evacuated and literally shut down. A decade later, however, in the early 1990s, both government and industry officials raised questions, based on the results of further scientific research, concerning the validity of those earlier concerns. Many condemned the dioxin scare of the 1980s as a classic overreaction to unjustified public fears and, accordingly, as a prime example of what was wrong with environmental law. With the passage of yet another decade, however, we seem to be coming full circle. The latest scientific evidence suggests yet again that dioxin does in fact present the kinds of serious hazards to human health that were feared in the 1980s.[10]

Another reason for the dynamic character of environmental law is that nonscientific changes can affect the types of controls that are thought to be necessary. Demographic shifts over time can warrant more or less regulation, or, at least, different regulatory emphases. Increases or decreases in population mean that the number of exposed individuals is higher or lower, which policymakers may conclude warrants correspondingly higher or lower compliance costs. Changes in the age or diet of the exposed population may similarly affect the risk presented from a fixed level of contaminants. Likewise, changes in technology may have a dramatic impact. A requirement that was once technologically or economically infeasible can, upon discovery of new technologies or new substitute commercial products, be quickly rendered feasible. In short, to the extent that environmental law turns on assumptions about market forces or available technology, shifts in those underlying assumptions inevitably drive similar shifts in environmental legal requirements.

Finally, environmental law necessarily changes over time because nature itself does so. Nature is not static, but quite dynamic. Ecosystems evolve over time—indeed, nature's capacity for evolutionary change is its principal strength. Because, however, nature changes in this ongoing way, so too must the environmental laws governing its protection. Regulations must reflect current ecological realities rather than the ecosystems of the past. For this reason, some argue that the entire notion of "preservation" of nature is both falsely premised and misguided.[11]

Precaution

Another significant aspect of environmental protection law that derives from the nature of ecological injury is its primary focus on the prevention, rather than redress, of environmental harms. Redress is rarely a viable option because of the sheer impossibility or at least limited effectiveness of cleaning up environmental harm once it takes place. Nature's complexity makes it extremely difficult to put the pieces back together again: the quality of individual human life cannot be readily recreated and human health frequently cannot be restored. Nor can sustainable aquifer formations or wetlands be "created," though some fledgling efforts have been attempted. In short, the irreversible nature of much ecological injury drives environmental law to reflect a precautionary principle and to focus, accordingly, on preventing the realization of environmental risks rather than the redressing of environmental harms.[12]

Environmental law's precautionary focus is further compelled by the continuing nature of ecological injury. While it may be relatively easy to address a threat at an early stage, it is often harder if one waits until there is an actual physical manifestation of the problem in the ecosystem. By then, the ecological stakes may not only be higher, but the dimensions of the threat may be so great that it is virtually impossible to do anything about it. Environmental threats have a tendency to persist, spread, and accumulate over time and space. The longer one waits, the harder it can be to eliminate the threat.

It is the exponential character of ecological injury, however, that not only renders the need for risk regulation especially compelling, but also leads inexorably to the regulation of low probability risks. As previously described, many ecological risks, and the attendant environmental stakes, do not persist or increase in a merely linear fashion. Ecological injury is instead frequently marked by exponential growth. The longer one waits, the far greater is both the likelihood of the risk being realized and the amount of injury threatened. Indeed, what was once a fairly small, low probability risk susceptible to relatively easy redress can become a very large, highly probable risk—one that resists elimination and is capable of producing catastrophic, irreversible consequences.[13]

For this same reason, prudence supports the precautionary regulation of risks while still small, before they reach those higher likelihood, potentially more threatening stages. When action is taken while the risk is small, the downside of a mistake is minimized, at least in terms of the environmental harm that might be realized. Yet, at the same time, the tendency for environmental protection law to focus on small risks generates other, less desirable, features of this area of lawmaking, including attendant scientific uncertainty of ecological cause and effect, severe and widespread distributional implications of environmental restrictions, and associated controversy arising out of the implementation of controls without a known harm. The latter two features of environmental law are discussed next.

Controversy

Environmental law is inherently controversial, for reasons rooted in the spatial and temporal dimensions of ecological injury. Environmental law's controversial nature is not, moreover, simply a recasting of the scientific uncertainty surrounding environmental law or its dynamic character. No doubt those features exacerbate much of the controversy surrounding environmental law, but they do not provide its essential fuel. What feeds much of what is controversial about environmental law is instead the enormous distributional conflicts unavoidable in the establishment of a legal regime for environmental protection. These include conflicts over enormous natural resource wealth, human health, and sharply contrasting values.

The distributional implications of any scheme of environmental law-making extend, of course, to both the associated benefits and the related costs. There are, on the one hand, the benefits that flow from preventing ecological injury and, on the other, the costs of such prevention. The former includes not only the direct ecological injury prevented, but also all of the proximately related consequences that are avoided (e.g., damage to human health and welfare). The latter includes the wide range of preventive steps that are taken in response to an environmental restriction, such as the installation of end-of-pipe treatment, the denial of access to certain natural resources, the curtailment of activities, and the requirement of lifestyle changes. The Office of Management and Budget (OMB) recently estimated in a draft report that, as of September 2001, the total aggregated annual costs associated with all major federal environmental regulations was between $120 billion and $203 billion and the annual benefits were between $120 billion and $1.78 trillion.[14]

Environmental law is riddled with controversy because there is almost always a mismatch in the allocation of those distributional costs and benefits. Those who receive the benefits will often not be required to absorb the related costs, and vice versa. Indeed, quite the opposite is true. Nature tends to ensure that there will be an inequitable distributional skewing of who benefits and who pays. The reason for this natural inequity is basic to the structure of the ecosystem and the nature of ecological injury. The ecosystem is dominated by shared resources, such as air and water, as well as by a series of interlocking chemical cycles that bind together otherwise seemingly distinct ecological subsystems. The nexus of resources is the fundamental and inevitable source of the spillovers from local causes to far-flung effects that environmental law addresses, and any such spillover is, by its very nature, a distributional conflict.

Natural resources such as air and water create a common pool over both space and time. The natural fluidity and mobility of those resources adds to their common pool nature by magnifying the impact of actions at one time and place on the same resource at other times and places. Actions upwind are likely to have impacts downwind, just as actions upstream are likely to have impacts downstream. So too, though less obviously, do animal and plant species exhibit common pool tendencies both because of their reproductive capabilities and their interdependencies with other parts of an ecosystem. An impact on one species not only affects the viability of that species, but may well have a significant impact on other species of plants and animals in both the present and the future. The classic instance, discussed in the previous chapter, of the chain reaction of ecological consequences unwittingly triggered in Borneo in the 1960s as a result of introducing DDT to kill malaria-infected mosquitos exemplifies a widespread, not atypical, ecological phenomenon.

Any of the host of chemical cycles throughout the natural environment produces similar distributional consequences. A disruption of one part of a cycle has effects throughout the cycle. These effects are felt in other places and at other times for the simple reason that the cycles are themselves physical links between different ecological subsystems and operate continuously over time. The destruction of rainforests in the Amazon may, because those rainforests had consumed carbon dioxide from the atmosphere, increase the amount of carbon dioxide in other parts of the globe. Such increases in turn can promote global warming and as a result a rise in ocean levels and changes, therefore, in the hydrologic cycle.

Spillover effects, whether flowing from restrictions on the exploitation of common pool resources or from the absence of such restrictions, are unavoidable. To be sure, so long as the pool is large enough, the spillover effect of no restriction may be so small as to be imperceptible. But with dramatic increases in technological capacity for resource exploitation, both the costs of restrictions and of the absence of restrictions are no longer so muted. Resources once assumed to be boundless are now susceptible to being irreversibly depleted. In extreme circumstances, a single misguided action may cause such catastrophic consequences. The more likely scenario, however, is damage owing to the cumulative impact of numerous actions, far removed in time and space, that in exponential fashion fail to reveal the full scope of their threat until it is too late to respond effectively.

It is, moreover, the tendency of all of these common resource pools both to spread out cause and effect over space and time and to preclude restriction of access to the pool. This tendency creates a natural distributional skewing in the related costs and benefits. An action in one place and time will cause injuries in other places and times. For this reason, restrictions on harmful actions impose costs on individuals in one place and time for the benefit of individuals in other places and times. Those who are absorbing the costs of the restriction, therefore, cannot naturally capture the related benefits. Society as a whole is better off, but there is no overlapping identity to those disparate in space and time who are paying the costs and receiving the benefits.

When such distributional inequities arise exclusively in the context of the production of benefits, controversies are less pronounced. So long as everyone is becoming better off (Pareto optimality), or at least as long as no one is getting worse off for the benefit of others, the controversy surrounding inequities in the distribution of benefits is not as pronounced. Where, however, the distribution of harms is at stake, the inherent inequities become apparent.

Environmental law, of course, invariably reflects the distribution of harms. The ecological injury to be redressed almost always involves actions that benefit some in one place or at one time, while causing harm to others at another place or another time. The homeowner building on a wetland, the farmer applying pesticide to a field, the car manufacturer producing sport utility vehicles would all characterize their activities as beneficial and productive. Those potentially subject to environmental restrictions, therefore, perceive those restrictions as harming them by reducing their own benefits and restricting their livelihoods and lifestyles for the benefit of others in other places and times.

Even when the effect of the environmental restriction is to avoid the tragic destruction of a common resource such as the ozone layer, an endangered species, a marine fishery, or a sole source aquifer of drinking water—all cases in which there would seem to be only winners and no losers—the environmental restriction is unlikely to be perceived as such. Especially because of the scientific uncertainty surrounding cause and effect, those subject to immediate restrictions on their economic activity will tend to perceive themselves as disproportionately burdened by substantial economic costs for the purpose of reducing speculative future risks to others. It is one thing to accept costs when one can perceive the very real harms that would otherwise be inflicted on others. But when, as is often the case with ecological injury, the related spatial and temporal features deny the certainty of that effect and render invisible its causal mechanics, such short-term, more immediate costs tend to be far less palatable.[15]

The spatial and temporal divide that ensures a mismatch in the spreading of the costs and benefits of environmental controls is also further exacerbated by the fact that the costs may sometimes have clearer implications for human health and welfare than do the benefits. The short-term economic costs of complying with environmental protection controls are almost always susceptible to being reconceived as having their own adverse implications for human health, which renders unavoidable a clash between competing human health concerns. A wealthier society, some argue, is a healthier society. Greater societal affluence means a higher standard of living; more people enjoy better and healthier food and drink, put less strain on their bodies, and receive better medical care, all of which result in significantly lower incidences of illness and longer life expectancies than in poorer societies. There are, accordingly, immediate human health costs that result from society's assuming higher pollution control costs now for the inherently speculative benefit of future generations.

For that same reason, if the purpose of a particular environmental protection program does not have a clear connection with human health, such as many natural resource preservation and species protection policies, the controversy surrounding the adoption of that policy is likely to be even greater. Even when public opinion polling suggests persistent public support for strong environmental protection laws, a divide is apparent between support for those policies perceived as necessary to protect human health in the short term and those designed to promote preservation of the natural environment in the long term. Public aspirations can be high for both kinds of policies, but individual commitment in terms of willingness to engage in self-sacrifice is much higher when immediate human health concerns are at stake.

Finally, it is not just the regulated community's perception of distributional inequity and the members of the public most concerned about human health that promotes persistent controversy, but also the contrasting perceptions of those within the environmental community who view environmental protection as a moral, ethical, or spiritual obligation. Many environmentalists equate environmental risks with assaults on their persons or on the natural environment. They begin with the premise that such assaults should be unlawful *per se* because no one has the right to subject another to health risks or to risk serious, irreversible damage to the natural environment. Other environmentalists derive their zeal for environmental protection, especially on matters such as endangered species protection, from their religious beliefs. For them, environmental degradation constitutes an affront to God. [16]

Many environmentalists are, moreover, hostile to application of cost–benefit analysis in environmental law. They question whether any methodology based on the market value of the use of a natural resource can possibly account for the value of its nonuse or preservation. They also believe, for similar reasons, that economic analysis, whether premised on market value or utility, is doctrinally predisposed toward the more immediate economic benefits presented by resource exploitation and development and against the long-term, uncertain, benefits of environmental protection. [17]

Though in direct opposition, similar moralistic overtones echo among those most resistant to environmental protection laws due to their erosion of private property and personal autonomy interests. By restricting some activities and, in particular, constraining the exercise of unlimited private dominion over natural resources, environmental laws transgress what their opponents claim to be fundamental rights linked to human liberty and freedom. These laws are also seen as promoting a regime of legal rules that promotes the collective over the individual and government regulation over free market forces. Such a legal regime, opponents claim, is antithetical to the basic cultural norms of liberty, property, and freedom from governmental restraint upon which the United States was founded (Don't Tread on Me!) and that are embedded in the U.S. Constitution and Bill of Rights. [18]

Accordingly, there are individuals on both sides of the environmental protection debate who summarily reject any characterization of environmental lawmaking as the attempt to balance competing economic interests. Each camp views their position as being supported by absolute, not relative, rights. The right to human health. The right to a healthy environment. The rights of nature itself. The right to private property. The right to individual liberty and freedom from the will of the majority.

Without a common economic denomination, the sharply contrasting nature of these highly moralistic perceptions of the role of environmental law makes compromise difficult. The fundamental disagreement about humankind's relationship to the natural environment and the proper role for law in addressing that relationship produces a polarization of positions. Each side tends to view the other as beginning from an unacceptable moral premise.

CHAPTER THREE

The Challenges for U.S. Lawmaking Institutions and Processes of Environmental Protection Law

Lawmaking institutions and processes in the United States have many distinct features, reflecting important public values of how legal rules should be adopted, implemented, and enforced. These values necessarily affect the substance of those laws that are enacted. Within the United States, these features are not incidental matters—they are a matter of deliberate design.

The basic design is supplied by the U.S. Constitution, which in its first three Articles establishes the essential lawmaking institutions of the federal government and declares the scope of their respective spheres of authority. The Constitution, particularly in the Bill of Rights, further defines the relationship of federal governmental authority to that retained by the states. Through a series of amendments, the Bill of Rights also expressly carves out specific limitations on the scope of the authority of lawmaking institutions to adopt certain kinds of laws that the Framers of those amendments deemed impermissible. At least as much as the constitutional design for the structure and operation of the various lawmaking institutions, these explicit substantive and procedural constitutional limitations on lawmaking authority reflect overriding preferences.

Environmental protection law, like any area of law, must work within the constraints and exploit the opportunities provided by this constitutional design for lawmaking, as well as by related political processes. Because that design purposefully makes lawmaking difficult, environmental law faces the same considerable challenges faced by many areas of law. It is not easy for those seeking the enactment of new legal rules to navigate the required horizontal and vertical pathways established among the various branches of government and levels of sovereign authority under the U.S. system of lawmaking.

But the difficulties that environmental law faces are even greater than those confronting many other areas of law. Not only does the Constitution lack any clear, unambiguous textual foundation for federal environmental protection law, its design for lawmaking and many of its implied values pose substantial hurdles to effective environmental lawmaking. Some of these difficulties can be traced to the ways in which the Constitution's framework for lawmaking is especially ill-suited for environmental law, especially the Constitution's preference for decentralized, fragmented, and incremental lawmaking. Other difficulties derive more directly from the ways in which the values and information underlying environmental protection policy generate tensions with what opponents of that policy contend are the substantive values and preferences expressed in the Constitution, especially the protection of private property rights.

A final source of difficulties faced by environmental law is not the Constitution itself, but the well-entrenched political processes that govern the nation's electoral and lawmaking processes. Here, too, environmental regulation faces both the same difficulties faced by any area of law and several unique obstacles more closely linked to the nature of environmental protection concerns.

This chapter discusses each of these difficulties, with special emphasis on those most endemic to environmental law. These obstacles include those derived from the constitutional structure for lawmaking, the substantive preferences reflected in several explicit constitutional limits on governmental authority, and the dominant political processes that have developed over the years around the nation's lawmaking institutions.

Structure of Lawmaking Institutions

There are two obvious central features of the structure of U.S. lawmaking institutions: first, our tripartite system of government, which separates lawmaking powers among the three branches of government, and second, our commitment to decentralized government and federalism, dividing sovereign responsibilities between the federal, state, tribal, and, to a lesser extent, local governmental entities.

Under our tripartite system of government, each of the three branches of government possesses its own distinct features, many of which have special relevance for environmental lawmaking. Even though the Constitution lacks any settled textual commitment to the existence of environmental protection law, any effort to enact, administer, and enforce such laws is remarkable for the large number of diverse and often conflicting governmental interests that are implicated, especially within the executive and legislative branches.

Within the executive branch of the federal government, for example, there are those administrative agencies responsible for developing the law

(e.g., the Environmental Protection Agency [EPA]), the Department of the Interior, the National Oceanic and Atmospheric Administration, and the President's Council on Environmental Quality), those charged with enforcing the law (e.g., the Department of Justice and the EPA), those primarily subject to the law's requirements (e.g., the Department of Transportation, the Department of Defense, the Department of Interior, and the Department of Energy), and those primarily concerned with its budgetary implications and economic impact (e.g., the Office of Management and Budget [OMB] and the Department of Commerce).

Within the federal legislative branch, there is a similarly large number of diverse and often conflicting interests implicated by environmental lawmaking. Underlying the workings of each chamber of Congress, a multiplicity of committees and subcommittees possess either primary responsibility for the development of proposals or formal bills authorizing legislation in the first instance, jurisdiction to appropriate monies for the operation of the federal government and its programs, or authority to oversee the actual operation of authorized federal governmental activities for which Congress has appropriated funds. Because the spatial and temporal distributional implications of environmental law are so large, both in terms of the associated environmental benefits and the economic burdens, a correspondingly large number of legislative committees are interested in influencing any environmental lawmaking efforts.

A fuller view of the structure of U.S. lawmaking institutions relevant to environmental lawmaking requires superimposing this essentially horizontal division of authority within the three branches of the federal government onto the vertical division of authority that simultaneously exists between sovereign authorities at the federal, state, tribal, and local levels. The same horizontal division of authority that dominates at the federal level is largely replicated at the other levels. Just as the Constitution takes care in dividing responsibilities among branches of government within the federal system, so too does it create a careful balance of authorities between the federal and state sovereigns. In many respects, federal law and the federal system dominate, but not without providing a strong role for the states, including some immunity from federal oversight.

For instance, of particular relevance to environmental law, the Constitution provides only specific, enumerated powers to the federal government, while preserving the general police powers of the states and excluding some essential state functions from federal control. Those enumerated federal powers include, *inter alia,* congressional power to spend its monies, exercise dominion over its property, and regulate commerce among the states, Native American tribes, and foreign nations. As interpreted by the Supreme Court, these powers do not include any general federal sovereign authority to enact environmental protection laws in order to promote public health or welfare.

The Constitution elsewhere carves out for state governments some special immunities from federal oversight in order to ensure against the federal government's encroachment on state sovereignty. According to the Supreme Court, the Tenth Amendment's reservation of powers to the states carries with it, by implication, a limitation on the extent of the federal government's authority to intrude on the sovereignty of states. The Court has further held, especially in recent years, that the Eleventh Amendment imposes significant limits on Congress's authority to subject states to suits in court (both federal and state) for monetary relief.[1]

Many of these features, both in combination and in isolation, present obstacles for any effort to create environmental protection law. Two that pose the more substantive difficulties are fragmentation of authority and federalism.

Fragmentation of Authority

The natural and deliberate effect of fragmenting authority among branches of government and between sovereign authorities is to make it more difficult to enact laws. Great effort is needed to secure the necessary congressional committee approvals; garner majority votes in both chambers; obtain presidential signature, agency implementation, and enforcement; and, if necessary, defeat challenges in court to the law's validity. There is, in short, a strong structural bias within our existing lawmaking institutions in favor of government's acting more slowly and incrementally. Whatever their ideological bent, sweeping law reforms in response to new information or values are very difficult to accomplish without institutional change. Yet, those same institutions needing reform resist just that possibility.

Environmental protection law's own features, moreover, make this an especially demanding undertaking. Its highly controversial nature makes it difficult to forge the coalitions needed, especially in Congress, but also between the relevant administrative agencies. Because of environmental law's redistributive thrust, there are almost always those resisting the change who, under existing law, possess considerable resources they will work hard to avoid losing. They can base their opposition to statutory enactments on the substantial scientific uncertainty and sheer complexity surrounding ecological injury. The latter, in particular, renders the process of legislating detailed statutory provisions especially difficult.

Environmental law's inherently dynamic nature creates further obstacles because it means that future statutes, statutory amendments, and regulatory revisions are likely to be necessary. Securing passage of environmental law is not just a matter of exploiting one opportune moment in time. It requires multiple debates and lobbying efforts, with any one failed effort potentially leading to an irreversible catastrophic environmental harm. Environmental law must be flexible and responsive to new information regarding ecological cause and effect, available technology, and changing lifestyles. The essentially conservative, fragmented, and deliberately cumbersome process for lawmaking in the United States does not readily lend itself to such responsive, iterative lawmaking initiatives.

That is why U.S. presidents have sometimes sought to circumvent the normal lawmaking processes to address what they perceive to be pressing environmental and natural resource concerns that demand more immediate attention. President William Howard Taft invoked what his supporters claimed to be the inherent powers of the presidency when he withdrew from private claims petroleum reservoirs on federal lands without waiting for specific legislative authorization. Presidents Teddy Roosevelt, Harry Truman, Jimmy Carter, and Bill Clinton each similarly invoked seemingly narrowly drawn provisions of the American Antiquities Act to prevent irreversible exploitation of significant natural resources rather than risk their loss during the time necessary to secure specific congressional legislation.[2]

Fragmentation also makes it difficult to address issues in a comprehensive, holistic fashion. Ecological injury resists narrow redress; due to the highly interrelated nature of the ecosystem, it is almost always a mistake to suppose that one can isolate a single discrete cause as the source of an environmental problem. Not only is a broader overview needed, accounting for the full spatial and temporal dimensions of the matter, but failure to pursue such an overview is likely to result in an approach that is at best ineffective and at worst unwittingly destructive because of unanticipated consequences. When, however, governmental jurisdiction over the host of diverse activities affecting the ecosystem is divided between many entities, necessary coordination and overview are surprisingly difficult. "The environment, rather than being treated holistically, is thus subdivided according to the organized principles of the social systems, not the natural world."[3]

The institutional obstacle of fragmentation not only arises among the various branches, but also within them. Fragmentation of congressional committee jurisdiction over environmental issues is inevitable given the ways in which ecological cause and effect span so many diverse human activities. Environmental law will invariably implicate the interests not just of congressional committees concerned with environmental law *per se,* but also of most major committees concerned with various aspects of the economy and society potentially subject to environmental regulations—

ecological injury's tremendous spatial and temporal dimensions guarantee it.

Because, moreover, of the separation of authorizing committees and appropriations committees in both congressional chambers, there are likely to be powerful factions on appropriations committees particularly skeptical of the thrust of environmental protection laws. Members named to appropriations committees are, due to self-selection or their experience on other committees primarily concerned with budgetary limitations, likely to be especially sensitive to economic costs. For that reason, they are apt to be disproportionately concerned with the more immediate and known economic costs of environmental controls than they are responsive to the more speculative, uncertain, long-term benefits of those same controls.

A similar division of interests is evident within the executive branch. While certain agencies, primarily the EPA, have defining missions that render them especially sensitive to environmental protection concerns, the same is not necessarily so for many other powerful forces within that branch. The Departments of the Interior, Agriculture (including the Forest Service), and Commerce (including the National Oceanic and Atmospheric Administration) each have mixed missions—they both enforce certain restrictions and, because of their own resource management activities, are subject to others. Other very powerful cabinet agencies, such as the Departments of Transportation, Energy, and Defense, are mostly the target of environmental regulation and, therefore, are more likely to be skeptical of tough restrictions that cabin their discretionary authority to pursue their primary agency agendas.

The result is a disjunction of sorts within the executive branch. The federal executive branch is simultaneously the regulator and the regulated. Portions of the branch take an expansive, supportive view of environmental protection law, while other parts embrace a narrower, more skeptical outlook. As described before, the highly uncertain nature of ecological cause and effect and its complexity provide much fodder for disagreement, which both informs and slows down the lawmaking process.

Under the unitary executive theory governing the executive branch, those agency disagreements are to be resolved by the president in his capacity as chief executive and not by the courts. Because of the structure of the Executive Office of the President, however, the divisions found elsewhere are repeated, though with economic concerns more likely to dominate. Based on their own primary missions, the OMB and the Council of Economic Advisors both tend to embrace an approach more sensitive to the concerns of the regulated community and economic growth. Only the Council on Environmental Quality, an invention of the 1970s, exists within the Executive Office as a possible pro-environment counterweight in its advice and counsel to the president.

Federalism and Decentralization

A second source of structural obstacles confronting environmental lawmakers is the Constitution's division of lawmaking authority between federal and state governmental entities. As described above, while the federal government possesses many sweeping lawmaking authorities, they are nonetheless limited to certain specific enumerated powers, reserving the exercise of general police power authority to the states. The states also enjoy certain immunities from federal direction and monetary liability.

The resulting preference for decentralization of authority shares some affinities with environmental protection. There are plainly advantages to the retention of lawmaking authority within those governmental bodies closest to the natural environment at stake. Those governmental entities are more likely to possess the relevant expertise regarding both the ecological causes and effects. They may well have had the opportunity to see the threats to the environment firsthand and thus be able to grasp the scope of the problem and anticipate how best to redress it. Local governmental officials and elected representatives are also those most accountable to people in the immediate geographic area, who are likely to have the most directly at stake in terms of the health and environmental threats and potential economic costs.

There are, nevertheless, significant countervailing factors associated with this decentralization emphasis that are problematic for environmental lawmaking. The most significant stumbling block is that the vast spatial and temporal boundaries of many environmental problems do not readily lend themselves to local control. The issues involved are transboundary in character. The risks posed are not confined to a single political jurisdiction, and a narrowly bounded regulatory authority cannot provide an effective remedy for their redress. To the extent, moreover, that both the risks and possible remedies are likely to persist over time, a more centralized approach is apt to achieve the long-term perspective and resources needed to devise and maintain an effective legal remedy.

Indeed, the more likely scenario is that the decentralized approach, lacking the necessary national and long-term perspective, would prompt the various states to pursue policies that maximize the potential benefits to those within their jurisdiction at the expense of persons and ecosystems in neighboring states. Under such a scheme, generating environmental contaminants would, quite rationally, be located near borders between political jurisdictions so as to maximize the export of environmental risks to other jurisdictions. It is no happenstance when a source of water or air pollution regulated by one state is strategically located or operated so as to send most of its effluent discharge into another neighboring state. Nor should it be unexpected for a state or local government to develop a regulatory approach that seeks to direct much of the costs of environmental protection on those residing outside the state's borders.[4]

Based on analogous logic, there are reasons for concern that the lack of national perspective would make a state more prone to bargain away the national interest. That potential may be less troubling where, as is sometimes the circumstance, any resulting harm is readily redressed. But where, as is often the case with environmental injury, the resulting harm is instead irreversible, the stakes are much greater. Just such concerns years ago prompted California to relinquish its control over Yosemite National Park to the federal government; the state was sufficiently concerned about its inability to protect such an irreplaceable national resource from the short- and long-term pressures of economic development that it agreed to transfer what is today considered to be one of the nation's "crown jewels" to federal control.

The limited nature of federal lawmaking authority under the Constitution is yet another structural obstacle. None of the specifically enumerated sources of federal governmental lawmaking authority provides a ready fit with environmental concerns. Each instead reflects a property and marketplace approach to governmental authority fairly antithetical to the values and premises of a legal regime for environmental protection. Only the states possess general police power authority.

The Constitution's Property Clause (Art. IV, § 3, cl. 2), though conferring on Congress plenary authority within the clause's scope, remains limited to the government's management of property that it owns. While the federal government in fact does own much of the nation's most valuable resources—approximately 30 percent of the nation's lands—the exercise of proprietary powers is far from coextensive with the scope of comprehensive authority needed to provide for environmental protection. The Property Clause is instead firmly rooted in the traditional property law model in which rights to the natural environment depend upon the assignment of property rights. The clause does not readily lend itself to the regulation of private property rights in natural resources, which is a primary thrust of modern environmental protection law. While natural resources law finds its common law precepts in property law, the common law roots of environmental law can be found primarily in tort doctrine's imposing liability on activities causing injury to persons or property.

The Constitution's Spending Clause (Art. I, § 8, cl. 1) is susceptible to a similar analysis. Because of the sheer size and scope of the federal budget, the clause certainly provides the federal government with extraordinary leverage over many activities affecting the natural environment. It is not tied to environmental protection *per se,* but it is also unbounded in its potential coverage of environmental matters. Perhaps even more important, like the Property Clause, its theoretical underpinnings are fundamentally inconsistent with the basic notion that lawmaking authority for environmental protection derives from governmental authority to prevent certain harmful results. Both clauses arguably presume instead that the federal government possesses no such inherent authority to make laws for the public welfare. The exercise of federal governmental authority instead depends for its legitimacy on the government's assertion of a formal property right (Property Clause) or its expenditure of taxpayer monies (Spending Clause).

At least in recent history, the only clause susceptible to a broader reading has been the Constitution's Commerce Clause (Art. I, § 8, cl. 3), which authorizes Congress to regulate interstate commerce. An expansive reading of that clause authorizes federal legislation for environmental protection based on the theory that activities adversely affecting the environment have substantial effects on interstate commerce. The vast majority of modern federal environmental legislation is based on just such a reading of the Commerce Clause and has, to date, been upheld by the courts when challenged. The fit is nonetheless theoretically uneasy. The rhetoric of the Commerce Clause itself suggests the problem: it makes congressional control dependent on a commercial nexus. Commerce possessing a substantial interstate dimension is what the Constitution isolates as being of sufficient national interest to warrant the exercise of federal authority. The problem for environmental protection lawmaking is that, although commerce is certainly of central relevance to environmental protection, it is not ultimately that area of law's central concern.[5]

To base the validity of federal lawmaking authority for environmental protection on a commercial nexus invariably invites the creation of tortured legal arguments and legal fictions. The ends pursued by many environmental protection laws are sometimes—but certainly not always—commercial in character. Indeed, many of those laws are intended to reject the very notion that the natural environment should be viewed primarily in commercial terms. Nor are all human activities that substantially affect the environment so obviously "commercial" in character. So long as the federal courts have been willing to discount these constitutional disfluencies between environmental protection and commerce, federal environmental protection law has been able to rely on the Commerce Clause for its expansive reach. But the federal role remains structurally vulnerable to legal challenge in the event that the federal courts decide to embrace a stricter, more literal reading of the extent of Commerce Clause authority.[6]

Somewhat paradoxically, the existing division of authority between federal and state sovereigns also creates obstacles to states' enacting laws that are more protective of the environment. The U.S. Supreme Court has interpreted the Commerce Clause's conferral of authority to Congress over interstate commerce to create, by negative implication, a limit on state laws that unduly burden interstate commerce. Interstate commerce, to that extent, maintains a privileged position in the constitutional scheme.

Whatever the merits of the Court's rulings, the impact on states' efforts to prevent threats to their ecosystems from sources outside their borders has been swift and without exception. Prompted by a series of uncompromising rulings by the Supreme Court, lower courts have struck down virtually every one of those laws based on their discriminatory and adverse impact on interstate commerce. The need to protect interstate commerce from discriminatory regulation and undue burdens has overridden the environmental protection concerns of the states.[7]

Constitutional Preferences

Further structural obstacles to the development of a legal regime for environmental protection are rooted in various preferences expressed by the Constitution. Environmental law is wholly lacking in a constitutional foundation because its tendency is to challenge rather than to find support in constitutional doctrine and preferences. These preferences all reflect the need to prevent governmental overreaching in general. Several, moreover, are more directly premised on the presumptive need to protect the operation of free market forces—especially private property rights and freedom of contract—from governmental interference. Missing from the constitutional scheme is any explicit endorsement of the legitimacy of environmental law's core objective to fundamentally redefine the relationship between humankind and the natural environment.

The various guarantees declared by the Constitution, particularly in the Bill of Rights, possess a common focus and premise: restraining certain types of governmental action. The constitutional right, accordingly, turns on the individual's freedom from governmental intrusion. The First Amendment, for example, prohibits governmental restraints on freedom of speech or the free exercise of religion; the Fourth Amendment bars unreasonable searches and seizures by the government; the Eighth Amendment denies government the power to inflict cruel and unusual punishment.

Whether the freedom announced is the First Amendment's free exercise of religion, the Fifth Amendment's right against self-incrimination, or the Eighth Amendment's bar on double jeopardy, the clear constitutional message is that the government, if left unchecked, is the greatest threat to human liberty.

To the extent that any legal regime for environmental protection relies on the government's restraining the behavior of individuals, it is unavoidable that the Bill of Rights will serve a limiting function. There is no reason to suppose that environmental protection law will be generally immune from those fundamental constraints on governmental action. To the extent, therefore, that bans on littering implicate freedom of speech, they may be unconstitutional or at least raise First Amendment concerns. To the extent that the enforcement of environmental law threatens individuals with *criminal* punishment, a host of constitutional protections will necessarily attach to the accused. To the extent that environmental laws restrict where a church or temple may be built or where individuals may otherwise gather to worship, free exercise concerns will be implicated. Like every other area of law, environmental law must work within these and all the other constitutional restraints on government actors.[8]

There are, moreover, certain constitutional limitations on government's lawmaking authority that can be particularly problematic for environmental regulation. These include the protection of private property rights found in the Fifth Amendment's Takings and Due Process Clauses and Article I's Contract Clause. The original meaning and precise scope of each is susceptible to much debate and disagreement. But, however answered, the general preference expressed by these provisions for limiting governmental interference with the working of the marketplace cannot fairly be gainsaid.[9]

For that reason, there is an inevitable tension between environmental protection law and these very same constitutional provisions. The premise of much environmental law is that private bargain and exchange in property rights in the marketplace cannot be safely relied upon as a guard against excessive ecological damage. The temporal and spatial dimensions of the environmental spillovers associated with human manipulation of the natural environment require substantial governmental oversight and, indeed, restraint of individual action, including governmental limitations placed upon the exercise of private rights in natural resources:

The real difficulty is that a modern ecological theory has eroded the notion of a bounded domain, often almost to the vanishing point. Many things that a short time ago were thought entirely the business of a landowner within the confines of his or her own land are now revealed to be intimately interconnected with other lands and with public resources that have never been thought to belong to the owner of a given tract.[10]

The government, therefore, may need to impose environmental restraints, notwithstanding their adverse impact on preexisting contractual rights. It may need to limit the exercise of private property rights in certain natural resources, irrespective of the economic harm to property owners that may ensue. Further, the government may sometimes need to act quickly in light of new information regarding environmental risks, even though doing so limits the procedural avenues available to individuals for challenging the government's action and subsequently raises due process concerns.[11]

None of these constitutional hurdles presents an insurmountable obstacle to fashioning an effective regime for environmental protection. The absence of such an obstacle, however, does not belie the existence of a fundamental constitutional tension requiring close attention and accommodation in creating environmental law.

The Political Process

The peculiar political systems that have developed around government in the United States, especially surrounding the election of the president, members of Congress, and many state and local officials, provide another source of obstacles for environmental law. No doubt the most obvious of these obstacles is the extent to which those running for office are dependent on campaign donations from those with considerable economic resources. Clearly, because of its inherently redistributive nature, environmental protection law tends to be most threatening to those who currently have many of the economic resources. Such persons and entities tend, notwithstanding some notable exceptions, to be understandably opposed to laws that would reduce their existing wealth and corresponding economic clout. As a result, those advocating environmental protection laws typically face well-funded challenges.

At the same time, those persons and entities favoring stronger environmental protection laws (environmentalists) are likely to face severe organizational barriers to their mounting effective political campaigns. To the extent that environmentalists are dominated by those currently "losing" under the existing system of laws, they are likely to have far fewer economic resources to enlist on their behalf. Furthermore, as environmentalist interests are often not economic in character at all, but are instead based on a different moral vision regarding the proper relationship between humankind and the natural environment, environmentalists are especially unlikely to be able to enlist allies from the business community to convert their vision into the campaign coffers needed for political success.

Moreover, the tremendous spatial and temporal dimensions associated with ecological injury create tremendous impediments to effective political organization in favor of environmental protection. The pool of those adversely affected is simply too spread out over space and time to effectively organize for collective action. Future victims don't yet know of the damage and might not yet even be born, and present victims are unlikely to understand the source of their harm given the extraordinary complexity of the natural environment and the associated scientific uncertainty. Present victims who are aware of the source of their harm may also take no action due to the perverse incentives generated by the prospects of "free riders," who exploit the common pool nature of the ecosystem to maximize their gains or minimize their losses by relying on others to make the necessary sacrifices.

Perhaps for these reasons, those seeking elected office tend to stress the importance of economic growth and promise short-term results: new businesses, new jobs, lower taxes, a broader tax base to support desired of government services. These tend to be the catchwords and slogans of those seeking elected office in relatively short election year cycles (typically two to four years), especially at the state and local levels. A candidate seeking elected office based on an environmental agenda that is not premised on traditional notions of economic growth, but instead on the imposition of short-term limits with the prospect of widely dispersed gain in the distant future, is substantially disadvantaged within the political system.

Finally, our political system is inherently dependent on bargaining and the forging of compromise. The ability to compromise competing interests and eliminate conflict is often the calling card of a successful politician or government official. For environmental protection, however, compromise is not always a viable option. In some settings, undertaking a series of compromises simply delays the ultimate destruction of the endangered resource. Effective environmental protection might require long-term adherence to absolute limits, not provisional objectives to be inexorably bartered away over time. Yet, the economic pressures on the environment are constant and unrelenting, and such nonnegotiable environmental regulation is rarely seen.[12]

One environmentalist succinctly described the situation this way: "In the environmental movement, our defeats are always final, our victories always provisional. What you save today can still be destroyed tomorrow, don't you see?" Thus lacking the ability to compromise, environmental advocates often find that they lack credibility in our political system. Branded as "zealots" and members of a "radical fringe," their views are systematically discounted as being extreme and insufficiently pragmatic.[13]

*   *   *

Making environmental protection law places enormous pressure on law-making institutions as the essential features of the problem to be addressed are not readily susceptible to legal redress. Indeed, our lawmaking institutions are particularly inapt for the task of considering problems and crafting legal solutions of the spatial and temporal dimensions necessary for environmental law.

Environmental protection law in the United States has not only overcome the substantial institutional and political obstacles to its initial enactment, but has persisted and strengthened over its three-decade-plus history. It has done so because of the compelling nature of the problem and the strength of the American public's commitment to environmental protection, a commitment that is rooted both in fear of threats to human health from environmental pollution and in aspirations for ecological preservation. The evolution of environmental regulation has required widespread changes in law, and it has required significant evolution by the lawmaking institutions themselves. The story of that legal transformation in the face of repeated waves of institutional and political resistance is the subject of the second part of this book.

The Road Taken

In her book *Silent Spring,* first published in 1962, Rachel Carson awakened a nation to the dangers presented by the unregulated use of pesticides. Borrowing from Robert Frost's poem "The Road Not Taken," Carson wrote movingly of the "other road" open to the nation for avoiding ecological catastrophe, advocating strict regulation of pesticide use as well as basic lifestyle changes.

Over forty years have passed since the first publication of *Silent Spring.* Although Rachel Carson would no doubt find fault in much of the road actually traveled during that time, it is equally clear that much has been accomplished in improving environmental protection efforts. The emergence of a comprehensive legal regime for environmental protection has served an important role in securing those accomplishments.

Part 2 of this book explains environmental law's development and evolution during the past several decades, emphasizing particular events that occurred in the 1970s through the 1990s. This part begins with a chapter that considers the origins of modern environmental law. A central focus concerns why environmental law emerged in the early 1970s notwithstanding substantial structural obstacles, discussed in part 1, and why environmental law has since persisted, despite the tenacity and strength of efforts favoring its undoing.

Some commentators have suggested that environmental law may have resulted from a "republican moment"—an " 'outburst of democratic participation and ideological politics' "—created by widespread and then-rising public demand for environmental protection. The term "republican" invokes the political tradition referred to as "civic republicanism," which stresses the willingness of individuals to undergo sacrifices to promote the public good. A "republican moment" is a time of such heightened civic-mindedness that it is possible to overcome substantial institutional and political obstacles to potentially radical social change. Under this view, the "original 1970 Earth Day looks very much like a 'republican moment.' An estimated 20 million Americans participated in a variety of public events that day. More than 2,000 colleges, 10,000 high schools and elementary schools, and 2,000 communities took part."[1] The theoretical significance of such a "republican moment" lies in the contention that, without such a moment, environmental protection law would never exist because of its radically redistributive nature.

The better answer to the riddle of environmental law's emergence in the 1970s distinguishes between the seeming suddenness of its emergence and the long-standing reasons that explain its development. A series of major laws came into existence very quickly, but both the relevant preexisting legal doctrine and the reasons for a more comprehensive legal regime were both long standing and deeply ingrained. As proponents of "republican moment" theories recognize, such moments can depend for their occurrence on social movements that existed for decades beforehand and on implementing actions that occur for decades afterwards.

It is an oft-repeated fiction that environmental law spontaneously began in the late 1960s and early 1970s. Environmental law no doubt had its first, most formal, expression during that time, but its historical legal roots are far deeper and broader. They extend to the nation's natural resources laws, which played such a dominant role in the country's first 150 years. Environmental law in the United States also stems from the statutory and public policy precedents in the areas of public health and worker safety that were steadily established throughout the twentieth century. It is not, as many in the media have seemed to assume, "a movement without a history."[2]

The second part of the explanation for environmental law's persistent expansion relates to the depth of the shift in public attitudes that prompted environmental law's initial embrace. This was no thinly developed public affinity with a social movement of the moment. Environmental law was then, and is still today, the product of the public's fundamental reconceptualization of time and space, which propelled environmental law's extraordinary series of legislative enactments and has since underlain the defeat of a series of major political challenges. The sheer depth and tenacity of the public's views, which are most often rooted in concerns about potential threats to human health and the dangers of exceeding ecological limits, explain why environmental law has been so persistent and inexorably expansive and why its repeatedly proclaimed demise has proven, on each occasion, to be premature. American environmentalism sweeps into its embrace both long-term altruistic beliefs about humankind's relationship to the natural environment and short-term, more self-interested concerns about the impact of pollution on specific individuals. On the other hand, much of the controversy and conflict surrounding environmental law since 1970 can be traced to an equally persistent gap between the public's aspirations for environmental protection and its willingness to sufficiently change individual behavior to realize those aspirations.

The first chapter of part 2 considers the origins of modern environmental law and is followed by individual chapters discussing each of modern environmental law's first three decades. The events described in each decade chapter are broadly related to the theoretical framework set out in part 1. That framework explains much about the peculiar and seemingly paradoxical manner in which environmental law has evolved. Some patterns emerge across the years, as do some discernible trends. Each decade has witnessed threshold moments of national consensus and aspiration, followed by periods of controversy and fundamental challenge that always result in environmental law's surprising persistence and expansion.

CHAPTER FOUR

Becoming Environmental Law

Environmental law is frequently characterized as paradoxical because of its peculiar twists, turns, and tendencies toward unintended, contradictory consequences. Its greatest paradox, however, may simply be the fact of its existence in the first instance. Given the enormous institutional and organizational obstacles to environmental law's creation described in part 1, dispassionate rational choice analysis would seem to lead ineluctably to the conclusion that no government would ever adopt such enormously redistributive legislation, especially when surrounded by tremendous scientific uncertainty. As described by one commentator, classic political theory makes plain that "environmental groups will not organize effectively and . . . environmental statutes will not be passed."[1]

The explanation of how this paradoxical situation came to be is twofold. The first relates to the temporal roots of modern environmental law; the second to the depth and breadth of shifts in public opinion that underlay the remarkable array of laws passed by Congress in the 1970s. Indeed, it is the remarkable strength of those roots and shifts, consistently underestimated by those seeking to cut back on environmental protection requirements, that has both defeated a series of such counterreform initiatives and fueled environmental law's further expansion.

Historical Roots of Modern Environmental Law

The term "environmental law" appears to have been formally coined at the September 1969 Conference on Law and the Environment held at Airlie House in Warrenton, West Virginia. Among those in attendance at the conference were lawyers and legal academics who went on to play significant roles in the development and evolution of environmental law, many of whom continue to do so today: law professors Joe Sax, Dan Tarlock,

Bill Hines, Jim Krier, Sheldon Plager, and David Currie; law student (now law professor) Nicholas Robinson; litigators David Sive, Jim Moorman, Jan Stevens, Tony Roisman, Victor Yannacone, and Ed Berlin; and policy advocates Tom Jorling, Mike McClosky, Ralph Nader, and Bill Van Ness. Conference recommendations included establishing an "Environmental Law Reporter," creating "an early warning system about major environmental modifications and proposals, permitting public comment and criticism before the event," founding a "national environmental law organization . . . similar to the American Civil Liberties Union," and undertaking "administrative reform" to support "hard analysis." The conferees were both strikingly influential and prescient. Shortly thereafter, they helped create the still-thriving Environmental Law Institute, which publishes *Environmental Law Reporter;* Congress enacted an "early warning system" in the National Environmental Policy Act; young attorneys established public interest law organizations such as the Environmental Defense Fund and Natural Resources Defense Council; and the judiciary began to "reform" administrative law, including the development of the "hard look" doctrine of more exacting standards of judicial review in direct response to ecological concerns.[2]

Intriguingly, those in attendance at Airlie House deliberately resisted "any attempt to define environmental law" and speculated that the best theory "might well be that there is nothing at all unique about environmental law. It is a way of applying other aspects of law to a particular set of facts or events." The apparent consensus was that environmental law was best defined in reference to the problems it addressed: the "hideous fact" of "environmental decay." The legal response "would, in turn, define the field." The conference participants disagreed sharply about which legal responses were potentially the most effective. Some favored "the broad, swift remedy of a constitutional attack," while others "preferred the philosophically more opaque strategy of mixing legislative and judicial remedies."[3]

The strategy that the nation ultimately pursued was the "philosophically more opaque" one. The year 1970 is popularly invoked as environmental law's formal commencement due to the extraordinary number of significant events occurring during the decade beginning with 1970. In that year alone, the nation witnessed the signing of the National Environmental Policy Act, the creation of the President's Council on Environmental Quality, the first nationwide celebration of Earth Day, the creation of the U.S. Environmental Protection Agency, and the passage of the Clean Air Act's demanding and uncompromising air pollution control program. Ronald Reagan, who was then governor of California, declared "an all-out war against the debauching of the environment," as "[g]overnors and legislative leaders in more than a dozen states . . . put environmental protection at or near the top of the list of priorities for action."[4] Further, the first environmental law journal—*Environmental Law*—was published in 1970; Professor Sax published his celebrated book *Defending the Environment: A Strategy for Citizen Action;* and several law schools held their first conferences on the topic.[5]

During the next several years, Congress added comprehensive, ambitious environmental legislation aimed at water pollution control, solid and hazardous waste management, endangered species protection, and a host of other regulatory targets. Each of those federal programs contemplated, promoted, and sometimes effectively compelled complementary state environmental policies and programs. The regime for environmental protection law appeared to come virtually out of nowhere as it exploded onto the scene—seemingly a "movement without history."[6]

Appearances, however, can be deceiving in law as in life. The environmental statutes and institutions that emerged in the 1970s were of a very different magnitude than any previously existing regimes for environmental protection, but they reflected a logical, albeit exponential, outgrowth of decades of legal evolution on closely related matters. The more accurate characterization of the origins of environmental law is, therefore, that a host of once-disparate strands of law and related social movements converged after decades to *become* what we now think of as modern environmental law.

There was, of course, a rich history of U.S. natural resource laws, and there existed long-standing environmental organizations, such as the Sierra Club, the National Audubon Society, and the National Wildlife Federation. Although natural resource laws had been dominated for much of the eighteenth and nineteenth centuries by policies designed to promote maximum resource exploitation, resource conservation objectives had risen to prominence by the turn of the twentieth century. By the early- to mid-twentieth century, with congressional passage of such laws as the Antiquities Act of 1906, the Migratory Bird Treaty Act of 1918, the Federal Power Act of 1920, the Mineral Leasing Act of 1920, the National Park Service Organic Act of 1916, the Taylor Grazing Act of 1934, the Historic Sites, Buildings and Antiquities Act of 1935, the Bald and Golden Eagle Protection Act of 1940, and the Submerged Lands Act of 1953, federal policies favoring disposition of resources into private hands for economic use were being displaced by laws favoring governmental retention, conservation, and, increasingly, preservation of natural resources as part of the nation's heritage. During the 1960s, Congress passed a series of resource preservation statutes, including the Refuge Protection Act of 1962, the Land and Water Conservation Act of 1964, the National Wildlife Refuge Administration Act of 1966, the National Historic Preservation Act of 1966, and, most important, two of the strongest preservation laws—the Wilderness Act of 1964 and the National Wild and Scenic Rivers Act of 1968.[7]

One of the most influential and eloquent environmental leaders of that time was Secretary of the Interior Stewart Udall. Secretary Udall spoke early on about a "quiet crisis" that demanded a broad and aggressive emphasis on natural resources conservation and preservation policies, while simultaneously drawing the connection between those progressive policies and the need for modern pollution control laws. Udall, who was instrumental in securing passage of the Wilderness Act of 1964, warned that "in the long run life will succeed only in a life-giving environment and we can no longer afford unnecessary sacrifices of living spaces and natural resources to 'progress.'"[8]

The environmental protection laws that emerged in the 1970s, however, were decidedly different than these earlier natural resources laws. Although they furthered similar values, the two relied on very different legal premises. For most of the nation's history, the primary, if not exclusive, basis for the government's assertion of authority over natural resources had been its proprietary ownership of the particular resource at issue. In 1970, the federal government owned over one-third of the nation's land, the vast majority of which was in the natural-resource-rich western states and Alaska. By exercising its proprietary authority, the government could manage and protect the resources by way of permits, licenses, patents, and leases and, if necessary, by filing suits against those who interfered with the government's dominion.[9]

The regulatory premise of environmental law that had emerged by 1970, however, was and remains markedly different. It ultimately challenges rather than embraces the kind of absolutist notions of property rights that underlie the claims of property owners, including the federal government—that ownership of natural resources confers plenary authority over their extraction and appropriation. The core regulatory premise of much environmental protection law today is the sovereign's police power to regulate private activities that adversely affect public health and welfare because of the impact of those activities on the natural environment notwithstanding property claims.

For this reason, the historical roots for modern environmental protection law cannot be simply derived from preexisting traditional natural resources laws. They are instead at least as likely to be found in the widespread social, urban justice movements concerned with public health in the United States, which led to the enactment of state and local legislation throughout the nineteenth and twentieth centuries. Viewed from this perspective, the environmental laws of the 1970s may be more accurately described as the "culmination of an era of protest" rather than as the beginning of an entirely new movement.[10]

Although many individuals during the late nineteenth and early twentieth centuries no doubt considered pollution to be an indicator of progress, there were many dissenting voices. There were early municipal efforts to control urban pollution, with problems of noise pollution, waste disposal, and air pollution as matters of particular public concern; the zoning movement in urbanized areas was largely a response to such negative spillovers between incompatible uses of neighboring properties. The Smoke Prevention Association was founded in 1907, and by 1912, twenty-three of the twenty-eight largest cities in the United States had smoke abatement laws, though these regulations saw limited enforcement and, presumably, minimal compliance. The sanitation movement similarly became a potent political force at the turn of the twentieth century, led by public health professionals and sanitation engineers concerned about both urban waste disposal and contamination of public drinking water. Congress, not coincidentally, enacted both the Food and Drug Act and the Meat Inspection Act in 1906, based on analogous public health concerns.[11]

Another important historical root of the congressional enactments of the 1970s was scientific research into occupational hazards and the associated labor movement of a half-century earlier. Concern with occupational health can be traced far back into the nineteenth century, extending to Benjamin McCready's 1837 report on workplace hazards in the United States. At least in the United States, however, it is only during the early twentieth century that distinct scientific inquiry appears to have been undertaken to examine the connection between environmental contamination in the workplace and disease.[12]

Much of the pioneering work in this field was performed by Alice Hamilton, who has been dubbed the nation's "first great urban/industrial environmentalist." In the early part of the twentieth century, while a professor of pathology at the medical school of Northwestern University, Hamilton conducted pathbreaking investigations of lead poisoning in the workplace, as well as of the possible adverse health consequences of using white phosphorus in industrial processes. Hamilton, who in 1919 became the first woman appointed to the faculty at Harvard University, discovered the dangers posed by white phosphorus, assisted in the development of an effective substitute, and advocated in favor of legislation to ban further use of white phosphorus.[13]

Hamilton's work, however, does not exist in historical isolation. She was joined by a number of individuals and organizations, many led by women, focusing on related issues of garbage, public health, urban industrialization, and occupational hazards. These organizations included the National Consumer League and the Women's Trade Union League, and important contributions were made by Florence Kelly, Jane Addams, Mary McDowell, and Ellen Starr.[14]

By the mid-twentieth century, environmental pollution remained a less prominent political issue, likely because of national attention to matters of war and peace, but it had nonetheless become a matter of importance to many Americans. There was considerable news media coverage of the air pollution disaster in Donora, Pennsylvania, in 1948, in which twenty persons immediately died, fifty more died within a month, and thousands became ill as the result of pollution during a dense fog caused by a lengthy thermal inversion that persisted for several days. William Vogt published *The Road to Survival* in the late 1940s, and Fairfield Osborne published *Our Plundered Planet* in 1948, both of which highlighted the potentially catastrophic environmental threats presented by technological advances, industrialization, and patterns of resource consumption. Congress enacted the first federal water pollution control program in 1948. Although twenty-one states had water pollution control laws by 1946, these laws exempted many industrial practices and, like the earlier smoke abatement laws, lacked any pretense of meaningful enforcement.[15]

Environmental issues steadily increased in prominence during the next two decades. The suburbanization of America during the 1950s prompted increased interest in environmental amenities and recreational use of the outdoors in particular. The decline in many diseases after World War II, thanks to the development of vaccines and powerful new antibiotics, both raised public expectations in health and longevity and shifted the public's focus to preventive care and to diseases, such as cancer, potentially linked to environmental pollution. Severe air pollution events similar to what had occurred in Donora recurred in London in 1952 and New York City in 1953, reportedly resulting in the deaths of at least four thousand and two hundred persons, respectively. Two new research institutions dedicated to providing environmental policymakers with outstanding, nonpartisan, and in-depth analysis—the Conservation Foundation and Resources for the Future—commenced operations in 1952.[16]

By the 1960s, Congress was ready and able to enact a series of new environmental statutes. In addition to the natural resource preservation laws previously mentioned, Congress passed a series of air and water pollution control statutes during that decade, each one of which incrementally upped the ante of the federal role. These laws included the Water Pollution Control Act Amendments of 1956, the Water Quality Act of 1965, the Clean Water Restoration Act of 1965, the Air Pollution Control Act of 1955, the Clean Air Act of 1963, and the Air Quality Act of 1967. None of these laws compares in jurisdictional scope or regulatory reach to the post-1970 laws, but they served as extremely important precedents for the subsequent environmental laws, which would borrow heavily from many of their provisions. They reflected public opinion trends of the 1960s that exhibited mounting concern for the environment, though far lower than they were to rise by 1970. Gallup public opinion polls conducted in May 1960 and then again in 1970 showed the percentages of Americans who saw "pollution/ecology as an important problem" rise from 1 percent to over 25 percent.[17]

Congress also passed a host of laws in the 1960s that, while more consumer oriented in their focus, simultaneously served as important legislative precedents for 1970s environmental legislation. These consumer protection laws reflected both the public's growing concern with threats to public health and its increasing unwillingness to rely on industry alone to ensure public safety. Between 1966 and 1968, new laws included the National Traffic and Motor Vehicle Act, the Fair Packaging and Labeling Act, the Federal Hazardous Substances Act, the Federal Meat Inspection Act, the Natural Gas Pipeline Safety Act, the Flammable Fabrics Act, the Child Protection Act, and the Hazardous Materials Transportation Act. For most of the 1960s, when the president and the leadership in both chambers of Congress were Democrats, the Democratic Party eagerly embraced the notion that the federal government should pass regulatory laws to address such public concerns.[18]

By 1969, with Republican Richard Nixon in the White House but the Democrats still in the majority in the Senate and House, no one political party dominated the federal government, which made lawmaking far more difficult. For both ironic and tragic reasons, however, the two parties' eagerness to join together to forge a bipartisan consensus and enact statutes that addressed matters of public concern was even greater than before. Buffeted by civil rights protests and opposition to the Vietnam War and awash in the demoralization resulting from the assassinations of President John F. Kennedy, the Reverend Martin Luther King Jr., and Senator Robert F. Kennedy, the nation by 1970 was desperate for a positive, consensus-building issue that could make a difference and turn public attention away from the war and the race riots then taking place in some of the nation's major cities. The public was no longer satisfied by modest, incremental steps; they sought immediate, dramatic change.[19]

Whether or not motivated by sincere belief in environmentalism, almost immediately after the 1968 presidential election both parties seized upon environmental protection as a source for political opportunism. Environmental issues had received virtually no attention during the 1968 campaign or in either party's platform. But by late 1969 and early 1970, both the Nixon

White House and the Democratic-controlled Congress were competing for the environmental mantle. Even many in industry were by the late 1960s in favor of an increased federal role in regulating potential harms to the environment. Especially as more states and major cities passed their own air pollution control laws—in 1967, states passed 112 pollution control laws—the possibility of a uniform, federal preemptive standard became increasingly attractive to those in the regulated community.[20]

The first part of the answer to the question posed by environmental law's seemingly paradoxical existence is, therefore, to dispute the notion that modern environmental law was simply an impulsive response to a social movement that, without any history, swept through national politics. The legal regime that emerged may well have seemed to erupt out of nowhere, but both the social movement and statutory precedent that underlay it had been a long time in development.

Changing Conceptions of Time and Space

The second part of the answer to the question posed by the seeming paradox of environmental law's emergence relates to the extent and depth of the public concerns about environmental protection. Ever since environmental law emerged in the early 1970s, there has been a tendency to equate what seemed like the suddenness of its appearance with the thinness of the public's commitment and underlying beliefs. For those highly skeptical of the efficacy of environmental restrictions, the public's dramatic embracing of environmentalism in 1970, which culminated in nationwide demonstrations on Earth Day, seemed a mere ephemeral fad, bound to have a short political shelf life. Environmentalism was simply the issue of the moment that, akin to the demand for a consumer product, would soon dissipate as the public's attention turned to other concerns.

But just as the apparent suddenness of environmental law's arrival was misleading, so too were the assumptions about the public's lack of actual commitment to environmental protection misguided. The public's concerns about public health and ecological limits did not emerge out of nowhere in the late 1960s and early 1970s. They were long standing. The absence of any prior comprehensive law reform in response to those concerns was more likely the reason why the changes of the 1970s occurred so rapidly. In nature, a volcano may erupt in dramatic fashion, as an earthquake will strike unexpectedly. But the apparent suddenness of the event belies years of geologic events at work and masks their inexorable quality.

The underlying social and political pressures for law reform in response to environmental protection concerns had similarly been building up over decades. And underlying the "eruption" of environmental law in the 1970s were years of pressure building from changing public attitudes, concerns, and values. These changes were occurring throughout the twentieth century and expressing themselves in diverse ways. The absence of a single point of focus on environmental protection does not, however, detract from the strength of the concerns being built up.

Indeed, by the early 1970s, a fundamental reconceptualization of both time and space underlay the extraordinary depth of public concern. The American public saw humankind and the natural environment differently than it had in the past. To some extent, this transformation in public perception captured the public's imagination and aspirations. Yet, in other respects, it generated substantial public concerns and, indeed, widespread fears, especially as they related to threats to human health and survival. In both respects, changing conceptions of time and space compelled a transformation in law generally and the emergence of a comprehensive legal regime for environmental protection in particular.

The relevancy of conceptions of time and space to societal change, including legal history, is not new. In *The Culture of Time and Space,* Stephen Kern insightfully describes how from 1880 to 1918 technological innovations and independent cultural developments combined to create new ways of thinking about time and space. Kern further draws from a variety of historical events during that time period, ranging from movements in art, developments in music, and even outbreaks of war, and places them in a wonderfully new and revealing light by explaining their common linkage to perceptions of time and space.[21]

While Einstein's theory of relativity challenged late-nineteenth- and early-twentieth-century notions of time and space, the wireless telegraph made it possible to coordinate the setting of clocks and therefore to create a standard time, collapsing the previously distinct worlds of "public" and "private" time. "Time is money" became the mantra of business as watches and clocks became more precise, increasing the importance of ever smaller bits of time. The bicycle developed a "cult of speed" and the automobile extended social lives beyond ten miles. Electrification merged night and day and was considered "the greatest environmental revolution in human history since the domestication of fire." Cameras and then film allowed for the capture of the present before it drifted into an unrecoverable past; time could even be manipulated in moving pictures. Airplanes gave humankind a new visual perspective on the planet, and prompted the emergence of modern art forms like cubism, which in turn led to the development of camouflage that made shape indiscernible from its surroundings. Technological advances in the machinery of war allowed for greater separation between decision and impact, obviating the need for generals to be close to the front lines; projectiles that could be volleyed only one to two hundred yards during the Napoleonic War could be fired from a distance of as many as nine thousand yards by the end of World War I.[22]

An analogous analytic framework applied to environmental law is equally revealing, particularly because ecological problems and lawmaking processes possess such dominant and clashing spatial and temporal dimensions. To a large extent, our understanding of ecological problems reflects the changing conceptions of time and space just described, as do our aspirations for environmental law. Many of our lawmaking processes, however, are rooted in very different assumptions about time and space—a condition that is the source of much conflict and controversy. Environmental law's challenge has been to bridge that gap.

The Spatial Dimension of Environmental Law

Perceptions about space changed throughout the twentieth century, but did so especially rapidly in the decades immediately before the 1970s. At the turn of the twentieth century, the nation was responding to what it perceived as a "closing" of the American frontier. A nation that had seemed for much of the nineteenth century to be boundless in its reach as it steadily spread westward had to face its physical limits with the settling of the far western United States. The change in mindset accompanying the closing of the American frontier had widespread cultural implications. With regard to natural resources law, in particular, it prompted a shift in national policies in the early twentieth century away from laws that promoted maximum resource exploitation in favor of policies and laws that increasingly emphasized resource conservation and even resource preservation.[23]

Changing technology during the first half of the twentieth century had similarly profound effects on public attitudes and, ultimately, on implications for environmental protection. Advances in engineering and aviation, mass production of the automobile, and even such seemingly incidental technologies as the bicycle and the elevator dramatically expanded spatial horizons and changed the landscape. Buildings could now be built taller than ever before. People could travel farther both horizontally and vertically and so could live either more closely together or much farther apart. The resource demand implications of these technological advances were enormous.

By 1970, a similar shift in mindset regarding physical space had occurred, with similarly far-reaching consequences for law and policy. Somewhat ironically, however, the changes resulted from what had first appeared to be expanding horizons. Space exploration in the 1950s and

1960s, commencing first with satellites and then manned spacecraft, expanded horizons and seemed to open up new frontiers. But the ultimate human psychological effect of the first photographs of Earth from the lunar orbiters in 1966 and the first manned flight to the surface of the Moon in 1969 was far different.

The Earth on which life depended seemed more, not less, fragile after these events. By expanding our horizons, we appeared smaller, more vulnerable, and less secure than ever before. It was, of course, hardly news that humankind resided on a planet traveling through space, but those first photographs from space drove home that reality in a way that was both exhilarating and unsettling. The Earth thereafter was frequently characterized as a "spaceship" and as a "lifeboat." Soon after the first walk on the moon, author C. P. Snow captured well the sentiment in an essay in *Look* magazine:

The solar system is dead, apart from our world; and the distances to any other system are so gigantic that it would take the entire history of mankind from paleolithic man to the present day to traverse—at the speed of Apollo 11—the distance to the nearest star. So that the frontier is closed. We can explore a few lumps in our system, and that is the end. . . . As a result of supreme technological skill and heroism, we are faced not with the infinite but with the immovable limits.[24]

Scientific advances and technological change also combined in unanticipated ways to make the world seem smaller, less autonomous, less exclusive, and less secure. Visually, the world looked smaller, but not just because of these most recent photographs of the Earth as a global system. Events and new technologies developed over the several decades preceding the 1970s had set the stage. The world wars had awakened the United States to the rest of the world. Radio stations, newspapers, and national news magazines now had stationed reporters all over the globe. Newsreels had become popular staples at movie theaters, and, of course, during the 1950s, television had begun to enter millions of American living rooms.

Accordingly, events occurring elsewhere had become far more real and were now seemingly closer than ever before. Expanding news coverage, especially on television, created more opportunities for these widening horizons. These changes were also fueled by significant advances in scientific understanding of the natural environment and the impacts of human activities. Partly in response to perceived threats posed by other nations, the federal government invested heavily in basic scientific research both to enhance national security and to promote industrial growth. The upshot, especially during the post–World War II years, was dramatic increases in scientific learning and eventually in the public's understanding of environmental threats.

The devastation caused by the two atomic bombs dropped on Hiroshima and Nagasaki had accelerated an end to World War II, but also fundamentally unsettled preexisting notions of individual security and autonomy. Ultimately, no place was secure, notwithstanding the proliferation of fallout shelters and nuclear war "disaster drills" during the 1950s. As public awareness of the actual dangers posed by radioactive fallout grew, the public discovered not only that the government's early reassurances about the benign effects of radiation were not accurate, but that the threat was far more persistent and broader in physical scope than initially understood. Radioactive fallout, it turned out, could spread hundreds of miles through the atmosphere, contaminating areas far removed from the site of a bomb's explosion. A scare concerning the possible pesticide contamination of cranberries in 1959 further fueled public concern about hidden dangers, a concern likewise reflected in pockets of vocal community hostility to the fluoridation of public water systems.[25]

In *Silent Spring,* Rachel Carson in 1962 gave passionate, foreboding expression to these fears. She wrote of how "[f]or the first time in the history of the world, every human being is now subjected to contact with dangerous chemicals, from the moment of conception until death." There is nothing tempered or equivocal about Carson's prose or her indictment of the chemical industry in general, and of pesticide use in particular. She directly linked the threats posed by nuclear fallout and pesticides, describing how they interrelate to erode steadily the natural environment for human habitation.[26]

Although the publication of *Silent Spring* was justifiably characterized as "an epochal event in the history of environmentalism . . . helping launch a new decade of rebellion and protest," there were other significant publications and subsequent events during the 1960s that drove home the essential message of the spatial dimensions of ecological threats. Murray Bookchin's *Our Synthetic Environment,* also published in 1962, attracted a widespread audience. Ralph Nader's popular book *Unsafe At Any Speed,* while concerned with auto safety, buttressed the overlapping theme that the public could not trust industry to safeguard their health and safety. Paul Ehrlich's celebrated *Population Bomb,* published in 1968, underscored the exponential, explosive, and potentially catastrophic nature of the threats faced by humankind.[27]

A series of events during the mid- to late 1960s seemed only to confirm the legitimacy of the public's fears. A fish kill caused by pesticides occurred in the Mississippi River in 1965. DDT contamination in Wisconsin similarly received widespread media coverage throughout 1968 and 1969, as did potentially toxic levels of mercury found in swordfish a few years later, prompting the *New York Times* to warn that "society would be criminally remiss if it failed now to do everything possible to arrest [mercury's] destructive spread." It seemed that no place was safe from these toxic chemical threats, as the suspected carcinogen, polychlorinated bi-phenyls, popularly referred to as "PCBs," could be found even in the remotest areas of Antarctica.[28]

Two of the most visually unsettling events, however, both occurred in 1969. These were the burning of the Cuyahoga River in Ohio and the Santa Barbara oil spill off the coast of California. Along with the horrors of the Vietnam War, images of burning rivers and seagulls suffocated in oil were now being brought by television and national news magazines directly into the living rooms of millions of Americans. The immediate, visual confirmation of threats to the environment intensified public demand for environmental protection. Direct experience of an ongoing threat necessarily increases pressure in favor of measures to prevent the threatened occurrence's taking place rather than merely to redress any consequential harm after the fact. Likewise, learning, and even visually observing, that an environmental harm has just happened not only makes that harm seem more real, but also naturally generates equally immediate responses to mitigate the amount of harm.[29]

Fear and threats to personal health were not, however, the exclusive source of the shift in public attitudes. As the spatial perspective grew to worldwide dimensions, many Americans found their imaginations and aspirations captured by parts of the world and aspects of the ecosystem previously unknown to them. They discovered that they cared about the preservation of certain places of natural beauty and life forms they had never visited and might never visit, but that nonetheless were now an important part of their lives. And rather than perceiving technological advances only as threats to preservation efforts, the American public believed that such advances offered potential hope for its protection. At least for many in the United States, the fulfillment of President Kennedy's promise to put a man on the Moon by the end of the 1960s demonstrated what American ingenuity and technology could accomplish. Such technological optimism was reflected, in turn, in the environmental laws of the 1970s that presumed that a similar national commitment to environmental protection would lead to technological advances sufficient for its accomplishment.

Spatial dimensions, accordingly, were expanding in two directions. The American public now not only felt threatened by actions that had previously seemed too far away to present such concerns, but also contemplated threats within spatial dimensions so small and immediate that they had previously escaped attention. Americans now knew that potentially harmful levels of contamination could be detected in concentrations that had until recently not been remotely measurable: parts per million, parts per billion, and even parts per trillion.

The threats seemed widespread, invisible, and seemingly impossible to avoid. If industry could not be trusted to eliminate these risks, neither did the government seem entirely trustworthy. The government had not been forthcoming regarding the extent of environmental risks posed by its own activities and had failed to prove its willingness to be vigilant in overseeing the safety and health hazards created by private industry. The government had promised peace, but had given the nation a polarizing, divisive war in Vietnam that, by the end of the 1960s or the beginning of the 1970s, Americans understood to lack even a possible pretense of the "victory" that many Americans had come to believe was their manifest destiny.

Americans also cared increasingly about adverse ecological effects in other parts of the world, regardless of whether they might lead to problems closer to home. For many Americans, increased awareness of the rest of the world, including other ecosystems and forms of life, had created a strong psychological tie. The connection they felt with the rest of the global ecosystem lacked any traditional physical nexus, yet its depth provided for widespread support for the environmental protection of other parts of the world. As depicted at the time by Barry Commoner, the world was literally becoming a "closing circle" as a result of technological "advances," population increases, and environmental degradation.[30]

The Temporal Dimension of Environmental Law

Public conceptions of time also changed in response to changing technology and culture and, as with space, in ways that prompted the emergence of modern environmental law in the 1970s. During the earlier course of the twentieth century, moreover, the collapse of spatial dimensions often implicated a collapse of temporal dimensions. The telegraph, and then the telephone, allowed instant communications between different parts of a state, the country, and, ultimately, the world. One could now travel across different time zones to arrive at a destination earlier than the "time" one had departed. It could be "Monday" for a person on one end of a telephone call and "Tuesday" for the person at the other end of the call. By sharp contrast, earlier in the nation's history, no such uniform notion of time even existed: Someone in 1870 traveling by train between Washington, D.C. and San Francisco would pass through two hundred different time zones—and Philadelphia time was five minutes behind New York City time.[31]

It was, however, the closing of the temporal frontier in the 1950s and 1960s, akin to that of the spatial frontier described above, that most influenced the emergence of modern environmental law, which thereafter reflected a deeper understanding that time was not unlimited. The nation had limited time to gain information and to make decisions because there were potentially adverse impacts of our actions today that could not simply be reversed in the future. The nation learned that it could not defer its environmental problems to some future time any more effectively than it could export them to another, insoluble, part of the globe. Indeed, the apparently catastrophic nature of the impacts of modern industrial technology were of such magnitudes as to threaten the extinction of plant and animal species, and, it seemed, the time left for even humankind itself.

Of course, the basic notion that time was finite, at least time for life on Earth, was not new in the twentieth century. Several religions have long included as a central eschatological tenet the proposition of a cataclysmic end to life on Earth. Moreover, at least since the 1850s, science had joined religion by asserting that our sun and, accordingly, life on Earth, had a limiting temporal boundary. Theories of atomic disintegration and the basic laws of thermodynamics compelled the conclusion that the sun would die at some definite time in the future.

The vast temporal dimensions of that unhappy fate, however, largely undermined its otherwise demoralizing impact. Scientific calculations left little doubt that the sun still had millions, indeed, billions of years left. No matter what the discount rate, there seemed little reason to adjust behavior or attitudes based on a consequence so remote in time as to defy any possible contemplation or personal identification. By the 1960s, however, increased public awareness of the potentially catastrophic environmental consequences of certain new technologies and industrial processes had rendered the finiteness of life on Earth a matter of ongoing concern. Nuclear weapons made the catastrophic destruction of human life a real, substantial threat. By publishing its "Doomsday Clock," the *Bulletin of Atomic Scientists* responded to contemporary worldwide events related to war, peace, and the proliferation of nuclear weapons by setting the "clock's" time either further or closer to "midnight" depending on whether nuclear war seemed less or more imminent.[32]

The finiteness of life and the ecological viability of the planet itself were no longer measured solely in billions of years. The Doomsday Clock used mere minutes as a measure. Nuclear weapons could be launched quickly, causing immediate devastation. In the aftermath of the United States' testing of a hydrogen bomb in 1953, the *Bulletin of Atomic Scientists* moved the Doomsday Clock forward to only two minutes before midnight.[33]

The immediate, potentially catastrophic nature of the threats presented by a "bomb" was not confined to nuclear weapons. No doubt in an effort to capture the emotion associated with such weapons, Paul Ehrlich similarly described the threats presented by overpopulation as the "Population Bomb" in his celebrated book of that same name. The analogy was plain. Rather than a nuclear explosion, this bomb was a demographic explosion demonstrating the potential and associated environmental implications of exponential increases in human population then projected to occur. According to Ehrlich, the impact for human welfare and the natural environment was no less severe than that presented by a nuclear weapon. Ehrlich predicted that "every American will probably be subject to water rationing by 1974 and food rationing by the end of the decade" and that pesticides like DDT "may have already shortened by as much as a decade the life expectancy of every American born since 1946."[34]

The controversy surrounding the promotion during the 1960s of a supersonic commercial transport plane, or "SST," reveals the depth of the public's heightened concern. The airplane promised to be able to go much faster than any previous plane—indeed, faster even than the speed of sound. But rather than being widely embraced by the public in a manner consistent with a long-standing fascination with new technologies and acceleration, the SST fell victim instead to the public's growing fears about technology and environmental thresholds. The breaking of the sound barrier is marked by a loud sonic boom, perhaps too disturbingly reminiscent of an exploding bomb.[35]

Increased awareness of the irreversibility of many environmental effects also caused people to think about time differently. At least in the nonquantum world of classic Newtonian mechanics where people live their lives, time goes only in one direction. Time itself cannot be reversed. Yet the consequences of actions taken at one time often can be reversed at some point in the future. The ability to reverse consequences falls far short of reversing time, but it does both offer the possibility of a fresh start and significantly reduce the stakes of making an initial mistake.

In the second half of the twentieth century, however, more and more environmental effects such as the Santa Barbara oil spill seemed irreversible in character and more extreme in scope. Some of this irreversibility resulted from the potential presented by new technology for exploitation of natural resources on much greater scales. As earthmoving equipment grew ever larger, increasing the scale of the impact it could have on the environment, landscapes could be literally transformed in their entirety. As pumping capacity grew exponentially, entire aquifers or deposits of petroleum and natural gas could be completely drained. Even natural resources long thought renewable in character could, because of the scope and pace of resource exploitation, be irreversibly depleted.

New technology was sometimes the precipitating factor for the public's increased awareness of irreversible consequences. Other times, it resulted simply from better scientific understanding of the effects of long-standing practices. The complexity of ecosystems naturally masks cause and effect, so advancing scientific inquiry into the interrelationships between humankind and the natural environment invariably reveals previously unappreciated problems as well as creates opportunities for improvement. One such problem increasingly revealed in the 1960s was species extinction. As more animal and plant species were identified, the number of them found to be at risk, threatened, or recently extinct also became better understood. At the same time, scientists began to appreciate, often for the first time, the distinct ecological importance of different species and subspecies and the disappearing nature of the critical habitats upon which they depended for their survival.

Enhanced knowledge also lay behind the public's increased appreciation during the 1960s of the irreversible nature of certain kinds of pollutants within the natural environment. Some wounds could not be healed by the passage of time. Some contaminants simply persist and continue to accumulate. The resulting increases in concentrations further present the potential for crossing threshold levels at which associated adverse environmental effects may increase exponentially and irreversibly. The biodegradability or nonbiodegradability of particular chemical compounds became, overnight, a matter of common parlance. Many plastics were found to be unexpectedly harmful to the environment because they were not biodegradable and, therefore, would not break down into their basic chemical elements when subjected to natural environmental processes over time. The same was true for many chemical compounds, including, most notoriously at that time, phosphates, which were then included in many popular laundry detergents and, as a result, had polluted the nation's waterways.[36]

The public was, accordingly, compelled to think differently about the nature of time in perceiving ecological cause and effect. Some environmental consequences do not occur immediately, but rather may take considerable time to manifest themselves. It may be months, years, decades, or even generations before the increasing effects resulting from human actions reach a level and form capable of normal human apprehension. As discussed earlier in the book, this ecological feature has distinct implications and challenges for lawmaking, adding to the scientific uncertainty surrounding the development of legal standards while contributing to a distributional asymmetry between regulatory costs and benefits that makes regulation exceedingly difficult to make, maintain, and enforce.

The lengthening of recognized periods of time between cause and effect also has significance for the way people think about time and, even more specifically, for their desire for environmental protection laws. Such temporal delays generate enormous insecurity and dread among those who believe that either they themselves or persons or things they care about are at risk of future harm. The concern never dissipates, because the risk persists over time. The only possible resolution of the threat is provided, ironically, if the risk is realized.

The sense of dread that pervades the affected population may cause considerable immediate harm, wholly apart from whether the risk is itself ever realized in the future. The harm may be both physical and mental. Severe anxiety can destroy mental stability and peace of mind, but it can also lead to a series of debilitating physical ailments, including gastrointestinal problems, high blood pressure, and increased susceptibility to infectious diseases.[37] Substantial economic harm may also result. Economic opportunities, including employment, may be forgone or precluded by looming fears. Property values are also highly vulnerable to public fear of future environmental harm. Such perceived environmental threats, whether or not realized or even whether or not reasonable, can destroy property values.

Whatever the character of the harm, personal or economic, the upshot is increased public demand for laws that purport to reduce or even eliminate the risks in the first instance. That demand may or may not be possible to meet. Still, the concerns associated with risk over time can serve as a powerful impetus in any political drive to overcome the institutional obstacles that make environmental lawmaking so difficult.

Both because lawmakers are responsive to public concerns and because they are, of course, susceptible to the same shifts in attitudes about time and space as the public at large, it is not surprising to see these same themes being struck during the late 1960s and early 1970s by members of Congress (both Democratic and Republican) and by President Richard Nixon in their arguments for more stringent environmental protection laws.[38] They all stressed the need to safeguard the natural environment for future generations, a purpose specifically incorporated into the National Environmental Policy Act of 1969, which stated its objective to "fulfill the responsibilities of each generation as trustee of the environment for succeeding generations."[39] Elected officials took explicit account of the spatial and temporal limits humankind then faced because of the "exponential increase in the pressure of man and his technology upon the environment."[40]

Lawmakers advised each other that they must be guided by the "humble idea" that "[w]e live today in what an engineer might call a closed system. Some of our resources, once used, cannot be replaced. Others of our resources are renewable, but finite."[41] "In one very real sense we are all passengers on the planet Earth."[42] President Nixon cautioned that "[c]onditioned by an expanding frontier, we came only late to a recognition of how precious and how vulnerable our resources of land, water and air really are."[43] Members of Congress, responding to the same concerns being expressed by the general public, described the need to enact laws to correct the past "failure to foresee and control the untoward consequences of modern technology": "[t]he radioactive poisons from nuclear tests, the runoff into rivers of nitrogen fertilizers, the smog from automobiles, the pesticides in the food chains, and the destruction of topsoil by strip mining."[44]

Elected officials also perceived the temporal urgency of the need for tough, new environmental protection laws. "Time is of the essence," one member of Congress warned. "[I]n our struggle to restore our environment[, m]an simply does not have an eternity to right the wrongs he has done to the land, sea, and air. Indeed, he may only have a generation."[45] The pressing nature of temporal limits were, in particular, a central reason why Congress was willing ultimately to provide such stringent protections for endangered species in the Endangered Species Act. The specter of humankind itself as an "endangered species" similarly became a refrain in congressional debates on proposed legislation. "[C]ontinued degradation of the environment through air pollution could cause serious changes in the natural systems regulating the biosphere and possibly destroy the earth's ability to sustain life."[46] "Man, no less than the peregrine Falcon, and the Mountain Lion, is an endangered species."[47]

Finally, although the judiciary (by deliberate constitutional design) plays a far more passive role in lawmaking, judicial opinions during the same time period struck similar spatial and temporal chords. Illustrative is Justice Hugo Black's 1970 dissent from the Court's denial of review in *Named Individual Members of the San Antonio Conservation Society v. Texas Highway Department,* a case in which environmentalists challenged a proposed highway. Reflecting the public mood of the day, Justice Black wrote passionately about the necessity for effective environmental protection laws to ensure humankind's "very survival":

The cars will spew forth air and noise pollution contaminating those acres not buried under concrete. Mothers will grow anxious and desert the park lest their children be crushed beneath the massive wheels of interstate trucks. [Environmental] legislation has come about in response to aroused citizens who have awakened to the importance of a decent environment for our Nation's well-being and our very survival.[48]

During the same era, Judge Skelly Wright, of the United States Court of Appeals for the District of Columbia Circuit, pointedly wrote about the significance for environmental lawmaking of scientific uncertainty joined by the threat of irreversible effects on a "massive scale." Judge Wright described in an opinion for the full appellate court how "[m]an's ability to alter his environment has developed far more rapidly than his ability to foresee with certainty the effects of his alterations." His opinion further explained the challenges government regulators face in "evaluating the effects of unprecedented environmental modifications, often made on a massive scale" and how they must "deal with predictions and uncertainty, with developing evidence, with conflicting evidence, and, sometimes, with little or no evidence at all."[49]

Based on analogous reasoning, judges in the early 1970s began to perceive the relationship between humankind and the natural environment differently and to incorporate those new perceptions into their legal reasoning, with potentially radical implications. For instance, in *Just v. Marinette County*, the Wisconsin Supreme Court held that the state "has a duty to eradicate the present pollution and to prevent further pollution in its navigable waters." The court stressed that while "[s]wamps and wetlands were once considered wasteland, undesirable, and not picturesque," society now understood that "swamps and wetlands serve a vital role in nature, are part of the balance of nature and are essential to the purity of the water in our lakes and streams." Based on such ecological reasoning, the court boldly declared that "[a]n owner of land has no absolute and unlimited right to change the essential natural character of his land so as to use it for a purpose for which it was unsuited in its natural state and which injures the rights of others."[50]

In sum, changes in how the public thought about time, like space, helped to drive environmental lawmaking. The increased public awareness of environmental injuries seemingly shortened time horizons in some ways and lengthened them in others. People now worried more about the finiteness of time, but they also grew more concerned about permanence or irreversibility of some harms and the never-ending persistence of many environmental risks. By the end of the 1960s, the basic political ingredients were well in place, at least in terms of public values and priorities favoring environmental protection, for the legal transformation in the legislative, executive, and judicial branches necessary for the emergence of modern environmental law.

CHAPTER FIVE

Building a Road: The 1970s

The 1970s were an extraordinary decade for environmental law. Prior to 1970, environmental protection was evident in only a handful of fledgling regulatory efforts scattered across offices in the federal government and a relatively few state governments. Those programs expressed the early ruminations of some good ideas but lacked overall coordination, resources, and even a pretense of enforcement. Within just a few years in the 1970s, the federal government brought together and dramatically expanded many of these programs in an effort to forge a comprehensive legal regime for environmental protection. The fifty states, some preceding and some following the efforts made by the national government, began to do the same.

This chapter first highlights the most significant environmental events of the decade, including an overview of the related statutory and institutional changes that occurred. The chapter then discusses the political dynamic behind the changes, with particular focus on the relationships between President Richard Nixon, Congress, the courts, and the emerging environmental public interest community. Finally, the chapter identifies several evolutionary legacies arising out of the 1970s that have since proved to be of enduring significance for environmental law.

A Revolution in Law

The first year of the decade was itself quite remarkable. The bookend events for 1970 were the signing into law of the National Environmental Policy Act (NEPA) on the very first day of the decade, followed in December by the creation of the U.S. Environmental Protection Agency (EPA) and the signing of the Clean Air Act on the very last day of the year. These three events, standing alone, were remarkable.

Although formally titled the "National Environmental Policy Act of 1969," NEPA became law on January 1, 1970, when it was signed with great fanfare by President Nixon. NEPA turned out to be a deceptively simple statute. Its far-reaching declarations of a national policy "to create and maintain conditions under which man and nature can exist in productive harmony" prompted its dubbing as the "Magna Carta of environmental law." NEPA also created a "Council on Environmental Quality" within the Executive Office of the President charged generally with advising the President on environmental issues and more specifically with ensuring governmental NEPA compliance.[1]

But it was NEPA's action-forcing procedural requirements, inspired by the path-breaking collaboration of political scientist Keith Caldwell with the then-chair of the Senate Committee on Interior and Insular Affairs, Henry "Scoop" Jackson, that fundamentally changed the way the U.S. government did business. With the strong backing of the courts, NEPA's straightforward requirement that each federal agency assess and consider the significant environmental impacts of its actions and alternative courses of action before the agency acts changed governmental behavior and policy. Environmental activists seized upon NEPA's sweeping purposes and mandatory language to challenge the lawfulness of federal agency actions with significant environmental impacts. The resulting barrage of NEPA litigation caused substantial delays in government projects because so many government agencies adopted narrow interpretations of NEPA in order to resist preparing "environmental impact statements." The courts repeatedly rejected "crabbed" readings of NEPA submitted by federal agencies as defenses in those cases and the courts, accordingly, routinely enjoined those federal agency defendants from acting until the proper environmental studies had been completed.[2]

Early on, environmental advocates argued with some success that NEPA's mandate extended beyond procedure to include a substantive mandate, which required federal agencies to take reasonable steps to minimize the environmentally harmful effects of their actions or to decline to undertake such actions at all. By the end of the 1970s, however, the U.S. Supreme Court had rejected any such substantive dimension to NEPA, ruling instead that NEPA's mandate was "essentially procedural."[3]

The EPA's creation in December 1970 had an even more profound and long-lasting impact on the nation's environmental laws and environmental quality. As the self-described "guardian" of environmental protection law, the EPA administers the laws enacted by Congress—but it has accomplished far more. Inspired by its first administrators during the early 1970s, William Ruckelshaus and Russell Train, the agency has since its inception served as the primary incubator of new statutory and regulatory innovations and as the primary protector of existing environmental programs.

The ability to play this role within the executive branch is very much the product of the agency's institutional origins. At the time of the EPA's creation, a major point of contention within the Nixon White House was whether the environmental protection functions then dispersed throughout several agencies should be consolidated along with those of the Department of the Interior in a cabinet agency for "Natural Resources and the Environment." The final decision opted for a noncabinet, separate agency concerned exclusively with environmental protection, which remains the EPA's institutional structure today. Those within the Nixon administration who supported that approach expressed the concern that, within a broader cabinet agency, environmental protection objectives risked being captured by competing governmental policies favoring resource exploitation.[4]

From the outset, therefore, the EPA's exclusive mission has been environmental protection. This mission necessarily attracts personnel who share a common interest. By its nature, those not interested in environmental protection are unlikely to be attracted to a job at the agency. While its career employees no doubt frequently differ in many of the particulars concerning how the agency might most effectively accomplish its objectives, those shared objectives remain their overriding concern. The ongoing and exclusive commitment of the EPA's staff to environmental protection has remained a significant constant in the political dynamic surrounding environmental law, notwithstanding significant shifts in the views of political appointees within the agency and elsewhere in the executive branch, the rhetoric of members of Congress, and the opinions of members of the federal judiciary.

The 1970s, however, witnessed a statutory and institutional transformation extending far beyond the creation of NEPA and the EPA. The federal environmental statutes of the early 1970s, beginning with the Clean Air Act, were dramatic, sweeping, and uncompromising. Seemingly every aspect of environmental protection and natural resource conservation was the subject of comprehensive congressional legislation during the decade, and congressional votes were overwhelmingly in support of the new laws. The average vote in favor of major federal environmental legislation during the 1970s was 76 to 5 in the Senate and 331 to 30 in the House, suggesting a broad bipartisan consensus. As one legislator put it in describing his reluctant vote in favor of safe drinking water legislation in 1974, "[a]fter all, if one votes against safe drinking water, it is like voting against home and mother."[5] A listing of the federal environmental laws enacted in the 1970s illustrates the dramatic nature of the virtual revolution in law that occurred (see table below).

The substantive terms of many of these laws were unprecedented in their reach. For instance, in the Clean Air Act of 1970, Congress mandated the achievement by 1975 of national ambient air quality standards necessary for the protection of public health (primary standard) and public welfare (secondary standard). Congress also instructed the EPA to publish an initial listing of "hazardous" air pollutants within ninety days and then, within a year of its listing, to publish final emissions standard regulations. Congress established a similarly rigid schedule for the EPA's listing of categories of stationary sources that "may contribute significantly to air pollution which causes or contributes to the endangerment of public health or welfare" and called for an even tighter schedule for promulgating regulations for new sources. The Clean Air Act also mandated that the administrator achieve a 90 percent reduction in existing levels of automotive emissions of hydrocarbons and carbon monoxide by 1975 and nitrogen oxides by 1976, with a narrow provision for a possible one-year extension.[6]

The statutory undertaking was enormous. It required strict regulation of twenty to forty thousand major stationary sources of air pollution and

Major Federal Environmental Protection Statutes Enacted during the 1970s

Statute	Year
NEPA	1970
Clean Air Act	1970
Federal Water Pollution Control Act	1972
Federal Insecticide, Fungicide, and Rodenticide Act	1972
Noise Control Act	1972
Coastal Zone Management Act	1972
Endangered Species Act	1973
Safe Drinking Water Act	1974
Forest Rangeland Renewable Resources Planning Act	1974
Federal Coal Leasing Act Amendments	1976
Toxic Substances Control Act	1976
Resource Conservation and Recovery Act	1976
National Forest Management Act	1976
Federal Land Policy and Management Act	1976
Clean Air Act Amendments	1977
Clean Water Act Amendments	1977
Surface Mining Control and Reclamation Act	1977
Outer Continental Shelf Lands Act	1978

millions of cars and trucks being driven by average citizens and reductions of 275 toxic air pollutants, many of which were emitted by industries vital to local economies. The short timescale contemplated by the federal law necessarily precluded resolving the tremendous scientific uncertainty associated with the complex mechanisms of air pollution and its reduction. The environmental standards that the EPA ultimately promulgated, therefore, were necessarily based on a fair amount of speculation about present and probable future circumstances. As fairly described by one recent historical account of how Congress and the EPA derived environmental standards, "EPA in those early days was flying blind."[7]

Distinct features of the 1970 Clean Air Act were also plainly reflective of the physical features of the ecological problem the act sought to address. The potentially interstate nature of air pollution prompted Congress to call for the promulgation of nationally uniform ambient air quality standards and for a strong federal role in overseeing state achievement of those standards. Because of the scientific uncertainty associated with determining the actual effects of various air pollutant levels on public health, however, the statute did not purport to announce those national ambient air quality standards itself, but instead delegated that task to an expert administrative agency (the EPA). In instructing the EPA to promulgate national ambient standards, Congress demonstrated its awareness of the complexities of determining ecological cause and effect in the air pollution context and the associated changing nature of scientific information. Congress told the EPA to account for the "latest scientific information," to consider "those variable factors (including atmospheric conditions) which of themselves or in combination with other factors may alter the effects on public health or welfare of such air pollutant," and to take into account the potential for some pollutants in the atmosphere to "interact" with other pollutants in a way that could create yet more or different adverse effects. To that same end, Congress mandated that the EPA undertake review and potential revision of the scientific bases for its national ambient air quality standards and the standards themselves every five years, as well as include "an adequate margin of safety" to ensure that standards were "requisite to protect the public health."[8]

The federal legislation addressing water pollution was no less sweeping, ambitious, or reflective of the distinct physical features of the problem it addressed. The Federal Water Pollution Control Act Amendments of 1972 sought "fishable and swimmable" waters throughout the United States by 1983 and zero discharge of pollutants by 1985. The statute made unlawful any discharge of pollutants into navigable waters absent a permit. The law also established a series of very strict, nationally uniform, technology-based effluent limitations applicable to new and existing categories of industry.

Moreover, the act required a further reduction of discharges when these already strict technology-based requirements proved insufficient to meet state water quality standards.[9]

In many respects, the Federal Water Pollution Control Act reflected the distinct features of aquatic ecology in general and the water pollution problem in general, some of which created challenges different from those presented by air pollution. Congress, for instance, deliberately decided against having water quality standards be the primary basis for pollution control because of the sheer complexity of determining cause and effect of pollutants in aquatic systems. The experience of regulators prior to 1972 was that there were so many factors that influenced the actual impact of pollutants on water quality, including temperature, flow, volume, and the presence of other pollutants, that regulation tied to such determinations would quickly become mired in protracted factfinding and scientific uncertainty. For that reason, and because Congress thought much industrial water pollution was susceptible to effective end-of-pipe treatment, the legislators embraced an approach that emphasized strong, nationally uniform technology-based effluent limitations on water pollutants in the first instance. As later described by the Supreme Court, quoting the 1972 law's legislative history, "[p]rotection of aquatic ecosystems, Congress recognized, demanded broad federal authority to control pollution, for '[water] moves in hydrologic cycles and it is essential that the discharge of pollutants be controlled at the source.'"[10] But, also because water (unlike air) seemed potentially susceptible to zoning for different uses (ranging from drinking, recreation, transportation, and manufacturing), Congress also decided against nationally uniform water quality standards in favor of allowing the states great leeway in promulgating such standards applicable within their own borders. Here too, however, as with the Clean Air Act, Congress included provisions intended to restrict interstate water pollution because of the obvious ability of water naturally to transport pollutants across state borders. Finally, because aquatic wetland areas that constitute the border between land and water are both invariably of great ecological value (and fragility), but simultaneously present heightened opportunities for economic gain based on their accessibility to water, Congress included in the 1972 act distinct provisions for the regulation of the potential filling of those waters and associated wetlands.[11]

Congress also passed a series of laws in the 1970s that focused on particular types of hazardous chemicals rather than on specific environmental media such as air or water. These laws reflected the potentially enormous reach of environmental protection laws into the nation's economy. The Federal Insecticide, Fungicide, and Rodenticide Act of 1972 required the EPA to regulate more than fifty thousand federal pesticides to guard against "unreasonable adverse effects on the environment." The Toxic Substances Control Act (TSCA), which became law in 1976, mandated the EPA's review of more than fifty thousand existing chemicals and approximately one thousand new chemicals each year to identify and, as necessary, to regulate their manufacture, sale, use, and disposal to prevent "unreasonable risk of injury to health or the environment." The Resource Conservation and Recovery Act (RCRA), enacted just ten days after TSCA, provided for the EPA's comprehensive regulation of the generation, transportation, treatment, storage, and disposal of hazardous wastes "as necessary to protect human health and the environment." Falling within the regulatory ambit of RCRA are hundreds of thousands of hazardous waste generators producing hundreds of millions of metric tons of hazardous wastes and thousands of treatment, storage, and disposal facilities of such waste.[12]

The infusion of new federal environmental protection laws prompted a parallel congressional revision of many of the nation's natural resource laws. Consistent with their nineteenth-century roots, these laws had generally reflected policies favoring disposition and exploitation of natural resources rather than their conservation and preservation. The legislation of the 1970s, by contrast, called for restriking the balance in favor of conservation and preservation. The Coastal Zone Management Act of 1972, the Forest Rangeland Renewable Resources Planning Act of 1974 and 1978, the National Forest Management Act of 1976, the Federal Land Policy and Management Act of 1976, the Surface Mining Control and Reclamation Act of 1977, and the Outer Continental Shelf Lands Act of 1978 each imposed both procedural planning requirements (modeled after NEPA) and substantive standards designed to conserve the nation's natural resources and reduce and eliminate certain types of ecological damage.

Perhaps the most far-reaching of these modern natural resources laws, the Endangered Species Act of 1973, did not seek to strike a balance between competing interests at all. It instead singled out the prevention of species extinction, both animal and plant, as an overriding federal policy objective. The act imposed inflexible procedural and substantive requirements on the activities of federal agencies. No "action authorized, funded, or carried out" by any federal agency can be undertaken if "likely to jeopardize the continued existence of any endangered species or threatened species or result in the destruction or adverse modification of habitat of such species." The act further imposed significant restrictions on activities of private persons, including on private lands, that harmed endangered animal species.[13]

Although all of the laws described above were federal in scope, the legal transformation during the 1970s was not confined to the federal government. The new federal laws contemplated a substantial role for state implementation, albeit subject to federal oversight. Under the Clean Air Act, states were responsible, in the first instance, for the preparation of state implementation plans necessary for the accomplishment of nationally uniform air quality standards established by the EPA. Pursuant to the Clean Water Act, states developed their own permitting programs, which allowed them to be responsible for overseeing compliance with the federal water pollution control law within their borders. Similar roles for states existed under most of the federal statutes, including other federal pollution control laws such as the Resource Conservation and Recovery Act, and natural resource conservation laws such as the Endangered Species Act. Despite some resistance to what some states characterized as federal mandates, most states had begun to develop their own environmental programs and agencies by the end of the 1970s.[14]

The task of translating these legal mandates into detailed regulations required new and changing lawmaking institutions. New executive branch institutions at the federal level included the EPA, the Council on Environmental Quality, and the National Oceanic Atmospheric Administration; new environmental protection agencies formed in many states. Other executive branch agencies that found themselves subject to the new laws as much as responsible for their implementation underwent a transformation resulting in changing priorities, personnel, and ultimately even agency culture. There were also new legislative committees and subcommittees and even much discussion regarding the creation of specialized "environmental courts" with jurisdiction over environmental law issues. In short, by the end of the 1970s, the entire legal landscape pertaining to environmental law had been transformed.[15]

Three U.S. presidents oversaw this transformative process: Presidents Nixon, Ford, and Carter. As chief executive, each necessarily played a significant role. President Ford signed a series of important laws, including RCRA, TSCA, the Federal Land Policy and Management Act, and the National Forest Management Act, while successfully vetoing surface mining control and reclamation legislation. During his first year in office, President Carter signed into law extensive amendments to both the Clean Water and Clean Air Acts as well as the Surface Mining Control and Reclamation Act previously vetoed by Ford. Carter also oversaw the passage in 1978 of an ambitious series of laws designed to address a widely perceived national "energy crisis" resulting from the country's dependence on petroleum imports, including the Public Utility Regulatory Policies Act, Energy Tax Act, National Energy Conservation Policy Act, Powerplant and Industrial Fuel Use Act, and Natural Gas Policy Act. While environmentalists generally praised those energy laws aimed at promoting conservation, they were unreceptive and often openly hostile to laws that appeared to roll back environmental protection requirements in order to bolster domestic energy supplies in pursuit of U.S. "energy independence" from foreign oil imports. Although both Ford and Carter played significant roles in influencing environmental law, the 1970s nonetheless belonged to President Nixon. His role was by far the most influential, both because of the timing of his presidency and because of his remarkable personality.

Richard Nixon: The Waxing and Waning of an "Environmental" President

President Nixon's environmental legacy is clearly considerable: he created the EPA and the National Oceanic and Atmospheric Administration; signed into law NEPA, the Clean Air Act, the Federal Environmental Pesticide Control Act, the Marine Mammal Protection Act, and the Endangered Species Act; delivered the first formal presidential message to Congress on the environment; and called for international negotiations for a new Law of the Sea treaty. Nixon's actual role in environmental law's early years, however, is far more complex than a mere listing of significant events that occurred under his presidency would suggest. Thanks to the scholarship of the historian John Brooks Flippen, who undertook exhaustive research of all of the primary historical documents pertaining to the Nixon White House, including the contemporaneous notes of Nixon's advisors and the audiotapes of meetings, Nixon's own words emerge from the historical record and allow for a fuller portrait of his views on environmental law.[16]

Everything was politics for Nixon and environmental law was no exception. Nixon became interested in environmental protection matters almost immediately after his election in 1968 out of concern that the Democrats would be successful in their apparent effort to seize the environmental initiative. Nixon's presidential transition team included a task force on natural resources and the environment consisting of twenty academics, environmentalists, and corporate officials and chaired by Russell Train, the president of the Conservation Foundation and a Republican with strong environmental credentials.[17]

Only one week after Nixon's inauguration, the Santa Barbara oil spill occurred, followed soon thereafter by images of the Cuyahoga River catching on fire. The Democrats, particularly Senator Henry Jackson, acted quickly to seize the issue by proposing environmental legislation. Nixon, not wanting to allow the Democrats to seize the initiative, responded with his own proposals based on his transition team reports.[18]

Nixon was especially concerned about ensuring that the Democrats did not gain any political advantage by campaigning on the environmental issue in the upcoming 1970 congressional elections, but he was even more concerned about Senator Edmund Muskie as a potentially viable Democratic candidate for the presidency in 1972. Running for vice president on a ticket with Hubert Humphrey against Nixon in the 1968 presidential elections, Muskie had emerged from the loss with a highly favorable public image. He was also well poised, as chair of the Senate Committee on Environment and Public Works, to exploit the environmental issue both by garnering favorable publicity for himself and by condemning Nixon for not doing more to address environmental issues.[19]

In late 1969 and throughout 1970, Nixon acted repeatedly to establish his environmental protection credentials. On December 23, 1969, the president ordered a halt to the construction of an environmentally controversial barge canal in Florida. On that same day, he also announced the federal government's use of the Refuse Act as authority to restrict water pollution in the nation's navigable waters. In 1970, the president chose the very first day of the year to sign NEPA into law during a widely publicized New Year's Day ceremony, and pursuant to that same law, Nixon appointed the first Council on Environmental Quality, naming Russell Train as the council's first chair. Nixon privately instructed his new council to "get the administration out front on the environment."[20] Soon afterward, he delivered a formal "environmental message" to Congress and the nation that set forth a sweeping agenda for law reform and institutional change in furtherance of environmental protection.[21] In July 1970, President Nixon proposed, by executive order, the creation of the EPA and the National Oceanic and Atmospheric Administration, both of which came into formal existence by the end of the year.[22]

In the fall of 1970, Nixon selected William Ruckelshaus to be the EPA's first administrator. He chose Ruckelshaus, a young, state government lawyer from Indiana with strong credentials as a vigorous enforcer of environmental protection requirements, over recently defeated congressional candidate (and future president) George H. W. Bush, because the latter's ties to the Texas oil industry were considered a potential political liability. Ruckelshaus quickly established a reputation at the agency as an aggressive enforcer and highly effective advocate for environmental protection.[23]

On December 31, 1970, President Nixon signed into law the Clean Air Act Amendments of 1970, the substantive terms of which he personally played a strong hand in drafting. Perhaps more than any other law, the Clean Air Act reflected the struggle between Nixon and Muskie over the environmental issue. Ralph Nader took explicit advantage by publicly declaring that Muskie might be "stripped of his title 'Mr. Pollution Control' "[24] should Nixon gain the upper hand on pollution control legislation. As Nixon and Muskie each sought to outdo the other in terms of their willingness to address the public's enthusiasm for environmental protection, the result was a remarkably sweeping and ambitious environmental protection law within the Clean Air Act that Congress enacted. To limit Muskie's receiving credit for the legislation, Nixon did not even invite the senator to the presidential signing ceremony attended by members of the national news media.[25]

Notwithstanding President's Nixon's reputation as a strong supporter of environmental protection, his interest in it was surprisingly short-lived. By 1971, the president was already beginning to question the efficacy of the environmental agenda, both as a matter of wise social policy and as a matter of political expedience. The Republican Party had not done as well as Nixon had hoped it would in the 1970 congressional elections. He repeatedly expressed frustration that environmentalists had refused to give him credit for all of his significant accomplishments and had instead continued their criticism that he was not doing enough.[26]

During the first few months of 1971, Nixon began to change course. He speculated to his close advisor Bob Haldeman that "[t]he environment is not a good political issue, only a good defensive one."[27] He began increasingly to view the environmental movement as a fad. In a private meeting with automobile company executives, Nixon declared that environmentalists are "enemies of the system" who wanted the citizens of the United States to "go back and live like a bunch of damned animals."[28]

In June, the president informed Haldeman that the administration should take on the environment and that it "was not a sacred cow." Nixon worried aloud that his administration had been "sucked in too much on issues such as the environment."[29] Events in the fall of 1971 further distanced the president from the environmental position. Environmentalists challenged under NEPA the Atomic Energy Commission's proposal to detonate a five-megaton nuclear device off Amchitka, an Aleutian Island off Alaska. Nixon was reportedly outraged. The White House defeated the challenge only after seven court decisions, including a 4 to 3 vote by the U.S. Supreme Court denying the environmentalists' request to enjoin the denotation. The litigation apparently confirmed Nixon's growing belief that the environmentalists were running amok.[30]

In 1972, Nixon's annoyance with his inability to gain political advantage for his earlier accomplishments persisted and he decided to ally himself with those in industry promoting a backlash to environmentalism. In opposing federal water pollution control legislation then pending in Congress, Nixon described environmentalists as "going crazy."[31] He subsequently vetoed the legislation, which Congress later overrode. The next month, two weeks after the November 1972 election, the president instructed EPA administrator Ruckelshaus not to spend the funds authorized by Congress in overriding Nixon's veto for expenditure under the new law. The Supreme Court ultimately ruled against President Nixon and ordered the EPA to spend the sums allotted by Congress.[32]

In 1973, the emerging oil crisis further solidified the president's opposition to environmental protection legislation. Nixon announced that industry would have a temporary exemption from certain Clean Air Act emissions standards and had his vice president, Spiro Agnew, cast the tiebreaking vote to exempt the Alaska pipeline from NEPA review. When Nixon named Russell Train to succeed Ruckelshaus as administrator of the EPA, he advised Train that the "earlier first blush of emotion and commitment had passed" and Train's job was now "to balance environmental protection with other pressing needs."[33]

By 1974, President Nixon had become one of environmental law's harshest critics. He advised his cabinet to "[g]et off the environmental kick."[34] The White House proposed a series of amendments to existing environmental laws intended to relax their requirements in response to the energy crisis. (EPA administrator Train refused to testify before Congress in support of the proposal.) Nixon also withdrew his support from national land use legislation, which, until his action, had seemed likely to secure congressional passage. And on his last full day in office later that year, the president vetoed the EPA's budget on the ground that it was too high.[35]

Nixon's turnabout is revealing of the inherent challenges of environmental lawmaking. Nixon correctly perceived a temporal disconnect between the politics of environmental protection and the law of environmental protection. Success and failure in the political arena is measured by a time frame far shorter and more episodic than is possible for the analysis of the success of new, complex, and comprehensive legal regimes. Because of the sheer complexity and associated scientific uncertainties of ecological problems, and the inherently compromising and conservative character of our nation's lawmaking institutions, palpable environmental improvements are likely to occur only after years, if not decades, of program experimentation, implementation, and enforcement. In many instances, it simply takes time to understand and address a complex ecological problem. And, even when the answer may be clear, the enormous distributional repercussions of its legislative embrace prompt the enactment of laws that may promise the world, but that are in fact riddled with the compromises and accommodations, which further stall the realization of environmental improvements. Hence, while the electoral politics of environmental protection occur over weeks and months during congressional and presidential election cycles, the yield of environmental protection law frequently presents itself only on a much longer time scale.

At the outset, Nixon, like Muskie and others, reaped the short-term political gains available to those who embraced environmental protection priorities and condemned past actors for creating current environmental threats. But, due to expectations placed on the presidency, it was only a relatively short time before the Nixon administration was held responsible for not solving environmental problems. The political dimension of environmental protection provided no defense for the fact that no such positive results could possibly be so immediately realized. With the help of Democratic Party rhetoric, the Nixon administration came to be perceived as part of the problem rather than the solution. That is the gravamen of Nixon's claim that environmental protection was not a good "political issue," only a good "defensive" one.[36]

Convinced that there was little to gain politically from echoing the seriousness of environmental problems, President Nixon was further faced with the far more immediate economic consequences of environmental protection. As previously described, the costs and benefits of environmental protection law are almost always marked by substantial temporal and spatial divisions. The trade-off between short-term economic costs and uncertain, long-term environmental benefits has never been a popular one for the persons and entities faced with justifying the economic costs. Members of the public are likely to be ready to blame the government officials charged with administering the laws, or, at the very least, they are less likely to be active, generous supporters of the president who oversees the work of those officials. Nixon, accordingly, apparently concluded that his greater political fortunes ultimately lay with the vested economic interests of the regulated community opposed to strict environmental regulation.

Congress, the Courts, and the Environmental Public Interest Community

Remarkably, notwithstanding President Nixon's opposition to the very regime of environmental law he helped create, that legal regime not only survived, but continued to expand in the 1970s. As support from the White House quickly ebbed, environmental law found its institutional supporters elsewhere. The most significant of these supporters were in Congress and the federal judiciary and in the rising environmental law public interest community.

The environmental laws that Congress passed during the 1970s changed tenor as the decade progressed to reflect increasing skepticism and distrust of the executive branch. The statutes imposed hundreds of stringent deadlines on executive branch agencies, primarily the EPA, and increasingly reduced that agency's substantive discretion in meeting those deadlines.

One-third of the deadlines in those early laws were for six months or less; 60 percent were for one year or less; 86 percent of the statutory deadlines applied specifically to the EPA. The comprehensive amendments Congress passed in 1977 to both the Clean Air Act and Clean Water Act were far longer and more detailed than the original acts, passed in 1970 and 1972, with Congress eliminating much of the discretion contained in the short, broadly worded provisions of the prior enactments.

The federal statutes were, however, only the most prominent strands in a detailed web of congressional efforts to oversee the EPA's work. Congress oversaw the executive branch through the budgetary process, mandatory reports to Congress, confirmation hearings on presidential nominations, and general oversight hearings. Congressional oversight of the EPA was remarkably intense because of the extraordinarily large number of congressional committees and subcommittees that could validly claim that the agency's work fell within their jurisdictions. Whether the subject of a given congressional committee was agriculture, marine fisheries, public works, transportation, commerce, small business, energy, science, or foreign affairs, the relationship to environmental protection policy was likely to be direct and substantial. The vast and crosscutting implications of both ecological injury and pollution control virtually guaranteed that the EPA would not lack legislative oversight.

During much of the 1970s, for instance, at least eleven standing House committees, nine standing committees in the Senate, and up to one hundred congressional subcommittees shared jurisdiction over the EPA. Congressional supervision of the agency each year included lengthy and rigorous appropriations hearings on its budget, numerous appearances by EPA officials at hearings, as many as one hundred reports to Congress, thousands of congressional inquiries, and, doubtless even more frequently, less formal direct contact with the agency. EPA officials testified before Congress 92 and 113 times, respectively, during the first two Congresses of the 1970s (the 92d and 93d) and 172 and 212 times during the last two Congresses of the decade (the 95th and 96th).[37]

The federal courts also served an essential supporting role in maintaining environmental law. The judicial review provisions that Congress had included in various environmental protection laws prompted a series of lawsuits challenging EPA rulemaking. Parties seeking judicial review naturally included those within the industry potentially subject to the new rules. But they also included many environmental public interest organizations taking advantage of the citizen suit provisions that Congress had included in the new federal environmental laws.[38]

The courts, moreover, were practically enthusiastic in their welcome of "what promises to be a flood of new litigation—litigation seeking judicial assistance in protecting our natural environment."[39] The first widely celebrated environmental case was *Scenic Hudson Preservation Conference v. Federal Power Commission,* argued in 1965 before the U.S. Court of Appeals for the Second Circuit. The *Scenic Hudson* court agreed with the environmental plaintiffs that the Federal Power Commission had not satisfied its "duty to inquire into and consider all relevant facts" prior to approving a proposal to construct a hydroelectric facility "in an area of unique beauty and major historical significance."[40] *Scenic Hudson* established a pattern for environmental litigation in general that persisted throughout the 1970s. In a series of rulings, the courts made plain their view that the judicial review provisions that Congress had included in the environmental statutes commenced a "new era" "in the history of the long and fruitful collaboration of administrative agencies and reviewing courts." The courts were "in a real sense part of the total administrative process."[41] The courts, accordingly, justified the application of a more exacting standard of judicial review (a "hard look") designed to ensure that agencies provided sufficient consideration to the public's environmental concerns. In similarly breathing substantial judicial life into the procedural requirements of NEPA, the D.C. Circuit declared that it was the court's "duty . . . to see that important legislative purposes, heralded in the halls of Congress, are not lost or misdirected in the vast hallways of the federal bureaucracy."[42] As further elaborated upon by that same court in a subsequent case, the new regime of environmental protection law reflected "the widely shared conviction that the nation's quality of life depended on its natural bounty, and that it was worth incurring heavy cost to preserve that bounty for future generations."[43] Environmental interests, by "touch[ing] on fundamental personal interests in life, health, and liberty," have "a special claim to judicial protection."[44]

Although nongovernmental in nature, both long-standing and newly created environmental public interest organizations played an equally critical role during the 1970s in maintaining environmental law's momentum before all three branches of government. They included those member organizations long associated with resource conservation and preservation issues such as the Sierra Club, the National Wildlife Federation, the National Audubon Society, and the Izaak Walton League. They also included a host of new groups that, modeling their strategy after the courtroom successes of the civil rights organizations of the 1950s and 1960s, adopted a more aggressive, litigation-oriented approach to promoting law reform on behalf of pollution control. The Ford Foundation, in particular, played a key role in this regard, providing several of these new organizations with the substantial initial funding that allowed them to commence operations.[45]

Professor Joseph Sax's early scholarship provided much of the strategic blueprint followed by the environmental public interest groups. In his celebrated 1970 book *Defending the Environment,* Sax argued that sustained citizen lobbying and lawsuits on behalf of the environment were necessary because government alone was not institutionally capable of withstanding industry pressures for ever greater resource exploitation. In his highly influential law review article that same year on the "public trust doctrine," Sax sought to reinvigorate what he argued were long-standing legal principles of state responsibility, based on notions of trusteeship, that he claimed citizens could effectively enforce in court as a means of safeguarding the natural environment. Finally, Sax was instrumental in the securing the passage of the Michigan Environmental Protection Act in 1970, establishing by statute the right of a citizen to initiate a lawsuit to enforce environmental protection requirements.[46]

Environmental organizations in the 1970s filed hundreds of citizen suits against the federal and state governments and private industry, typically using the strict deadlines in the federal laws and legal theories inspired by the public trust doctrine as leverage in negotiating favorable settlements. They lobbied members of Congress and established themselves as invaluable advisors to, and sources of credible information for, congressional committee staff. They also worked, often informally, with career staff within the federal agencies, especially those workers at the EPA and the Department of the Interior who had strong commitments to environmental protection. Those career staff, in turn, often used the threat of lawsuits by environmental public interest organizations as leverage in internal governmental deliberations on policymaking.

The courts, including the U.S. Supreme Court, were generally receptive to environmental citizen suits. Especially noteworthy is that in a series of landmark rulings, the Supreme Court ruled that environmental plaintiffs could meet the "standing" requirements derived from Article III of the Constitution's "case or controversy" requirement for federal court jurisdiction. The Court specifically recognized noneconomic environmental and aesthetic injury as a cognizable injury sufficient to support standing and upheld exceedingly attenuated and speculative allegations of causation as satisfying Article III's requirement that the injury alleged have a sufficient "causal nexus" with the action being challenged. In all of these rulings, the Court eschewed doctrinal rigidity in favor of a process of legal reasoning that accounted for environmental law's features, including the uncertain and speculative nature of such injuries and the more attenuated chains of causation between action and injury. Standing analysis, then, was fairly straightforward and flexible.[47]

When denied access to governmental lawmaking forums, these new activist environmental organizations also knew how to enlist the news media to publicize their concerns and generate public support. The League of Conservation Voters, for example, soon developed "The Dirty Dozen" label for Senators and Representatives who most consistently voted against the environment, and came up as well with a system for scoring members of Congress based on their support for environmental protection legislation. Greenpeace was one of the more successful organizations in generating international media attention through its efforts on behalf of whales and in opposition to nuclear weapons testing.

Environmental nongovernmental organizations grew dramatically both in size and in influence during the 1970s. This included decade-long increases of membership in existing groups such as the Sierra Club (from 113,000 to 165,000 members), the National Wildlife Federation (from 540,000 to 811,000 members), and the National Audubon Society (from 120,000 to 400,000 members), as well as the creation of new organizations ranging from such smaller, national groups as the Environmental Defense Fund and Natural Resources Defense Council to more grassroots organizations such as Greenpeace and Friends of the Earth. By the end of the 1970s, these organizations boasted a combined membership of several million.[48]

As the decade came to a close, many activists who had worked for environmental public interest groups in the early 1970s had become high-ranking policymakers in the Carter administration. Former attorneys from the Natural Resources Defense Council and the Environmental Defense Fund were running programs at the President's Council on Environmental Quality, at the Department of the Interior, at the EPA, and at the Department of Justice's Land and Natural Resources Division. The assistant attorney general who headed the Land and Natural Resources Division, James Moorman, had himself come from the Sierra Club Legal Defense Fund. Moorman dramatically expanded the size of the division, creating new sections concerned exclusively with environmental enforcement, hazardous waste, energy conservation, and wildlife, and he hired attorneys with environmental public interest backgrounds for many of those new positions.[49]

No doubt many of the extraordinary strides environmental law made during the 1970s would not have occurred without the effort and commitment of several remarkable persons working within the government and in nongovernmental organizations. In addition to national environmental leaders such as Russell Peterson of the National Audubon Society, Michael McClosky of the Sierra Club, Rick Sunderland of the Sierra Club Legal Defense Fund, and David Brower of both the Sierra Club and Friends of the Earth, such a list of individuals would include scientist activists such as

Rachel Carson and those academic scientists like Charles Wurster who, in challenging the spraying of DDT in Wisconsin and on Long Island, created the Environmental Defense Fund. The list would also plainly have to include politicians like President Nixon and Senators Muskie and Gaylord Nelson, and congressional staff like Leon Billings, Phil Cummings, Tom Jorling, and Frank Potter, dedicated public servants like William Ruckelshaus and Russell Train, and jurists like Justice William O. Douglas and Judges James L. Oakes, Harold Leventhal, and Skelly Wright. Also included would be environmental lawyers such as David Sive (often referred to as the "father" of modern environmental law), Tony Roisman, and Jim Tripp, who brought some of the earliest environmental public interest lawsuits; John Adams, who helped to create the Natural Resources Defense Fund; Brock Evans, lobbyist for the Sierra Club; Fred Anderson, who was the first president and inspirational force in the creation of the Environmental Law Institute; Gus Speth, a founding attorney of the Natural Resources Defense Council who went on to create the World Resources Institute, chair the President's Council on Environmental Quality, and serve as the head of the United Nations Development Program; and Professor Joseph Sax, who authored pathbreaking legal scholarship on defending the environment through litigation, lobbying, and law reform. Also deserving of mention would be journalist John Oakes of the *New York Times*, whose behind-the-scenes work in shaping that newspaper's editorial policy on environmental policy undoubtedly influenced public opinion and political decisions nationwide.

As important a role as each of these individuals and their respective institutional entities plainly played in the formation of modern environmental law, it would nonetheless be mistaken to characterize them as root causes of that transformation. Their essential role lay in responding to changing public attitudes and priorities and assisting in the effective and creative translation of those public policy preferences into law.

Understanding the 1970s

The 1970s have had a lasting influence on environmental law's subsequent evolution. As the formative decade for modern environmental law, the 1970s left the United States with an extensive array of statutes and legal institutions that have served as the fundamental building blocks for subsequent changes. The legacy of the 1970s, however, extends beyond these basic building blocks to more amorphous, yet no less significant, developments with implications for environmental law's long-term evolution. There were important lessons learned, institutional relationships established, and countermovements born during the decade that have continued to express themselves in the years since. A few of the more significant are discussed below.

The Power of Information Disclosure

NEPA is famous for its bold declarations of environmental policy and for its strictly enforced requirement that federal agencies prepare detailed written statements of the environmental impacts of their actions that may significantly affect the quality of the human environment. NEPA's more far-reaching legacy, however, has been its demonstration of the power of information disclosure as an effective means of regulation.

As it became apparent during the 1970s that NEPA's mandate was "essentially procedural" rather than "substantive," many environmentalists concluded that the "unhappy truth" was that the law lacked any meaningful long-term regulatory impact.[50] The truth about NEPA, though, has been far different. NEPA's mandate that agencies disclose the environmental impacts of their actions resulted in substantial changes in agency behavior with positive effects on environmental protection.

There are many reasons for NEPA's effectiveness. One underestimated reason is that adverse environmental impacts, once publicly disclosed, prove difficult to ignore. Environmentalists are unlikely to have the resources necessary to produce that information on their own. Yet, once armed with NEPA's statutory requirement of information disclosure, environmentalists proved quite capable of forcing the federal government to produce that information for them and, upon its subsequent public disclosure, to use the information as an effective organizing tool.

Even more subtle, but no less significant, the information disclosure requirement turned out to change agency behavior. Most career agency decisionmakers act in good faith. They may be initially reluctant to expend scarce agency resources to develop information, but once the information is before them, they are unlikely to simply ignore it. Most are instead apt to act based on that new information.

Of course, political forces within the agency are always free to ignore that information or even to try to influence its substantive content. Their ability to do so, however, is less than might be assumed. A political appointee who ignores or confronts career staff often does so at her peril. Leaks by career staff to the national news media can seriously damage political careers, and internal staff memoranda critical of agency policy can readily lead to a judicial reversal of the final agency action once litigators subject the agency action to judicial review.

NEPA also made such internal agency confrontations more likely by changing the nature of the workforce employed by federal agencies. Faced with an environmental information disclosure requirement, federal agencies had to hire individuals with educations relevant to the preparation of the necessary documentation. Persons with training in the relevant environmental sciences are unlikely to discount the importance of scientific information related to their chosen profession. The pool of those who choose to study biology, hydrogeology, biochemistry, or wetland aquatics are naturally dominated by individuals who care about those matters. As an agency hires more such persons and their seniority increases over time, a natural environmental constituency develops within the agency itself. NEPA had just such an impact on offices, including environmental assessment offices, within federal agencies throughout the federal government. These offices extended beyond the "action agency" formally preparing the impact statement to include expert environmental offices within other agencies, such as the Fish and Wildlife Service at the Department of the Interior, which is responsible for commenting on a draft impact statement. An adverse comment by such an office can prove fatal to the government's position in subsequent litigation.

NEPA also led to a proliferation of similar environmental disclosure requirements in virtually all of the states (and, more recently, tribes). These laws, referred to as "SEPAs" (and "TEPAs"), closely followed NEPA's model and had as their centerpiece a requirement that the environmental impacts of certain kinds of proposed actions be disclosed. Some of the state laws, however, went further than their federal predecessor. In some states, the information disclosure requirement was not confined to state governmental action but could be triggered by purely private activity with a potentially significant environment impact on the human environment. In other states, the statutory mandates were also not confined to procedural requirements and the preparation of the impact statement. Unlike NEPA (as construed by the U.S. Supreme Court), some state SEPAs included substantive mandates as well, meaning that environmental concerns were entitled to special weight in the determination of whether a proposed activity should proceed.[51]

The information disclosure model was further replicated in another important way throughout the various federal environmental pollution control laws Congress enacted during the 1970s. Virtually all of those laws depend for their enforcement on self-reporting by those subject to federal and state pollution control permits. By federal statute, one of the conditions in a permit issued by the EPA or by a state agency pursuant to a federally approved state program is that the permitee file publicly available self-monitoring reports on regulated emissions. These reports provide

those seeking to ensure the permitee's compliance with applicable requirements with an effective means of oversight and, if necessary, an evidentiary
basis to bring an enforcement action. Indeed, the self-monitoring reports
proved to be the linchpin of citizen suit enforcement under the federal environmental laws during the 1970s.

Finally, open meeting laws were yet another early product of the first
years of environmental law. Congress enacted the Federal Advisory Committee Act (FACA)in 1972, which mandated sweeping reform in the use of
federal advisory committees. As the federal government's executive branch
grew in the post–World War II years, so did the use of outside committees
giving advice to agencies charged with implementing regulatory statutes.
These committees often included members of the business community
subject to those regulations. For instance, at the same time that President
Nixon created the EPA in 1970, he also created the National Industrial
Pollution Control Council (NIPCC), which worked with the Commerce
Department in overseeing the EPA's implementation of the new federal
environmental laws. The members of the NIPCC were from industry
and they held private sessions designed to influence EPA's environmental
standard setting. It was partly because of Senator Lee Metcalf's frustration
with his inability to obtain the minutes of those NIPCC meetings that he
sponsored in the Senate a tough federal open meeting law that, combined
with similar efforts in the House, resulted in FACA, which revolutionized
agency decisionmaking process by mandating greater transparency for the
public.[52]

The Tragedy of Distrust

The modern environmental law movement was born partly from fear
of pollution and partly from public distrust: distrust of industry and distrust of governmental efforts and reassurances. The legislation of the early
1970s responded with sweeping, ambitious goals, but at a cost to the resulting environmental laws. The legal area of environmental protection
came to be dominated by unkept promises and the promotion of a culture within that area dominated by adversarialism, polarization, and distrust.

The early statutes promised dramatic, immediate change, but both the
ecological problems and the regulatory solutions created to resolve them
proved far more complicated and nuanced than had been thought. The
science was far behind the legislative mandates, and early gains in scientific
knowledge seemed mostly to underscore how much we did not understand
rather than to provide clear answers and pathways to the desired environmental improvements. The short time periods provided by statute made it

exceedingly difficult to determine both environmental standards and the controls necessary to achieve them.

Implementation and enforcement also proved to be far from self-executing. It was one thing to get the law on the books. It was quite another to take the steps necessary to implement and enforce the law in a meaningful way. Implementation efforts invariably reveal unintended consequences and inequities that policymakers must consider and address. It takes time and resources to fill in the programmatic details from the statutory outlines. Enforcement decisions, moreover, are inherently discretionary and suffused with policy. There are policy implications implicit in deciding when and against whom to bring enforcement action and in determining the stringency of the sanctions to be imposed for noncompliance. A seemingly strong and inflexible legal mandate can be rendered a practical nullity through lack of enforcement.

Furthermore, many of those subject to the newly emerging environmental protection requirements were powerful economic entities. They did not welcome laws that sought to impose significant economic costs for seemingly speculative benefits to be realized, if at all, in distant times and places. These entities accordingly sought ways to resist and delay implementation and enforcement. None was likely to change its long-standing practices very quickly, especially to the extent that the entity might naturally harbor legitimate concerns that its competitors would not be similarly complying and, therefore, not incurring the same expenses.

The EPA was, accordingly, faced with a dilemma. The statutory mandates were unforgiving, as was the public expectation of results, but the achievement of immediate, discernible change was proving increasingly elusive. The situation was complicated by the fact that members of the public demanding environmental improvements were themselves generally unwilling to undertake any of the lifestyle changes necessary for those mandates to be achieved. The public vigorously opposed parking restrictions, car pooling requirements, and other regulatory measures designed to reduce air or water pollution by regulating individual behavior. Congress often responded to the public outcry against some measure by limiting EPA authority while simultaneously criticizing the agency for failing to achieve environmental statutory deadlines.

Equally unforgiving were members of the regulated community and officials of state and local governments who found themselves subject to the EPA's jurisdiction. Industry fought EPA efforts to implement the statutes, challenging agency regulations and statutory interpretations in court. State and local governments chafed under the threat of federal usurpation of regulatory authority over matters of public health, safety, and welfare that they viewed as within the ambit of their exclusive control. Both those in industry and many in state and local governments naturally sought their own champions in the Congress to question the EPA's efforts.

Any EPA effort to accommodate the complaints of the regulated community or the states, however, was met by stiff opposition from environmental groups, which insisted on strict adherence to statutory mandates and deadlines. Environmentalists joined litigation brought against the agency by states and the regulated community, effectively sandwiching the EPA between the two opposing positions that it was doing too much and too little. And, like industry and the states, environmentalists also sought advocates in Congress who would guard against the EPA's neglecting its statutory responsibilities.

A pathological cycle involving national environmental policy in general and the EPA in particular emerged from the 1970s. When the EPA failed to meet a statutory deadline or to otherwise accommodate the regulatory community, members of Congress, especially those on the authorization committees who had drafted the relevant law, and the environmental community widely condemned the agency. On the other hand, when it demanded strict compliance with the law, members of the regulated community, some state governments, and members of Congress, especially those on appropriation committees more sensitive to economic concerns, similarly denounced the agency.

Constituencies that were naturally skeptical of the EPA's mandate and implementation efforts developed within the executive branch itself. President Nixon's NIPCC, whose members included industry officials charged with advising the federal government on federal pollution control policies, ended in 1975 after Congress refused to appropriate staff funds, but not equally short-lived was the regulatory oversight role that the Office of Management and Budget (OMB) assumed soon after the EPA commenced operations. Pursuant to a series of executive orders throughout the 1970s, the OMB increasingly scrutinized the context of EPA regulations based on their potential adverse impact on the national economy. Moreover, because of the OMB's primacy on matters of agency budgeting, there was always at least a veiled threat of budgetary retaliation in the event that the EPA ignored OMB advice on pending EPA rulemakings.

The EPA was often caught in a whirl of clashing political forces. Senator Muskie's Air and Water Pollution Subcommittee of the Senate Committee on Public Works was sharply critical of the agency for failing to implement federal environmental laws with sufficient vigor, as was Representative Paul Rogers's Subcommittee on Public Health and Welfare of the House Committee on Interstate Commerce. The subcommittees sponsored several highly publicized oversight hearings at which EPA officials were criticized.[53]

The congressional criticism was not confined to those who believed that the EPA was not doing enough. There were plenty of congressional overseers concerned with potential agency overreaching. For instance, as a result of internal compromise, the EPA's budget was initially within the jurisdiction of the House subcommittee chaired by Representative Jamie Whitten, an outspoken critic of many environmental laws. Whitten accordingly used the appropriations process to conduct lengthy inquiries into the details of the agency's implementation of those laws. He quite openly opined that Congress may not actually have intended full implementation of the environmental laws it had passed: "Sometimes a fellow might feel that if he writes a law three times as strong as he wants it to be, maybe it will be carried out 100 percent." Whitten also described his ability to "limit use of money" in order to cut back on environmental laws.[54]

By the close of the 1970s, there was considerable distrust of the EPA. The agency had consistently failed to meet statutory deadlines and had continuously been subject to denunciations based on allegations of over- or underregulation. The high degree of scientific uncertainty, the human emotions triggered by threats to public health, and the tremendous costs of regulation combined to ensure the constantly high volume of those complaints. "By making promises that [could not] be kept, and thus forcing EPA to reformulate public policy, Congress indirectly undermined public confidence in the Agency's competence and good faith."[55] When, moreover, members of Congress themselves treated the agency as "every elected official's favorite whipping boy," they directly eroded the public trust of the EPA that any agency charged with safeguarding public health must maintain in order to be effective.[56]

The culture of adversarialism and distrust that pervaded much of environmental lawmaking during the 1970s also led to sharp divisions within the environmental community. There were many heated disagreements about tactics, especially the propriety of compromising on environmental values for either short- or long-term returns. David Brower, a leading figure within the Sierra Club, broke away from that organization over disagreements on policy and strategy. The organization Friends of the Earth resulted from that clash, but later suffered from its own internal disputes, with Brower's leaving and forming the Earth Island Institute.[57]

Both the EPA's difficulties and those within the environmental community are directly traceable to the challenges faced by environmental lawmaking described in the opening chapters of this book. Significant conflict and controversy naturally result from the nature of ecological injury, the kinds of strains placed on lawmaking institutions seeking to fashion environmental law, and the clashes in personal values implicated by any effort to decide upon the appropriate level of environmental controls.

For that reason, the EPA's dilemma could be viewed positively as part of the small price to pay for the nation's first effort to reshape its relationship with its natural environment. The conflict and controversy surrounding the EPA were, from that same positive perspective, simply a necessary evil: the inevitable consequence of administrative agency implementation of fundamental social change in our system of government, which depends heavily on skeptical and critical oversight by competing branches and sovereign authorities. By their very nature, moreover, environmental problems promote just such intragovernmental conflict in lawmaking. Each conflict is directly traceable to the spatial and temporal features of environmental degradation and, accordingly, are a necessary expression of our lawmaking system rather than evidence of institutional failure. Regardless of the accuracy of such a positive "spin," the culture of adversarialism and distrust that developed around environmental law in the 1970s has had a powerful and long-lasting legacy in the decades since.

Developing Fissures in Environmental Lawmaking: Federalism and Regulatory Reform

Although consensus in lawmaking marked the birth of modern environmental law at the inception of the 1970s, deep fissures were evident by the end of the decade. Some problems were less directly tied to environmental law *per se* than to broader concerns about lawmaking apparently being promoted by environmental law. Others, however, did relate directly to the environmental protection requirements themselves, based on mounting claims that those requirements were so unreasonably demanding and inflexible as to be destructive of public welfare and the nation's economy. These two movements, which emerged largely in response to the apparent substantive and institutional thrust of environmental lawmaking, ultimately came in subsequent decades to be known as "federalism" and "regulatory reform."

Federalism. The federalism movement in environmental law has many strands, but its common thread is a concern about the possible diminution of the essential prerogatives of the states as independent, autonomous sovereigns—and that concern is not without basis. To a large extent, both industry and environmentalists promoted a dominant federal role in a deliberate effort to diminish the role of the states. The automobile industry, for instance, began to promote federal clean air legislation for the purpose of precluding the possibility of each of the fifty states' insisting on their own separate emissions controls and thereby complicating manufacturing standards. In particular, California's imposition in the late 1960s of its own pollution control requirements on automobiles prompted the industry to favor some form of preemptive federal legislation, even if fairly strict.[58]

No doubt, however, the primary impetus for the federal government's taking a dominant position in environmental protection came from those favoring more, rather than less, regulation. The most oft-stated concern of those advocating a strong federal role was that the states were less likely to enact tough environmental pollution control laws. The reasons were several. First, the state governments were likely to be sensitive to complaints made by local industry about the costs of pollution control and, therefore, less likely to possess the political will needed to impose and maintain those controls. For similar reasons, states might engage in a "race to the bottom," competing for new industry by imposing less demanding environmental controls than neighboring states. Finally, at least for many in the emerging environmental public interest community, there were decided practical advantages to a national focus. It was far easier for an environmental organization to concentrate its limited resources on lobbying efforts before Congress or a federal agency than to mount such an effort in each state.[59]

The federal environmental laws were, however, directly responsive to "race to the bottom" concerns. The Clean Air Act imposed nationally uniform air quality standards on all states, overriding the objections of economists that such national uniformity made little economic sense. Why, those economists asked, should air quality standards be uniform when neither the benefits of those standards nor the costs of their achievement were similarly uniform? The Clean Water Act was similarly directed. It imposed a series of minimum uniform, technologically based effluent limitations on categories of industries throughout the nation, limitations that no single state had the power to relax.[60]

The states also likely suffered in the debates about their proper role in federal environmental law from skepticism arising out of the civil rights movement that dominated so much of the period immediately preceding the 1970s. Many environmental activists had also been active in the civil rights movement. Justly or not, these environmentalists still viewed many states as obstacles to social change rather than as potential allies.[61]

The spatial dimensions of the pollution problem also weighed heavily in favor of national legislation. While the value of local solutions to local problems could not be gainsaid, the logic of national approaches to problems that defied state jurisdictional boundaries proved overwhelming. Environmental advocates constantly reminded lawmakers that pollution does not stop at state borders and that, in the absence of federal restrictions, states could be expected to minimize the costs to their own citizens by promoting economic activities that brought jobs and taxes to the state while exporting the harms of environmental pollution to other states.

Nature, without more, provided the ready means to export pollution. By their physical nature, air and water could transport pollutants to states and localities downwind and downstream from their industrial sources. A state need not, therefore, even "race to the bottom" in terms of degrading its own environmental quality to promote its competitive economic advantage over other states. It need do no more than take advantage of the natural tendency of the flow of water and the movement of air to disperse pollutants beyond its own borders. The Clean Air Act, accordingly, specifically addressed the interstate pollution issue, as did the Clean Water Act.[62]

Finally, the new federal pollution control laws were not the only cause of the heightened tensions between federal and state sovereigns arising out of environmental law. Equally controversial during this time were the amendments being made to federal natural resources laws that portended both greater federal oversight of the management of resource-rich lands, located mostly in the West, and a greater emphasis on resource conservation and preservation. These laws included the Wilderness Act of 1964, the Endangered Species Act of 1973, the Federal Land Policy and Management Act of 1976, the National Forest Management Act of 1976, and the Surface Mining Control and Reclamation Act of 1977.

These laws brought to the surface long-simmering controversies between the federal government and many western states. Almost all of the public lands owned and managed by the federal government are located in the western part of the nation, including Alaska. In the continental United States, the percentage of federal ownership ranges from approximately 29 percent of the state of Washington to 87 percent of the state of Nevada. Many western states have long been wary of the threat to their sovereignty presented by such a large, powerful landowner within their borders. At the turn of the century, these states and their supporters in Congress argued vehemently against the national government's retaining ownership of such a vast western territory. They believed that it would be unduly destructive of their sovereign prerogatives to allow for a competing sovereign landowner within their borders, especially when the Supremacy Clause of the federal Constitution might mean an ousting of state regulatory jurisdiction over federally owned lands. Of particular concern, the Supremacy Clause might mean that states could regulate and tax activities on a substantial proportion of the territory within their respective borders only with congressional acquiescence.[63]

So long as the federal government pursued a policy both promoting private commercial exploitation of the public lands and state taxation of those activities, the economic concerns within the western states were dampened. When, however, the federal natural resource laws began in the 1970s to suggest significant limitations on such exploitation in favor of environmental protection, a political coalition in opposition naturally arose. Opponents included both private economic interests hostile to the substance of the new federal laws as well as state government officials protective of their regulatory prerogative to determine the pace of natural resource development within their borders. The movement, which later became known as the "Sagebrush Rebellion," even prompted some western states to enact laws that formally denounced the federal government's retention of ownership of public lands and called for its relinquishment of ownership of much (and in some instances all) of the National Forest lands, subsurface mineral rights, and lands then administered by the federal Bureau of Land Management.[64]

By the end of the 1970s, moreover, those opposed to the redistributive thrust of environmental protection laws began to question more broadly the notion that the nature of ecological problems justified such a dominant federal role in either pollution control or natural resource conservation. The states themselves were not, however, the sole voice behind this increasing sentiment. Members of the regulated community joined in, perhaps owing to the demanding federal environmental legislation that had ultimately been passed, now believing that they would fare better under state control. Many states, now joined by industry, increasingly promoted state autonomy as an essential value of such independent constitutional import that it should cast doubt on the legitimacy of any legal regime, including environmental law, that undermined state sovereignty. This federalism theme, raised at the outset in the 1970s, became an increasingly powerful evolutionary force in subsequent decades.

Regulatory Reform. One striking aspect of the vast array of sweeping environmental protection laws enacted by Congress in the 1970s was the relative ineffectiveness of any industry opposition. Industry leaders warned that the new laws were too extreme, were too expensive, and would cripple the nation's economy and produce significant unemployment. Some industry leaders accused environmentalists of being communist sympathizers and drew parallels between the writings of environmentalists and *Das Kapital* and *Mein Kampf.* But neither the U.S. public nor, even more significant, many members of Congress seemed persuaded by such exaggerated rhetoric. The once prevailing notion of "what's good for General Motors is good for the United States" had been replaced by the public's rising distrust of industry assurances and dread of the unknown adverse health consequences of industrial pollution.[65]

Many in business assumed in the early 1970s, as did then-President Nixon, that the environmental movement was a passing fad, fed by an upsurge of emotion, that would subside as quickly at it seemed to them to have emerged. Such thinking misapprehended both the breadth and depth of the roots underlying environmentalism and the public's embrace of environmental protection concerns. By the mid-1970s, however, industry leaders began to recognize the tenacity of the public's commitment and, accordingly, initiated a series of deliberate, long-term strategic steps to try to recapture the high moral ground and cast doubt on the wisdom of the new environmental protection laws. They sought to characterize the environmental laws as irrational and extreme and as the product of emotion and national hysteria rather than sound thinking. The auto industry, for example, made exorbitant doomsday claims, in speeches and congressional testimony, that compliance with the new Clean Air Act standards would be "impossible" and cause "business catastrophe" (only soon thereafter to adopt the catalytic converter that succeeded in reducing emissions and improving fuel economy).[66]

The regulated community's strategy for changing public attitudes was deliberate and extensive. Among those crafting the strategy were William Simon, who became head of the Olin Foundation in 1977; Irving Kristol, an influential conservative writer; and Richard Scaife of the Mellon Foundation. They, along with others, sought to persuade the business community that ideas were important and that social philanthropy should be affirmatively used to promote ideas sympathetic to the interests of business. Kristol wrote at the time that it was "absurd" to give money to institutions whose views or attitudes they disapproved of and that business should instead give to those who "believe in the preservation of a strong private sector."[67] "American business," Simon contended, should stop "financing the destruction of free enterprise." What was instead "desperately needed" was to give "funds to scholars, social scientists, writers and journalists who understand the relationship between political and economic liberty."[68]

Accordingly, a group of conservative business and intellectual leaders identified those charitable foundations that had played instrumental roles in promoting the efforts of environmental public interest groups, such as the Environmental Defense Fund and the Natural Resources Defense Council, and lobbied those foundations to cease their funding. The leaders of this new conservative movement decided to create their own foundations to support new think tanks and conservative public interest law firms— for example, the Heritage Foundation, the American Council on Science and Health, the Institute for Educational Affairs, the Washington Legal Foundation, and the Pacific Legal Foundation—that would be philosophically supportive of business concerns. Industry leaders also sought ways to influence the national news media that they believed had been unduly sympathetic to the claims of environmentalists.[69]

These counteroffensive efforts by business to reshape public attitudes and influence the future development of environmental law had both immediate and longer term effects. Henry Ford III argued vehemently for the Ford Foundation, which had been instrumental in providing critical seed money that launched groups like the Natural Resources Defense Council, to cease its funding of environmentalists. He declared that it was time "to examine the question of our obligation to our economic system" and argued that "[t]he Foundation exists and thrives on the fruits of our economic system." Soon thereafter, a newly appointed head of the Ford Foundation decided to end its funding of those national organizations.[70]

Simon, Mellon, and others funded industry-sympathetic research by think tanks and independent scholars. Walter Wriston, then the chief executive officer of Citibank, explained: "It takes about twenty years for a research paper at Harvard to become a law. There weren't any people feeding the intellectual argument on the other side." More conservative, pro-business philanthropic foundations, such as the Olin and Mellon Foundations, sponsored research and scholarship by establishing chairs and fellowships at the Heritage Foundation, the Hoover Institute, the American Enterprise Institute, and Murray Weidenbaum's Center for the Study of American Business at Washington University, all of which were heavily funded by business donations.[71]

The influential role played by the national news media was also a focal point of industry's response to the newly enacted environmental laws. The editors of the editorial page at both the *Washington Post* and *New York Times* were, according to one account, dismissed for being too "antibusiness" in their outlook. The *Times* fired John Oakes in 1976; under Oakes, the *Times* editorial page had run a series of editorials advocating environmental causes. Philip Geyelin, who left his position at the *Post* in 1977, had similarly promoted positions favored by environmentalists.[72]

Business interests also sought other avenues to influence news media coverage. They established the Media Institute in 1976 for the purpose of monitoring the media's coverage of business. The Mobil Oil Corporation started buying advertising space on the op-ed page of the *New York Times* in 1971, a practice it later extended to similar space in the *Washington Post, Boston Globe, Chicago Tribune, Los Angeles Times,* and *Wall Street Journal.* Many of these "ads" simply expressed Mobil's view on current environmental issues. In the mid-1970s, the American Electric Power Company similarly commenced a multimillion-dollar advertising campaign in opposition to the mandatory use of scrubbers for air pollution control and in favor of greater reliance on coal and nuclear power. In 1976, the Advertising Council initiated its own multimillion-dollar effort to inform the public about the importance of the U.S. economy. Corporations spent $100 million and

$140 million in advocacy advertising on environmental and energy issues in 1975 and 1976, respectively.[73]

The business community also sought ways to improve its own public image. As described by one chemical industry strategy document prepared in 1979, industry needed to engage in a multimillion dollar advertising campaign to counter "growing evidence that the public image of the chemical industry is unfavorable, and this has a negative results on sales and profits."[74] One apparent industry effort was to increase grants to entities such as the Public Broadcasting Service (PBS). Even absent formal advertising, PBS nonetheless provided those corporate sponsors with prominent favorable images simply by directly associating their names with popular PBS shows. Corporate donations to PBS increased from $3.3 million in 1973 to $22.6 million in 1979.[75]

None of these undertakings had any perceptible impact on environmental laws themselves during the 1970s. Yet, their long-term effect has been quite substantial. As described in the next two chapters, the actions taken by the business community effectively established the political and intellectual foundation for a series of subsequent reform efforts that have challenged the basic tenets of the environmental protection laws that Congress enacted in the 1970s.

CHAPTER SIX

Expanding the Road: The 1980s

Modern environmental law's second decade was marked by immense contradiction and persistent expansion. The first year, 1980, itself witnessed the election of Ronald Reagan as president in November, immediately followed by congressional passage during the lame-duck session in December of two extraordinarily far-reaching laws of the very kind Reagan had campaigned against: the federal Superfund imposed sweeping liability on generators, transporters, and disposers of hazardous substances, and the Alaska National Interest Lands Conservation Act reaffirmed the legitimacy of federal ownership of vast acreage in Alaska and limited commercial exploitation of much of its resources in favor of conservation and preservation objectives. Moreover, when Reagan sought in the early 1980s to make federal environmental protection and natural resource conservation policies more friendly to business, his efforts were rebuffed with such ferocity that they led to the enactment of a series of new federal environmental laws even more demanding than their predecessor statutes. But the 1980s ended much as the 1970s had begun, with a surface consensus favoring environmentalism masking sharp disagreements about environmental law. The presidential candidates of both major political parties, including Vice President George H. W. Bush, vied for the mantle of "environmental candidate," the Pope declared the lack of environmental protection a "moral crisis," and *Time* magazine celebrated Earth itself as the "Planet of the Year" in favor of its normal practice of announcing a "Man of the Year."[1]

Like the preceding chapter, this chapter first describes the environmental highlights of the decade, including the reform efforts of the Reagan administration, the significant changes in environmental law, and the ways that environmentalism began to transform both U.S. law in general and the U.S. legal profession in particular. The chapter then discusses the reasons for these developments, with particular focus on why the Reagan reform effort failed and why environmental law evolved so expansively during the 1980s. The chapter concludes by identifying several broader trends established in the 1980s that portended significant changes for environmental law in the 1990s.

The Reagan Revolution That Wasn't

When Ronald Reagan was elected president in November 1980, there was good reason for the confident predictions that the nation's environmental and natural resources laws would soon undergo major changes favored by industry. Environmentalists had been far from effusive in their praise of the Carter presidency, especially its national energy policy that had threatened to promote resource development and energy production at the expense of environmental protection and resource conservation. But environmentalists' preference for Carter over Reagan in 1980 was nonetheless quite clear.

As a presidential candidate, Reagan had made little effort to conceal his skepticism of the wisdom of the environmental laws of the 1970s. Reagan's core philosophy favored less government regulation and more economic freedom for business to expand the economy and, according to the Reagan formula, thereby build the wealth of the nation. Candidate Reagan had promised "a total review of thousands and thousands of regulations" and the elimination of those unnecessary and burdensome "to the shopkeeper and the farmer and the individual as well as to business and industry."[2]

The environmental laws of the 1970s seemed to Reagan and to many of his supporters in the business community to be the epitome of federal governmental overreaching. They imposed needless "bureaucratic red tape" on business and threatened to cripple the nation's economy with the exorbitant compliance costs. Reagan questioned whether the regulatory costs were worth their uncertain benefits. In a comment that inspired much ridicule, he suggested that trees produced far more nitrogen oxide air pollution than did industry, confusing nitrogen oxide with nitrous oxide, which does result from the natural decaying of trees but which does not contribute to air pollution endangering public health and the environment.[3]

Reagan, the former governor of California, was also naturally hostile to the environmental laws of the 1970s to the extent that they expanded the authority of the federal government seemingly at the expense of state sovereignty. He campaigned in favor of greater deference to state authority in general and proudly announced that he was a "Sagebrush Rebel," formally linking himself with those in the western states who favored the federal government's relinquishment of ownership and management authority of the public lands in the West. Reagan even went so far as to embrace the notion that federal retention of the ownership of the public lands was "contrary to the Constitution [and] contrary to the basic law when the thirteen colonies first came into the Union."[4]

The Republican Party's formal platform in 1980 was similar in tone and substance to candidate Reagan's rhetoric. It promised redress for the "crushing burden of excessive federal regulation"; it isolated "EPA's . . . excessive adherence to 'zero risk' policies" for special criticism; and it emphasized the need to make "rational" "clean air, water, and waste disposal" policies. The platform literally declared "war on overregulation."[5]

Both the formal transition to the Reagan administration in December 1980 and the first few months of the new administration in 1981 signaled just such a major shift in national environmental policy. The new conservative think tanks funded by business during the 1970s, such as the Heritage Foundation, quickly published detailed blueprints for the administration's sweeping reform of the nation's environmental and natural resource policies. These studies identified specific offices that should be headed by persons more sympathetic to business concerns as well as individual programs and regulations that warranted reform. David Stockman, the president's pick to head the Office of Management and Budget (OMB), warned in a memorandum soon before Inauguration Day "of a 'ticking regulatory time bomb' " that required "strict, comprehensive and far reaching policy corrections." According to Stockman, "a whole new mindset down at EPA" was necessary because otherwise EPA rules "would practically shut down the economy if they were put into effect."[6]

Immediately after his inauguration, President Reagan announced that Vice President George Bush would head a cabinet-level Task Force on Regulatory Relief that would be responsible for reviewing new regulatory initiatives as well as reassessing existing regulatory programs. The task force, within a week of its creation, suspended approximately two hundred pending regulations. Vice President Bush asked industry leaders to identify for the task force particularly burdensome regulations, which resulted in a "hit list" of 119 existing regulations that the task force concluded warranted reconsideration, over half of which were EPA regulations.[7]

The centerpiece of the regulatory reform effort, spearheaded by Stockman at the OMB, was Executive Order 12,291, issued by the president in February 1981. That new executive order required all executive branch agencies to submit proposed and final regulations to OMB for prepublication review and further required that all "major rules"—those with an annual impact on the economy of more than $100 million—be accompanied by a cost–benefit analysis (dubbed "regulatory impact analysis") modeled in many respects after the National Environmental Policy Act (NEPA). OMB authority under the executive order was significantly stronger than it had been in prior administrations, because it provided for OMB review of proposed regulations, purported to authorize OMB to block final publication of rules until OMB approval, and declared overarching cost minimization and cost–benefit standards to guide OMB's review.[8]

Reagan's appointees to head the most important federal environmental agencies held similar outlooks on the need for regulatory reform. James Watt, the new secretary of the interior, had been president of the Mountain States Legal Foundation, a conservative, pro-development public interest organization that had challenged a number of natural resource conservation and preservation programs on behalf of commercial interests. Watt made little secret of his intention to reduce restrictions on the economic development of federal lands by miners, loggers, and ranchers. He seemed to invite "confrontation with [his] emphatic, colorful, and frequently inflammatory rhetoric."[9] Watt described the Department of the Interior as "oppressive," and he condemned as "environmental extremists" those who "would deny economic development" of the nation's natural resources and thereby "weaken America." Watt acknowledged his general support of the objectives of the Sagebrush Rebellion, and, soon after becoming secretary of the interior, he advocated transferring millions of acres of federal lands into private ownership.[10]

Anne Gorsuch (née Anne Burford), Reagan's first EPA administrator, had been a state legislator in Colorado, where she earned the reputation of being skeptical of the efficacy of environmental protection laws, hostile to heavy-handed federal oversight of state programs, and sympathetic to business complaints about regulatory burdens. Reagan's candidates to head the EPA were reportedly asked by the president's transition team whether they were willing "to bring EPA to its knees."[11] If this is so, Gorsuch may well have given the desired answer. Fairly or unfairly, her early actions at the agency were quickly perceived by environmentalists and reported by the national news media as designed to undercut environmental regulation and enforcement. Gorsuch's repeated efforts to reorganize sections of the agency, including its enforcement branch, were characterized as eliminating enforcement. Her proposals to reduce the EPA's budget by as much as one-third simply confirmed for her critics her anti-environmental agenda. And her attempts to render environmental regulations more flexible and cost sensitive, especially newly promulgated hazardous waste regulations, were met by waves of public criticism and condemnation.[12]

While Watt and Gorsuch served as the primary lightening rods for President Reagan's environmental policies during his first years in office, they were only two of several controversial actors. Reagan himself caused a political firestorm by announcing the abolition of the President's Council on Environmental Quality, a decision from which he subsequently retreated in the wake of significant political opposition. The president's appointees to other key environmental policymaking positions shared, like Watt and Gorsuch, a pro-business, deregulatory agenda. The new assistant secretary of agriculture overseeing the Forest Service and the management of the national forests was John Crowell, who had been lumber corporation Louisiana-Pacific's general counsel; the new head of the Bureau of Land Management was Robert Burford, who had championed the rights of ranchers on public lands, both in his individual capacity as a rancher himself and as a Colorado legislator; and Reagan's newly appointed head of the Department of the Interior's Office of Surface Mining was Robert Harris, a leading critic of federal surface mining control legislation who had brought litigation challenging its constitutionality.[13]

Quite surprisingly at the time, the otherwise very popular President Reagan achieved very little of his regulatory reform agenda in the area of environmental law. Both Watt and Gorsuch left their positions in the wake of considerable controversy and criticism within the first four years of the administration, with Gorsuch departing the EPA after only two years. Her departure was no doubt the more tumultuous. Congressional committees investigated allegations that she had engaged in "sweetheart" deals, agreeing to not bring some enforcement actions and to settle others on terms favorable to industry. When Gorsuch, based on advice from Justice Department lawyers, declined Congress's request that she turn over enforcement documents for committee review, Congress voted her in contempt. The executive branch ultimately turned over the documents, but twenty high-ranking EPA officials, including Administrator Gorsuch, were effectively forced out of office as a result of the document controversy, and an independent counsel was appointed to investigate whether there had been criminal misconduct in the prior refusals to release documents. Gorsuch was never indicted, although one of her assistant administrators was ultimately convicted of perjury and sent to prison.[14]

Of the two agency heads, Secretary Watt no doubt accomplished more of his agenda. He had previously worked at Interior and, therefore, knew how to accomplish bureaucratic change more quickly. Watt also knew that a secretary of the interior has a distinct policymaking advantage over an EPA administrator because the relevant statutes had historically conferred on the secretary considerable discretionary authority as manager of the nation's public lands. Secretary Watt could accomplish substantial change without congressional agreement and often in a less politically visible, decentralized fashion. From this position, Watt expanded oil and gas leasing on the outer continental shelf, accelerated mineral leasing of public lands, reduced land acquisitions for national parks, and transferred more authority to private ranchers for the management of federal rangelands.[15]

Watt did not achieve his more sweeping proposed reforms, however, because he failed to anticipate the extent to which public land law had gradually changed during the decades preceding his tenure, incrementally reducing the secretary's discretionary authority. By the time Watt became secretary, the position no longer enjoyed virtually unchecked authority to manage the public lands. During the 1970s, Congress had added significant procedural and substantive requirements to many public land laws, and the federal judiciary had displayed a willingness to oversee the enforcement of those requirements. As a result, although Watt certainly accomplished more at Interior than Gorsuch did at the EPA, his accomplishments, too, had a surprisingly brief impact. Watt was forced out of office a few months after Gorsuch in 1983, resigning in the wake of a tidal wave of criticism after he publicly referred to the membership of a federal advisory committee as including "a black, . . . a woman, two Jews and a cripple."[16]

Even more important, Congress enacted none of the Reagan administration's proposals to reduce the various federal environmental and natural resource laws. Nor were any of the administration's formal efforts to reduce the reach of the environmental protection laws through administrative and regulatory change enduring. Many of these initiatives were so poorly received when proposed that they were abandoned as soon as they were challenged. Many other policies resulted in lawsuits by environmental organizations and were ultimately struck down by the courts. The federal courts, especially in the years before Reagan's own appointments to the federal bench rose in their influence, included many judges generally sympathetic to the goals furthered by the environmental laws of the 1970s. These judges stood ready to guard against the misdirection of environmental policies by the executive branch, striking down what they perceived to be the Reagan administration's flouting of federal environmental statutory mandates.[17]

To be sure, some of President Reagan's proposed reforms survived political controversy and formal legal challenge. There was increased exploitation of natural resources on public lands and on the outer continental shelf, and there were administrative changes to environmental protection programs, including regulatory flexibility under the Clean Air and Clean Water Acts. The administration redefined the meaning of "source" under the Clean Air Act in a way that permitted major sources of pollutants to increase some emissions without triggering the strictest control requirements. And the U.S. Army Corps of Engineers expanded the use of "nationwide permits" under the Clean Water Act to allow for more development within wetlands in the absence of individual permitting proceedings.[18]

It is nonetheless far from clear that the modicum of reform that did occur during this time period was more than what would likely have occurred during a second Carter administration. The EPA during Carter's presidency, led by Douglas Costle, had been contemplating many of its own reform measures during the last year of the administration. President Carter had also proposed a series of energy initiatives, including the creation of a fast-track consolidated permitting agency (the Energy Mobilization Board), opposed by environmentalists, which would have expedited the development and production of domestic energy supplies. Many of the reforms that happened under Reagan might well have taken place even if Carter had been reelected president.[19]

Ironically, it might well be that more reforms intended to increase environmental law's flexibility and cost sensitivity would have been successfully adopted and implemented in the absence of a Reagan presidency, because those measures could have been debated without the tremendous political controversy surrounding Reagan's environmental policies. Even some supporters of President Reagan have openly speculated that his environmental appointees managed to retard any possible reform effort by discrediting their own initiatives. The president's own chair of the Council of Economic Advisors publicly declared, "We will be lucky if, by January 1985, we are back where we were in January 1981 in terms of the public's attitude toward statutory reform and social regulation."[20]

Simply put, officials in the Reagan administration struggled to sell any meaningful reforms, regardless of their actual merits. The mere association of the reform with the administration tended to destroy its credibility, as both Watt and Gorsuch further polarized debates surrounding environmental matters. No doubt for this reason, the harshest critics of the early Reagan environmental policies were conservatives who had supported the significant reforms that the administration itself had discredited.[21]

Even the purported beneficiaries in industry of the Reagan regulatory reform effort became disenchanted with the administration. Business interests generally favored a reduction in regulation, but many far preferred a tough regulatory regime to an uncertain one. The controversy and regulatory instability created by Gorsuch and Watt made long-term investment difficult. When it became clear that first Gorsuch and later Watt could not provide such stability, even their political support in industry diminished, and their departure from the administration quickly followed. Perhaps the death knell for Gorsuch's tenure at the EPA came when former EPA administrator Russell Train, who had served under President Nixon and had strong ties in both the business and environmental communities, published an op-ed piece in the *Washington Post* suggesting that Gorsuch "budget and personnel cuts, unless reversed, will destroy the agency as an effective institution for many years to come."[22]

For these reasons, much of the last six years of the Reagan administration and the first two years of the subsequent Bush administration, closing the 1980s, were marked by efforts on the part of those administrations to distance themselves from the debacle of the first two years of the decade. To restore the credibility essential to the working of the EPA, President Reagan was effectively compelled to turn to William Ruckelshaus in 1983 to replace Gorsuch as EPA administrator. While Ruckelshaus was with the timber industry when asked to return to the agency, he still possessed the stature and credibility necessary for the position based on his successful term as the EPA's first administrator. When Ruckelshaus quietly left the agency just before Reagan's second inauguration in January 1985, he was replaced by his deputy, Lee Thomas. Thomas was not nearly as well known as Ruckelshaus nationally, but he brought to the position a similar reputation as a professional, nonideological administrator committed to responsible implementation of the agency's statutory mandates.

Secretary Watt's successor, William Clark, was not nearly as well received as either Ruckelshaus or Thomas, but he took care during his tenure at Interior to avoid the political landmines both laid and set off by his predecessor. The rhetoric of the Sagebrush Rebellion that had dominated the 1980 campaign and the Reagan administration's first heady months all but disappeared. Indeed, except as mere political rhetoric, such extravagant proposals lacked substantial support even among many Republicans in the western United States. Most westerners enjoyed the substantial recreational opportunities offered on the public lands; those opportunities, however, were at risk if those public lands either went into private ownership or were managed pursuant only to state laws that lacked the kind of protection for recreational interests found in federal law. In addition, there was reason to believe that the federal government's selling off grazing lands might lead to *less,* not *more* grazing, because environmental and recreational interests might be able to outbid ranchers for the property. Somewhat paradoxically, therefore, selling the public rangelands could have left ranchers worse off, as they lost not only the subsidy of federal management, but even any possible right of access.[23]

The political necessity for the Republicans to restore their environmental credentials did not end at the close of Reagan's second term. To avoid the political taint created eight years earlier by Watt, Gorsuch, Stockman, and Reagan himself, then-Vice President Bush campaigned to be the "environmental" president, a far cry from the antiregulation rhetoric of Reagan's 1980 campaign speeches and the Republican Party's 1980 platform. Bush famously attacked his opponent, Massachusetts governor Michael Dukakis, for the seriously polluted waters of Boston Harbor. Upon his election, Bush not only appointed William Reilly, president of the World Wildlife Fund, as EPA administrator, but followed through on his campaign pledges by providing essential sponsorship to significant new national air pollution control legislation. In the 1970s, President Nixon and Maine senator Muskie had competed in their support for tough air pollution control policy. As the 1980s came to a close, it was President Bush and another Democratic senator from Maine, George Mitchell, who were both collaborating and competing in their efforts to secure passage of new, comprehensive amendments to the federal Clean Air Act.

As described in more detail below, the ironic upshot of the Reagan attack on federal environmental law was most likely more, not less, demanding federal environmental legislation. Possible positive reforms designed to make environmental standards less rigid and more flexible in their application became harder, not easier, to achieve. The sum total of affirmative reforms achieved during the Reagan years certainly fell far short of any fundamental retrenchment of federal governmental regulation for environmental protection, let alone the promised "revolution."

Solidifying Environmental Law

Partly because of and partly notwithstanding the Reagan administration, the scope of environmental protection dramatically expanded rather than contracted during the 1980s, as environmental laws became more far-reaching and demanding. This included the passage of several new laws, as well as extensive amendments to the pollution control laws of the 1970s. As a result, environmental law became a settled part of the legal landscape and, therefore, ingrained in both public and private expectations.

Remarkably, Congress enacted the two most extraordinary environmental laws of the 1980s during the few weeks following Reagan's election in a December lame-duck session of Congress that occurred just prior to his inauguration. Normally, there is little, if any, significant legislation enacted during such transitional periods, especially when, as occurred in late 1980, a presently minority party would soon take control in both the White House and the Senate. The party about to take over the reins of leadership has every incentive to block any significant lawmaking during the interregnum. In 1980, there was also particular reason for that to be true in the environmental area given that the incoming president had campaigned against the enactment of sweeping environmental laws. The Republican leadership in Congress, however, did not block the legislation, but instead worked closely with their Democratic counterparts in fashioning acceptable compromise bills.

The first significant bill was the Alaska National Interest Lands Conservation Act (ANILCA), signed into law by President Carter on December 2, 1980.[24] ANILCA represents one of the single most significant federal natural resource laws that Congress has ever enacted. As described by Carter, the legislation "set[ ] aside for conservation an area of land larger than the State of California." ANILCA doubled the size of the National Park and Wildlife Refuge Systems, adding more than 97 million acres; doubled the size of the Wild and Scenic River System; and tripled the size of the Wilderness System by adding 56 million acres.[25]

Wholly apart from the practical dimensions of the new law, it was of substantial precedential significance. It reaffirmed, just as the Sagebrush Rebellion was purportedly on the rise and about to find its way into the White House, the legitimacy of federal retention and management of public lands. It also promoted both resource conservation and preservation objectives on an unprecedented scale, notwithstanding considerable commercial pressure to relax restrictions on resource development. By December 1980, moreover, passage of the Alaska legislation had become a political necessity for both sides of the aisle in Congress. Neither the then-impending inauguration of President-elect Reagan nor the Republican's ascendancy a few weeks later to the leadership of the Senate was sufficient to impede congressional action. The historic withdrawal by President Carter and Interior Secretary Cecil Andrus in December 1978 of millions of acres of public lands in Alaska from mineral and other commercial development provided the White House with considerable leverage. The advantages to all of the congressional compromise reflected in ANILCA outweighed the risks of starting the negotiations again under a new Congress and new president.[26]

The single statute, however, that most transformed environmental law and the environmental law profession in the 1980s was the Comprehensive Environmental Response, Compensation, and Liability Act (CERCLA), which also became law in December 1980.[27] Unlike all the other major environmental laws of the preceding decade, CERCLA, popularly known as "Superfund," was a *liability* rather than a *regulatory* statute. By imposing monetary liability on those entities that contributed to releases and threatened releases of hazardous substances, CERCLA sought the cleanup of the numerous abandoned and inactive hazardous waste sites littering the nation's landscape.

The existence of such sites was partly the result of decades of underregulation of disposal activities by state and local governments. Absent regulatory oversight, companies would dispose of their hazardous wastes either on- or off-site in unsecured containers, often burying them in landfills lacking any liners, leachate collection systems, or monitors. Unless one is in the waste control business, waste is inherently a nonproductive aspect of most activities. Neither a business seeking to maximize profits nor a governmental agency seeking to minimize costs is likely to spend any more on waste control than the minimum required by law.

But the hazardous waste sites targeted by CERCLA were also partly the natural result of the tough regulatory statutes that Congress and the states had enacted in the 1970s. Because of the expense of complying with those statutes, many hazardous waste disposal businesses shut down. The unintended consequence of tough prospective laws was, consequently, even more abandoned dump sites across the nation with hundreds and sometimes thousands of barrels and tanks eroding and leaking onto the land and into nearby surface waters and groundwaters. By their nature, waste disposal laws are difficult to monitor and to enforce. There are many clandestine ways to dispose of hazardous wastes, making violations easy to commit, difficult to discover, and, if the cost of compliance is high, a seemingly easy way for a business to save a lot of money.

Driven by public concern over publicized hazardous waste sites such as Love Canal in Buffalo, which reportedly leeched suspected carcinogens "into the backyards and basements of 100 homes and a public school," Congress intended CERCLA to be a drastic, short-lived remedy for a national emergency.[28] It imposed monetary liability for the costs of cleanup on those responsible for creating the hazardous waste sites. It also imposed a tax on the chemical industry (later amended to apply to corporations in general) to create a fund to pay for the cleanup costs. This "Superfund" was used both to pay for cleanup costs in advance of the recovery of those costs from those legally responsible and to pay for cleanup at those orphan sites where no solvent responsible parties could be identified.[29]

The standard of liability was strict, meaning that it did not depend on any showing that those responsible for creating the site had, at the time of their actions, acted negligently, recklessly, or in an otherwise legally culpable manner. As further interpreted by the courts, CERCLA also imposed liability on a "joint and several" basis in those circumstances in which the injury to be redressed was deemed legally "indivisible." Joint and several liability allows a plaintiff to compel any one of several legally responsible parties to pay the *entirety* of damages—here, the cleanup cost of the site. Because, moreover, of the combined effect of deliberate mixing and leaking, poor recordkeeping at the sites, and the ways in which the forces of nature (namely, wind and water) further commingle contaminants, most Superfund sites were legally indivisible.[30]

What made strict, joint and several liability so transformative of the law, however, was its potential scope of application. CERCLA identified as potentially responsible parties not only the current owners and operators of the sites where the hazardous substances were located and those who transported the substances to the site. It also extended liability to (1) all past owners and operators at the time of disposal and (2) any entity that arranged for the transportation or disposal of discarded hazardous substances.[31]

The category of past owners and operators extended the scope of liability back in time to prior landowners who might have had no active involvement in the waste disposal activity beyond passive ownership of the property. The impact of such a temporal expansion of liability on a strict, joint and several basis was tremendous. Not only did it retrospectively sweep in persons and entities who had long assumed that their responsibilities had ended with formal relinquishment of land ownership, but it also sent a strong signal throughout the real estate and banking industry regarding the implications of the ownership of land. The result has been that few purchasers of real estate now consider the transaction without detailed inquiries into the past uses of the property, including the possible presence of hazardous substances. Possible environmental liability became a normal part of the negotiation of real estate transactions, especially of industrial property. At the very least, the price of such property reflected possible cleanup costs, and some sales of contract made cleanup an express condition of sale. Several states made investigation into possible contamination and remediation of any environmental hazards discovered a formal condition of a lawful sale.[32]

The practical impact of CERCLA's extending its liability scheme to so-called arrangers was, however, even greater. The federal statute did not make liable only current and past owners and operators of the sites and those who had transported the hazardous substances to them. It also singled out for liability those persons who "arranged" for the transportation, treatment, storage, and disposal of the hazardous substances now located at the sites and requiring cleanup. The single most significant category of such arrangers comprises the original generators of the hazardous substances. This category of responsible parties is extraordinarily broad, including representatives of nearly every manufacturing and industrial activity in the United States, ranging from the most powerful Fortune 500 company to the family-owned neighborhood dry cleaner. It also reaches many federal agencies, including the Department of Defense and the EPA, many state agencies, all municipal governments and hospitals, and public and private universities and colleges. Under CERCLA, each was potentially subject to strict, joint and several liability for the cleanup of all hazardous substances located at the same site where their own hazardous substances had been disposed.[33]

After CERCLA became law, liability for environmental contamination was no longer just someone else's problem. It became everyone's problem,

and the impact of this change was immediate and far-reaching. It generated a huge demand for environmental lawyers to represent those concerned about their potential exposure. It also made public and private
entities more aware of the implications of not taking every possible measure to guard against liability based on future activities. Indeed, although
CERCLA was formally only a liability law concerned with existing conditions based largely on past conduct, CERCLA's greatest impact was likely
on future behavior. The threat of such sweeping liability in the future indirectly prompted industry proactively to seek out ways to change their
manufacturing processes to minimize the production of hazardous wastes.

Congressional passage of CERCLA and ANILCA in 1980 were not,
however, the only significant environmental laws of the decade. Congress
substantially amended in the 1980s the Clean Water Act; CERCLA; the
Federal Insecticide, Fungicide, and Rodenticide Act; the Resource Conservation and Recovery Act; the Safe Drinking Water Act; and the Toxic Substances Control Act. Each of these legislative amendments reflected similar
characteristics, all in response to Congress's distrust of the Reagan administration's willingness to implement fully the federal environmental laws.
Each eliminated substantial EPA discretion, and imposed tighter and more
deadlines on agency action.[34]

For instance, the 1986 amendments to CERCLA dramatically expanded
the size of the Superfund from $1.6 billion to more than $4 billion, imposed more stringent cleanup standards on Superfund cleanups, and reduced EPA discretion in settling cases. Indeed, the amendments were so
strict that the White House staff recommended that Reagan veto the bill,
but he declined to do so, apparently because of concerns voiced by Republicans in Congress that such a veto could hurt their reelection prospects a
few weeks later in November.[35]

The best illustration of congressional attitudes toward the EPA during
the Reagan administration, however, is provided by Congress's amendments in 1984 to the Resource Conservation and Recovery Act (RCRA),
which governs solid waste management and the treatment, storage, and
disposal of hazardous waste. When first enacted in 1976, RCRA conferred
on the EPA very broadly worded authority to promulgate treatment, storage, and disposal regulations for hazardous waste "as may be necessary
to protect human health and the environment." As amended in 1984, the
statute imposed sixty additional deadlines on the agency and extended jurisdiction to 130,000 small-volume generators of hazardous waste and 1.4
million underground storage tanks.[36] The law dictated precisely when each
of a series of regulations had to be published, the dates by which permits
had to be issued, and the substantive criteria that the permits had to contain.

The statute also imposed a series of default prohibitions on the disposal of specified categories of hazardous wastes should the EPA fail to meet certain deadlines. Under these prohibitions, the agency's failure to meet a deadline meant that land disposal of the waste was effectively prohibited. In the face of such an inflexible and harsh result, both the EPA and the regulated community had great incentive to ensure that all deadlines were met. As described by two commentators at the time, the amendments were "dripping with evidence that Congress [did] not wish to entrust EPA with too much."[37]

Finally, environmental law also rediscovered in the late 1980s the power of information disclosure as a regulatory tool. The modern era of environmental law began in 1970 with NEPA, which was exclusively an information disclosure statute requiring federal agencies to prepare environmental impact statements for major federal actions significantly affecting the quality of the human environment. During the rest of that first decade and throughout much of the 1980s, however, information disclosure mandates like NEPA seemed supplanted in significance by the next generation of comprehensive command-and-control permitting requirements that, like the Clean Air and Clean Water Acts, imposed specific numeric limitations on pollution sources. Information disclosure requirements came to be viewed as representative of an early legal regime for environmental protection that had not yet matured into a full-fledged program dominated by environmental quality standards and effluent and emissions requirements.

In 1986, however, information disclosure again proved itself to be a powerful supplementary basis for promoting environmental quality. The impetus for the renewed legislative attention was, as is often the case for environmental law, an environmental accident with tragic consequences. In December 1984, a Union Carbide plant in Bhopal, India, accidentally released a toxic compound, methyl isocyanate, killing more than three thousand people and seriously injuring many thousands more. When, in August 1985, another Union Carbide plant in West Virginia accidentally released a toxic compound resulting in the hospitalization of nearby residents, Congress responded with new legislation. In neither instance did the surrounding communities have notice of the potential for releases of such toxic compounds, let alone emergency plans to minimize the public health impacts in the event of such a release.[38]

Passed by Congress in October 1986, the federal Emergency Planning and Community Right to Know Act (EPCRA)[39] required emergency planning by industry in anticipation of such accidental releases, as well as the public reporting of chemical releases so that residents would know what chemicals were being released into their communities. EPCRA required annual reports of toxic releases by manufacturing companies employing more then ten full-time employees in widely defined industrial manufacturing activities. Both the reports themselves, known as the "Toxics Release Inventory," and their practical impact surprised government regulators and the regulated community alike. Industry reported annual releases much greater than had been anticipated, and the general public showed unexpected interest in the data. Many citizens requested information regarding releases and the national newspaper *USA Today* published in August 1989 a list of "The Toxic 500," referring to the nation's industries reporting the highest volumes of toxic releases, as did several national environmental organizations.[40]

The information, while far from either comprehensive or timely, proved to be invaluable. Government regulators learned that some chemicals were being released in quantities far greater than had been suspected. The magnitude of such releases made government officials aware of the need to regulate releases previously thought too incidental to warrant systematic control. Industry also gained new knowledge and discovered new opportunities, as better understanding of their own releases sometimes suggested new ways to reduce the amount of waste they generated through the adoption of pollution prevention strategies.[41]

Industry also reacted to public disclosure by reportedly unilaterally reducing toxic releases. The most widely publicized of such actions was the 1989 pledge by the chief executive officer of the agricultural company Monsanto to reduce its air emissions of hazardous chemicals by more than 90 percent by 1992. By the end of the 1980s, some in government and many commentators were touting information disclosure and voluntary reductions as the single most promising source of achieving a next generation of pollution reduction.[42]

The most innovative form of environmental regulation, however, was achieved by the state of California. In November 1986, voters in that state approved by referendum Proposition 65, entitled the "Safe Drinking Water and Toxic Enforcement Act of 1986." Proposition 65 imposed flat bans on the discharge of certain carcinogenic or reproductive toxics into drinking water and also imposed a duty to warn on those persons responsible for exposing individuals to those toxins. What made these requirements especially effective was that they shifted the burden of scientific uncertainty from government regulators to the party responsible for the discharge. Accordingly, the discharge ban was lifted only if the discharger could establish that the release would not be "significant." Likewise, the duty to warn was lifted if the person responsible for the release could establish that there would be no significant risk even assuming a lifetime of exposure.

Even more than the federal experience with the Toxics Release Inventory, Proposition 65 provided companies with a substantial economic incentive to reform their manufacturing processes and reformulate their products so as to reduce toxic releases and exposures. The Safe Drinking Water Act had such an immediate effect on those products, like water faucets and well water pumps, that are intimately involved in the physical delivery of water to people. But the broader warning requirements also proved extremely effective. No company could easily bear the adverse market impacts of tying their product to an explicit warning of possible carcinogenic or reproductive toxicity. The resulting pressure for technological innovation led in turn to a series of significant reductions in toxic exposures in California. No formal emissions limitation or design standard was necessary—the general duty to warn, coupled with the threat of adverse public reaction in the marketplace, proved sufficient.[43]

The Greening of American Law and the Legal Profession

The significance of the 1980s for environmental law was not confined solely to the nation's rebuff of the Reagan administration's deregulatory efforts, Congress's detailed amendments of both first- and second-generation environmental statutes, or the rediscovery of the power of information disclosure. Virtually all U.S. law was "greened" during the 1980s. The environmental protection and natural resource statutes were simply the most obvious, surface expression of the legal transformation. The emergence of environmental law in the United States, especially during the 1980s, involved an assimilation of environmental law by U.S. law generally. The new scientific understandings, public values, and societal goals expressed by environmental law were not confined to environmental protection statutes, but rather infused one category of legal rules after another, transforming U.S. laws in response to the public's demand for environmental protection.

Law expresses a tentative equilibrium struck between competing values and priorities at a moment in time. Yet, like any equilibrium, law is always susceptible to destabilization and, accordingly, possible modification in response to changes in any of the factors underlying it (e.g., factual assumptions, values, or distribution of political or economic power). In the process of legal evolution, areas of law reflecting different factual and policy premises can confront and inform each other and result in changes in legal doctrine.

It became evident during the 1980s that modern environmental law was sufficiently entrenched and widespread in the United States to have just such a transformative effect on the law in general. Environmentalism and modern environmental law challenged many of the equilibria upon which legal doctrines in a variety of crosscutting areas rested. Indeed, because of the pervasive contextual reach of activities subject to environmental protection restrictions, hardly an area of law was left untouched.

The development of administrative law provides a telling example. It is fair to say that the reformation of modern administrative law occurred primarily on an environmental law slate. Judges responded to what they perceived to be a pressing need for a heightened judicial role in environmental controversies. According to these judges, environmental disputes warranted closer judicial scrutiny both because of the interests of future generations not formally represented in court and because of the substantial costs of complying with environmental standards. The courts, accordingly, developed the "hard look" doctrine, which called for especially searching judicial examination of agency decisionmaking records; they imposed extra procedural requirements on agencies to ensure that all interested parties had a full opportunity to bring to the agency's attention their concerns prior to the promulgation of an environmental standard; and they relaxed standing requirements to provide for easier access to judicial review. Congress, in turn, created new administrative procedural devices, such as enhanced rights of public participation in the Clean Air Act. Finally, the executive branch agencies developed new decisionmaking techniques such as negotiated rulemaking, which provides a nonadversarial forum where agency officials can meet with environmentalists, representatives from industry, and officials of state and local governments to forge agreements on how environmental regulations should be fashioned.[44]

Tort law likewise evolved in response to environmental concerns. Traditional tort doctrine proved unable to provide meaningful redress to the new class of environmental injuries. For instance, the latency period between a defendant's negligent conduct in exposing a plaintiff to harmful substances and the manifestation of physical injury decades later had repercussions both for what kind of evidentiary showing a plaintiff could reasonably make regarding causation as well as when a plaintiff could reasonably be expected to initiate a lawsuit. A reformation of tort doctrine was therefore necessary for tort law to provide meaningful remedies to injured persons. The result has been the emergence of an entirely new area of law referred to as "environmental torts," as well as some, albeit still relatively modest, modification of long-standing tort doctrines such as nuisance law and causation as well as statute of limitation periods for the filing of lawsuits.[45]

The interaction between property and environmental law has also been significant, but far less one-sided in character. Because environmental law challenges many of the scientific, economic, and sociological assumptions underlying much of private property doctrine, environmental law's rise in the 1970s and 1980s seemed to portend a corresponding erosion of private

property rights in natural resources. Yet, because property rights enjoy constitutional protection, that confrontation led to a series of claims that environmental protection laws were themselves unconstitutional. The most
frequent legal complaint was that environmental restrictions on the use of
property were so harsh as to constitute the legal equivalent of a "taking" in
violation of the Fifth Amendment's prohibition on governmental takings
of private property for public use in the absence of just compensation.[46]

Similar evolutionary patterns of environmental law and environmental
concerns prompting legal change were repeated throughout other areas of
law. They occurred in fields as diverse as alternative dispute resolution,
banking, bankruptcy, corporate, criminal, First Amendment, insurance,
remedies, securities, and tax law. Each discipline underwent a significant
process of transformation in response to the public's desire to have a legal
system that better reflected environmental protection goals.[47]

Finally, because of sweeping new laws like CERCLA and the large
number of areas of law constantly intersecting with environmental statutes,
the field of environmental law increased correspondingly the number of
practitioners and their prominence. By the end of the 1980s, no major law
firm in the country lacked environmental law expertise. No major corporation could afford not to have in-house environmental expertise in both its
legal and engineering departments, and most corporations hired vice presidents who were primarily responsible for environmental matters. Most
large municipalities also began to hire in-house environmental law experts,
as did state agencies and federal agencies, such as the Departments of Defense and Energy that were themselves liable "arrangers" under CERCLA
and, consequently, potentially responsible parties.[48]

The increase of environmental lawyers in the U.S. Department of Justice during the 1980s is also illustrative of the overall national trends. The
Justice Department's Land and Natural Resources Division grew into a
potent force with several hundred lawyers in the latter half of the 1970s,
but its Environmental Enforcement Section still had only approximately
fourteen lawyers at the end of the Carter administration in 1980. By the
beginning of the George H. W. Bush presidency in January 1989, that same
section included about 110 lawyers and there was an entirely separate section of approximately thirty attorneys working on environmental criminal
enforcement. The EPA exhibited a similarly large increase in its number
of environmental lawyers. The agency employed about fifty-two lawyers
when it commenced operations in the early 1970s, but employed more than
six hundred by the end of the 1980s. The American Bar Association's section on Environment, Energy, and Resources had grown to 10,772 members by 1989. The term "environmental law" did not even merit a separate
entry in the *Index to Legal Periodicals* until 1973. By 1989, "environmental

law" had been joined by separate headings for "coastal zone," "environmental protection," "endangered species," "U.S. Environmental Protection Agency," "fish and game," "forests and forestry," "hazardous waste liability," "hazardous waste sites," "international environmental law," "wetlands," and "hazardous substances." The number of pages in the *Index* devoted to listing articles related to environmental law correspondingly grew from four in 1970 to nine by 1989 (and twelve by 1990).[49]

In short, as the decade of the 1980s came to a close, environmental law and the associated legal profession were booming. The regulatory reform response to the stringent requirements of the 1970s—sought by some and feared by others—had essentially failed.

Understanding the 1980s

The 1980s marked environmental law's adolescent years. Rebellion and conflict replaced any remaining pretense of political unity and social consensus on environmental policy matters. They were tumultuous years for environmental law. Although neither Anne Gorsuch at the EPA nor James Watt at the Department of the Interior served in their respective government positions for especially long, they cast a shadow over the entire decade. They influenced the development of environmental law in significant respects, albeit not at all in the direction they had likely hoped. The environmental laws that emerged from the 1980s were even more demanding, pervasive, and settled than those existing at the beginning of the decade.

As with the 1970s, however, the legacy of the 1980s is not simply the establishment of formal legal requirements. The 1980s confirmed environmental law's surprising persistence, the depth of which had been hinted at but far from established by the close of the 1970s. The 1980s also witnessed the laying of the foundation for the evolutionary shifts in environmental law that would be realized in subsequent years. Some of these shifts were more expansive in direction; others were more supportive of regulatory retrenchment. Some of the more significant shifts are discussed below.

Environmental Law's Persistence

Environmental law's surprising persistence was the most important environmental lesson of the 1980s. Its obituary had been repeatedly written. In the 1970s, environmental law withstood mounting criticism from a president (Nixon), but one whose political popularity was ultimately on the wane. By contrast, in the 1980s, a highly popular president (Reagan) repeatedly sought to reduce the stringency of federal environmental regulation throughout two terms in office. But here again, Reagan's reform efforts, like those of Nixon before him, largely failed. Environmental law proved capable of tenaciously maintaining, and even expanding, itself in the face of withering presidential criticism.[50]

The fundamental mistake made by Presidents Nixon and Reagan, and by Reagan's environmental advisors, was their failure to appreciate the depth of the public's aspirations for environmental protection as well as the public's fears of human health threats from environmental pollution. The Reagan administration repeated Nixon's mistake of assuming that public support for environmentalism was thin and ultimately reversible. The administration thought, incorrectly, that it could manipulate the kinds of fears harbored by the public in the 1970s that had favored more environmental regulation into a shift of public opinion in favor of less regulation.

Revealing in this respect was OMB director David Stockman's attempt to appropriate the term "bomb" in arguing in favor of regulatory reform. Presumably playing upon public dread associated with nuclear weapons, environmentalists in the 1960s and 1970s had referred to "bombs" and "ticking time bombs" in describing the threats presented by overpopulation and poor hazardous waste disposal. In the 1980s, Stockman sought to co-opt the term by characterizing the threat to the nation presented by overregulation as a "ticking regulatory time bomb."[51]

Members of the general public, however, simply rejected the characterization. They accepted the basic premise that environmental threats were serious and substantial, and governmental regulation was, therefore, necessary. Rather than perceiving regulations as posing an equivalent threat, the public saw attacks on environmental regulation as confirming their fears that government would be "captured" by the regulated industry and, at industry's behest, seek to enrich business at the expense of the public health and the environment. The public's innate distrust of government and business had been an important factor in environmental law's genesis in the 1970s. Watt and Gorsuch unwittingly retriggered that distrust and ultimately became its political victims.

The Reagan administration also underestimated the ability of the environmental community to organize effectively against administration reform efforts. The day immediately after Reagan's inauguration, leaders from the ten major national environmental organizations met at a restaurant just a few blocks away from the White House to develop an opposition strategy. They pursued during the following years a coordinated strategy, working with members of the news media, sympathetic career employees within the federal government, political opponents to the administration in Congress, and skeptics in the federal judiciary. The series of news reports hostile to Watt and Gorsuch throughout the early 1980s, the plethora of oversight hearings held in Congress, and the numerous victories in litigation were not mere happenstance or the result of simple good fortune.

The environmental community tapped into the public's hopes and fears. Unlike the Reagan administration, environmentalists could understand the extent of the public's desire for environmental protection because they shared that desire and similarly feared the consequences of pollution and resource destruction. Environmental activists converted those public concerns into their own political muscle. At the beginning of the 1980s, the ten largest environmental organizations had a combined membership of 3.3 million. By the end of the decade, they boasted 8 million members. The perception environmentalists promoted that the Reagan administration was attacking federal environmental laws also boosted fundraising. By 1985, the ten largest environmental organizations had increased their combined receipt of donations to $218 million per year; by 1990, those donated sums had increased to more than one-half a billion dollars.[52]

Moreover, because the 1970s were the formative years for many national environmental organizations, their members understood the aura of distrust surrounding environmental law and how, if necessary, they could use that to their strategic political advantage. Those interested in reform of environmental law within the Reagan administration, by contrast, not only overestimated the public's willingness to compromise its aspirations for environmental quality, but they further failed to appreciate the significance of those institutional forces within government that historically had been supportive of strong environmental protection laws. These included career employees within the EPA and the Department of the Interior who were upset at what they perceived to be the new administration's undermining of the statutes that they were charged with administering.

Environmentalists also took advantage of the fragmented structure of lawmaking within the federal system by effectively tapping into the legislative branch's natural interest in overseeing (and criticizing) the executive branch. The congressional committees that had been primarily responsible for the initial passage of environmental legislation were especially interested in ensuring the legislation's faithful implementation by the executive branch. For those members of Congress principally interested in securing the attention of the national news media, oversight hearings critical of an executive agency's performance on environmental protection had proven to be an effective means of obtaining such exposure. Perhaps for both of these reasons, an adversarial relationship developed between the two branches, promoting a culture within congressional committees of vigorous nondeferential oversight of the executive branch on environmental matters.

Intense congressional scrutiny of both Gorsuch and Watt began soon after their respective confirmations. In 1981, the chairs of six different committees and subcommittees began to investigate the EPA, including Senator Robert Stafford of the Senate Committee on the Environment and Public Works; Representative John Dingell of the Subcommittee on Oversight and Investigations of the House Committee on Energy and Commerce; Representative James Florio of the Subcommittee on Commerce, Transportation, and Tourism of the House Committee on Energy and Commerce; Representative Elliott Levitas of the Subcommittee on Investigations and Oversight of the House Committee on Public Works and Transportation; Representative Mike Synar of the Subcommittee on Environment, Energy, and Natural Resources of the House Government Operations Committee; and Representative James Scheuer of the Subcommittee on Natural Resources, Agricultural Research, and Environment of the House Science and Technology Committee. There were pervasive congressional concerns raised that Gorsuch and other political appointees at the agency were entering into "sweetheart deals" with industry, manipulating programs for political ends, and attempting to cripple the agency through requests for budget reductions.[53]

Secretary Watt was similarly subjected to intense congressional scrutiny and criticism. The House Committee on Interior and Insular Affairs held an oversight hearing on the secretary just two weeks after his confirmation. The Senate confirmation hearings had themselves lasted two days, with over forty witnesses testifying. The chair of the House Committee made clear at the first oversight hearing that he had not been "enthused about [Watt's] appointment."[54]

Like Gorsuch, Watt found himself subjected to scrutiny from multiple congressional committees and subcommittees because of the sheer reach of concerns implicated by environmental protection. For instance, additional oversight legislative hearings followed Watt's decision, less than a month after taking office, to reverse former Interior Secretary Cecil Andrus's decision not to lease for oil and gas exploration four areas off the shore of northern California. The committee chair at that hearing openly criticized the secretary for having made "controversial decisions which in [his] view suggest[ed] a predetermination to simplify the complex and to eschew any effort to balance and resolve competing environmental and energy issues."[55]

The resulting whipsaw created by damaging reports and occasional leaks from career employees within the environmental agencies and legislative oversight hearings at which administration actions were denounced overwhelmed much of the Reagan administration's efforts to reform federal environmental policies. As previously described, the administration's confrontation with Congress and its massive institutional oversight machinery was the decisive factor in ultimately causing Gorsuch, Watt, and a number of other lower-cabinet-level environmental appointees to resign.

Reforming the Reformers

The highly visible failure of the Reagan administration to reform environmental law and policy masked the planting and fertilization of the intellectual seeds of a more powerful reform movement, the significance of which has only become apparent in subsequent decades. The reformers succeeded during the 1980s to build an effective constituency of lawyers, economists, and scientists ready, willing, and able to challenge many of the fundamental premises of modern environmental law.

The most remarkable of these organizations was the Federalist Society for Law and Public Policy Studies. The Federalist Society originated in 1981 in response to the perception of many conservative law students and business leaders that liberalism unduly dominated discourse at the most prestigious academic institutions. The society started out informally, but with the financial assistance of conservative foundations, it spawned active chapters at law schools throughout the nation, ultimately creating a powerful network of politically engaged conservative lawyers, many of whom subsequently gained high positions in the executive and judicial branches during the Reagan and George H. W. Bush administrations.[56] Environmental law was not its primary focus, but the society's agenda was dominated by tenets that questioned the legitimacy of environmental law's legal regime. This was not wholly coincidental. There was a natural, indeed fundamental, antipathy between the agendas of the environmental and Federalist Society movements.

The Federalist Society, for instance, advocated a diminished role for national government and heightened constitutional safeguards for the individual states. It opposed national laws that its members believed improperly usurped the states' prerogative to decide for themselves how to regulate their economies, as well as laws that conscripted state apparatus to achieve nationally dictated social policies. The federal pollution control statutes, however, were deliberately national in perspective. They routinely created national standards and then, based on a variety of legislative carrots and sticks, sought to coerce and encourage states to enact the necessary implementing legislation and to undertake the necessary administration and enforcement.

Another major concern of the Federalist Society was so-called judicial activism. The examples of such activism routinely denounced by the society included a disproportionate number arising out of environmental litigation. The Federalist Society, accordingly, opposed judges exercising equitable authority to fashion remedies that depended on substantial, ongoing judicial oversight. In a speech widely heralded by the society, President Reagan's first attorney general, William French Smith, in 1981 singled out a court order in an environmental law case as just the kind of judicial overreaching that needed to be curbed. So, too, did the Federalist Society identify relaxed judicial barriers to citizen standing to bring enforcement actions as encouraging undesirable judicial activism. Here too, however, environmental law's promotion of a more "active" judiciary and increased citizen access to courts fundamentally clashed with Federalist Society policy.[57]

Finally, the property rights and the law and economics movements became closely identified with the Federalist Society during the 1980s, adding intellectual weight to what had previously been an emotional political issue that lacked a coherent legal theory. A major intellectual force behind the Federalist Society's involvement in the issue was University of Chicago law professor Richard Epstein. With financial support from William Simon's and Irving Kristol's Institute for Educational Affairs, Epstein's 1985 book *Takings: Private Property and the Power of Eminent Domain* laid out a virtual legal blueprint for Fifth Amendment "regulatory takings" challenges against environmental laws that diminished property values by limiting the exercise of private property rights in natural resources. Epstein argued that virtually any government regulation (short of a mere codification of a traditional common law nuisance) that diminishes property value amounts to a taking of private property for public use that, under the Fifth Amendment, requires the government's payment of "just compensation." The essential premise of much environmental law is, in contrast to Epstein's theory, that the physical characteristics of the ecosystem generate spatial and temporal spillovers that require restrictions on the private use of natural resources far beyond those contemplated by centuries-old common law tort rules. In short, what Epstein merely acknowledges as an incidental limit on the exercise of private property rights in natural resources—the possibility of physical spillover effects—modern environmentalism perceives as a dominant characteristic justifying comprehensive governmental regulation.

A similar pattern emerged in related areas of science and economics. In prominent publications, some scientists and economists expressed greater skepticism of the wisdom of existing environmental laws and policies. They questioned the ecological premise of modern environmental law, suggesting that the problems being addressed were not nearly as substantial as had been presumed. These writings accused environmentalists of "gloom and doom" exaggerations unsupported by "sound science." They further questioned the priorities of existing laws, contending that too much attention and societal resources were being paid to environmental concerns and that public welfare could be more effectively promoted by enacting policies that fostered economic growth.[58]

By the end of the 1980s, the EPA itself was embracing the basic proposition that its priorities and resources had been misdirected. In 1983,

Administrator Ruckelshaus first publicly agreed with industry's long-standing contention that environmental laws should be reformed to allow for environmental protection standards to be strictly based on a formal "risk assessment" and a more deliberate consideration of social costs. In 1987, the EPA issued a widely trumpeted report, *Unfinished Business,* that even more broadly echoed industry's claim that the agency was spending too many resources on environmental problems wrongly prioritized due to public misperceptions of relative risks. The report identified both environmental problems that were the object of a disproportionately large amount of agency resources, such as hazardous waste disposal, and environmental problems, such as wetlands destruction and global climate change, which received too little agency attention.[59]

What transpired during the 1980s was the beginning of the realization of the ambitions of those business leaders who, as described in chapter 5, undertook to influence future national environmental policy by influencing the marketplace of ideas. Those business leaders had understood that it would require a long-term investment strategy to create a generation of scholarship more reflective of their values and priorities. Such a change could not be expected overnight, as it would take "twenty years for a research paper at Harvard to become a law."[60] Almost exactly twenty years after beginning their efforts, the business leaders of the 1970s had achieved their goal: an intellectualization of the conservative movement favoring reform of the nation's environmental laws. Environmental law had yet to be fundamentally reformed in the pro-business manner they sought, but they had laid the intellectual groundwork necessary for significant reform.

Splitting the Environmental Community

Somewhat ironically, just as the regulatory reform movement's losses during the 1980s masked its growing cohesiveness, the converse was true for the environmental movement, which appeared increasingly divided by the decade's close. The "Reagan Revolution" had provided a common target, which initially brought environmentalists together. But the afterglow of environmental successes in resisting that revolution revealed a sharply splintered movement.

The principal fissure that developed in the environmental movement during the 1980s was between the so-called national environmental organizations, such as the Sierra Club, the National Wildlife Federation, the World Wildlife Fund, the Natural Resources Defense Council, and the Environmental Defense Fund, and the more decentralized, grassroots, community-based organizations. The former responded to the challenge of the Reagan presidency, especially its early years, with enormously successful fund-raising and membership drives. That injection of resources converted what had once been fairly informal, ad hoc operations into more professional, hierarchical, bureaucratic organizations almost exclusively led by white males as their chief executive officers. The gap between these organizations and the local communities widened, and the formal organizations focused more on national and international environmental issues. In operational style, the national environmental groups began to resemble their business counterparts who lobbied Congress and litigated in the courts on behalf of the regulated community. These organizations were highly sophisticated, effective, and relatively well funded, and their professional staffs included teams of scientists, economists, and lawyers trained at many of the nation's most prestigious academic institutions.[61]

The grassroots environmental movement also increased significantly during the 1980s, but in very different ways. This movement was marked by community-based neighborhood associations, sometimes linked across geographic regions, rather than national organizations. The local groups were not so concerned with broad national issues as they were with threats in their own backyards. Many grassroots leaders were women, racial minorities, or members of low-income communities. While these activists lacked the formal training of the professional staffs of the national groups, they possessed an expertise born out of personal experience and passion.[62]

Grassroots environmentalists were distrustful both of government officials and of the businesses that they believed were locating a disproportionate number of polluting facilities in minority communities. Local environmental activists made accusations of "environmental racism" and made claims for "environmental justice," with the latter ultimately becoming their rallying cry. However, these groups were similarly suspicious of the national environmental organizations. The national organizations seemed too little interested in the plight of local communities, too seduced by their own fund-raising efforts, and too willing to compromise local concerns for the pragmatic fashioning of national compromises.[63]

There was also an increasing cultural divide in style and background between rank-and-file national environmentalists, who were increasingly white and from elite social and educational backgrounds, and their grassroots counterparts, who were often poor racial minorities who lived in the very communities being threatened. Some minority leaders described the work of the national environmental groups as being "irrelevant" at best and, at worst, "a deliberate attempt by a bigoted and selfish white middle-class society to perpetuate its own values and protect its own lifestyle at the expense of the poor and underprivileged."[64] Mainstream national environmentalists were seen as ignoring both the urban environment and the needs of the poor in favor of seeking "governmental assistance to avoid the unpleasant externalities of the very system from which they themselves have already benefitted so extensively."[65] As one commentator opined, socially elite environmentalists "would prefer more wilderness . . . for a more secure enclave in nature from the relentlessness of history and the demands of the poor."[66]

Like the regulatory reform movement, the emerging grassroots environmentalism of the 1980s resulted in little, if any, meaningful legal change. For both movements, the decade was a time for political organizing, for establishing networks, and for developing intellectual bases. Both did so quite successfully, and for that reason, notwithstanding their starkly clashing philosophical inclinations, both reform movements rose dramatically in prominence and influence during the 1990s. As described in the next chapter, the 1990s saw these movements substantially transform the terms of the debate surrounding environmental law, yet ultimately accomplish far less formal change than anticipated at the decade's outset.

CHAPTER SEVEN

Maintaining the Road: The 1990s

The 1990s saw enormous political upheaval that promised tremendous changes in environmental law. The environmental justice movement exploded to the surface, accusing industry, government, and traditional environmentalists of engaging in "environmental racism." Those seeking to relax the nation's environmental laws likewise upended the political dynamic that had governed the nation's lawmaking institutions since the early 1970s. Environmental law had persisted, notwithstanding repeated challenges in prior decades, largely because of members of Congress and the federal judiciary who successfully resisted any efforts by the executive that seemed intended to cut back on environmental protections. During the 1990s, both the federal legislative and judicial branches began questioning the basic precepts of environmental law rather than safeguarding them. Leaders within both branches questioned environmental law's failure to take greater account of economic costs. They even questioned its constitutional validity, resurrecting limits on congressional authority that had been dormant for decades.

Even more remarkable than the vigor and identity of those challenging environmental law during the 1990s is that, just as in the 1980s, virtually none of these efforts succeeded. Environmental law once again persisted, and domestic U.S. environmental law exited the 1990s much as it entered. With the exception of the Oil Pollution Act of 1990 and the extensive amendments that same year to the Clean Air Act, both of which occurred before any of these challenges, and congressional adoption of the Safe Drinking Water Act Amendments and the Food Quality Protection Act a few weeks before midterm elections in the fall of 1996, there were only minor statutory amendments of any of the domestic environmental laws during the 1990s. For better and for worse, the extraordinary dynamism of the earlier decades that had subjected the major federal environmental laws to extensive amendments every few years abruptly paused in the 1990s. Only in the international arena did U.S. environmental law continue to evolve rapidly.

Following the approach of the two preceding chapters, this chapter first describes the environmental highlights of the decade of the 1990s, including the shifting attitudes toward environmental law evident in both Congress and the federal judiciary, the full-fledged emergence of the environmental justice movement, the rise in the role of the states in environmental law, and the internationalization of environmental law. The chapter then discusses the significance of these developments for environmental law's future, including their implications for environmental law's ongoing evolution.

Shifting Winds in the Politics of the Environment

The winds of politics are notorious for their abrupt and unpredictable shifts in direction and force. The influences surrounding environmental law are no exception. During his first two years in office, President Nixon promoted himself as an advocate for the environment, but he quickly abandoned that pretense upon concluding that the political rewards were too few and the political opportunities in developing alliances with powerful business interests were too great. What commenced as an embrace became, by the turbulent end of his presidency, a series of vituperative denunciations of environmentalists.

The first President George Bush displayed a similar, albeit less extreme, change of heart in the early 1990s. As described in chapter 6, Bush had campaigned for the presidency by stressing his deep commitment to environmental protection—for instance, he pledged a policy of no net loss of wetlands and famously condemned his Democratic challenger, Massachusetts governor Michael Dukakis, for his failure to clean up Boston Harbor. Early in his presidency, Bush delivered on some of his environmental promises. He appointed a distinguished environmentalist, William Reilly, then-president of the World Wildlife Fund, to head the Environmental Protection Agency (EPA) and supported significant increases in that agency's budget. Bush also deserves credit for securing passage of the Clean Air Act Amendments of 1990, which included some of the most ambitious and far-reaching environmental provisions ever enacted by Congress. Additionally, Bush made large portions of the outer continental shelf off New England, Florida, and California off-limits for oil and gas development.[1]

Like Nixon before him, however, Bush seems ultimately to have concluded that he was unable to capture sufficient political advantages for his efforts to justify the costs to his core constituency in the business community.

No matter what he did, the environmental community seemed only to criticize his administration for not doing enough. The short-term political price of alienating the business community was simply too great to warrant advocating environmental benefits that would be realized only in the distant future and sometimes in distant places. By midterm, the Bush administration no longer seemed ready to cater to the concerns of environmentalists and instead appeared to be looking for opportunities to be more responsive to the regulated community's criticism of existing law. Bush's director of the Office of Management and Budget (OMB), Richard Darman, publicly derided the environmental movement, declaring that "America did not fight and win the wars of the 20th century to make the world safe for green vegetables."[2]

Bush, accordingly, proposed oil and gas exploration in the Arctic National Wildlife Refuge and supported limits on the public's ability to challenge plans to increase resource exploitation on public lands. His vice president, Dan Quayle, initiated the Council on Competitiveness, charged with reviewing environmental regulations to assess their adverse impact on business. Although the council came under heavy fire from Congress for delaying the implementation of environmental regulations, Quale eventually instigated a moratorium on regulatory initiatives, including many significant pending environmental regulations. The Justice Department also became embroiled in a controversy with Congress concerning whether the department was failing to prosecute environmental criminals.[3]

As Bush completed his presidency in 1992, he seemingly abandoned his earlier support of efforts to forge international environmental law agreements. Bush threatened to not attend the United Nations Conference on Environment and Development, popularly referred to as the "Earth Summit," in Rio de Janeiro, and although he agreed at the last moment to attend, while there he declined to have the United States sign the Biodiversity Convention and insisted on a weakened version of an agreement on global climate change. Here, too, Bush was unwilling to have the U.S. economy absorb what seemed to be potentially high costs in the short term for uncertain benefits to be enjoyed in the distant future and by the peoples of other nations. However, the international condemnation of U.S. recalcitrance at Rio was so embarrassing to U.S. environmentalists that Administrator Reilly wrote a memorandum to all EPA employees critical of the administration and the president.[4]

The single largest shifts in the politics of environmentalism, however, occurred within the other two branches of the federal government. As described in chapters 5 and 6, Congress during the 1970s and 1980s had been environmental law's primary champion. Congress had consistently resisted executive branch efforts to eliminate or soften the laws and, sometimes unfairly, characterized the White House, the EPA, and the Department of the Interior as undermining environmental protection by their reform efforts. Congressional committee chairs had held numerous oversight hearings at which they closely questioned executive branch officials, had often held press conferences critical of executive branch initiatives, and had repeatedly rejected White House proposals for legislative change. Individual members of Congress had even filed briefs in court opposing executive branch action.

The courts likewise had served as major bulwarks against fundamental reform of environmental law during the 1970s and even for much of the 1980s. The judiciary had opened the courts to citizen suits, had heightened judicial review of agency action, and had strictly enforced deadlines and statutory language that imposed uncompromising requirements on the regulated community and the federal regulators themselves. The courts had shown themselves to be especially willing to embrace expansive readings of federal Superfund liability.

In the 1990s, however, both Congress and the federal judiciary acted very differently. The Democratic Party took over the White House for the first time in twelve years with an administration that included a vice president, Al Gore, who in 1992 had written a book *(Earth in the Balance: Ecology and the Human Spirit)* embracing the imperative of environmental protection. But in a virtually simultaneous conversion, the two other branches became environmental skeptics. The political roles were effectively reversed from what they had been in the 1970s and 1980s, but the political conflict remained just as stark. Clinton appointed individuals with strong environmental credentials to important policymaking positions in the executive branch, including at the EPA, Interior, the Council on Environmental Quality, Justice, Agriculture, Energy, and the White House Domestic Policy Office. However, congressional leaders and influential judges simultaneously evinced their increasing skepticism of environmental law's efficacy, and many leaders within those two branches of government became proponents of fundamental changes in environmental law. Congress sought to amend environmental laws to make them more responsive to economic costs and, in the interim, to impose riders on appropriation bills that restricted the implementation of existing laws. The federal judiciary, especially the U.S. Supreme Court, began to limit the constitutional reach of federal environmental protection law in a wide variety of contexts.

The Contract with America and the 104th Congress

The sea change in the relationship of Congress to environmental law was marked by the election of the 104th Congress in 1994. In that election, the

Republican Party took over the majority in both chambers for the first time since the mid-1950s. The ascendancy of the Republican Party to majority status in both houses of Congress significantly changed environmental law's long-standing political dynamic.

During the fall of 1994, Republican candidates campaigned against the Democrats and the Clinton administration on the basis of a common agenda formally referred to as the "Contract with America." During the campaign itself, the full implications of that agenda for environmental law were never explored, but those implications quickly became apparent in the immediate aftermath of the election of Republican majorities to both the Senate and House. As the new Republican majorities translated the Contract's aspirations for reduced government bureaucracy and a stronger economy into concrete legislative proposals, they targeted federal environmental protection programs more than any other area of the law for significant curtailment.[5]

The Republican leadership in both chambers moved swiftly on several legislative fronts to convert their agenda into positive law. The majority leaders reorganized legislative committees to emphasize such priorities as protecting private property rights, expanding commerce, and exploiting natural resources. They proposed legislation to replace environmental standards based on minimum standards of human health and on technology-forcing requirements with environmental standards based on cost–benefit analyses, comparative risk assessments, and other economic efficiency criteria. Environmentalists had long complained that such standards inevitably decrease environmental protection by discounting environmental values not susceptible to monetary valuation and environmental risks not certain to occur.[6]

Other aspects of the new Republican majority agenda similarly promised a radical overhaul of the existing federal environmental law programs. Many of these initiatives derived from the kind of conservative think tanks that business leaders had deliberately created for that very purpose in the 1970s. Proposed bills included legislation that would limit Congress's ability to enact so-called unfunded mandates, which require actions by state governments without providing the states with the funding necessary to carry them out. Proponents of this legislation repeatedly cited federal environmental laws as examples of laws that, because they rely on state and local implementation, included such improper mandates.

Other bills promised "regulatory relief" designed to make it harder for government to promulgate regulations that impose economic costs on industry. Here too, proponents singled out costly environmental requirements as justifying these reforms. The bills proposed, *inter alia,* placing on federal agencies multiple layers of procedural requirements and imposing

heightened standards of judicial review to ensure against "excessive" regulation. In a wholesale reversal of the National Environmental Policy Act
(NEPA), these proposed laws would require greater consideration of the
economic impact of compliance with *environmental* laws. Purportedly following up on the EPA's 1987 report *Unfinished Business,* the proposed laws
also would require greater consideration of the relative benefits of *alternative* uses of societal resources in addressing competing risks. Academic
think tanks supported by pro-business interests had promoted these reform
initiatives, while environmental interest groups contended that such measures would unduly chill agency implementation of needed environmental
protection rules.[7]

Finally, the Republican Contract with America sought to rein in environmental law's reach through budgetary reductions and disincentives.
For instance, within the broader context of reducing the national debt, the
new Republican legislative majorities proposed budgets that singled out
environmental protection for some of the most severe reductions. These
budgets reportedly would have reduced the EPA's enforcement dollars by
up to 30–40 percent, and they included as many as seventeen riders on appropriation bills specifically aimed at curtailing enforcement of the Clean
Air and Clean Water Acts.[8]

The even-more-sweeping proposals, however, related to proposed budgetary disincentives. The Contract included bills that called for compensating private property owners for any economic loss suffered because
of federal restrictions on the use of their property. The legislative proposal singled out for such treatment environmental restrictions, especially
those related to protection of wetlands and endangered species. The legislative hearings in support of such a compensation requirement accordingly
sought to highlight the plight of small landowners who allegedly retained
no economic use of their land because of environmental restrictions.[9]

The practical effect of the proposed laws would have been to confer
an economic right—compensable if diminished—on property owners to
engage in the very kind of environmentally destructive conduct that the
environmental laws had deemed unlawful. The most likely programmatic
effect of such a damage remedy—which was estimated to cost the federal
government billions of dollars if enacted and if existing environmental laws
were fully implemented and enforced—would be for the federal agencies responsible for administering those environmental laws to minimize
their liability by curbing their implementation and enforcement efforts. No
doubt to ensure just that result, the proposed legislation called for the damage remedies to be paid out of individual agency operating budgets, rather
than out of general U.S. Treasury funds.[10]

Any one of these legislative proposals, if enacted, could have fundamentally changed the structure of federal environmental law. Their cumulative impact would have been almost as revolutionary as the lawmaking effort that had created modern environmental protection law in the early 1970s. Moreover, for much of 1995, congressional passage of at least several of these initiatives seemed a virtual certainty. Many of the most powerful members of Congress, including both the Speaker of the House and the Senate Majority Leader seemed to favor enactment of major reform while the environmental public interest groups, by comparison, seemed diminished in their political muscle.[11]

Remarkably, however, with the exception of two limited bills that imposed procedural requirements on unfunded mandates to state and local governments and regulations of "small business," practically none of these varied proposals became law. The congressional environmental reform efforts dissipated almost as quickly they formed. In a reversal of roles, while the legislative branch sought to reduce environmental protections, the executive branch fought to preserve them.

Unlike President Bush, President Clinton did not enter the presidency either highlighting his environmentalist credentials or even seemingly interested in environmental issues. Balancing the budget, enacting health care reform, and expanding civil rights were his announced core concerns. Environmental protection was not a priority, and environmentalists had been widely critical of Clinton's environmental performance while governor of Arkansas.[12] However, Clinton surpassed Bush and Nixon before him in realizing the political value of seizing environmental issues, and thanks to the 104th Congress, he had a ready target for partisan condemnation. Clinton's rhetoric reflected his political conversion to the environmental cause: "Roll back health and safety? No. Let DDT back in our food again? Not on your life. Create more tainted water or toxic waste . . . ? Never. No. . . . Just say no to what they are doing."[13]

Somewhat ironically, the executive branch under Clinton used the same tactics against Congress that Congress had used against the Nixon, Reagan, and Bush administrations during the 1970s and 1980s. Just as Congress had effectively exploited the public's distrust of government to defeat earlier retreats from environmental protection, so did the Clinton administration block Congress in the 1990s. President Clinton, Vice President Al Gore, EPA administrator Carol Browner, and Interior Secretary Bruce Babbitt repeatedly characterized Congress as seeking to undermine public health and environmental quality for the sake of industry profits. The U.S. public responded with such hostility to any proposed change that the legislative reform effort was effectively sapped of its political viability. Once again, a major effort to reform fundamentally the demanding framework of U.S. environmental law fell fairly flat, this time during the 1990s, just as similar efforts had in the two prior decades.

The Changing Nature of the Federal Judiciary

As described in chapter 5, the federal judiciary during the 1970s served as a significant catalyst in support of sweeping, far-reaching, and stringent environmental protection law. Many judicial rulings made it easier for environmental plaintiffs to bring suits against polluters. And through a series of expansive (and sometimes thinly based) interpretations of existing law, courts effectively provided environmentalists with the political leverage necessary to obtain strong environmental protection laws from both the executive and legislative branches.

During the 1980s, however, the seeds of a transformation in judicial attitudes were planted, and they finally came to fruition during the 1990s. More than a decade of conservative judicial appointments by Presidents Reagan and Bush to the federal judiciary systematically replaced federal judges more sympathetic to environmental concerns with judges apathetic to, skeptical of, or even seemingly hostile toward the efficacy and wisdom of environmental laws. Increasingly lost was any judicial notion that environmental concerns were somehow "special"—perhaps akin to civil rights—and thus deserving of heightened judicial safeguarding.[14]

The most portentous of the judicial rulings of the 1990s were those of the U.S. Supreme Court. In a series of decisions arising in a host of constitutional contexts, a bare majority of five justices actively promoted a view of the federal constitution that systematically unsettled the constitutional foundations of many of modern environmental law's most distinctive features. In form, environmental law is classic New Deal regulatory legislation—it rests on expansive notions of congressional power under the Commerce Clause, presumes the need for significant governmental restrictions on market transactions and private property rights, and anticipates the need for judicial oversight of executive branch implementation by providing for judicial review. Modern environmental law, like many of those New Deal laws that preceded it, also presumes a dominant preemptive role for federal law at the expense of substantial state autonomy over public welfare, including enlisting the machinery of state government in furtherance of federal programs.

As described in chapter 3, each of these features is endemic to environmental law. Each is a direct, not incidental, expression of the nature of the problem environmental law seeks to address. The physical nature of the problem promotes a national, rather than state-by-state, approach to solutions, yet the dual-sovereign framework contemplated by the Constitution makes the federal government dependent upon partnerships with the states for full implementation and enforcement. The Fifth Amendment provides that private property may not be taken for public use without just compensation, but environmental law unavoidably and constantly limits private property rights to address problems seen only in broad temporal and spatial spillovers. Finally, Article III of the Constitution limits the jurisdiction of federal courts to lawsuits where plaintiffs can allege imminent and concrete injury, but the complexity of ecological cause and effect frequently makes it difficult for environmental plaintiffs to make such showings.

In earlier decades, the Supreme Court appeared to avoid rigid application of constitutional doctrines that would stand as obstacles to comprehensive federal environmental law, environmental restrictions on private property, or broad citizen suit standing in environmental litigation. The 1990s were decidedly different. Both in environmental and nonenvironmental cases, the Supreme Court began to rethink certain presumptions of U.S. constitutional law and thereby unsettled some precepts upon which modern U.S. law rested.

In 1992, the Court in *Lucas v. South Carolina Coastal Council,* 505 U.S. 1003 (1992), ruled in favor of a landowner who claimed that environmental restrictions on his use of coastal property without compensation amounted to an unconstitutional taking. It was not so much the result in that particular case as the Court's reasoning that called into question environmental restrictions. The Court in *Lucas* held that land use restrictions that deprived land of *all* economic value or beneficial use amounted to *per se* takings unless the restrictions at issue did no more than codify what otherwise amounted to long-standing "background principles" of law. The Court's willingness to embrace economic value as the determinative touchstone of a law's constitutionality was troubling because it seemed to accept too easily the precept that the economically profitable exploitation of a natural resource is somehow constitutionally guaranteed or at least preferable. The teaching of the modern environmental statutes regarding the propriety of government's restricting uses of natural resources based on the related spatial and temporal spillovers—"the economy of nature"—was rendered a second-class concern. So too was the importance of nondevelopmental values of preserving natural resources that are not readily translated into market or economic value.[15]

At least as troubling was the *Lucas* Court's ruling that the only exception to the *per se* taking rule occurs when the environmental restriction merely codifies "background principles of law," such as the common law of nuisance. The premise of much modern environmental law has been that such common law doctrines, especially nuisance law, have failed to deal with environmental issues. A nuisance standard that makes the lawfulness of an activity turn on its "reasonableness" does not give a court any meaningful guidance in resolving the multiplicity of complex factors that must be weighed in deciding how much environmental degradation is too much. In short, these "background principles" have never been adequate to deal with environmental concerns, which is why environmental law evolved beyond those principles to fill the gap with detailed standards and regulatory controls. Therefore, to have the constitutionality of environmental restrictions turn on the extent to which those restrictions merely codify preexisting law places a constitutional obstacle in the path of the law's evolution that environmentalists would argue is both necessary and proper.

To similar effect were the Supreme Court's decisions during the 1990s regarding the legal standing of citizens to bring lawsuits enforcing federal environmental law. The Supreme Court had long held that Article III's "case or controversy" requirement meant that a plaintiff in federal court must possess "standing" to bring the lawsuit. As interpreted by the Court, to have standing, a plaintiff must allege a "concrete injury," the action of the defendant must be a "cause" of that injury, and the injury must be susceptible to "redress" through the lawsuit.[16]

As described in chapter 5, the Court during the 1970s handed down a series of decisions that were responsive to the peculiar nature of ecological injury and made clear that such citizen allegations of injury could satisfy the requirement for standing. The Court's decisions during the 1990s were precisely the opposite in their jurisprudential thrust. The Court repeatedly ruled against the citizen's ability to maintain environmental lawsuits to promote environmental protection, while ruling in favor of the standing of economic interests that alleged that they were suffering from "needless economic dislocation produced by agency officials zealously but unintelligently pursuing their environmental objectives."[17] Indeed, the Court's rulings were so systematic in raising barriers to citizen standing in environmental cases that one justice, frustrated in dissent, openly complained about what he described as the majority's "slash-and-burn expedition through the law of environmental standing."[18]

For example, the Court required that in order to bring a lawsuit an environmentalist plaintiff alleging injury to a wildlife species would have to show either that her profession includes the study of that particular species or demonstrate that she had planned to visit the precise location where the species is located in the near future. The Court's opinion expressed disdain for the environmentalist plaintiff's claim that citizen standing should be sufficiently established by her strong personal interest in the species survival. According to the Court, mere caring, no matter how strongly held, could not establish a legitimate constitutional injury. Entirely missing from the Court's analytical framework was any acknowledgment of the legitimacy of the very psychological and emotional ties to aspects of the natural environment that Congress sought to safeguard by enacting laws such as the Endangered Species Act.[19]

In enacting the Endangered Species Act, however, Congress was not simply responding to the narrow category of concerns represented by those very few individuals who might have actual, immediate plans to interact with the threatened species in its habitat. Congress instead was responding to the broader category of persons who care deeply about the survival of those species for any of a number of reasons, ranging from scientific interest to deeply held views about the responsibilities of humankind to other species. Such a concrete, individualized concern need not be based on the party's having the personal resources necessary for actual travel and some sort of a physical communing with the species. The Supreme Court, however, effectively ruled that such a legislative judgment was constitutionally out of bounds, at least for the purpose of establishing that an individual possesses the kind of personal injury necessary to maintain a lawsuit.

The Court's decisions regarding the proper sphere of federal legislation were even more unsettling for their implications for environmental law. The federal environmental statutes rest on decades of judicial precedent that endorsed expansive notions of congressional Commerce Clause power. The Court's long-standing test of Commerce Clause authority had been strikingly broad: as long as the activity being regulated bore some, even minimal, relation to interstate commerce, it fell within Congress's Commerce Clause regulatory authority, even if the activity was noncommercial and occurred wholly within a single state.[20]

Largely prompted by Congress's insatiable appetite for expanding federal criminal jurisdiction (and thus the workload of the federal judiciary), the Court finally rebelled during the 1990s by announcing a more restricted scope of congressional Commerce Clause authority. The new test seemingly required that the activity being regulated be "economic" in character and bear a substantial relationship to interstate commerce. The problem for environmental law was that the jurisdictional bases for environmental regulation in existing federal statutes did not anticipate that new test's analytic framework and therefore did not neatly reflect it.[21]

To be sure, much environmental regulation does, in fact, apply to economic activity that bears a substantial relationship to interstate commerce. Virtually any industrial activity, such as those involved in the production and sale of paper, steel, and agricultural products, would constitute a class of "economic activity." But that fact does not, by itself, necessarily satisfy the Court's constitutional test. The constitutional inquiry seems under the

Court's current formulation to turn on how the statute itself defines its jurisdiction, not how the statute might be amended to define its jurisdictional bases. The jurisdictional provisions of the federal environmental statutes, however, are not uniformly couched in terms of the economic nature of the activity to be regulated.

For example, the actual terms of federal environmental statutes such as the Clean Air, Clean Water, and Endangered Species Acts do not turn at all on whether a particular activity to be regulated is economic in nature or possesses some interstate commercial nexus. They turn exclusively on a finding that the activity pollutes the air or the water or harms an endangered species or its habitat. Such activity need not be commercial in origin and can occur within a single state's boundaries. These are laws that, at bottom, seek their justification not in their relationship to commerce, but in their promotion of a system of values in which commerce is no longer government's principal, let alone exclusive, legitimate end. This is particularly true of the Endangered Species Act, which would seem to be especially vulnerable to the new constitutional standard. Although it might be fairly easy in theory to recast those jurisdictional provisions of the Endangered Species Act to focus on the commercial character of the regulated activities, the political hurdles to passage of such curative legislation would likely be substantial. At the very least, environmentalists would have to be prepared to agree to the significant substantive compromises that would be called for in forging the political alliances necessary to achieve such legislation.

As the 1990s came to a close, the extent to which a majority of the justices would be willing to take the logic of their Commerce Clause precedent outside of the criminal law arena to strike down major public welfare laws, such as environmental laws, remained unclear. It was clear, however, that those in the federal government and the environmental community who defended the constitutionality of Congress's passing environmental laws could no longer confidently rely on the single fact that pollution and its reduction have substantial implications for the national economy. Those defenders would instead have to try to develop legal arguments that coincided with the Court's new analytic framework. The opportunity to develop those arguments soon presented itself when a series of plaintiffs, prompted by the Supreme Court's recent pronouncements, attacked in the lower courts the constitutionality of several environmental statutes based on legal theories that would have been completely unthinkable in either the 1970s or 1980s.[22]

The shift in judicial attitude was not, however, confined to the Supreme Court. The lower federal courts do not respond only to the Supreme Court's precise holdings. Federal district court and court of appeals judges also read beyond those holdings and frequently anticipate in their own decisions where they believe the Court is going. The lower courts, accordingly, more regularly denied standing to environmental plaintiffs and the federal government lost more cases in which it was defending its authority to promulgate and enforce strict environmental protection requirements, especially under the Superfund law.[23]

The 1990s, in short, witnessed an extraordinary shift in the federal judiciary's treatment of environmental law. In the 1970s, federal judge Skelly Wright famously wrote in an environmental case that it was the court's "duty . . . to see that important legislative purposes, heralded in the halls of Congress, are not lost or misdirected in the vast hallways of the federal bureaucracy."[24] In the 1990s, Supreme Court justice Antonin Scalia directly challenged Wright's characterization of the judicial function. Writing even before his appointment to the Court, Scalia decried the judiciary's apparent "long love affair with environmental litigation." And taking direct issue with Judge Wright, Scalia made quite explicit his view that "it would be a good thing, too" to have policies such as those furthered by federal environmental protection laws get "lost and misdirected in the vast hallways of the federal bureaucracy. . . . The ability to lose or misdirect laws can be said to be one of the prime engines of social change."[25] By the end of the decade, the constitutional foundations of environmental law may have been far from eroded, but those foundations were certainly destabilized.

"Environmental Racism: That's What It Is"

In early 1990, representatives of more than a hundred community-based grassroots environmental groups on the Gulf Coast and in the Southwest publicly confronted the mainstream environmental groups. The grassroots organizations sent highly publicized correspondence to the chief executive officers of the ten leading national environmental organizations accusing their organizations of ignoring the plight of the poor and people of color. The letters demanded that the groups respond within sixty days to describe how they would make changes in their programs to give a higher priority to the environmental concerns of low-income communities and communities of color, and what measures they would take to increase by 35–40 percent their total percentage of minority employees and to include more persons of color on their governing boards.[26]

This action by grassroots environmental justice organizations signaled an escalation in the effort to bring attention to their concerns. The basic tenets of much of the environmental justice movement were most obviously rooted in the civil rights movement. The foundation of the movement, however, can also be easily traced back to the sanitation and public health movements of the late nineteenth and early twentieth centuries, as described in chapter 4. These earlier social movements had responded to serious public health problems, especially in urban areas, caused by open sewers, uncontrolled garbage disposal on the streets, absence of distinct residential and industrial zoning classifications, and the unregulated processing and manufacturing of food. The cities afflicted with these conditions suffered from extraordinary population density and disease.[27]

Both government agencies and the mainstream environmental groups simply assumed during the 1970s and much of the 1980s that the modern environmental laws were addressing the public-health-related concerns of low-income communities and communities of color. Indeed, to the extent that sources of industrial pollution might be disproportionately located where the poor and racial minorities lived, as many of those communities claimed, governmental officials and environmentalists believed that environmental laws were likely only to be socially progressive in their positive impact. There was certainly no reason to suspect that the implementation of such laws might perversely leave those communities in worse circumstances.

But the counterintuitive nature of the problem is also why the environmental justice movement succeeded in garnering so much national attention. It was newsworthy that there was a racial dimension to allegations of environmental injustice particularly when environmental justice advocates named some liberal environmental public interest organizations as being part of the problem. The Rev. Dr. Benjamin Chavis, a well-known civil rights activist in North Carolina and later head of the National Association for the Advancement of Colored People (NAACP), reportedly coined the phrase "environmental racism" in 1987 as he was preparing to present to the National Press Club a report he authored on toxic waste sites and race in the United States: "[I] was trying to figure out how [I] could adequately describe what was going on. It came to me—*environmental racism*. [T]hat's what it is."[28] The report was the influential study on the siting of hazardous waste facilities that Chavis co-authored with Charles Lee, then with the United Church of Christ Commission for Racial Justice: *Toxic Wastes and Race in the United States*.

Also receiving widespread attention in 1990 was sociologist Robert Bullard's celebrated book *Dumping in Dixie*.[29] Bullard described a pattern of hazardous disposal sites being located by industry and government in communities of color throughout the southern United States, which triggered an avalanche of further academic inquiry. Beginning with the University of Michigan in January 1990, major universities and many of their law schools sponsored academic conferences on environmental justice.[30] Prior to 1990, no law review had published an article on the subject, but by the end of that decade, there had been at least ten formal law review symposiums exclusively dedicated to environmental justice issues and at least three hundred law review articles published on the topic.

Networks of grassroots environmental justice organizations formed throughout the United States. In October 1991, approximately three hundred representatives of local organizations from around the nation joined two hundred other attendees from state and federal governmental agencies, academic institutions, and mainstream environmental organizations at the First National People of Color Environmental Leadership Summit in Washington, D.C. Congress held hearings on environmental justice in 1992 and members of both the House and Senate, including then-Senator Al Gore, sponsored environmental justice legislation that would have both compelled analysis of allegations of social injustice and imposed substantive limits on the aggregation of sources of environmental risk in disproportionately burdened communities. With Gore's election to the vice presidency in 1992 and Chavis's appointment to head the NAACP a few months later, significant new federal environmental justice legislation seemed likely in the early 1990s.[31]

Political events far broader than the environmental justice movement, however, simply overwhelmed any possibility of securing federal legislation. Political shifts in Congress and the resulting "divided government"— the Democratic Party controlling the executive and the Republican Party gaining the leadership of both chambers of Congress in 1995—brought new environmental legislation to a standstill throughout the remainder of the 1990s. The upshot was that environmental justice concerns were no more formally codified in environmental law at the close of the 1990s than they had been when the decade began. The only clear exception was President Clinton's 1994 executive order on environmental justice, which required each federal agency to "mak[e] environmental justice part of its mission by identifying and addressing, as appropriate, disproportionately high and adverse human health or environmental effects."[32]

Significant changes nonetheless did occur in environmental law in response to environmental justice concerns even in the absence of comprehensive legislative enactments. For instance, in response to the 1994 presidential executive order, the EPA reformed its enforcement policies to consider environmental justice factors in targeting facilities and geographic areas for enforcement, in remedy selection, and in settlement. Environmental justice concerns also resulted in significant changes in the setting of environmental standards. Both EPA programs for curbing toxic "hot spots" under Section 112 of the Clean Air Act in inner cities and for reducing vehicle miles traveled pursuant to that same law reflected a desire to increase environmental justice. The latter redirected transportation funds that subsidize the commuting needs of suburban dwellers to increase funding to offset the costs for those dependent on more environmentally friendly mass transit options.[33]

The EPA similarly began to pay greater attention to cumulative impacts and synergistic effects (caused by mixing of pollutants) when setting standards. For instance, the agency had for years based its water quality standards on assumptions about fish consumption that were generally correct but that nonetheless dramatically understated the amount of subsistence fishing actually engaged in by members of certain minority communities. The EPA had simply never considered the real cultural differences that exist between communities, sometimes along racial lines, that lead to different diets, eating habits, and lifestyles and, therefore, also create some pathways for exposure to toxic accumulation that do not exist for the population generally.[34]

Finally, the dynamics surrounding the siting of environmentally risky facilities changed dramatically during the 1990s in response to claims of environmental injustice in general and environmental racism in particular. As the voices of local communities became stronger, the "deals" surrounding siting determinations were dramatically restruck. Sometimes, companies seeking permits simply abandoned their plans in the face of organized, knowledgeable, and effective community opposition. Other times, federal and state regulatory agencies denied the necessary environmental permit altogether. More often, however, the deal surrounding a siting decision was renegotiated on terms far more favorable to the community than had historically occurred.[35]

The environmental justice movement taught the nation in the 1990s that, if left to the normal workings of political, economic, and social forces (including race discrimination), environmental laws could make society as a whole much better off, but still affect adversely racial minorities and the poor. Environmental protection laws can reduce air, water, and land pollution, but the residual waste captured by a scrubber or filter is ultimately redirected elsewhere, perhaps to an incinerator or a landfill placed in a minority community. Residual pollutants will invariably find the path of least regulatory resistance. The environmental justice movement, in short, affected environmental lawmaking in the 1990s by changing the terms of the debate and the faces of those debating.[36]

State, Tribal, and Local Environmental Law

So much of modern environmental law's early focus was on the president, Congress, the EPA and the Department of the Interior, and the federal courts that it is easy to overlook that by the 1990s most environmental law was *state* rather than federal law. Each state administers air pollution, water pollution, and hazardous waste management programs. States also regulate the utilization and development of natural resources including water, minerals, forests, parks, and wildlife. Virtually all states and many major metropolitan areas have environmental agencies analogous to the EPA with authority to set environmental standards, issue permits, and initiate administrative or judicial enforcement actions. During the 1990s, most environmental enforcement actions were brought by state and local governmental officials rather than the EPA, Interior, or the U.S. Department of Justice. In addition, Native American tribes, as a further expression of the environmental justice movement, emerged as a distinct and potent sovereign environmental regulatory authority during the decade.

As significant as state environmental laws became during the 1990s, they retained a strong relationship to, if not heavy dependency on, federal law. Although some states initiated their own programs in the 1960s prior to congressional passage of comprehensive federal environmental legislation, most of the state environmental laws were themselves the direct or indirect product of federal environmental statutes. The Clean Air Act prompted the states through a variety of strategies, including the threat of more intrusive federal regulation, to enact detailed implementation plans to achieve uniform, national ambient air quality standards. It is a state agency that develops, administers, and enforces the plan, but the resulting state laws retain a federal character that simultaneously renders them subject to federal government oversight and to enforcement as "federal" law as well.[37]

Other federal environmental programs similarly promoted the creation of state programs, including the Clean Water Act; the Resource Conservation and Recovery Act; the Safe Drinking Water Act; the Federal Insecticide, Fungicide, and Rodenticide Act; the Endangered Species Act; and the Surface Mining Control and Reclamation Act. According to a survey conducted by the Environmental Council of the States, the number of states with delegated programs created under these federal statutes had dramatically increased by 1998 to 757 out of 1,167 federal environmental programs, with fifty-three states and territories responsible for those delegated programs.[38]

The overall impact of such a shift of law to the states plainly had positive aspects. While a federal agency like the EPA is necessary to overcome obstacles to the establishment of demanding environmental laws, greater involvement by state and local officials is a practical necessity for those laws to mature beyond theory and to change actual individual and business behavior. Absent a revolutionary change in the nature of the federal government, a federal agency such as the EPA will never, standing alone, possess the resources needed to implement and enforce the multitude of pollution standards and controls that it develops. Unless the EPA can persuade the states and municipalities to stand and work with the federal government, those standards and controls would be no more meaningful or effective than those found in nations that have exceedingly strict laws on the books but no actual implementation and enforcement.

As state programs and expertise grew, however, federal–state relations worsened during the 1990s. States openly complained about federal dictates regarding how their programs should be run, especially when federal funding of their programs did not increase in proportions commensurate to the increase in delegations. States argued in favor of greater program flexibility and state autonomy to decide where and how to regulate economic activity. One result was the National Environmental Performance Partnership System, established in 1995, under which the EPA signed agreements with individual states that, *inter alia,* gave those states greater administrative flexibility and required less federal oversight in state implementation of federal statutory programs. By April 1997, twenty-seven states had signed performance partnership agreements with the EPA.

The federal–state divide nonetheless further deepened in the late 1990s. Heads of state environmental agencies complained that the EPA was interfering with state effectiveness, while insisting that "states are not branch offices of the Federal Government."[39] At the same moment, however, the EPA was becoming more skeptical of the effectiveness of some state efforts after agency assessments concluded that many states lacked either the capacity or the will to enforce environmental requirements aggressively. The EPA threatened on several occasions to withdraw federal approval of state programs but did not carry out those threats, no doubt because doing so would have required it to take over the administration of those state programs. At most, the agency succeeded in cajoling some states to change policies to which it had objected.[40]

In addition, as some state programs matured, state enforcement actions against the federal government and industrial facilities located in upstream or upwind states proved politically attractive. Such enforcement had the advantage of promoting environmental quality at home while exporting the compliance costs to other sovereigns or jurisdictions. The federal government also provided plenty of potential enforcement targets. Many federal agencies, such as the Department of Energy, either operated polluting facilities or hired private contractors to operate facilities on the agencies' behalf. The EPA's own ability to force those facilities to comply with federal requirements was limited by its inability to bring an enforcement action in court against another executive branch agency. The executive branch has long taken the view—under the so-called unitary executive theory—that one executive branch agency may not sue another in court because to do so would allow another branch, the judiciary, to resolve an intrabranch dispute that should be resolved only within the executive branch.[41]

During the 1990s, states increasingly stepped into that enforcement gap and sought to impose civil penalties and obtain injunctive relief against federal facilities allegedly in violation of applicable requirements. Their success in obtaining such relief turned on their ability to persuade the federal courts, including the U.S. Supreme Court, that Congress had both subjected federal facilities to environmental requirements and waived federal sovereign immunity that would otherwise preclude such state lawsuits.[42]

The state enforcement actions against other states and facilities located within those states based on interstate pollution were similarly a reflection of state environmental law's maturation. To meet federal and state environmental law standards within their own states' borders, businesses naturally had an incentive (as did state regulators) to locate and/or operate facilities in a way that exported pollution to other jurisdictions. The interstate provisions in laws like the Clean Air and Clean Water Acts, that were designed to prevent such extraterritorial exports of pollution, lay largely dormant. The politics were too controversial, given the competing distributional stakes for the various states, and the science was too complicated for the EPA to use these provisions.

At the instigation of downwind and downstream states, the law of interstate pollution finally became active in the late 1990s. During the 1980s, downwind and downstream states initiated a series of lawsuits against the EPA and upstream and upwind states. Downwind and downstream states also imposed considerable administrative and political pressure on the EPA to finally act after many years of recalcitrance. By the end of the decade, the agency itself was taking the initiative to improve the science and to enforce those federal statutory provisions that limited interstate pollution, especially air pollution. The EPA granted downwind states' petitions under the Clean Air Act that the agency must require upwind states to develop plans that further reduced air pollution emissions because of their adverse effect on downwind states. The EPA formally declared the existing controls of upwind states to be inadequate and promulgated more demanding requirements to be imposed on them. Finally, the agency proposed the creation of innovative air pollution "banks" that permitted states to buy and sell emissions rights to allow the more stringent requirements to be met at the lowest possible costs. The interstate air pollution initiative included some of the most innovative and far-reaching administrative rulemaking ever attempted by the EPA.[43]

Finally, state and local governments were not the only sovereign entities rising in significance for environmental lawmaking during the 1990s. Tribal governments also rose in prominence in many respects. To be sure, Native American tribes had long played a significant role in natural resources law, to the extent that they both managed natural resources within tribal boundaries and exercised broader sovereign rights that they possessed under treaties with the federal government, especially with regard to fisheries. What occurred in the 1990s, however, was that the tribes began to assert comprehensive regulatory authority over pollution control issues. In addition, as many essential natural resources—especially fish, water, and some energy resources—became scarcer and conflicts between competing users inevitably multiplied, tribal sovereign rights in those same resources correspondingly increased in their relative importance. The environmental justice movement, moreover, promoted tribal demands that its sovereign voice and natural resources rights be respected.[44]

In 1987, Congress amended the Clean Water Act to allow for Native American tribes to exercise sovereign authority for the purpose of tribal implementation of that act. Tribes were, accordingly, authorized to assume primary responsibility for the issuance and enforcement of permits for sources within the reservation, as well as for the promulgation of water quality standards. What made the latter especially significant was its potential application to sources of water pollution outside tribal boundaries that affect the quality of waters within them. Such extraterritorial application of tribal standards promised an injection of tribal authority into a context where disputes between bordering states and between states and the federal government had already undermined effective regulation. Based upon congressional and executive action, tribes obtained similar express regulatory authority under other federal environmental laws, including both the Clean Air Act and the Safe Drinking Water Act.[45]

By the end of the 1990s, tribal governments had joined states as sovereign entities with substantial authority over natural resource management and pollution control matters. The EPA's organizational structure included an American Indian Environmental Office. President Clinton's executive order on environmental justice expressly extended its mandate to Native Americans. Most of the EPA's regional offices, accordingly, established offices specifically charged with working with tribal leaders to enhance their management of pollution concerns. In recognition of their expanding sovereign role and responsibilities, the tribes themselves established in 1991 the National Tribal Environmental Council for the purpose of enhancing tribal ability to protect, manage, and preserve air, land, and water for current and future generations.

Internationalization of Environmental Law

A prominent justification in the United States during the 1970s in favor of national environmental legislation was that pollution does not stop at state borders. If states were allowed to set their own environmental requirements absent any national oversight, each state would likely enact laws that encouraged interstate pollution adversely affecting bordering states. In addition, to the extent that many states shared common resources, including major bodies of water and the air, coordination of their respective environmental requirements was necessary.

The Bhopal tragedy in 1984, the massive fish kills in the Rhine River and the Chernobyl nuclear power plant accident in 1986, continuing acid rain damage in European forests, and evidence of a deepening hole in the ozone layer all brought home the analogous need to look beyond U.S. borders in crafting a legal regime for environmental protection. Just as the environmental laws of the 1970s responded to the need to look beyond the borders of individual states, the environmental problems of the 1980s underscored the futility of relying solely on domestic law.

In the 1990s, international environmental law became environmental law's most engaging and dynamic area. The United Nations listed only fifty-two treaties related to environmental issues in 1970. By 1999, the number of environmental treaties was 215, and the number of international environmental agreements of one kind or another was about one thousand.[46]

Part of the reason for the tremendous growth was that, because of increased technological capability and increased populations, countries were putting more pressure on common global resources. The number of global commons that required international coordination and cooperative efforts grew significantly in the latter half of the twentieth century, especially as developing nations increased their own technology capacity. When the relatively few developed nations, such as the United States and several Western European and Soviet Bloc countries, had industrial and manufacturing sectors with the technological capacity to operate on massive scales, the global commons were only slightly threatened. Environmental degradation was more regional and localized in its impact. The impacts on the global ecosystem grew exponentially, however, as the number of nations possessing significant technological ability increased along with the demands of their populations for more modern amenities. Endangered species, depleted fisheries, ozone layer destruction, and global warming all became prominent subjects of international negotiation and bilateral and multilateral agreements.[47]

Another significant source of demand for international environmental law was the globalization of the economy and the concomitant growth in international trade. The relationship between trade and the environment has two distinct strands. The first relates to the impact of trade itself on the environment. As international markets for any one country's domestic goods increased, so too did the demands on that same country's natural resource and industrial base. Meeting rising demands for production often meant accelerated extraction of natural resources and increased industrial output, both of which have direct implications for environmental quality.

The second strand linking trade and the environment is differently derived. It stems from how environmental regulations can stand as obstacles to international trade. Not all nations, of course, have the same environmental standards—some are more demanding than others. Businesses located in countries subject to more rigorous requirements are likely to believe that they are being unfairly placed at a competitive disadvantage. A steel plant outside of the United States, for instance, does not have to comply with air pollution control standards established by the Clean Air Act and, therefore, would likely be able to produce its steel at lower cost and sell it at a lower price than could a plant operating in the United States.

Of course, what is perceived as a competitive disadvantage for some is viewed as a competitive advantage for others, including for countries seeking to attract new industrial facilities from multinational corporations. A more relaxed environmental standard can be an effective inducement for business, whether it is a new automobile manufacturing plant or a hazardous waste disposal facility willing to accept waste from other nations. From an environmental perspective, a country using its laws to that end might seem to be engaged in the very "race to the bottom" that U.S. environmental laws sought to avoid by imposing minimum, national uniform standards on new sources of pollution throughout the nation. For a developing nation more interested in the short-term advantages of attracting new business than the long-term implications of environmental degradation, the race might seem to be more to the top than to the bottom, if not simply a race for sheer survival.

In either event, the resulting disparity generates pressure to create a level global playing field for business. This can be accomplished either by relaxing the more environmentally demanding laws or by increasing those that are less demanding. Either possibility, however, is quickly mired in the controversy of pitting international free trade objectives against environmental protection concerns. To demand that another country increase its environmental standards contravenes free trade principles, which oppose one country's conditioning its imports on the exporting country changing its own domestic laws. But achieving a level playing field by lowering the environmental standards in the country that currently has more demanding requirements is no less controversial. Those favoring strict environmental standards strongly object to making those standards subordinate to the promotion of trade, especially when the resulting increases in economic activities are likely to burden the environment even more.

Also heavily implicated by the trade–environment debate are matters of national sovereignty. Just as individual states in the United States continue to resist the loss of sovereignty implicit in national environmental legislation, so too do many nation-states find it difficult (if not wholly unacceptable) to agree to surrender any of their sovereignty to international authorities. Indeed, the sovereignty obstacle is far greater in the international context—small and large nations alike resist any such acquiescence. Wholly apart from the underlying merits of the problem to be addressed, these states react adversely to any notion that their laws must be either strengthened or relaxed in order to accommodate the concerns of other countries.

The United States is no exception in this respect, having declined in the 1980s to sign agreements such as the Law of the Sea Convention, and then again in the 1990s having failed to join the Biodiversity Convention at the 1992 Earth Summit. Congress similarly declined, notwithstanding U.S. formal ratification, to enact any legislation implementing the Basel Convention on the Control of Transboundary Movement of Hazardous Waste.[48] On each of these occasions, powerful interests in the United States were opposed to the treaties. Some of that opposition was based on conflicting economic interests, while other opposition was based on professed political principle regarding the impropriety of the United States subjugating its autonomy to the will of the international community.

During much of the 1990s, it seemed as though environmental law was seeking to catch up with international free trade law. No doubt because of the powerful, vested economic resources promoting free trade, the infrastructure for free trade agreements and its associated political constituency developed far more quickly in the twentieth century than did the infrastructure and constituency for related areas, including environmental protection law. One result was that both international agreements promoting free trade and international legal institutions for their implementation not only developed first, but the latter also became the forum for resolving conflicts between trade and environmental objectives.

International environmental law lacked the kind of unified agreement and political constituency that marked international trade law, which therefore had "an advantage based on seniority. The body of international trade law is long-standing, well-defined, and backed by a powerful business constituency."[49] The General Agreement on Tariffs and Trade (GATT) was completed in October 1947 and has since been amended several times. GATT's general purpose is to promote liberal trade policies by restricting barriers to trade, such as tariffs, quotas, taxes, and regulations that discriminated against imports. GATT includes provisions to allow nations to seek relief from trade barriers. And, in 1994, GATT negotiations led to the creation of the World Trade Organization (WTO), which provides a more developed institutional structure for promoting free trade and ensuring compliance with the various multilateral trade agreements.[50]

In contrast to international trade law, "the large collection of international environmental legal instruments is largely unconnected and has only a diffuse public behind it."[51] There are a host of legal agreements relating to environmental issues, with many gaps and some overlapping provisions. Entirely missing for the framework for international environmental law is any unified international institution for the harmonization, implementation, and further development of those proliferating agreements.

When the inevitable conflicts between environmental protection requirements and free trade developed during the 1990s, the former were invariably perceived as "obstacles" to the latter's realization. Because, moreover, only free trade possessed an institutional framework for dispute resolution, it was within that institutional setting, with its distinct set of preferences and values, that various conflicts were addressed. Had the tables been turned, it might well have been free trade that was perceived as the obstacle.[52]

Be that as it may, as international environmental law emerged during the 1990s, it was GATT and then the WTO that addressed in the first instance the conflicts that arose. A GATT panel ruled in 1991 that a U.S. ban on tuna imports from Mexico restricted trade in violation of GATT. The ban had been based on the Mexican fishing fleet's noncompliance with the U.S. Marine Mammal Protection Act's restrictions on incidental killing of dolphins in tuna fishing that occurred outside U.S. territory. The panel rejected the U.S. claim that the ban fell within the exemptions for measures either "necessary to protect . . . animal . . . life" or "relating to the conservation of exhaustible natural resources."[53] The panel narrowly construed the reach of each exemption. In 1998, a WTO dispute settlement panel, affirmed on appeal, similarly ruled against the U.S. effort to enforce a domestic law that banned the importation of shrimp harvested in the absence of turtle excluder devices that prevent turtles from drowning in shrimp nets.[54]

By the late 1990s, the making of international environmental law had become one of the globe's most pressing and contentious concerns. There was a series of discrete confrontations between nations around the globe. Downwind and downstream nations in Europe were increasingly complaining about cross-boundary air and water pollution. In the Middle East, tensions were rising as nations already in sharp conflict had to grapple with scarce supplies of their shared water resources. In seas around the globe, the fishing fleets of various nations competed for diminishing fish stocks that risked ecological collapse absent coordination. Communities in developing nations that found themselves the locus of pollution and hazardous waste exported from industrialized nations increasingly complained of "eco-imperialism." Finally, issues of global warming and climate change dominated international diplomacy in a way that no environmental issue previously had, albeit yielding little, if any, real progress.[55]

Over the course of the 1990s, accordingly, international environmental law formally had become a matter of "national security," as global instability was increasingly linked to environmental degradation and conflict. In 1996, Secretary of State Warren Christopher declared that "addressing natural resources issues is frequently critical to achieving political and economic stability, and to pursuing our strategic goals around the world. [W]e must also contend with the vast new danger posed to our national interests by damage to the environment and resulting global and regional instability."[56] The Woodrow Wilson International Center for Scholars soon thereafter established an Environmental Change and Security Project, which has both tracked and underscored the connection between national security and environmental concerns. In February 1999, EPA administrator Carol Browner likewise embraced the compelling need to strengthen national security through environmental protection initiatives.[57]

By the decade's final few months, international environmental law was not just a matter for quiet reflection in closely knit and highly structured diplomatic circles. There were literally riots in the streets of Seattle when thousands passionately demonstrated against the WTO during its meetings there, protesting that the organization paid too little attention to social issues, including environmental protection, in promoting free trade. For the first time in modern U.S. history, environmental protesters included groups who used violence to achieve maximum disruption as they sought to emphasize the seriousness of their cause and the depth of their passion.[58]

Understanding the 1990s

The 1990s are potentially misleading because one change of widespread portent for environmental law's future was in the form of a nonevent. What was most strikingly missing from the 1990s was the kind of persistent statutory overhauls that had occurred during both the 1970s and 1980s. During each of those two prior decades, hardly any significant area of federal pollution control or natural resource law remained untouched. In assessing modern environmental law's first two decades, legal commentators in the

early 1990s routinely remarked on the changing nature of federal environmental statutory law.[59]

The 1990s stand in sharp contrast. Following the passage of the Oil
Pollution Act and the Clean Air Act Amendments at the decade's outset,
there were relatively few comparable legislative statutory products. Long-
ballyhooed legislation to reform the Superfund program never passed.
Repeated efforts to amend the Clean Water Act or pass long-overdue
amendments to antiquated federal mining law met a similar fate. Notwithstanding widespread bipartisan support, Congress could not even pass legislation that would have elevated the EPA to cabinet status; when the 1990s
commenced, the enactment of that seemingly benign, symbolic legislation
had seemed a virtual certainty.[60]

The absence of statutory changes comparable to those of prior decades
was not, however, because change was no longer necessary. Environmental law's need for ongoing reform and experimentation was no less in the
1990s than it had been before. As always, new information regarding health
benefits, variations in compliance costs, advances in technology, issuance
of judicial rulings, and discovery of unanticipated consequences of prior
regulatory programs produced a demand for new approaches. Environmental justice advocates sought new legislation to address their claims
of discrimination and distributional unfairness. Property rights advocates
sought relief from environmental restrictions or at least compensation for
their resulting economic losses. States sought reductions in so-called unfunded federal mandates either by an increase in federal funding or by a
decrease in the number of the mandates themselves. And the regulated
community sought increased regulatory flexibility that allowed for greater
consideration of economic costs and for voluntary industry initiatives.

There are several reasons why Congress during the 1990s proved unable
to enact new authorizing legislation in response to any of these competing
constituencies. One reason is that the institutional equilibrium within the
federal government that had sustained prior lawmaking efforts finally col-
lapsed. A second reason is that the executive branch tried to step in to fill
the void, which both diminished the need for legislative action and further
polarized relations among all three branches of government. A final reason
is that those seeking reform failed to account for changing attitudes within
industry regarding the efficacy of environmental protection requirements.
Each of these reasons is discussed more fully below.

The Demise of Bipartisanship

At environmental law's birth in the early 1970s, environmentalism was
prominently nonpartisan. As described by the *New York Times,* "Conser-

vatives were for it. Liberals were for it. Democrats, Republicans and Independents were for it. So were the ins, the outs, the Executive and Legislative Branches of Government. It was Earth Day and like Mother's Day, no man in public office could be against it."[61]

President Nixon deliberately sought to prevent the Democratic Party in general, and presidential aspirant Senator Ed Muskie in particular, from capturing all the political capital arising out of the public's growing concern with environmental protection. Congressional votes on environmental bills were overwhelmingly in favor of passage and generally nonpartisan. There were leading supporters of the legislation on both sides of the aisle, as there were skeptics. Finally, the federal judiciary's pronounced interest in ensuring that the laws were not lost or misdirected in the "vast hallways" of the federal bureaucracy further underscored the absence of partisan politics. Judges at the time, more so than today, were not closely identified with one political party or the president who appointed them, though it appears likely a myth that the appointment of judges was devoid of political partisanship.[62]

This largely nonpartisan spirit dominated during the remainder of the 1970s and for much of the 1980s. The executive branch waxed and waned on environmental matters, regardless of the political affiliation of the president. President Gerald Ford signed significant legislation, including the Resource Conservation and Recovery Act, the Toxic Substances Control Act, the National Forest Management Act, and the Federal Land Policy and Management Act, while vetoing federal surface mining control legislation. President Jimmy Carter promoted energy conservation but also promoted fast track permitting for accelerated domestic energy resource development that environmentalists strongly opposed. President Ronald Reagan began to reorient the Republican Party in opposition to what he perceived to be the excesses of environmental protection law, but then politics ultimately compelled Reagan, too, to return to those moderates in his party who embraced the basic premises of the federal statutes, such as Bill Ruckelshaus, twice the EPA's administrator. And, as Nixon had done in his bid for reelection, George H. W. Bush sought to capture the environmentalist mantel in his successful run for the presidency in 1988.

Congress during the 1980s similarly resisted the identification of strong environmental protection policy with a single political party, in spite of the fact that a new class of young "Reagan Republicans" was elected to both chambers over the course of that decade. Unlike such Republican predecessors as California's Pete McCloskey, Kentucky's John Sherman Cooper, Illinois's Everett Dirksen, or Massachusetts's Edward W. Brooke III, who had joined bipartisan efforts in support of tough environmental protection laws during the 1970s, these new Republicans were more socially conservative, more skeptical of government regulation, and less pragmatic and willing to compromise. Yet the Republican leadership positions were then still dominated by moderates such as Howard Baker of Tennessee, Robert Stafford of Vermont, Mark Hatfield of Oregon, John Chafee and Lowell Weicker of Connecticut, and Charles Percy of Illinois, who continued to support demanding environmental laws. As chair of the powerful Senate Committee on the Environment and Public Works when the Republicans claimed the Senate in 1980, Senator Stafford may well have been the most influential because he and his staff were willing to work closely with their Democratic counterparts in the minority in opposition to the Reagan administration's environmental policies. The committee held frequent hearings that criticized administration policy, Senator Stafford and his staff repeatedly blocked administration efforts to pass laws that would relax existing requirements, and they secured passage of extensive amendments that both increased the EPA's regulatory responsibilities and limited the Reagan administration's discretion to reduce existing controls.

During the 1990s, however, the political dynamic in Congress changed. In the early 1990s, the Republicans in Congress mirrored the Bush administration's change of heart on environmental matters. They now openly questioned the wisdom, fairness, effectiveness, scientific grounding, and economic cost of strict environmental laws. Because, moreover, the skeptics in the Republican Congress were no longer newly elected, but veteran legislators by the 1990s, they began to rise to leadership positions both within the party and within Congress. It was therefore not surprising that environmental laws became a disproportionate target for reform in the Contract with America when the Republicans took charge of both chambers of Congress following the November 1994 elections. With the notable exception of an isolated few such as Senator John Chafee of Rhode Island, whose seniority entitled him to become chair of the Senate Committee on the Environment and Public Works, those Republicans who ascended to the relevant leadership positions in the House and the Senate were no longer party moderates who supported the existing laws. They were instead skeptics who supported fundamental change.

If even a pretense of nonpartisanship was then possible, the Democratic members of Congress and the Clinton administration eliminated it altogether by their response. Democrats seized the political initiative, either because they legitimately believed that Republicans sought to eliminate meaningful environmental protection or because they perceived a political opportunity to weaken the political opposition. In either case, the resulting rhetoric furthered the partisan divide. Democrats in Congress and Clinton administration officials at the EPA, the Department of the Interior, and the White House unleashed a steady, highly moralistic denunciation of the Republican legislative agenda. Democrats accused Republicans in Congress of gutting environmental laws and selling out public health and the protection of the nation's natural resource heritage in return for greater profits for their business allies.[63]

The immediate-term political impact was palpable. Virtually none of the Republican leadership's proposed reforms survived the Democratic attack. In addition, to guard against voter backlash, Republicans joined Democrats just before the 1996 elections to secure passage of significant safe drinking water and food quality legislation. The longer-term impact within the decade, however, was the wholesale political polarization of the environmental legislative agenda. Meaningful legislative debate and compromise essentially disappeared in both chambers. The political battle lines between the parties had, in effect, been drawn on environmental protection. For the first time in the three-decade-long history of modern environmental law, consensus legislation was no longer a politically viable option.

Annual statistics compiled by the League of Conservation Voters (LCV) provide some corroborating quantitative evidence of these qualitative political shifts. Since 1971, the league has published annual scores for individual members of Congress based on its assessment of their respective voting records for or against environmental protection. An examination of these voting records, broken down by party affiliation and region of the nation, reveals an ever-widening partisan divide.[64]

The results for both the House and the Senate from 1971 through 2000 are reproduced in the figures below. The same general pattern is evident in both sets of scores, although the Senate scores (as shown in the figure on page 154) are the more striking. In the Senate, the average score over thirty years generally remains within a fairly narrow range, between forty and fifty points. The two endpoints are virtually identical, between forty-three and forty-four points. There are nonetheless both marked differences between the Democrats and Republican scores throughout as well as discernible trends. The Democratic scores are always higher than the Republican scores, but the difference between the two increases dramatically in each succeeding decade.

Even more particularly, during the 1970s, the Democratic and Republican scores were quite different than in the 1990s, with the former about twenty points higher than the latter, but they also rose and fell together. When one political party's scores went up or down, so did the other's, almost to the exact same extent. Members of the two parties appear to have been reacting similarly to bills before Congress, sometimes in support of positions favored by environmentalists and sometimes not. They both increased at the outset of the decade, decreased in response to the energy

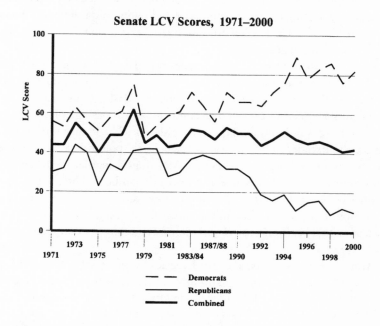

Points awarded by the League of Conservation Voters for support of environmental initiatives in the U.S. Senate, by party, 1971–2000

crisis, and then rebounded in response to congressional passage of a series of important bills in 1977 and 1978. Only at the very end of the decade, during the final years of the Carter administration, did the Democratic score fall rapidly down and the Republican score plateau to such an extent that they end the decade virtually identical, fewer than ten points apart. That phenomenon was likely the result of President Carter's National Energy Plan and its emphasis on the exploitation of domestic energy supplies, which resulted in a precipitous drop in the Democratic score.

After 1980, however, the two political parties began to oppose each other far more. There was a general tendency for one party's score to rise as the other's fell. The overall pattern generally showed the Democratic score on the rise and the Republican score falling, but there were still some periods where the converse occurred and other times when the two scores still tended to work in tandem. By the end of the decade, however, there was almost a forty-point difference between the two major political parties.

During the 1990s, the partisan divide was made complete. The two political parties were in virtual opposition, even before the formal emergence of the 104th Congress and the Contract with America in 1995. At the very outset of the decade, during the final years of the Bush administration, a partisan split erupted, with the Democrats and Republicans staking out polarized positions on environmental issues. By the end of the decade, party scores in the Senate were more than seventy points apart. The Democrats appeared to have cast their political lot largely with those favoring more environmental protection, while the Republicans had done the same with the regulated community. Any vestige of 1970s bipartisanship was gone.

The House LCV scores over time were similar, as shown in the second figure, but their oppositional tendency was slightly dampened in comparison to that of the Senate. The Republican scores remained fairly constant throughout the 1970s and 1980s. The Democratic scores, however, remained constant in the 1970s but took a significant upward leap in response to the early Reagan years before holding constant. Interestingly, during the first few years of the 1990s, the House Democratic scores followed more closely the same trend as their Republican counterparts by decreasing substantially. It was not until the Republicans surprisingly took over the leadership of the House in the 104th Congress that the House

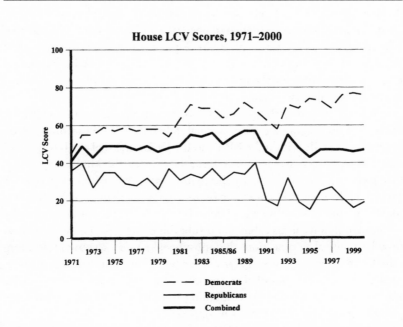

Points awarded by the League of Conservation Voters for support of environmental initiatives in the U.S. House, by party, 1971–2000

Democrats, like their Senate colleagues, began to systematically work in opposition to Republicans on environmental matters.

There is also evidence to suggest that the regulated community now perceives such a partisan divide in environmental law and has, accordingly, adjusted its support of candidates for office. In particular, an analysis of contributions by industry subject to environmental regulation to the political campaigns of Democrats and Republicans reveals shifts over time that are virtually identical to the shifts in the LCV scores of the two parties. Between 1990 and 2002, the amount of money that the energy and natural resource industry contributed to Democrat candidates significantly decreased (from 42 percent to 26 percent) while the amount contributed to Republican candidates correspondingly increased during that same time period (from 58 percent to 74 percent). A more focused inquiry into the campaign contributions of the coal industry is even more striking. Coal industry campaign contributions went from 59 percent Republicans, 41 percent Democrats in 1990, to 88 percent Republicans, 12 percent Democrats in 2002.[65]

The Rise of Executive Branch Lawmaking and of Legislation by Appropriation Rider

A second reason for the relative lack of statutory accomplishments in the 1990s is that the executive branch stepped in to fill the void left by Congress. The federal agencies did so partly in response to apparent congressional paralysis. Reforms were needed, regardless of Congress's ability to address them, and a governmental entity with lawmaking authority needed to provide some regulatory redress.

The executive branch, however, also took its action for the deliberate purpose of prolonging the congressional stalemate. Clinton administration officials, especially within the EPA and the Department of the Interior, did not want congressional action. Indeed, they feared the kinds of laws that Congress might pass, especially the 104th, 105th, and 106th Congresses. A presidential veto was, of course, an option, but never a sure thing. The president's willingness to veto a particular bill does not turn so simply on the recommendations of his cabinet and subcabinet officers. There are always broader political ramifications that must be taken into account in deciding whether to exercise that singular authority. In addition, legislative enactments are frequently bundled in a manner intended to make it even harder for the president to veto, by combining in one package matters that the president supports with matters he opposes.

For this reason, Interior and EPA officials repeatedly sought to develop regulatory initiatives that would both further their environmental objectives and, not incidentally, undermine the momentum of reform efforts on

Capitol Hill. Secretary of the Interior Babbitt spearheaded a series of programs that tried to be more responsive to the concerns of business and small property owners by making less harsh and more flexible the department's oversight of private exploitation of public resources within Interior's jurisdiction. Babbitt trumpeted comprehensive reforms in the administration of the Endangered Species Act, including habitat conservation plans and safe harbor plans intended to make that act more effective in its long-term ability to protect species and less onerous in its application to individual landowners. He displayed a willingness to broker pragmatic deals that discarded absolutist positions and that, by addressing the economic concerns of affected communities, had potentially greater staying power.[66]

At the EPA, Administrator Browner assumed a similar stance toward both the regulated community and state governments. She sought to promote regulatory approaches that would allow the regulated community to achieve pollution control requirements at lower costs and to provide states with more autonomy in their administration of federal programs. Browner promoted, for instance, the National Environmental Performance Partnership System, which allowed for greater state autonomy in administering federal environmental programs. By entering into more detailed agreements with the federal government, state environmental agencies could escape the kind of close monitoring those agencies had long found objectionable and also receive more federal technical and financial assistance.[67]

To similar effect, Administrator Browner sought to "reinvent" environmental law by reforming existing permitting regimes that the regulated community complained had the perverse effect of discouraging initiatives that could achieve greater environmental protection at lower cost. The gist of industry's complaint was that command and control erred by considering separately each part of a facility's operation with little, if any, attention paid to either the cost of pollution reduction or other more cost effective ways to reduce overall environmental harm. The result, according to some commentators, was too much money spent for too little return and the failure to exploit existing opportunities to reduce adverse environmental impacts at far lower cost.[68]

To address this concern (and no doubt also to forestall more far-reaching regulatory reform bills then pending before Congress), Browner's EPA embraced a series of reforms, such as Project XL, the Common Sense Initiative, and the Environmental Leadership Program, that contemplated a more holistic, less adversarial approach to facility regulation. Under these programs, the agency would, in effect, allow an individual facility to "trade" strict compliance with one environmental mandate for its "voluntary" agreement to achieve even greater environmental standards elsewhere. To similar effect, the EPA also expanded on the use of so-called supplemental environmental projects in the settlement of enforcement actions. This arrangement typically allows a defendant in an enforcement action to reduce substantially its payment of potentially applicable civil penalties in return for the defendant's "voluntary" agreement to support specific environmentally beneficial projects or facility reductions in pollution not otherwise required by law.[69]

While the business community and some within the environmental community applauded many of these reforms at the EPA and Interior, other environmentalists and many academic commentators expressed concern. They worried about the lack of meaningful public participation and absence of transparency in a system of decentralized decisionmaking that would allow for permits to be issued in the absence of complete information. They further objected to the lack of effective monitoring and compliance assurance resulting from a shift away from enforceable obligations and toward "voluntary" steps, and away from federal overseers and toward state and local officials who might be too close to those being regulated. Finally, many questioned the legality of these reforms on the ground that the existing environmental and natural resource statutes did not authorize the EPA and Interior to adopt reforms that in effect waived or "adapted" the statute's strict terms.[70]

What may have begun, however, as an administrative effort intended to fill the void left by Congress and deter congressional intervention transformed into a highly activist, ambitious lawmaking agenda during the decade's final years. Beginning in 1997, Secretary Babbitt wielded a sledgehammer to underscore the significance of Interior's new policy of destroying dams that were environmentally harmful or had otherwise outlived their functions. He further adopted sweeping reforms of long-standing rangeland policies and hardrock mining law, placing significant environmental restrictions on economic exploitation of the public lands without the benefit of any new, intervening federal statutory authority. Each new regulatory regime imposed new restrictions on environmentally destructive activities on public lands. Babbitt's solicitor at Interior, John Leshy, issued a series of "Solicitor Opinions" that similarly modified long-standing Interior policies in a manner more sensitive to resource protection and conservation concerns. Finally, in what may prove to be Babbitt's greatest legacy, he persuaded the president to designate as national monuments millions of acres of public lands of extraordinary ecological significance.[71]

EPA administrator Carol Browner was similarly ambitious during the final years of the Clinton administration. She overcame substantial opposition both in the regulated community and within the Office of the President to promulgate stricter national ambient air quality control standards for ozone and particulate matter. She also oversaw the EPA's invigoration

of the Clean Air Act's long-dormant interstate air pollution control provisions, promulgated tougher regulations applicable to diesel engines and
diesel fuel, and initiated an aggressive nationwide enforcement campaign
against electric utility companies for allegedly modifying their facilities
without complying with tougher requirements applicable to new sources.
Browner also issued regulations that sought dramatic improvement in
the quality of the nation's waters by focusing more on so-called nonpoint
sources of pollution, such as rain runoff from agricultural and construction
activities, that had historically been subject to less regulation.[72]

Unable to enact substantive legislation either to reform the environmental laws or to stop EPA and Interior's new regulatory initiatives, congressional opponents sought other legislative avenues to have their voices heard.
The result was a relative rise in the power of the congressional appropriations committees and their use of so-called appropriation riders, which
denied an executive branch agency the authority to spend any sums to implement specific programs or policies.

Since the 1970s, there had always been tension within Congress between
members overseeing authorization and members overseeing appropriation.
Those members of Congress who sat on the authorization committees, especially in the 1970s, were frequently more accepting of the environmental
protection premises of the statutes Congress was then enacting than were
members of the appropriations committees. During the 1970s and most of
the 1980s, the authorization committees took the leadership role in environmental policy matters. However, as their ability to enact legislation generally
waned during the 1990s, the appropriation committees became correspondingly more powerful. Indeed, appropriation riders became a common congressional legislative technique. Appropriation committees would simply
add a rider to budgetary legislation that denied the EPA or the Interior Department the authority to make certain proposed regulations final, implement final regulations, or take certain specific action, such as listing additional endangered species or designating new tracts of their critical habitat.[73]

Some riders even further required that certain actions be taken regardless of what other applicable environmental laws might dictate. The controversial Timber Salvage Rider that Congress enacted in 1995 is likely the
most notorious example in the 1990s. That rider effectively suspended applicable environmental laws such as the National Forest Management Act
and Endangered Species Act and required the harvesting of healthy and
valuable timber on public lands. The stated purpose was prevention of fire
and insect infestation, but the rider's actual reach was far broader in geographic and substantive scope.[74]

The placement of riders within massive budget bills also invariably rendered the price of a presidential veto too high. The president would be

presented with a Hobson's Choice. To prevent a rider from becoming law, he would have to veto a bill that authorized the annual appropriations for several agencies. The price of such a veto might be giving up hard-fought gains in welfare legislation or politically popular federal highway funding. The 1995 Timber Salvage Rider is illustrative. Environmentalists lobbied in vain to obtain a veto of the legislation that included that rider, and there was considerable misunderstanding regarding the precise legal effect of the rider. The mere title of the relevant legislation, however, well demonstrates why a veto, even in the face of such uncertain stakes, was not possible: the Emergency Supplemental Appropriations for Additional Disaster Assistance, for Anti-Terrorism Initiatives, for Assistance in the Recovery from the Tragedy that Occurred at Oklahoma City, and Rescissions Act. A suspension of environmental restrictions on timber harvesting, in other words, had been coupled with relief for those needing assistance in the aftermath of the Oklahoma City bombing.

As the 1990s came to a close, the clash between the executive branch and the appropriations committees grew in depth and breadth. Whenever the EPA or the Department of the Interior promulgated a new program in the face of substantial industry opposition, Congress seemed to respond with an applicable rider or an equivalent budgetary technique for blocking the administrative effort. One rider delayed the implementation of the EPA's new national ambient air quality standards for ozone and particulate matter under the Clean Air Act. Another rider delayed implementation of new Interior regulations that sought to limit mining activities on public land that caused undue environmental degradation.[75]

The tug-of-war between the two branches became especially confrontational during the final months of the Clinton administration as both industry and Republicans in Congress sought to respond to what they perceived as an effort by administration officials to rush into law sweeping new environmental restrictions. When, for instance, Congress passed a rider to prevent Administrator Browner from promulgating as final then-proposed regulations that significantly expanded the agency's authority to ensure the meeting of water quality standards under the Clean Water Act, the president simply delayed signing the bill for several days. The delay allowed Browner, the White House, and the OMB to broker a deal in marathon meetings over the substance of the final regulations, which Browner then immediately promulgated. The rider, which became effective a few hours later when the president signed the budget bill, had the legal effect of delaying implementation of the final rules but did not prevent them from formally becoming law.[76]

In short, although the political dynamic of the legislative branch limiting the discretion of the executive branch was reminiscent of the 1970s and 1980s, the situation in the 1990s was also strikingly different. Before it had been the authorization committees that had spearheaded legislation designed to restrict the executive branch's ability to render environmental regulation more sensitive to short-term economic concerns. By 2000, in the final months of the Clinton presidency, it was the appropriations committees now seeking to restrict the executive branch from undertaking environmental protection measures that legislators perceived as failing to take adequate account of those very same economic concerns.

The "Greening" of the Nation's Economy

A third reason for the legislative stagnation that persisted during much of the 1990s was the failure of many of those within the regulated community or within environmental organizations to appreciate the business community's shift in attitudes toward environmental law that had begun to take hold by the mid-1990s. Representatives both of industry and environmental organizations wrongly presumed that economic interests harbored a natural antipathy toward strict pollution control and resource preservation laws. While perhaps an accurate premise in the 1970s and much of the 1980s, it was no longer true as the century was coming to a close. Indeed, for much of the economy, quite the opposite was true.

Hence, while the conservative think tanks first launched by business interests in the 1970s continued in the 1980s to propound "reforms" for relaxing environmental protection requirements, there was a decided lack of unity within the business constituency in support of such reforms. So too, unity within the environmental community splintered, undermining its ability to present a cohesive, consistent position in its lobbying efforts. Some environmental organizations steadfastly persisted as they had in the past in treating business as necessary antagonists. Other organizations, however, began to forge alliances with business.

What many on both sides of the legislative debate failed to apprehend was the effect on industry of the fact that environmental protection laws had, by the mid 1990s, been in place for virtually a generation. Powerful economic interests had, during that time, invested millions if not billions of dollars in compliance with those laws. Companies had purchased expensive pollution controls. They had modified the production processes within their manufacturing facilities. They had hired highly trained engineers, scientists, and lawyers within their organizations whose primary mission was to address environmental protection matters and not to eliminate them (and their professions) from the industry's scope of concerns.

By the end of the 1990s, many of the larger companies within the nation's most powerful industrial sectors had largely internalized environmental law into their business organizations. Accordingly, they no longer so naturally welcomed the destabilization and legal uncertainty that would likely result from widespread reinvention and reformation efforts, especially if such efforts gave new business entrants a competitive advantage over existing companies. The failure to appreciate that countervailing industry concern played a large part in the downfall of the regulatory reform efforts of President Reagan's first EPA administrator, Anne Gorsuch, in the early 1980s. The same kinds of industry concerns regarding regulatory destabilization had only increased in the succeeding years. To be sure, these businesses did not welcome new, tougher environmental controls, but they remained wary nonetheless of uncertain change in existing standards and rules.[77]

Three decades of modern environmental law had also created a billion-dollar pollution control industry in the United States. Pollution control and waste management had themselves become big business. The Civilian Conservation Corps of the New Deal had created over 3 million jobs during the 1930s and 1940s. The Clean Air Act, the Clean Water Act, the Resource Conservation and Recovery Act, Surface Mining Control and Reclamation Act, and Superfund law had created millions of jobs worldwide.

By the late 1990s, the global market for the pollution control industry was approximately $500 billion per year. The market for the United States alone was more than $200 billion per year by 2000. The pollution control industry in the United States employed then more than 1.4 million individuals, or as many people as were employed by several of the nation's major industries, such as the aerospace industry. Approximately thirty thousand private entities and eighty thousand public entities engaged in the business of pollution control. Like ecotourism, the growth and viability of the pollution control industry had become dependent on maintenance and enforcement of the nation's pollution control and resource conservation laws. For better or for worse, depending on one's perspective, the nation's powerful economic interests included those who wanted more, not less, environmental protection.[78]

The environmental protection and natural resources laws had also succeeded in underscoring the value for the nation's economic well-being of the "ecosystem services" provided by productive natural systems. Watersheds, for instance, provided billions of dollars worth of high-quality drinking water and flood protection. New York City could either pay as much as $8 billion for a drinking water filtration plant and another $300 million for its annual maintenance, or it could opt instead to spend only about $1.5 billion to acquire critical watershed lands to produce the same supplies of drinking water. A 1997 publication in *Nature* concluded that total annual value of ecosystem services was at least $16–54 trillion dollars, or three times that of the global gross national product.[79]

For-profit business, too, had begun to appreciate better the economic value of specific "services" provided to their activities by productive natural systems and hence the dependence of such business on maintaining the ecological viability of those natural systems. Manufacturing processes saved money when available water supplies were cleaner and less likely to interfere with industrial operations or require costly pretreatment prior to its utilization. The billion-dollar fishing and shellfish industries now well understood their dependency on laws that prevented catastrophic events, ranging from massive oil spills to population collapses caused by persistent toxic contaminants. The real estate industry similarly recognized that laws that maintained clean air and water or restored land to its natural condition enhanced and maintained property values for residential development. Manufacturing enterprises seeking to purchase former industrial property had come to enjoy the benefits of laws that limited the ability of sellers to convey property with hidden, unwelcome surprises, such as leaking underground storage tanks of oil or other hazardous substances that could require costly remediation.[80]

Moreover, by the mid-1990s a smaller percentage of the U.S. economy was directly involved in polluting activities. The nation's economy was by then increasingly engaged in the provision of services other than heavy industry and manufacturing. The service sector had become responsible for about 75 percent of the gross domestic product and 80 percent of employment, and the trend was decidedly in favor of the service sector of the economy increasing its newly gained dominance. In 1970, one out of every four workers in the United States was employed in the manufacturing sector; it is now projected that only one out of every eight will soon be.[81]

To be sure, at the end of the 1990s, much of that service industry was itself dependent on the production of enormous amounts of electricity and heavy motor vehicle use, activities that are responsible for massive amounts of pollution. Accordingly, the growth of the service industry has hardly been environmentally benign. Even while the service economy was growing in relative proportion, manufacturing and industry were growing in absolute numbers and often as a direct result of the demands created by the expanding service economy. Yet, because the burden of the pollution control laws remained primarily on industry and manufacturing in the first instance, those laws were becoming less controversial (and therefore also potentially less effective) for that increasing percentage of U.S. businesses in the service industry and their employees.

In addition, because some of that emerging service industry was directly dependent on environmental protection, the number of powerful economic interests affirmatively in support of environmental laws was increasing. Ecotourism, for instance, had become big business. The same public values that supported enactment of tough environmental laws also fueled consumer demand for the enjoyment of pristine environments. Closing beaches because of ocean pollution could have catastrophic consequences for a community dependent on such tourism. The collapse of a fishery population because of pollution or overfishing by "factory boats" could likewise have severe economic consequences for small businesses that utilized charter boats. Emissions from a power plant that undermined visibility in a state or national park could adversely affect tourism-dependent businesses in the surrounding community.[82]

By the mid-1990s, businesses and communities dependent upon ecotourism understood these causal relationships. They no longer assumed that they had to be the unwilling victims of upstream or upwind activities that could destroy their economic livelihoods. Environmental laws had by now become sufficiently settled in their economic expectations to confer instead a sense of entitlement. Rather than favor relaxation of tough air, water, and hazardous waste disposal laws, affected businesses and communities were now more likely to rise up in opposition to any such relaxation of standards.

Moreover, because of environmental laws such as California's Proposition 65, that sought to change consumer behavior by information disclosure, there was also now a billion-dollar industry for environmentally friendly products. Millions of Americans were apparently willing to pay a premium for such products or to forgo altogether purchasing some products deemed too environmentally destructive. Americans, for instance, were willing to spend millions of dollars each year to purchase their drinking water from stores and specialized water companies rather than simply rely on tap water as they had in the past. Many Americans expressed a disdain for purchasing tuna that had been harvested with techniques that unduly threatened marine mammals. Americans preferred not to purchase wood products that were linked to the destruction of the rain forest, and they would pay more for fruits and vegetables that were less aesthetically pleasing if grown more "naturally" without the use of environment-threatening pesticides. Each of these sources of consumer demand supported a corresponding business that employed voters and that paid taxes.

Finally, societal attitudes had changed over time, including within the regulated community. The criminalization of environmental law, beginning in the 1980s, and the growth of environmental curricula in the nation's schools was not without effect. Corporate officers themselves must live within communities and within families. As the law settles over time, a moral stigma naturally attaches to its violation. One does not want to be classified a felon. Employees "don't like going home and being scorned for being part of a dirty enterprise as soon as they mention their job."[83]

In short, the regulated community no longer presented the monolithic opposition to modern environmental protection law that many of its purported pundits and environmental opponents once presumed. The leaders of the business community now were those who had succeeded in a regulatory regime that included environmental protection requirements. They had learned how to earn profits both notwithstanding and increasingly because of such requirements. They led a workforce that had gained competitive advantages over others; enjoyed the economic advantages of a cleaner air, water, and land; sold pollution control equipment and services; and tapped into markets that addressed consumers' environmental fears and aspirations. Some even held strong personal beliefs in environmental protection, having been involved in the environmental movement themselves. Both for better and for worse, just when those favoring major reforms of environmental laws were finally gaining powerful policymaking positions, the regulated community they purported to champion was no longer uniformly in favor of such fundamental reform.

PART III

Environmental Law in the New Millennium

Environmental law beat the odds during the 1970s, 1980s, and 1990s. Its supporters overcame massive institutional and political obstacles to develop a comprehensive series of federal environmental protection statutory programs. Environmentalists defeated repeated efforts to reduce environmental law's reach and stringency, and environmental protection laws steadily became, notwithstanding or perhaps because of these challenges, more comprehensive, far-reaching, demanding, and pervasive than ever. Now, as the United States enters a new century, much of the actual implementation and enforcement of environmental law occur at the state and local level, and pressure is building to create a similar international institutional framework for environmental protection law.

Notwithstanding environmental law's persistence, the disputes surrounding its implementation today are no less contentious or fundamental than those of the past. Many of the debates of the last three decades continue virtually unabated today. States still complain of excessive federal mandates and oversight. Industry still complains of excessive regulatory rigidity and too little consideration of compliance costs. Economists still complain that economic incentives could achieve environmental quality at a far lower cost than the "command-and-control" requirements that they contend dominate existing environmental statutes. And environmentalists still complain that, either because of regulatory loopholes or lack of adequate monitoring and enforcement, the existing statutory program contains too many exceptions that too often prevent the accomplishment of environmental goals. Controversy and distrust, produced by the combination of the inherent features of ecological injury and their proposed redress by the nation's lawmaking institutions, continue to impede candid and informed public discussion of environmental issues.

Yet, notwithstanding the familiarity of the themes being struck in the ongoing policy debates surrounding environmental law, its role since the 1970s had plainly changed by the new millennium. It was no longer so easy to characterize environmental law as "radical" or to see it as a temporary "fad." Environmental law had come of age as environmentalism became deeply embedded in all aspects of American life, including law. Of course, as described in this final part of the book, age has its own costs. What renders law more settled and less controversial may simultaneously render it less effective.

The final three chapters of this book reflect on the present state of U.S. environmental law and speculate about its future. There are distinct patterns evident in the way that environmental law has evolved during the past three-plus decades that strongly suggest the kinds of legal rules that are most successful in regulating the extent and pace of ecological transformation. There is also evidence that environmental law's aging process has unduly ossified the necessary lawmaking processes—some have dubbed it a "green arthritis"[1] —preventing environmental law from always evolving as it should. With regard to the future, it seems clear that environmental law faces significant challenges. At the most fundamental level, many of these challenges are related to yet another shift in the public's conceptions of time and space that is likely to make environmental protection goals even harder to maintain. Furthermore, future environmental law will doubtlessly be challenged by the changing nature of the domestic and international economies. The production and delivery of goods and services in the twenty-first century is plainly not the same as it was in the late 1960s and early 1970s, when modern U.S. environmental law was largely conceived. Effective environmental protection law will accordingly require different regulatory touchstones and perspectives in the future.

CHAPTER EIGHT

The Emerging Architecture
of U.S. Environmental Law

In 1987, former Senate committee staffer Ronald Outen captured the structure of U.S. environmental law and the dynamics of legislative amendment with this wonderfully evocative comparison to the "architecture of Tobacco Road":

If you have traveled in the remote parts of the Deep South, I am sure you have seen the architecture of Tobacco Road—shacks built of whatever materials were available at the time, often by a series of owners. Maybe the roof is corrugated tin, but one wall is made from a billboard and the door step is a cinder block. No part matches any other part, and there are holes here and there. Still, it provides a measure of basic shelter, and there comes a point where it is easier to tack a new board over a gap that appears than to redesign the entire structure.[1]

Well over a decade later, many environmental lawyers would likely still ascribe to the same depiction. Certainly, the various components of environmental law, including the Clean Air Act, Resource Conservation and Recovery Act, the Federal Land Policy and Management Act, and the Surface Mining Control and Reclamation Act, appear to be nothing less than a crazy patchwork quilt of statutory provisions only loosely falling under the common rubric of environmental law.

Efforts to "redesign the entire structure" have largely fallen flat, for reasons that Outen no doubt well understood from his days on Capitol Hill. When, for instance, the Conservation Foundation and the (senior) Bush administration Environmental Protection Agency (EPA) sought in the mid- and late 1980s to promote the kind of "cross-media" or "multimedia" approach to environmental pollution control that had long been highly touted and that seemed to make so much sense in theory, the proposal had turned out to lack any political legs. The existing system comprising the

Clean Air Act, Clean Water Act, Safe Drinking Water Act, Resource Conservation and Recovery Act, and similar initiatives subjected single sources of pollution to several largely uncoordinated regulatory schemes, each focused on just one environmental media—such as air, water, groundwater, or land. The result of such hobnailed regulation could be nonsensical and potentially perverse as industrial pollution would simply seek out the path of least regulatory resistance rather than the path where it might cause the least harm or be controlled at the least cost. But even more threatening to competing stakeholders and interest groups was the prospect of writing a unified cross-media statute that would place back on the legislative agenda their respective past political gains. Environmentalists further feared a regulatory scheme that depended on years of developing new information about cross-media pollutant pathways and, therefore, portended great implementation delays. Environmentalists remembered well the difficulties of enforcing the Toxic Substances Control Act of 1976 (TSCA), which had long provided the EPA with the statutory authority for the multimedia approach. Faced with the regulatory uncertainties and lack of clear mandate underlying TSCA's command to address "unreasonable risk of injury to health or the environment" in all aspects of a chemical's pathway in the marketplace, the EPA had accomplished hardly anything at all.[2]

However, even absent a repeat of the kind of legal revolution that occurred in the early 1970s, there has been discernible evolution in environmental law over the past three decades—largely in the form of convergence. Statutory programs have, in effect, "borrowed" from each other as years of experience have shown which approaches to pollution control and natural resource management are more or less successful. Environmental law is still far from satisfying any academic expectation for unitary rationality, but it is far less ad hoc and circumstantial than it once appeared to be.

The regulatory schemes that have prevailed within environmental law are also very much a product of both the environmental problems that the laws seek to address and the lawmaking institutions and processes within them. There are reasons why certain kinds of legal regimes have systematically proven to be more or less successful. So, too, are there structural reasons why alternative approaches, long touted as improvements, have been little utilized. This evolution is not mere happenstance—the development of environmental law reflects physical, political, economic, and societal challenges derived from competing spatial and temporal dimensions.

Some regulatory approaches may prevail over time because they in fact work well; they promote environmental protection at an acceptable level and fair distribution of cost, even if not by minimizing such costs. Quite possibly, however, other approaches may prevail over time not because they are environmentally successful, but instead only because they are "politically" successful. These approaches may even owe their political success to the fact they appear to achieve major environmental protection gains (and thereby appeal to environmentalists) that are in fact largely illusory because of hidden loopholes and gaps in regulatory coverage (which may appeal to powerful economic interests in the regulated community). Indeed, given the inherent tendency of our nation's lawmaking system to act incrementally and to seek accommodation and compromise, there is reason to suspect that the political pressures favoring just that kind of legal evolution are fairly constant.

This chapter first describes the phenomenon of convergence within environmental law that is gradually creating common ground between legal regimes that otherwise seem unduly fragmented and uncoordinated. Because convergence is largely prompted by the growing consensus of what kinds of regulatory approaches work best (or worst)—environmentally, politically, or both—the chapter next highlights some of the essential components for an environmental law program and touches on how the relative success of each component derives from its ability to address the challenges that face environmental lawmaking.

Convergence within Environmental Law

In the late 1970s, environmental law professors routinely asked their students to explain how and why Congress regulated the pollution of air and water so differently. Today, the more interesting question would be to ask the law student to explain how and why the two pollution control programs have become more similar during the past three decades. Indeed, the convergence of the Clean Air Act and Clean Water Act is representative of an overall trend in environmental law. Even the traditionally distinct areas of environmental law and natural resources law increasingly overlap in their regulatory focus and operation. Of course, significant differences between regulatory programs remain, but those that do are more likely than in the past to be explained by actual physical differences between the regulated resources or economic activities.

The Clean Air and Clean Water Acts

Congress enacted the Clean Air Act Amendments of 1970 (CAA) and the Federal Water Pollution Control Act Amendments of 1972 (FWPCA), renamed the Clean Water Act (CWA) in 1977, within two years of each other. Many legislators and committee staffers were intimately involved in drafting both laws. Each statute represented an ambitious and aggressive effort to establish a comprehensive federal regulatory role over pollution control.

However, the structures and essential features of the two laws had surprisingly little in common.

The 1970 CAA relied principally on state implementation plans (SIPs) developed by the states as necessary to achieve a series of uniform national ambient air quality standards (NAAQS) promulgated by the EPA for the entire nation. The agency would review each SIP to ensure its adequacy for achieving the NAAQS, and could, at least in theory, write its own "federal implementation plan" if a state repeatedly failed to produce an adequate SIP. But the primary regulatory responsibility for the achievement of the NAAQS remained with the states. The states would determine and apply specific emissions limitations to individual sources and otherwise decide how to regulate economic activity to ensure compliance with the NAAQS.[3]

The CAA included two major exceptions to exclusive reliance on a SIP to achieve the NAAQS: regulation of motor vehicles and regulation of new stationary sources. As described in chapter 5, the automobile industry had been the driving force behind national regulation of their industry, due to its desire (largely achieved by the CAA) to preempt state regulation. Congress singled out new stationary sources, drawing a sharp distinction between "new" and "existing" sources of pollution, but for different reasons. Under the CAA, new stationary sources alone were subject to nationally uniform emissions limitations, called "new source performance standards." The standards did not require a specific source to apply any particular control technology, but instead simply to meet numerical emissions limitations based on the EPA's determination of the capacities of "adequately demonstrated" control technology (and perhaps also on the availability of less polluting fuel).[4]

Congress structured the 1972 FWPCA very differently. Unlike the 1970 CAA, the linchpin of the FWPCA was neither confined to certain pollutants nor aimed just at achieving ambient standards. The FWPCA broadly applied to all pollutants and, focusing on point source discharges of pollutants such as industrial discharge pipes, sought to have point sources remove as much pollution as could be technologically accomplished, regardless of the actual impact of these efforts on water quality. Hence, while ambient standards determined the amount of required pollution control under the CAA, this was not the case under the FWPCA.[5]

FWPCA implementation also did not depend, as did the CAA, on state implementation in the first instance. Under the FWPCA, the primary basis for implementation of the statutory mandate was the "national pollutant discharge elimination system" (NPDES) permit program, a federal permit requirement that effectively rendered all discharges without a permit *per se* unlawful. No such permit requirement had been expressed in the CAA, which instead purported to confer maximum discretion on the states to determine how best to achieve the NAAQS through SIPs. The FWPCA allowed for a state agency to secede from federal administration of the permit program, but the minimum effluent limitations were dictated by the federal government.[6]

Nor did the FWPCA remotely mirror the CAA regarding treatment of new versus existing industrial facilities. Unlike the CAA, the FWPCA did not confer on existing industrial facilities any immunity from the application of nationally uniform technology-based effluent limitations. The FWPCA instead imposed a series of technology-based effluent limitation levels on distinct categories of both existing and new sources. The precise relevant factors for determination of particular standards under each allowed for consideration of the different circumstances possibly presented by existing and new facilities, but not a blanket exception.[7]

Finally, under the FWPCA, ambient standards were not nationally uniform as they were under the CAA. In effect, the FWPCA permitted states to zone their waters for different uses and to promulgate water quality criteria consistent with such uses. A state could, accordingly, decide that some waters would be better used for fishing and swimming, other waters for noncontact recreation, and still others for industry and transportation purposes. State determination of water quality standards was subject to some federal review, but this oversight was not remotely similar to the CAA's imposition of the NAAQS.[8]

In short, the differences between the CAA and FWPCA in the early 1970s were so stark, pervasive, and contrary that it made it difficult to say which was more stringent than the other. Regardless of the merits of any debate regarding the relative stringency of the two pieces of legislation in the early 1970s, what is more striking from a historical perspective is the extent to which their once-stark differences were largely obscured by the end of the 1990s. Incrementally, and without much explicit acknowledgment, the two statutory programs merged. To be sure, some overlap had always existed in many of their miscellaneous provisions respecting matters such as judicial review, citizen suit oversight, and non-preemption of more stringent state controls. Conversely, there were also significant differences between the two laws that persisted, especially those differences rooted in the distinct physical characteristics of air and water. For example, water is much more susceptible to being "zoned" for uses; accordingly, the FWPCA has continued to decline to apply to water the uniform national ambient standard approach that the CAA applies to air. Nevertheless, the converging shifts in regulatory perspectives that occurred within the two statutes were substantial.

By congressional amendment and executive branch regulation, the essential framework of the 1970 CAA was transformed in 1990 into a regulatory program quite similar to the 1972 FWPCA. This transformation was the product of two simultaneous, related phenomena: the decrease in the relative importance of ambient standards and state implementation plans and the concomitant rise of CWA-like technology-based emissions limitations and permit requirements.[9]

Soon after the CAA's initial passage in 1970, technology-based pollution controls like those that dominated the 1972 FWPCA began to increase in the CAA. The original notion that the federal government would simply announce the NAAQS and the states would be responsible for all the details became unworkable due to an avalanche of federal commands. Congress had divided the regulatory world into "attainment" and "nonattainment" areas, prescribing specific additional measures that SIPs must contain for each kind of area. The former were subject to detailed requirements designed for the "prevention of significant deterioration" (PSD); the latter were subject to increasingly prescriptive requirements to ensure reasonable progress toward attainment. Moreover, because every part of the nation was either an attainment or nonattainment area for each pollutant, and every place was an attainment area for at least one pollutant, these new federal commands were universally applicable.[10]

Technology-based controls became the norm and the NAAQS themselves, lacking any direct applicability to particular sources, became more incidental. New and modified major stationary sources in nonattainment areas became subject to a technology-based standard called "lowest achievable emission rates" (LAER). Existing major stationary sources in nonattainment areas became subject to emissions limitations based on "reasonably available control technologies" (RACT). Major new or modified stationary sources in PSD areas had to comply with emissions limitations based on "best available control technology" (BACT). Existing sources in areas federally designated for enhanced visibility protection had to "procure, install, and operate . . . the best available retrofit technology [(BART)] . . . for controlling emissions."[11]

In 1970, the imposition of technology-based emissions limitations and/or specific pollution control design standards had been the exception. By deliberate congressional design, that ceased to be true under the CAA within a few decades—at least for major stationary sources. The CAA's LAER, RACT, BACT, BART, and NSPS (new source performance standard) had now joined the CWA's competing technology-based acronyms, including BPT (best practicable control technology), BAT (best available control technology), BDT (best demonstrated control technology), and BCPT (best conventional pollutant control technology). It marked the beginning of what the U. S. Court of Appeals for the District of Columbia Circuit later described as the "mind numbing" quality of environmental law.[12] This alphabet soup of acronyms also directly contributed both to the promotion of professional expertise in environmental law and to the growing inaccessibility of the law's protections to communities lacking the necessary expertise to enlist those protections on their behalf.

The once-clear distinction between new and existing stationary sources also became increasingly blurred in the 1990s because of administrative reinterpretation/clarification of long-standing statutory terms. Those who drafted the CAA had understood the environmental risks of drawing such a sharp regulatory line between new and existing sources. An existing source could, in order to avoid more stringent controls, simply stay in operation many years longer rather than build a new plant. If enough existing facilities stayed in operation long enough, the perverse result of imposing much tougher pollution controls on new sources would be more, rather than less, air pollution. Congress anticipated that possibility partly by providing that the "modification" of an existing source could trigger the "new" source requirements, thereby limiting a source's ability to postpone indefinitely new source requirements. In the late 1970s, however, the EPA explicitly exempted "routine maintenance" from the scope of "modification," and neither the agency nor the states implementing the CAA aggressively policed the new/existing borderline until the late 1990s. During the final years of the Clinton administration, the EPA announced a more expansive reading of the "modification" trigger and, on that basis, initiated a series of nationwide enforcement actions against existing sources. The practical effect of this more demanding approach was the elimination of the prior grandfathering of existing facilities that had prolonged their useful lives (with the aid of much "routine maintenance") far longer than lawmakers had anticipated in the 1970s.[13]

Perhaps the most fundamental convergence between the CAA and CWA, however, involved the permit requirement, which had been the mainstay of the 1972 FWPCA but had not played any part in the 1970 CAA. The NPDES permit requirement had worked well within the CWA, providing some certainty to the regulated community, which wanted assurances that it could operate a facility under explicit conditions for a specified number of years without violating federal law. The CWA permit requirement had also given both government and environmental regulators a basis for effective enforcement. Absent a permit that included specific pollutant limits and monitoring and self-reporting requirements, there was no ready means of deciding whether an individual source of pollutant was or was not in violation of federal requirements. A SIP itself was not even a unified document, let alone one that readily linked individual sources to the applicable

NAAQS. In practice, SIPs were little more than theoretical constructs of numerous documents and records reflecting shifting polices. A SIP fell far short of providing any accessible means of setting limits for the emissions by any one source at any one time. It was practically impossible, as a result, to determine whether most air pollution sources were in violation of any applicable emissions limitations.

CWA enforcement, by contrast, had proven relatively easy. All that was required was to compare the discharge monitoring reports that had to be filed by the permitee with the effluent limits prescribed by the permit itself. Discharge in excess of those limits provided a prima facie case of a permit violation. All the citizen suit plaintiff (or government agency) had to do was file a complaint, along with a motion for summary judgment that included a copy of the permit and permitee's own monitoring reports. The plaintiff was guaranteed success, meaning a recovery of substantial attorney's fees and the violator's facing a substantial penalty payable to the federal Treasury and possibly injunction. For this reason, many such citizen suits were readily settled, with the terms of the settlement calling for substantial payments by the defendant to support environmentally beneficial projects in addition to (or instead of) payments to the Treasury. Not surprisingly, almost all the environmental citizen suits brought in the 1970s and 1980s were based on the Clean Water Act rather than on any of the other environmental laws, including the Clean Air Act.[14]

In 1990, Congress responded to the growing consensus that the CAA's lack of a CWA-type permit requirement worked to the CAA's disadvantage by adding to the CAA a broadly applicable permit requirement applicable, *inter alia,* to major stationary sources. Many of the details of the CAA's new permit program, including monitoring and reporting requirements, were modeled directly upon the CWA's NPDES permit system applicable to point sources. As with the CWA, the new CAA provisions allowed for individual states to take over the administration of the permit program, so long as they met a list of statutorily prescribed criteria. As a result, while the NAAQS may have been the ultimate driving force behind much of the CAA, they were no longer the actual, immediate basis of pollution controls any more than ambient standards were the basis of the CWA.[15]

It is especially intriguing that just as the CAA became more like the 1972 FWPCA, the new CWA was becoming more like the original CAA. Ambient standards, which had long been a dormant component of the CWA and far less important than similar standards in the CAA, became the source of a major new CWA regulatory initiative in the 1990s. The 1972 FWPCA had resulted from a conflict between the House and Senate regarding whether federal pollution limits should be rooted in technology-based controls or in water quality ambient standards to be determined by the states. The proponents of technology-based controls won out, largely because of their contention that ecological cause and effect was too complex to be the touchstone for federal regulation. As a result of a political compromise, however, the 1972 FWPCA provided for additional controls in the event that technology-based controls proved insufficient to meet state water quality standards.[16]

In particular, the 1972 FWPCA required each state to identify waters for which the technology-based effluent limitations would not be sufficient to meet water quality standards, determine the total daily maximum load of pollutants that would be consistent, and then assign those loads to the sources as necessary to ensure that water quality standards would be met. Congress, the EPA, and the states, however, largely ignored the water quality standard provisions of the CWA for the act's first two decades, until environmental groups successfully prodded them into action with a series of successful citizen suits.

Governmental reluctance was threefold. First, government regulators were understandably preoccupied with the challenge of implementing the technology-based provisions, which Congress had made clear were the federal statute's first order of business. The development of technology-based effluent limitations for multiple categories of industry in the context of changing technology, developing scientific information, and defending against constant massive litigation brought by industry and environmentalists was, to say the least, time and resource consuming. Second, the administrative burden of converting water quality standards into supplementary effluent limitations was huge. Because of the sheer complexity of the aquatic system, determining applicable pollutant loads necessarily depended upon calculations factoring not just pollutant amounts, but also numerous other site-specific factors such as temperature, water quantity, flow rates, and presence of other pollutants, all of which are seasonably variable. In short, it required the EPA and the states to develop the very information that had proved so elusive in the past that Congress had decided in 1972 to turn primarily to technology-based pollution controls instead. Finally, the EPA and the states had naturally shied away from the ambient standard side of the CWA because of the enormous political controversies that would invariably be triggered by trying to allocate pollution loads: facilities already subject to strict technology-based controls would strongly resist any further reduction of their effluent discharges; and nonpoint sources (especially agriculture) would exercise the same political leverage they had used in largely escaping from CWA regulation in the past.[17]

Notwithstanding each of these obstacles, the Clinton administration's EPA in its final years proposed and ultimately promulgated a water quality program for the CWA. As described in chapter 7, Administrator Browner nonetheless prevailed in this respect only with the assistance of some extraordinary White House behind-the-scenes maneuvering: delaying the presidential signing of a budget bill that included a limiting appropriations rider until after the administrator could complete the rulemaking proceedings. Although the future of this regulatory initiative is still uncertain—the Bush EPA's first administrator, Christine Todd Whitman, declined to implement the new regulations—the terms of the program underscore the full circle that the CAA and CWA are coming to in tandem: they rely heavily on state "implementation plans" strikingly reminiscent of the SIP approach first advanced in the 1970 CAA.[18]

Pollution Control and Natural Resources Law

The term "environmental law" came into common usage only in the 1970s, mostly in reference to the laws then being enacted for the purpose of regulating pollution or waste disposal activities. The actual field of environmental law, however, extends more broadly than the pollution control laws that triggered environmental law's formal naming. As described in chapter 4, modern environmental law seemed to many in the 1970s to be a "movement without a history," but actually its historical pedigree was quite extensive. Not only did a smattering of federal, state, and local air, noise, and water pollution laws exist before 1970, but the nation's natural resources laws had played a central role in the founding, expansion, and industrialization of the country. These natural resources laws are a necessary and significant aspect of what constitutes environmental law in the United States today.

Perhaps because they evolved during different moments of history, pollution control laws and natural resources laws in the United States have reflected different hierarchies of values and different theoretical foundations. Natural resources laws historically equated the public interest with the economic exploitation and development of natural resources, although resource conservation and "public trust doctrine" principles had emerged as a significant counterweight by the late nineteenth and early twentieth centuries, followed more recently by increased emphasis on preservation. The legal principles underlying natural resources law, however, were primarily grounded in *property law* principles, which emphasized the prerogatives of owners of property to decide how property should or should not be used. Pollution control law, by contrast, emphasized limits on the exercise of private rights over natural resources, especially common resources such as air and water, which had historically been freely used for waste disposal activities. Pollution control law, accordingly, sounded primarily in *tort law*—the law of civil liability governing intentional and accidental injuries—rather than in property law.

The institutional framework within the executive branch of the federal government for enforcing environmental law illustrates the difference in emphasis and theoretical foundation. The EPA is the federal agency primarily responsible for the administration of the federal government's pollution control programs. The most apt historical analogue to EPA regulation is found generally in tort law and more specifically in governmental regulation of public or private nuisances. A "public nuisance" is an "unreasonable interference with a right common to the public" and historically extends to interference with the public's use of common resources, such as air and water. A "private nuisance" is generally defined as an unreasonable interference with the use and enjoyment of privately owned land.[19]

The modern pollution control laws seek, in effect, to answer questions regarding allowable pollution levels that were once largely addressed by courts in common law nuisance litigation, but which now elude the institutional competency of courts in the more technologically and economically complex modern society. Because, however, the federal government does not possess the general police powers of a state, Congress and the EPA must instead rely principally on expansive notions of congressional authority under the Commerce Clause to regulate "channels" of interstate commerce and "economic activities" substantially affecting interstate commerce to justify federal pollution controls. Moreover, because such federal controls invariably limit the exercise of private property rights, the EPA and state agencies implementing federal programs are regularly the targets of claims that their regulations are unconstitutional "takings" of private property without just compensation in violation of the Fifth Amendment.[20]

The Department of the Interior is quite differently situated as the federal agency primarily responsible for federal natural resources law policy. Interior derives its authority principally from the federal government's ownership of almost 30 percent of the nation's lands. These properties are managed primarily by Interior but also by several other federal agencies, such as the Forest Service within the Department of Agriculture. The "public lands" include many of the country's most economically valuable and ecologically invaluable natural resources: national forests and parks, wildlife species, wild and scenic rivers, coal, oil, natural gas, minerals, old-growth forests, and wilderness areas valued because of the absence of humankind. Unlike the EPA, Interior's primary authority to regulate exploitation and protect these natural resources is not found in the Commerce Clause. Congress and Interior instead base their authority on an expansive reading of the Constitution's Property Clause.[21] Indeed, Interior's plenary authority to manage public natural resources is ultimately rooted in the very kind of absolutist notions of the prerogatives of property ownership that pollution control laws tend to question.

Notwithstanding their historically contrasting origins and doctrinal tendencies, these two distinct aspects of modern environmental law have become more alike during the past three decades. This is partly because the two kinds of laws invariably interact in their daily operations. Ecosystem management and protection does not, at bottom, readily separate into either "pollution control" or "natural resource" issues. Mining, for instance, involves both a threshold question of how much mining to allow as well as a series of distinct questions regarding what mining techniques should be used; how the extracted mineral should be transported, processed, and exploited; and ultimately how wastes resulting from the exploitation of the mineral should be disposed. While the first and last issues might neatly fit into the categories of "natural resources" and "pollution control," respectively, the many activities occurring within those endpoints can logically fit into either or both.

So too, governmental efforts to protect an endangered species or to preserve beautiful pristine lands cannot rely exclusively on the invocation of either property rights or the police power. Long-term species protection requires both the attainment and exercise of property rights essential to the species' survival and the limitation on the exercise of the private rights of others that would jeopardize the species' survival. The same is true for any natural resources of exceptional ecological significance. An essential element of long-term maintenance and protection is the acquisition and exercise of some necessary property rights in those resources. But, equally essential is the limitation of some private property rights that, because of ecological interdependencies, would otherwise harm the protected resource.

Most simply put, each theory of sovereign authority underlying environmental law—whether property or tort—has its limits. There are constitutional and political limits on the extent to which government can impose ever more stringent restrictions on the exercise of private property rights that threaten environmental values. At some point, the only effective and fair recourse is a formal purchase by the government of a property right in the natural resource of concern. There are similarly limits on the extent to which government can afford to, or should be required to, pay for every decrease in economic value occasioned by its restrictions on private rights. Private property rights in land and other resources cannot fairly be understood to confer on the owner an inviolable right to alter their physical state. Whether or not such absolute property rights ever truly existed in the United States, and there is reason to doubt that they did, it is doubtful that such rights can survive current scientific understandings of the spatial and temporal reach of ecological transformation made possible by modern technology.[22] In order to safeguard the environment, government must, whether under the guise of state police power or federal Commerce Clause authority, be able to restrict the exercise of private rights in natural resources without having to compensate the property owners for each and every diminished economic expectation.

Both pollution control law and natural resources law have, during the past three decades, worked within these competing property and tort law paradigms, with each increasingly borrowing from the other. Property law doctrine initially dominated natural resources laws, but during the past several decades those laws have increasingly imposed tort law limitations on property rights. At the same time, pollution control law began in the early 1970s by relying almost exclusively on tort doctrine notions about the need to curtail property rights based on their potential spillover effects. During the past thirty years, pollution control law has increasingly looked to property law theory to provide supplemental bases for achieving environmental protection.

Federal public land law, for instance, historically promoted its resource exploitation goals by conferring private property rights in natural resources to those individuals and private entities that made sufficient showing of their willingness and ability to develop the resource. Thus, the Homestead Act of 1862 conferred hundreds of thousands of acres of public lands to homesteaders; the General Mining Law of 1872 gave millions of dollars worth of mineral rights in public lands to miners who discovered valuable mineral deposits in commercial quantities; and a series of nineteenth-century federal railroad laws granted over 100 million acres of public lands to railroad companies in exchange for their construction of railroads that would further open up lands for settlement and economic exploitation. Even when federal natural resources law in the early twentieth century began to promote resource conservation, Congress relied on expansive notions of its authority under the Property Clause both to retain ownership of public lands and to manage those lands for greater economic return. Preservation policies were likewise grounded in principles of the government's formal ownership of national parks.[23]

During the past thirty years, however, federal natural resources law has increasingly relied on tort-like principles as federal policies have shifted toward greater promotion of resource preservation and the prevention of undue resource degradation of those resources selected for development. Like any other landowner, the federal government discovered that a property doctrine that emphasizes the inviolability of physical boundaries from discrete physical invasion does not readily lend itself to addressing external threats. Air pollution, water pollution, and noise pollution, although commencing far outside the borders of a federal property, may incrementally, yet severely, destroy the property's essential ecological features. Accordingly, either expansive notions of congressional authority under the Property Clause or supplementary laws based on a Commerce Clause/police power theory became necessary to protect federal proprietary interests from such external threats.[24]

Similarly, federal natural resources law increasingly limited private rights to natural resources that had been conveyed by the government. The same was true for many state governments with regard to natural resources formally owned by the state or simply subject to state plenary control. Based on a formal legal instrument such as a license, lease, or permit, the government initially conveyed a private right to exploit a natural resource. But that conveyance would now contain an express condition that barred activities that would cause, invoking the traditional rhetoric of tort law, "unreasonable" or "undue" environmental degradation in the exercise of that right. A tort or police power limitation was, accordingly, explicitly incorporated into whatever private rights were created, thereby creating tremendous uncertainty about what rights in the natural resource the individual had obtained. By the late twentieth century, rights to mine coal and minerals, develop oil and gas, harvest trees, and appropriate water routinely included such statutory or regulatory limitations on development rights.[25]

A property right expressly limited by tort principles was created by these conveyances that balanced the government's desire to promote resource exploitation and earn revenue with its goal to guard against irreparable ecological damage in the face of great scientific uncertainty. The explicit conditions potentially limited the government's exposure to successful regulatory takings claims in the event that the government subsequently decided to ban an activity in light of new awareness of the activity's ecologically destructive impacts. These conditions necessarily limited the economic value of what the government was offering, which lowered what people were willing formally to pay or otherwise do in order to acquire these private rights in natural resources from the government.

The resulting convergence with pollution control law occurred along two distinct dimensions. First, both natural resources law and pollution control law were restricting the exercise of private rights in natural resources. Natural resources law did so by limiting the property rights that the government was willing or able to convey. Pollution control law accomplished the same general end by limiting the exercise of private property rights in resources, especially land, because of potential spillover effects on other environmental media, especially air and water. The two kinds of environmental laws commenced from different legal premises—public versus private property—but each was shifting toward a middle ground in addressing the same kinds of ecological problems. The upshot was the emergence by the close of the twentieth century of a new widely accepted principle of law that private rights in essential natural resources such as air, water, and soil are ultimately no more than usufructary.[26]

The second impetus for convergence between pollution control and natural resources law occurred because as the drafters of natural resources law were relying increasingly on tort law principles, those crafting pollution control laws were seeking ways to utilize the advantages of property law concepts more effectively. Economists and many environmental policymakers have long contended that pollution control laws could achieve greater environmental protection at lower cost if they relied more on property rights and market incentives than on the kind of "command and control" regulation that generally dominates the federal pollution control framework. Instead of dictating to each facility how much pollution it can emit, many economists believe it would be more efficient to create a system that encourages those who can reduce pollution more cheaply to do so. At least in theory, a market of tradeable emissions rights could accomplish just that result by assigning to individual facilities a property right to release a specified number of emissions that the facility could then either apply to its own emissions or sell to another facility for application to the latter's emissions. If a particular source had the option of either reducing its pollution by a prescribed amount or purchasing the reductions that another facility could achieve less expensively, both environmental protection and economic efficiency would be simultaneously promoted. Those with higher pollution control costs would buy emissions rights from those with lower pollution control costs. Overall emissions would be reduced, and the actual reductions would be achieved by those who could do so less expensively. Indeed, if the government conditioned the sale of emissions rights on the seller of emissions reductions decreasing its own emissions slightly lower than the level that would have otherwise been required of the buyer, then the market approach could result in even greater environmental protection.

For a variety of reasons, however, such tradeable emissions policies and other market-based environmental policies were largely dormant within modern pollution control law in its first few decades in the United States. Some environmentalists questioned the morality of creating tradeable "property rights to pollute" at all. Others raised a number of issues regarding the efficacy and reliability of such a program. How would one determine the amount of pollution to allow? How would one account for pollution reductions that were otherwise likely to occur anyway, such as plant closings? Should trades be allowed between chemical pollutants in any circumstance or only when the two different chemicals contribute to a common environmental problem (e.g., biological oxygen demand or acidity in water or particulate matter or ozone in air)? How broadly should one define the market geographically? The larger the boundaries the greater the likelihood that there will be sufficient participants to create a viable, competitive market. On the other hand, the larger the boundaries the more questionable the assumption that the same environmental systems are affected by pollutants being discharged from either facility.[27]

Although no wholesale transformation of pollution control law from command and control to market incentives has taken place, some tradeable emissions policies and other market-based approaches have made some significant inroads. In a variety of settings, both at the federal and state levels, pollution control programs have incorporated tradeable emissions policies that seek to exploit the profit maximization incentives created by markets and private property rights. The most noted is the 1990 CAA's acid deposition program, which created a nationwide tradeable emissions program for emissions of sulfur dioxide. The program, however, was not a substitute for preexisting requirements, but the basis for even further emissions reductions. In fact, the CAA spawned a series of tradeable emissions programs: new sources are allowed to enter "nonattainment areas" as long as their additional emissions are more than offset by reductions in emissions from existing sources; specific regions such as southern California have created programs that allow emissions reductions of one kind (e.g., retirement of older, higher polluting motor vehicles) to substitute for industrial emissions reductions that might otherwise be required; and the EPA in the late 1990s promulgated an ambitious program for the sale and banking of nitrogen oxide emissions in order to obtain the reductions necessary to address significant interstate air pollution problems.[28]

Market trades have similarly been permitted in the CWA and greater use of these trades has been proposed to facilitate compliance with water quality goals. Both the Clinton administration's EPA in the late 1990s and the subsequent Bush administration's EPA promoted trading systems as part of a water quality standard compliance program. The Department of the Interior has also been experimenting with ways to achieve greater species protection on private property by granting private property owners enhanced protections from new government regulations. And, in Lake Tahoe, straddling the border of California and Nevada, the bi-state Tahoe Regional Planning Agency is implementing a complex land use plan that allows individuals who own especially ecologically fragile parcels that are, as a result, highly limited in their development to sell development rights to those who own parcels not similarly restricted. Property rights potentially make environmental controls fairer and more politically acceptable by providing for a fairer distribution of their respective burdens and benefits.[29]

Each of these initiatives illustrates ways in which pollution control and natural resources policies are becoming more alike. Each seeks to establish a new equilibrium between traditional tort and property concepts in developing legal frameworks that can best effectuate their goals. For natural resources law, that has meant greater utilization of tort doctrine to limit private rights in natural resources. For pollution control, it has meant, albeit still tentatively, greater utilization of the advantages of property law to create additional incentives for environmental protection. The result has been that these two historically distinct strands of modern environmental law are converging in myriad ways.

Evolutionary Trends in Environmental Lawmaking

Environmental protection law is far from settled, but it is certainly settling. The significance of the convergence phenomenon within environmental law is that certain kinds of regulatory approaches have proven more (or less) successful environmentally, politically, or both. With the benefit of more than three decades of experimentation, it is now possible to identify some approaches to environmental lawmaking that appear to be emerging as the more successful. It is also possible to explain their success in terms of their ability to respond to the ways in which the features of the ecological problems they address challenge our lawmaking institutions and processes.

Information Disclosure

It is no coincidence that the statute that marks the commencement of the modern environmental law era, the National Environmental Policy Act (NEPA), includes information disclosure as one of its important purposes. NEPA mandates that federal agencies learn and disclose the possible environmental impacts of proposed major federal actions significantly affecting the human environment and thereby addresses one of the central challenges to environmental lawmaking—scientific uncertainty. The degree of uncertainty surrounding ecological cause and effect creates the risk, absent such an assembly and disclosure requirement, that the environmental effects would simply be ignored. Because it is otherwise difficult to learn the necessary information regarding environmental effects, and because the results of that information can be so controversial due to its potentially wide, deep and long distributional import, there is a natural tendency *not* to learn and certainly *not* to disclose possible environmental effects.

NEPA's legal revolution represents an effort to overcome that natural tendency. It mandates the inquiry necessary to learn what the impacts will be, including their comparison to the impacts of possible alternatives to the action being proposed. And, with very limited exceptions, NEPA mandates the public disclosure of the information to ensure that those who might be adversely affected are provided advance notice.

NEPA's reporting requirements also respond directly to the spatial and temporal dimensions of ecological cause and effect that are the root of so much of the scientific uncertainty and social controversy surrounding environmental lawmaking. NEPA, especially as elaborated upon by regulations promulgated by the President's Council on Environmental Quality, can require one environmental impact statement (EIS) at the site- or facility-specific level and another EIS at a programmatic level. The latter type of EIS addresses potential environmental impacts from a far broader spatial and temporal perspective. NEPA regulations further require supplemental EISs to be issued upon the government's encountering "significant new information or circumstances." The regulations also expressly define the environmental "effects" to be disclosed as including "indirect effects," described as those that are "caused by the [government's] action and are later in time or farther removed in distance, but still reasonably foreseeable." Whether the environmental effects are significant turns in part on whether they are "highly controversial."[30]

The statutory language of NEPA also makes explicit the necessarily long-term dimension to environmental planning. NEPA describes the "continuing responsibility" of the federal government as extending to "each generation as trustee of the environment for succeeding generations." An EIS is required to include discussion of "the relationship between local short-term uses of man's environment and the maintenance and enhancement of long-term productivity." Further mandated is discussion of "any irreversible and irretrievable commitment of resources which would be involved in the proposed action."[31]

Information disclosure requirements are more readily susceptible to statutory enactment than are pollution control standards and emissions limitation requirements. They can be less controversial because they are procedural rather than substantive in nature. They promote intelligent planning and decisionmaking, but do not, at least on their face, dictate a particular result. For that reason, mandatory disclosure of information does not have the kind of obvious distributional dimension that readily generates political opposition, as do pollution control standards and emissions limitations.

Information disclosure is also consonant with notions of economic freedom and free market principles and, therefore, finds allies in those who favor market incentive approaches over command-and-control regulatory regimes. After all, one of the fundamental premises of a free market is "perfect information." It is that information that allows both the buyers and sellers to make rational choices in their respective purchases and sales. Environmental disclosure requirements, accordingly, promote the workings of a free market.

For these and other reasons, information disclosure not only marked the commencement of modern environmental law, but it also turned out to be among the most hardy of environmental law's elements during the subsequent decades. NEPA has also likely been the nation's most significant environmental law export, both domestic and international—at least thirty other nations have adopted their own versions of NEPA, as has virtually every state in the United States.[32]

NEPA's information assembly and disclosure requirements also led to the proliferation of planning requirements throughout most areas of environmental law. Almost every one of the major federal natural resources laws now includes long-term planning requirements that begin with NEPA's premise of information assembly and then extend it to require long-term planning to guide agency decisionmaking. Long-term resource planning is the central element of the National Forest Management Act (managing national forests), the Federal Land Policy and Management Act (managing public lands), the Magnuson-Stevens Act (governing fisheries), the Coastal Zone Management Act (managing coastal zones), and the Federal Coal Leasing Act Amendments of 1976 (regulating federal coal lands). Such planning is also important in pollution control laws such as the CWA, which relies primarily on areawide planning for nonpoint source pollution control, and the Resource Conservation and Recovery Act, which provides for the development of state and regional solid waste management plans.[33]

Wholly apart from their promotion of long-term planning requirements, information disclosure requirements have become one of the linchpins of contemporary recommendations for reforming environmental law. Buoyed by the apparent successes of the federal Toxics Release Inventory and California's Proposition 65, discussed in chapter 6, some policymakers began advocating broader use of information disclosure requirements. During the 1990s, the Clinton administration significantly expanded toxic release reporting requirements under the Emergency Planning and Community Right to Know Act (EPCRA) by extending the requirements to federal facilities, federal contractors, and additional industrial activities and by increasing the number of chemicals covered by the disclosure requirements.[34]

Eco-labeling requirements and certification programs, which make it easier for consumers to buy more "environmentally friendly" products, are now among the most widely touted of disclosure requirements. Labels facilitate consumers' expressing their preferences for environmentally responsible products in a way that directly encourages, but does not formally require, businesses to make their products differently or make different products altogether. The Energy Policy Act of 1992, for instance, expanded the list of household appliances that require energy efficiency labels and water flow information. There are currently two major nongovernmental eco-labeling programs—Green Seal and Scientific Certification Systems—and the EPA has sponsored a labeling program called "Energy Star" that rates the energy efficiency of specific consumer products. Labeling requirements have naturally prompted some environmental groups, the World Wildlife Fund among them, to promote utilization of formal certifications of certain industry practices, such as timber harvesting, as being more or less environmentally acceptable.[35]

A potentially effective information disclosure requirement under already existing law that has been largely underutilized, however, is the federal Securities and Exchange Commission (SEC) requirement that publicly traded firms disclose financially material information to current and potential investors in the firm's securities. Although the SEC long ago ruled that such disclosure requirements extended to a firm's environmental risks, such as the release of contaminants or noncompliance with applicable environmental requirements, there has apparently been neither much actual disclosure nor significant SEC enforcement. More widespread compliance would both allow investors to make better informed decisions about the actual liabilities and assets of particular firms and, not coincidentally, provide those same firms with a major incentive to minimize environmental risks.[36]

Finally, notwithstanding environmental law's many and varied information disclosure and planning requirements, it still suffers from a dearth of basic scientific information about actual environmental conditions, necessary both to target those areas where environmental problems may be the greatest and to evaluate the effectiveness of existing programs. As previously explained, the extraordinary complexity of ecological cause and effect prompted lawmakers to seek out environmental controls, such as technology-based pollution controls, that did not depend on the development in the first instance of a fuller understanding of the workings of the ecosystem. An unfortunate casualty of those laws, however, is that relatively few resources have been directed to create the kind of environmental data base needed now, thirty years later, to understand where pollution controls have and have not worked well, and how the laws could be better directed. The development of a broad and deep data base of scientific indicators is long overdue.[37]

Public Participation and Citizen Suit Enforcement

Another mainstay of successful regulatory schemes for environmental protection is significant and ongoing public participation in the development and enforcement of legal rules. Here, as in other areas of environmental law, the need for public participation derives from the nature of the problem being addressed by environmental law and, in particular, from the broad spatial and temporal dimensions of ecological cause and effect. Because cause and effect occur over such a wide span of time and space, the distributional implications of choosing one environmental protection standard or method of control are similarly widespread. The winners and losers—those who receive the respective benefits and costs of environmental protection—are not identical. Furthermore, there are those whose primary motivation is not to influence the resulting costs and benefits to humans, but rather to influence the resulting costs and benefits to the natural environment itself. It is difficult, if not impossible, for a lawmaker to fashion an equitable rule without first providing a meaningful opportunity for those affected and concerned to provide substantive input.

Nor is this just a matter of letting people talk for the sake of talking. The experience of environmental lawmaking is that public participation makes the resulting rules much more effective and better received. It is simply not possible, in the absence of meaningful public participation, for any lawmaker to anticipate all the ways in which alternative regulatory approaches may affect human behavior and ultimately environmental quality. The workings of the marketplace, technology, and the ecosystem itself are too complex. No one has the requisite expertise in all the relevant areas, let alone the unique perspectives of all members of the public. For this reason, in the absence of substantial and ongoing public participation, there are likely to be significant mistakes in lawmaking, including unintended economic and environmental consequences. Public participation does not, of course, eliminate such consequences, but it can reduce them considerably.

Public perception of environmental risk may, moreover, systematically depart from the results of scientific expert risk assessments in ways that lawmakers should take into account rather than discount as "irrational." For instance, "public intuitions about risk can often be unpacked to reveal concern about a whole set of values that rational people may legitimately consider, values which are captured only dimly (if at all) in the technical risk estimates used by risk analysts."[38] The public can legitimately take into account the equity of risk spreading, the voluntariness of risk, and the very real dread of long-term catastrophic environmental consequences unanticipated by science. These are factors that scientific experts generally ignore in their efforts to quantify risks on absolute scales and compare the risks of activities competing for scarce societal resources.

Indeed, learned largely by the environmental law experience, this central insight regarding the advantages and necessity of public participation in administrative lawmaking triggered a broad reformation of U.S. administrative law. Agencies came to be viewed not simply as "transmission belts" mechanically converting legislative directions into detailed, technical regulations. Under the new, reformed administrative law model, agencies such as the EPA or the Department of the Interior were responsible for "the provision of a surrogate political process to ensure the fair representation of a wide range of affected interests in the process of administrative decision."[39] At the very outset of the modern era of environmental law, Professor Joseph Sax claimed that environmental law's achievements would ultimately turn on its ability to revolutionize administrative lawmaking in just this manner. The past several decades have confirmed the accuracy of his prophecy.[40]

There is also an independent value to public participation wholly apart from its ability to make substantive differences. The greater the participation the more likely it is that those who are affected will be willing to accept the decision, including the consequences adverse to them. Inclusion itself is meaningful to people, wholly apart from the decision that results. Environmental lawmaking is, for reasons previously detailed, inherently and unavoidably controversial. There are distributional winners and losers. For some persons, the choice between one environmental standard or another poses no less than a choice between competing moral absolutes. Public participation provides a means to reduce the polarization and conflict that environmental lawmaking otherwise seems to attract. Feeling that one was involved in crafting the policy ultimately arrived at can make the risks ultimately imposed seem less involuntary in nature and can foster public trust in the process of government decisionmaking. "The most tragic images of environmental harm are those involving hapless victims, those who without sufficient knowledge or involvement, and without exercising choice, have had risk and damage imposed upon them."[41]

Finally, environmental law has taught the value of extending citizen suit participation to the courts. This includes two types of suits: citizen suit enforcement of environmental lawmaking requirements against the agencies charged with lawmaking responsibilities and citizen suit enforcement of the resulting environmental standards against the facilities to which those standards apply. Both types of citizen suit have proven essential to the successful operation of an environmental lawmaking regime because each has shown its ability to respond to structural problems that would otherwise undermine the regime's effectiveness.

The considerable challenges to environmental lawmaking place a natural brake on governmental lawmaking efforts. This inherent friction can prevent, or at least considerably slow down, the development, implementation, and enforcement of environmental protection and resource conservation standards. It is always easy simply to postpone necessary decisionmaking in the face of great scientific and technological uncertainty, especially when the economic implications of taking action are themselves so substantial as to erect formidable political opposition. That is especially so for environmental lawmaking, because among those counseling for cautious implementation are government officials who oversee governmental programs that are subject to strict environmental laws. For environmental protection lawmakers, therefore, it is not just a matter of dealing with outside forces that advocate a slowing down of the lawmaking process—there will inevitably be powerful resistance within the government itself.

Citizen suits, accordingly, have proven critical both in forcing government to act and in guarding against executive branch lawmaking compromises that are not true to the statutory mandates under which the relevant federal agency is operating. Such suits have likewise proven essential to enforcing environmental protection standards directly against the facilities to which those standards apply. The sheer number of regulated entities limits government's ability to engage in effective compliance oversight by itself. There are also some pollution sources, such as other federal agencies and state and local governmental activities, for which the government is either legally or politically constrained in its enforcement. Because of the unitary executive theory—which provides that intra-executive branch disputes must be resolved within that branch—one federal agency generally cannot bring another federal agency to court. Additionally, the federal government has historically proven reluctant to bring enforcement actions and seek significant civil penalties against state and local governments. In all of these contexts, citizen enforcement has served as a useful supplement, often welcomed by the government officials responsible for enforcement.

Broad Delegations of Agency Lawmaking Authority under Prescribed Deadlines

Another feature of environmental law that has proven essential to its successes is the broad legislative delegation of lawmaking authority to executive branch agencies, albeit under fairly strict deadlines. These two characteristics—"broad" and "strict"—may seem to contradict each other, but they are in fact complementary. Each renders the other more palatable and effective.

Broad delegations of lawmaking authority are necessary in the first instance because of the sheer complexity of environmental standard setting. The setting of specific environmental standards, whether health, cost, or technology based, requires deliberations based upon a vast array of informational inputs, regardless of whether the standards are to be applied to an entire industry of air or water pollution sources or to a subset of surface coal mining practices on or off public lands. The relevant information often requires considerable technical expertise for comprehension, is often riddled with assumptions and uncertainties, is constantly changing in light of new information and technology, and always has enormous distributional implications in terms of spreading economic costs and environmental risks.

In short, the dynamic and experimental nature of the kind of lawmaking necessary to promulgate environmental standards within that setting does not readily lend itself to the legislative arena. A legislature is institutionally disadvantaged in making the necessary technical evaluations and determinations. Even more fundamentally, there is nothing in our nation's history of lawmaking to suggest that our legislative processes are institutionally capable of making the kind of frequent incremental changes in response to changing circumstances and information that are necessary in setting environmental standards.

Furthermore, the politics of the legislative process render attractive broader delegations of authority to administrative agencies. The opportunities presented within the various committees and chambers of Congress to hold legislation hostage to competing agendas are simply too great to be responsive. Legislative log jamming is made a virtual certainty in light of the distributional ramifications of environmental lawmaking. The virtual paralysis of congressional action on significant environmental legislation since 1990 underscores the risk of heavy reliance on Congress for environmental law reform, be it for more or less stringent requirements.

For these reasons, the 1999 ruling of the U.S. Court of Appeals for the District of Columbia Circuit that the EPA's construction of its lawmaking authority under the CAA was unconstitutional dealt a potentially major setback to federal environmental law. In *American Trucking Association v. Browner,* the federal court of appeals relied on the "nondelegation doctrine," a Supreme Court-created constitutional doctrine that promotes separation of powers principles. The nondelegation doctrine provides that a legislative delegation of lawmaking authority to an executive branch agency must be based on an "intelligible principle" sufficient to guide the agency's exercise of that authority. The appellate court in *American Trucking* faulted the EPA for setting NAAQS (national ambient air quality standards) without deriving from the CAA any identifiable "determinate criterion" to justify why, in the face of tremendous scientific uncertainty, the agency had chosen one pollution limit over another.[42]

In 2000, however, the Supreme Court unanimously reversed the lower court's decision in *American Trucking* and effectively confirmed the legitimacy of the kind of broad delegations of legislative lawmaking upon which modern environmental law has depended. The unanimity of the Court's ruling was all the more striking because the Court had otherwise in the 1990s seemed ready to question many of the constitutional underpinnings of modern federal environmental law on issues of Article III standing, federalism, and property rights. On the nondelegation doctrine issue, however, the Court was little troubled by the scope of the congressional delegation.

The *American Trucking* Court accepted wholesale the federal government's assertion that the nondelegation doctrine was satisfied by the CAA's requirement that the EPA administrator "establish uniform national standards at a level that is requisite to protect public health from the adverse effects in the ambient air." Even more particularly, the Court addressed the relevance of scientific uncertainty and found it not constitutionally problematic that the pollutants at issue were " 'nonthreshold' pollutants that inflict a continuum of adverse health effects at any airborne concentration greater than zero, and hence require the EPA to make judgments of degree."[43]

A competing, yet ultimately complementary, feature of broad legislative delegations of environmental lawmaking has been a prescriptive deadline for their exercise. The executive branch agencies have commonly been given authority to promulgate rules of virtually unprecedented breadth—but under strict, often impossible deadlines. A distinctive feature of environmental law, accordingly, is that statutes often regulate the executive branch agencies as much as, if not more than, the regulated facilities themselves. As previously described in chapter 5, there have been substantial downsides to this legislative equation, most notably that impossibly short deadlines have triggered inevitable agency failures that have undermined much-needed credibility. But apart from the precise terms of the judicially enforceable deadlines themselves, many of which have no doubt been far too short, their very existence has proved to be effective and important.

The deadlines have often helped an agency by providing it with the legal leverage necessary to overcome obstacles to lawmaking efforts. The deadline has provided a ready answer to efforts by the regulated community and other government agencies to slow down the promulgation of rules. Hence, while EPA attorneys have often publicly complained of the "deadline suits" brought by environmental organizations, those same attorneys have sometimes privately encouraged their initiation. The result of those suits, moreover, has been, as a practical matter, repeated judicial extensions of the statutorily prescribed deadlines rather than judicial injunctions compelling strict adherence.

Emblematic of the potential effectiveness of deadline provisions are those that were included in the 1984 Hazardous and Solid Waste Act Amendments to the Resource Conservation and Recovery Act. Under that act, Congress imposed a series of deadlines for the EPA's promulgation of land disposal restrictions applicable to hazardous wastes. Congress did not, however, merely impose deadlines for the promulgation of those standards —it further divided the universe of hazardous wastes into discrete categories, established different deadlines for each category, and created very demanding default standards that would apply in the absence of deadline compliance. The practical effect of this legislation was that the regulated community now had even more incentive than the EPA or the environmental community to ensure that the statutory deadlines were met. Largely eliminated were industry efforts to slow down the rulemaking process, and virtually all of the deadlines were, in fact, ultimately met.[44]

Permit Requirements and Criminal Sanctions

Another clear lesson from three decades of experience with modern pollution control laws is the importance of coupling permit requirements with criminal sanctions for their violation. The advantages are both practical and symbolic. The permit requirement, as typified by the CWA, makes plain that no one possesses an unfettered right to use environmental commons as waste disposal facilities. Whatever environmental standard is ultimately applied, a permit must first be obtained to render pollutant disposal lawful. The legal default position is that the disposal is *per se* unlawful in the absence of a permit.

The practical advantages to this system are considerable. The regulated facility has the burden to seek out the government regulator in the first instance. Because there are so many potentially regulated sources, such a burden shift can be of enormous importance to government regulators. It is generally far easier for the facility that knows that it will be emitting pollutants to find the relevant governmental agency than it is for the government agency to locate all potential sources of pollution.

In addition, the permit provides a ready basis for aggregating into one formal document the various restrictions to be imposed on any one facility. Under the CAA, for instance, a single facility may be subject to a variety of environmental performance standards applicable to different kinds of pollutants being emitted. A plant may emit hazardous air pollutants that trigger one technology requirement; be located in a "nonattainment area" for another pollutant, thereby triggering another series of technology-based requirements; and be in a "prevention of significant deterioration" area for another pollutant, which calls for the application of yet some further technology-based standards. The CAA's permit requirement contemplates a single permit that incorporates each of the different standards applicable to multiple sources within an individual facility.[45]

Such a single permit approach is advantageous to all. It provides greater certainty within a regulated industry, as individual facilities know what they and their competitors both must do to meet applicable pollution control standards. The permit further promotes equity by facilitating enforcement by making both governmental and citizen suit enforcement much easier. Further, when the issuance of a permit includes, as do the CWA and CAA today, a self-reporting requirement, governmental and citizen enforcers can easily discern whether a source is in violation of applicable requirements. Unless the permit is itself written in vague and ambiguous terms, an entity seeking to ensure its own compliance (or the compliance of a competitor) need only compare the numerical limits set forth in the permit with the numerical data reported by the source's own required monitoring equipment.

Partly to ensure the integrity of the permit requirement, criminal sanctions have become an essential element of an effective environmental law regime. Because self-reporting has become the linchpin of permit enforcement, it is essential to provide permitees with a strong incentive to ensure that their monitoring and reporting is accurate. Criminal sanctions provide that incentive. A noneconomic criminal sanction cannot be readily converted into a mere cost of doing business ultimately reflected in a higher price charged to consumers. Criminal sanctions, most particularly sentences of incarceration, are personal. As described by one member of Congress, a "chief executive can't pass jail time on to consumers."[46]

The need for criminal sanctions in environmental law, however, extends beyond simply preserving the integrity of the self-reporting process. The more expensive it is to comply with an environmental protection requirement, the more money there is to be saved by noncompliance. Stringent environmental controls, accordingly, create an incentive for their violation by raising both the cost of lawful activity and the profit to be gained by their violation. Of course, any economic incentive to violate a law can be diminished if the likelihood of detection is high and corresponding sanctions certain. Environmental violations, however, are by their nature apt to be difficult to detect because of the sheer number of regulated entities and the myriad opportunities for noncompliance. Clandestine dumping of hazardous wastes, for instance, can save a lot of money and is not easily detected.

For some in the regulated community, simple respect for the command of the law is sufficient to ensure compliance. Others, however, will comply only if the government demonstrates its intent and ability to impose sanctions against violators, thus eliminating the economic incentive otherwise favoring noncompliance. Even the most law abiding are likely to at least reduce their compliance efforts if they perceive the absence of enforcement against noncomplying competitors.

It can be argued that environmental violations are no less deserving of criminal sanction than are traditional crimes. Violations can cause substantial, widespread, and irreversible harm to public health and to natural resources of enormous ecological significance. The conduct constituting the violation can be just as deliberate and as motivated by profit incentives as crimes that have long been the subject of felony sanctions. In fact, the same organizations are increasingly implicated in both environmental and nonenvironmental crimes. The rise of environmental law in the 1970s led to a corresponding rise in organized crime's involvement in environmental pollution, as the economic value of crime, in effect, rose.[47]

The criminal sanction also sends a unique symbolic message. Precisely because it can trigger one of society's harshest punishments—the loss of liberty caused by incarceration—a moral stigma uniquely attaches to its imposition. The long-term effect of this stigma can be severe. For many high-ranking corporate officials, the potential loss of social status and the associated community condemnation implicated by a criminal conviction is far more threatening than a multimillion-dollar fine.

While the modern environmental law experience has demonstrated the necessity of a criminal dimension to environmental violations, it also suggests that care must be taken in fashioning such sanctions. The inherent tensions between the features and aims of environmental law and criminal law must be resolved in fashioning environmental criminal law. Criminal law, for instance, requires the highest standard of proof to convict (namely, beyond a reasonable doubt by a unanimous jury), but environmental law makes such a showing problematic because of scientific uncertainties and fragmented corporate decisionmaking authority. Criminal law emphasizes settled norms, while environmental law is dynamic, changing, and seeks fundamental and dramatic change. And although criminal law employs clear, determinate, and readily accessible legal standards familiar to the general public, environmental law is replete with obscure, indeterminate, and highly technical standards that few can genuinely master.

None of these tensions means that there is something "wrong" with environmental law or its criminalization. There are legitimate, often unavoidable, reasons for this conflict inherent in the nature of environmental pollution and the traditions of U.S. lawmaking institutions and processes.

But, regardless of their legitimacy, these tensions nevertheless present a challenge for lawmakers, and while environmental criminal law is robust and successful in the United States, it is far from clear that those challenges have yet been adequately addressed.[48]

Hybrid Health- and Technology-Based Environmental Performance Standards

Perhaps the most persistent debate in environmental law has been over what should be the primary basis for environmental performance standards applicable to pollution control or resource development activities. There are a host of options available to achieve reductions in environmental degradation, each of which is reflected in at least one environmental law.

The CAA (for, e.g., catalytic converters), the Resource Conservation Recovery Act (for, e.g., double liners and leachate collection systems), and the Oil Spill Pollution Prevention Act (for, e.g., double-hulled vessels) all include *design standards* that prescribe a particular technology that must be used. A *cost–benefit standard* is evident in the Federal Insecticide, Fungicide, and Rodenticide Act, based on its application of a standard of "unreasonable adverse effects on the environment" that considers both the "costs and benefits of the use of any pesticide." The CAA also includes *health-based standards* and *technology-based standards;* the NAAQS are the most obvious example of the former, and the myriad standards applicable to stationary sources, ranging from BACT (best available control technology), LAER (lowest achievable emissions rates), and maximum achievable control technology all exemplify the latter. The CWA, of course, includes its own alphabet soup of technology-based standards (e.g., BPT, BAT, BCT, and BDT) but also offers an example of an *environmental-based standard.* The water quality standards promulgated by the states under EPA supervision pursuant to the CWA represent the latter standard insofar as they require the achievement of effluent limitations as necessary to achieve levels of environmental quality consistent with different uses of water, ranging from industrial use to swimming. There are also, scattered within the various statutory laws, a host of standards that dictate particular ecological results, such as the Resource Conservation and Recovery Act's "no migration of any hazardous constituent" standard and the Surface Mining Control and Reclamation Act's requirement that mined areas be restored to their "approximate original contour." Finally, there are examples of *taxes* (e.g., Superfund's chemical feedstock tax), emissions fees (e.g., CAA's sulfur dioxide emissions fees), deposits (e.g., state recycling laws), and huge subsidies (e.g., CWA's multibillion dollar construction grants program for publicly owned water treatment works) designed to produce market incentives favoring less environmental degradation and resource consumption.

No single basis for control is always the best. The propriety and effectiveness of one alternative or another is necessarily highly contextual. Cost–benefit analysis may be appropriate, for instance, where, as in federal pesticide regulation, the immediate object of regulation is a useful product (e.g., pesticide), but such analysis may be less useful or at least require more nuanced application for, as with the CAA or CWA, the disposal of waste. The regulator must somehow take into account the positive value of the pesticide product. Design standards usually make the most sense where it is clear that there is a simple technological fix of widespread applicability and there is an urgent societal need to have that improved technology be adopted as quickly as possible. The advantages of such a design standard can overcome the advantages of allowing the marketplace to create the economic incentive necessary for the possible discovery of a better technology.

Some generalizations regarding the relative value or political feasibility of differing regulatory approaches can be made based on the past several decades of experience. For instance, environmental emission fees or taxes have fared remarkably poorly. Whatever theoretical advantages they may offer in terms of their potential economic efficiency seem, after more than three decades of largely failed efforts, to be overcome by the political volatility of any proposal for increased taxes. Widely touted sulfur and carbon taxes proved politically moribund.

By contrast, the best or at least most politically viable approach to pollution control seems to be one that combines health-, environment-, and technology-based standards. The first two work best as either a basis for triggering the need for pollution reduction in the first instance or for supplemental controls. But the sheer complexity of ecological cause and effect makes it exceedingly difficult to base precise pollution reduction requirements on either health or environmental standards. The failed early efforts of both the CAA and CWA in regulating hazardous and toxic pollutants well testify to these pitfalls. The result for each was a paralysis of regulatory efforts as the EPA was unwilling to face the political heat that would have been generated had the agency sought strict implementation of those standards, particularly as they potentially mandated zero emissions of certain pollutants.

Health- or environment-based standards can work well as a trigger for the need to apply controls, much as they have for NAAQS under the CAA. NAAQS do not themselves apply to particular sources or directly require the reduction of precise amounts of pollution. Instead they trigger other requirements under applicable SIPs and attainment and nonattainment provisions of the CAA. By establishing overarching goals, while still allowing for flexibility in the means and timing of their attainment, NAAQS are more politically acceptable.

Water quality standards under the CWA are similarly designed, even though their implementation has been more delayed. Although those standards are not a trigger for the application of the CWA's technology-based controls, they are the trigger for supplementary controls. Under the CWA, if technology-based controls prove incapable of achieving water quality standards, then additional pollution reductions must be imposed as necessary to meet those standards. In that manner, the CWA's technology-based standards are not allowed to become less stringent than water quality standards. Where the CWA's water quality standards have fallen short, however, is in their translation into precise numeric TMDLs (total maximum daily load allocations) applicable to individual sources of pollution. The process of translation necessarily reinjects all the scientific complexities and distributional controversies that the technology-based standards were intended to avoid. It would likely prove more worthwhile to have the violation of water quality standards trigger a host of different regulatory efforts, including an expansion of the scope of sources covered and an increase in the types of controls applied—such as including land use controls and tradeable emissions policies.

The second generalization of the relative success of different regulatory efforts is that technology-based standards work fairly well once a determination has been made that some controls are necessary in a particular context. Such standards provide a basis for regulation that does not require resolution of the tremendous uncertainty surrounding ecological cause and effect. They also provide the regulated community with a continuing incentive to discover better, cheaper methods to reduce pollution because, unlike design standards, technology-based standards do not dictate the use of one particular technology.

To be sure, technology-based standards are no panacea. There is a risk of ossification: under these standards, facilities also have an incentive *not* to develop new pollution control technologies, as doing so will lead to more-demanding requirements. There is also a risk that an aggregation of facilities may lead to certain locations being subject to excessive risks to human health and the environment. Therefore, technology-based standards must generally work in tandem with health- and environment-based standards at the front end (deciding whether pollution controls are necessary), the back end (deciding whether further controls are needed), or both. But even with these caveats, technology-based pollution control standards can be judged to have accomplished much by overcoming many of the obstacles to pollution reduction efforts.

A third generalization is that tradeable emissions policies provide a potentially useful supplement to command-and-control regulation efforts. The marginal cost of pollution control generally rises as controls become more demanding. It costs far more to reduce pollution from 10 units to 5 units than from 100 to 95 units, even though each is a 5-unit reduction. Therefore, as the degree of pollution reduction being sought increases, so too does the need to have that reduction accomplished by those who can do so most efficiently. A market-based policy, such as a tradeable emissions program, provides for just such administrative flexibility by allowing facilities with higher pollution control costs to, in effect, buy reductions from those facilities with lower pollution control costs.

There have been some notable tradeable emissions successes over the past several decades and ambitious initiatives in more recent years. The EPA has estimated that its lead trading program in the early 1980s, which allowed gasoline refiners to meet lead content reduction requirements through trading, resulted in cost savings of more than $250 million per year. The agency's experience with the 1990 CAA Acid Deposition Program, which allows for sulfur dioxide permit trading to reduce emissions to 10 million tons lower than 1980 levels, may have saved as much as $1 billion per year in compliance costs. During the Clinton administration and the George W. Bush administration, the EPA launched several even more ambitious tradeable emissions programs. In 1998, the agency promulgated a sweeping final rule under the Clean Air Act that required twenty-two states and the District of Columbia to significantly reduce nitrogen dioxide emissions within their borders in order to reduce interstate transport of ozone. As an essential element of that rule, the EPA set forth a "cap and trade" program for the achievement of the emissions reductions. In particular, the agency announced a nitrogen oxide "budget" for each of the affected states that declared the total amount in tons of nitrogen oxide that could be emitted into the ambient air within each state. The agency further offered to allow states to adopt an emissions trading program in which regulated sources could buy and sell the rights to emit nitrogen oxide within that budget, thus providing a market incentive for reduction by those sources who can do so at the lowest cost. In December 2003, the Bush administration proposed two new emissions trading programs under the Clean Air Act, similarly described as allowing for further reductions of air pollution at lower cost. The first proposed to impose a regional "cap" on sulfur dioxide and nitrogen oxide emissions from thirty states, which amounted to emissions reductions significantly below current requirements, but then allow sources within that large geographic region to buy and sell rights to emit those pollutants. The second proposal was to create a similar cap and trade program for mercury emissions from power plants as part of a program to require further reductions in such emissions.[49]

A competing generalization that can fairly be made, however, is that such tradeable emissions schemes are most effective as a *supplement to* rather than as a *substitute for* the command-and-control approach that presently dominates modern environmental law. It is the presence of the formal command-and-control threshold framework that renders those other, more flexible, programs and policies attractive options and, therefore, potentially effective. In other words, there is a viable market for trading pollution credits because of the economic value to the purchasers of avoiding direct application of the command-and-control requirements to their facilities. A tradeable emissions policy can possibly work once pollution control objectives and reductions are set, but it cannot itself define those objectives or work in isolation from those applicable reductions. One commentator has accordingly properly described a possible evolutionary shift in environmental law from "command and control" to "command and convenant."[50]

In the absence, moreover, of significant scientific advances, tradeable emissions policies are unlikely to achieve the pervasive presence long forecasted and desired by some environmental policymakers. To work effectively, a tradeable emissions policy depends upon the presence of a sufficiently high number of market participants. Otherwise, the degree of bargaining and exchange occurring will fall far short of that necessary for the creation of the requisite market incentives for pollution control. Even the highly touted CAA Acid Deposition Program has suffered because those who participate in the defined market—public utilities—are not really themselves market participants. Public utilities are instead highly regulated private entities that are not susceptible to the normal workings of market forces.[51]

Perhaps the largest stumbling block limiting greater reliance on tradeable emissions policies is that current scientific understandings do not yet support the assumptions of pollution fungibility over type of pollutant emission, time, and space that are necessary to create widespread "pollution" markets with sufficient numbers of participants. A market trade, allowing one entity to reduce pollution less and another entity more, works most easily if the environmental effect remains constant when shifting the locus of pollution from one place to the other or from one time to another. Unfortunately, scientific understandings of ecological cause and effect are finding fewer rather than more instances of such geographic or temporal fungibility, let alone between different types of pollutants or emission sources.[52]

Finally, because higher cost savings also means greater incentives to cheat, trading provides less of an opportunity for reduced governmental administration than often advertised. Significant oversight is required to ensure that companies are not simply trading away their pollution reduction responsibilities in exchange for phantom or bogus offsets. There is similarly a need to guard against the very real possibility that those reductions that do occur might have occurred in the absence of a trade—for instance because of a plant closing—and may have even been delayed for the primary purpose of capitalizing on their potential economic value in a tradeable emissions program. In short, the kind of ongoing monitoring and oversight necessary to prevent any such corruption of a trading program can depend on the maintenance of the very kind of substantial government bureaucracy the program is intended to eliminate.[53]

A final generalization concerns the viability of drawing sharp distinctions between *new* and *existing* sources in the application of pollution controls. The threshold justification for such a distinction is fairly compelling. As an equitable matter, the two sources are not in the same circumstances, because a new source can clearly adapt its facilities to modern pollution control equipment more readily than can an existing facility, and a new source does not otherwise have sunk investment costs at risk. Recognizing a differential between the two also makes implementing pollution controls far more politically palatable because it reduces the opposition from the existing sources who, being current employers, are likely to be the more politically powerful. Based on just such logic, the CAA essentially exempted existing sources from stringent technology-based controls, with the expectation that those existing facilities would eventually be retired or sufficiently modified to allow for application of the tougher new source controls. The CWA, by contrast, simply applied a differential, but still rigorous, standard.

With the benefit of hindsight, it now seems clear that the CAA's blanket exemption was a mistake. Such a large differential between the regulatory requirements applicable to new and existing sources has been inequitable and inefficient, and has likely even led to worse environmental degradation. Existing facilities have simply stayed in operation far longer than they otherwise would have by undertaking upkeep that they contend constitutes "routine maintenance" rather than the "modification" that would trigger the new source standards. The result has been far more pollution, because aging, dirtier facilities have been kept in operation far longer than they otherwise would have been had the controls on existing sources been greater or the controls on new sources been less strict. The CAA would likely have been far more effective if it had either followed the CWA example, which applied some standards to existing sources, or simply allowed for a specified number of transitional years before applying a standard that then became more demanding over time. A mere prescribed number of years to allow for a transition would have given industry the certainty of information needed for long-term investment in pollution control, while reducing short-term political opposition to controls. Congress did just that in the Wilderness Act of 1964 when it banned all mining in wilderness areas, while simultaneously providing that the ban would not take effect for twenty years. Although twenty years may well have been too long a transitional period for imposing requirements on existing facilities, even that might have been better than the CAA's exemption, now well more than thirty years old and showing no signs of ending.

Cooperative Federalism

A final lesson learned from the U.S. experience with modern environmental law is the need for both the federal and state governments to play significant roles in the law's development, implementation, and enforcement. The nature of ecological problems is such that a legal regime for environmental protection cannot be effective without each layer of government serving a substantial role. Neither the federal nor the state sovereign can be effective without the substantial cooperation and involvement of the other.

The transboundary and temporal nature of ecological problems demands a national perspective and expertise, but the simultaneously local character of many of the causes and effects means that the federal government cannot and should not have exclusive authority—especially with regard to the implementation details. The past ramifications of federal pollution control laws, moreover, support a general thesis that the federal government should establish minimum national pollution control standards and objectives, and then the states should implement those standards subject to the federal government's close supervision and oversight. It may well be that, over time, states can be allotted greater degrees of responsibility and autonomy as their respective environmental programs mature and settle. But, as a general matter, there is little reason to believe that such an evolutionary progression can occur broadly across the nation in the absence of a strong and ongoing federal presence in the field. The distributional nature of environmental protection controls, especially their imposition of significant costs "here and now" for significant benefits "there and then," are otherwise too likely to erode effective protection efforts because they will inevitably produce local political forces that constantly seek such erosion for short-term economic gain. The often irreversible nature of environmental degradation, moreover, is such that environmental protection depends on constant vigilance. Even seemingly isolated setbacks can accumulate over time and space so as to overcome and render forever ephemeral any past successes. As evocatively described by one longtime observer of environmental law's evolution, relying exclusively on state and local governments for the accomplishment of national clean air and clean water objectives is "like trying to encourage spaghetti through a keyhole."[54]

The fundamental need for a strong national government presence in environmental protection is why the U.S. Supreme Court's emerging framework for defining the limits of congressional authority under the Commerce Clause is potentially so threatening to environmental law. As described in chapter 7, the threat to environmental law of the notion that Congress can regulate only "economic activities" that substantially affect interstate commerce remained largely theoretical during the 1990s. While it was apparent during that decade that there was a widening gap between the ecological focus of the jurisdictional provisions of federal environmental laws and the commercial focus of the Supreme Court's new Commerce Clause framework, the Court had yet to face the issue in a truly significant context. In early 2001, however, the Court in *Solid Waste Agency of Northern Cook County v. U.S. Army Corps of Engineers (SWANCC)* directly confronted that gap in the CWA and, in response, narrowly construed the act's jurisdictional scope—defining "navigable waters" to exclude so-called isolated waters.[55]

The *SWANCC* Court's conclusion that the plain meaning of "navigable waters" cannot extend to isolated, nonnavigable, intrastate waters not physically adjacent to waters satisfying what the Court described as the "classical understanding of that term" is not, standing alone, remarkable. To anyone approaching the question as a matter of first impression, the ruling might well seem logical, if not compelling. What made the Court's ruling so unsettling to environmental law was that the legal issue before the Court was *not* a matter of first impression: the relevant federal agencies (and arguably Congress as well) had embraced a view broader than that "classical understanding" for more than twenty-five years.[56]

The most remarkable aspect of the Court's reasoning was, however, its statement that such a narrow interpretation of the CWA's jurisdictional reach would have been necessary even in the absence of the statute's plain meaning because of the "significant constitutional questions" that would otherwise be raised. The Court questioned whether Congress even possessed the constitutional authority under the Commerce Clause to reach a broader definition of navigable waters, and singled out for discussion the gap existing between the CWA's focus on "navigable waters" and the "precise object or activity" that, under the Court's Commerce Clause analysis, must, "in the aggregate, substantially affect[ ] interstate commerce." The Court also expressed the view that permitting a broader federal jurisdiction "would result in a significant impingement of the State's traditional and primary power of land and water use."[57]

The Supreme Court's analysis was rooted in antiquated nineteenth-century notions that congressional Commerce Clause authority turns on the navigability of a body of water. To be sure, a water body's navigability may once have been a valid touchstone for assessing the legitimacy of national legislation when navigability established a water body's ability to serve literally as a highway of interstate commerce. The premise of modern environmental law, however, is that the national interest, including relationship to commerce, is much more extensive. Bodies of water provide essential supplies of drinking water; critical chemical and biological components for manufacturing, industry, and agriculture; a source of human recreation and enjoyment; a basis of enhanced property value for homes; a habitat for wildlife and plant life; and a substantial source of energy. Moreover, our knowledge of aquatic ecology makes clear the complex interdependencies of the ecosystem. Whether or not a specific water body is "navigable," "nonnavigable," or physically "adjacent" to another navigable water body is generally irrelevant to all of the above concerns and is certainly not dispositive of the question of whether national regulation is needed or appropriate.

Environmental laws inevitably regulate and affect commerce because the nation's natural resources supply, after all, what are literally the basic ingredients of commercial life. But that is not to say that the objectives of those laws are commercial or that the reason the laws regulate certain activities is their commercial character. What frequently makes environmental laws, whether the CWA or the Endangered Species Act, so historically unique and important is that they promote a different vision of the relationship between humankind and the natural environment, one that is deliberately not commercial in its emphasis.

The Court in *SWANCC* also seems to be suggesting that federal regulation of activities affecting environmental media—such as land, water, and, presumably, air—or natural resources, such as endangered wildlife, is inherently suspect as a matter of constitutional law because it interferes with matters traditionally regulated under state authority. Even if once tenable, such a constitutional subjugation of the legitimate role of the national government in environmental protection law is probably no longer viable. Such a policy seems inconsistent with our modern understandings of the workings of the ecosystem and its degradation, and is contrary to what hard-earned experience has shown to be required for effective environmental protection law.

Creating strong federal environmental law frameworks within which state environmental law develops has been the dominant path for environmental law's evolution, and it may well be an evolutionary path in which states' laws play an increasing role over time, both in implementation and as laboratories to experiment with innovative environmental policies. Yet, it is still fair to depict modern environmental law in the United States today as being firmly based on an active, demanding federal presence working in cooperation with, and not in displacement of, state governmental agencies.

Thus, under the CAA, the federal government has promoted and overseen the development of SIPs and state permitting programs. Under the CWA, the EPA has overseen the states' development of water quality standards, implementation of areawide waste management planning, and administration of pollutant discharge elimination system permit programs. The same pattern is evident in other pollution control laws, such as the Resource Conservation Recovery Act, and in such natural resources laws as the Surface Mining Control and Reclamation Act. Under the latter, the U.S. Department of the Interior is responsible for the establishment of "minimum national standards" for surface mining that may be implemented by individual states, subject to federal approval.[58]

To similar effect has been the increasing role of the federal government in working with state and local governments in fashioning natural resources law, as recently seen in Interior's use of habitat conservation plans under the Endangered Species Act but even for resources, like water, thought to be within the exclusive province of state law. Based on federal interest in water ranging from wetlands regulation under the Clean Water Act to endangered species protection, federal water reclamation, and federal hydroelectric facility licensing under the Endangered Species Act, the Reclamation Act of 1902, and the Federal Power Act of 1920, federal agencies now increasingly work collaboratively with state and local agencies and stakeholders. The result has arguably been a metamorphosis of Western water law in the fashioning of comprehensive watershed planning.[59]

In short, what has worked most effectively in environmental law, because of the nature of the problem being addressed and its accompanying political dimensions, has been a cooperative relationship between the national and state governments in which each sovereign is respectful of the expertise and relative autonomy of the other. But, at the end of the day, the federal government remains responsible for safeguarding the interests of the nation as a whole, and this requires vigilant oversight of state implementation of federal environmental objectives.

*   *   *

A snapshot portrait of environmental law in the United States today is still evocative of the "architecture of Tobacco Road." The nation's environmental law remains ramshackle, replete with inconsistencies and paradoxical gaps, and surrounded by critics urging its fundamental redesign. Viewed historically, however, it is apparent that there is more sense than nonsense to environmental law's existing structure. There are discernible evolutionary convergences in regulatory approaches based on decades of actual experience with what works well and what does not. Some of those persistent gaps, moreover, now seem less paradoxical than they once did and are now better understood as expressions of competing values in our lawmaking institutions rather than as fundamental flaws in environmental lawmaking. The process of environmental lawmaking is no doubt far from set. Indeed, as discussed in the next chapter, current environmental laws will likely require redirection and modification in response to the changing conceptions of the nature of the causes and effects of the ecological problems they address. However, even granting the possibility of such significant future changes, the basic architectural features of U.S. environmental law seem essentially in place.

Changing Conceptions of Time and Space Redux: Environmental Law's Future Challenges

To posit that environmental law in the United States is settling is a far cry from declaring that the environmental lawmaking process is complete. There remain significant regulatory gaps to be filled, fundamental shifts in policymaking focus to be made, and major reforms in the means as well as the ends of environmental protection law to be undertaken. The ecological problems that the nation currently faces challenge and will continue to challenge our lawmaking institutions and processes.

The sources of many of these current challenges to lawmaking are the same as those that triggered the revolution in environmental lawmaking that commenced in the 1970s. However, addressing the complex issues that led to regulatory gaps has become relatively more pressing over the past thirty years, because these issues have risen in proportionality as other regulatory targets of opportunity have been more directly and effectively addressed. The need for more systematic regulation of the environmental impacts of the agriculture industry and the need for greater attention to be paid to the possible synergistic effects of multiple pollutants are two obvious examples of problems long experienced whose time for regulatory redress is correspondingly long overdue.

There are, however, also newly evolving challenges with potentially complex lawmaking implications. As described in chapter 4, changes in the world, and particularly the public conceptions of the nature of those changes, drove environmental lawmaking decades ago. Environmental law was then necessary in part to respond to the increased demands the nation was placing on its natural environment, the enhanced appreciation of the environmental consequences of those demands, and the heightened concern of those consequences deriving from the public's fundamental reconceptualization of time and space.

The world, of course, has not stood still for the past several decades. World circumstances today, or at least our understanding of them, are very different in many respects from those that existed during modern environmental law's early years. Because of technological and societal changes, the ecological problems that the United States and the world now face are very different from those of the past—sometimes they are different because of actual changes in the physical world, and sometimes they are different simply because they are now better understood. Where there once was an "agricultural revolution" followed by an "industrial revolution," some observers contend that we are now in the midst of an "information revolution" in which the most current knowledge is quickly made available to all. But whatever their ultimate derivation, changing societal circumstances are once again not only altering the nature of the ecological problems that we face, but they are also changing how the public understands time and space in ways that may present heightened challenges for environmental lawmaking.

This chapter describes some of those challenges, including both their sources and their implications for environmental law's future. More particularly, the chapter first singles out for discussion specific ways in which notions of space and time appear to be shifting. Next discussed are the general implications of those shifts for environmental protection law. Finally, the chapter identifies several specific areas of environmental law that are likely to warrant reform.

Changing Conceptions of Space

The beginning of the twentieth century in the United States marked the closing of the American frontier. From long-established families to newly arrived immigrants, Americans had settled lands from one coast to the other. The nation's natural resources laws could no longer presume, as they had for much of the nineteenth century, unlimited domestic spatial horizons for natural resource development and exploitation.

During the final decades of the twentieth century, the spatial horizons of Americans were in many respects both expanded and even further limited. The Hubble space telescope revealed in striking detail solar systems and galaxies that had previously been a distant flicker—but it made them no closer or reachable. The exponentially longer amounts of time and increased expense necessary to send humans beyond our own moon had already dampened the once formidable American enthusiasm for endeavors more ambitious than the Apollo program. We seemed best able simply to peer into outer space, to make things visually closer, but without any actual physical presence in those distant worlds. Instead, the public learned that the dream of space exploration had led to a littering of space, as the debris from humanity's efforts resulted in thousands of discarded objects orbiting the planet.[1]

The U.S. public at the close of the twentieth century also became more aware of its increased vulnerability to broader global environmental degradation caused by activities not confined to the nation's own borders. Only a worldwide ban on the use of certain chemical compounds could hope to prevent destruction of the atmospheric ozone layer, which threatened to have potentially devastating worldwide human health effects, including in the United States. Even now, however, in some parts of the world, such as Chile, the government warns its citizens against exposure to the sun for more than a few minutes during certain seasons and times of day.

Increased harvesting of fish outside of U.S. territorial waters similarly threatened a very different but equally ominous ecological collapse of fisheries upon which the U.S. fishing industry and U.S. consumers depended. By the close of the twentieth century, eleven out of fifteen of the world's fishing areas and approximately 70 percent of its major fish species were declining in numbers and faced exigent circumstances. Atlantic cod, once the dominant species in the North Atlantic and a major foodstock, was already in serious decline. Catch of Atlantic cod decreased by 69 percent between 1968 and 1992. Atlantic bluefin tuna stock fell by more than 80 percent during the same time period.[2]

Potentially catastrophic consequences of global climate change could result from either increased emissions of carbon dioxide worldwide or the global destruction of natural "carbon sinks," such as tropical rainforests, that consumed carbon dioxide. Annual global carbon emissions reached 6.55 billion tons in 2001, as fossil fuel combustion activities released into the atmosphere carbon that had been removed from circulation over the course of millions of years and stored in plants, coal, and oil. It was at the time the highest level of carbon emissions in at least 420,000 years and perhaps as many as 20 million years.

The public learned, however, that more than just the carbon cycle is being subject to such disruptive amplification. The nitrogen and phosphorus cycles are being similarly disrupted. Nitrogen occurs naturally in both an inert form that is not biologically available and a "fixed" form that is. Production of fertilizer, fossil fuel combustion, and the destruction of forests and wetlands have combined to double the annual release of nitrogen to the more biologically available fixed form. Fertilizer production worldwide is simultaneously increasing by a factor of 3.7 (to 13 million tons of year) the amount of phosphorus being released. Such rapid increases in both these chemicals could potentially cause pervasive ecosystem damage on a global scale, including accelerated eutrophication of water bodies, increased plant susceptibility to disease, and acid deposition.[3]

Horizons far closer to home, however, did seemingly expand with human understanding. Exploration of the microbial world, of subatomic forces, and of the human genome accelerated during the final years of the century. Each suggested the possibility of massive reservoirs of untapped potential for human understanding and progress. Somewhat paradoxically, it was in the workings of the smallest parts of the world immediately before us rather than in the vast expanses of outer space that untapped spatial horizons seemed the most promising.

Biologists began to understand the extraordinarily important role that microbes play as the planet's ultimate recyclers. By breaking down complex chemical compounds over time, microbes supply many of the discrete chemical elements needed for sustaining life. As physicists further examined the workings of the atom through faster and more powerful "atom smashers," new horizons were similarly revealed in the smallest of spaces. Nanotechnology—the manipulation of individual molecules to create useful materials and devices invisible to the naked eye—proliferated as engineers sought to develop practical applications of atomic forces. Scientists began to speculate with increasing confidence about the prospect of even molecular-scale computing devices. Finally, the human genome project unraveled the basic blueprint of human life itself. Both exciting and unnerving, this new genetic insight made people think differently about both the world within and outside them. What had always seemed as fixed factors of life now seemed subject to possible manipulation, and other species that had long seemed impossibly different now turned out to be genetically similar to humankind.

Endocrine (hormone) disruptors emerged in the late 1990s as environmentalism's latest unsettling threat. *Our Stolen Future* strived to match *Silent Spring* as a warning to humankind of the invisible threats to human health and welfare and to the environment from synthetic chemicals. But now it was not just the season of spring that could be silenced; at stake was our very future. Ecologists warned that synthetic chemicals could be responsible for decreased fertility, lowering of male sperm counts, reduced intelligence, and dramatic increases of disease, of which cancer was just one example. As described by the book's authors, harmful exposure could arise at extraordinarily low concentration levels in the *parts per trillion,* which they described as the equivalent of one drop of liquid in a train of tank cars six miles long. The contaminants themselves were simultaneously "unfathomabl[y] small," "beyond people's wildest imaginations," but they presented risks that were literally "Here, There, and Everywhere" reaching "To the Ends of the Earth."[4]

No doubt the greatest impact on public conceptions of space, however, resulted from the emergence of what has become known as "virtual space." Advances in computer technology, especially those directed toward graphics and the Internet, created a virtual natural environment that people could experience in ways just short of actual physical presence. In past eras, technological advances had similarly profound spatial impacts. Glass windows invited the outside environment indoors and revolutionized the construction industry in previously undeveloped locations where the natural environment could be visually enjoyed. The elevator, by making the second and third floors as accessible as the first, allowed for greater exploitation of the vertical world, and skyscrapers soon proliferated. Just as the railroads had promoted the economic exploitation of natural resources in the western states during the second half of the nineteenth century, highways and automobiles allowed for the horizontal expansion of U.S. cities in the second half of the twentieth century. The resulting suburbanization of the nation's landscape increased developmental pressures on undeveloped lands, including wetlands and prime farmland, and contributed to increased air pollution from greater vehicular traffic.[5]

Even more effective than film or television, "surfing" the Internet in the late twentieth and early twenty-first centuries allowed individuals to choose for themselves the "sites" that they wished to "visit." A personal computer with an Internet connection enabled someone to seemingly travel to other parts of the world instantaneously, without ever leaving one's home or office. In the early 1970s, Harvard Law School professor Laurence Tribe famously noted that the significance for environmental protection of "plastic trees" replacing real trees was that the public might become increasingly disinterested in preserving the real thing.[6] By the century's close, "virtual" trees and ecosystems were becoming the modern equivalent of those earlier plastic replicas. Screen savers offered virtual natural environments, ranging from the sights and sounds of a forest or ocean to an aquarium with fish.

The emergence of virtual space coincided with a broader loss of the kind of physical nexus to the world that had long been so fundamental to the human experience. People seemed less tied than ever to any particular "place." By the close of the twentieth century, the average American was moving more than twelve times during his or her lifetime. The same shops, restaurants, and "outdoor" amusement parks proliferated across the nation, replacing regional differences with homogeneity and further eroding distinctiveness of place. The most popular places within national parks often became formal "visitor centers," where multimedia presentations on the park were given. One could now simply see a movie or study a display about the park rather than take the time necessary to experience the park itself, especially if the weather was too wet, too hot, or too cold. Even those nominally committed to experiencing the outdoors discovered the seductiveness of simply using the Web to "visit" instead. And, for those few truly hardy enough to venture into true wilderness areas, many would invariably bring along with them cellphones or satellite communication technology to allow them to maintain contact with the "real world."[7]

Of particular relevance to environmental protection policies, changing technology and markets and shifting attitudes during the final decades of the twentieth century promoted a cognitive severance of environmental cause and effect. The globalization of the world's economy then occurring meant that the physical distance between decisionmakers and the environmental impacts of their decisions became much greater than before. Corporate officials deciding how much oil to produce, silver to mine, crops to produce, fertilizer or pesticide to apply, or land to clear no longer lived where those activities were to take place. Executives no longer lived with the physical consequences of their decisions or even saw them firsthand. The environmental impacts of economic decisions frequently did not even reveal themselves in the country where the decision had been made. More restrictive domestic environmental protection laws contributed to such globalization by encouraging the export of environmentally destructive activities to nations with less demanding laws.[8]

American consumers similarly could not readily perceive the environmental impact of their purchasing decisions, as the impact on the world environment was effectively masked by distance. One could purchase a hamburger in a fast food restaurant or a wood chair in a discount furniture outlet in the United States while remaining oblivious to the related environmental consequences. The inexorable forces of supply and demand may, in fact, have linked the purchase of the hamburger or chair to the destruction of tropical rainforests or the filling of wetlands purportedly necessary to support the raising of cattle or the harvesting of timber. The loss of rainforests or wetlands may, in fact, have meant the decimation of an endangered species or the consequent erosion of an unprotected landscape. But the sheer physical distance of the consumption from the production had dissipated the consumer's sense of connection to environmental consequences that he or she might find deplorable.[9]

Finally, at least in the United States, the end of the twentieth century witnessed the public's response to the potential scarcity of personal space by demanding *more* rather than *less* of it. The fascination of Americans in the 1970s and early 1980s with compact and subcompact cars seemed by the year 2000 to be a distant memory. Much larger minivans and ever larger sport utility vehicles (SUVs) became the norm for middle- and upper-class Americans. U.S. consumers wanted larger cars that offered more internal space, notwithstanding the direct losses in fuel efficiency that had made smaller cars so economically attractive a few decades earlier. From 1991 to 2001, the market share for small cars decreased from 23 to 14.2 percent; the combined market share for SUVs, vans, and light trucks rose during that same period from 33.3 to 44.9 percent. Between 1987 and 2001, notwithstanding that the average weight of SUVs increased by 638 pounds, their acceleration rates increased by approximately one-third, with corresponding decreases in gas mileage. Some municipalities even began to eliminate the special parking spaces for compact cars that had been introduced in the 1970s. Average fuel economy for model 2003 cars and passenger trucks was 6 percent below that which had been achieved fifteen years earlier.[10]

The same phenomenon occurred with house size and land use. Wealthier Americans sought increasingly larger living space, even as the average family size decreased. The average house size in the 1950s was 1,100 square feet; by 1996, it was over 2,000 square feet, with almost 14 percent of those homes over 3,000 square feet. The "mansionization" of the suburban United States placed even greater economic pressure on land development, especially valuable wetlands on or about the aesthetically pleasing border area between land and water. In the Chicago metropolitan area, the amount of acreage used for residential land development grew between 1970 and 1990 eleven times faster than the population; in Cleveland, where population has been declining since 1970 by approximately 11 percent, the amount of urbanized land use has increased by 33 percent.[11]

The same pattern is evident throughout the nation. In every region of the country, metropolitan areas are developing land acreage at a rate that far outpaces corresponding population increases (and sometimes decreases) from 1983 to 1997. In the West, which witnessed the greatest increase of population (32.2 percent), the amount of land being developed increased by 48.9 percent. In the South, population increased by 22.2 percent, but land development increased by 59.6 percent. In the two areas of the country in which the population increases were the smallest—the Midwest (7.1 percent) and Northeast (6.9 percent)—the corresponding pace of land development was larger by a factor greater than five (32.2 and 39.1 percent).[12]

Even the average size of Americans themselves has increased significantly in recent decades. In keeping with McDonald's famous invitation to customers to "supersize" their meals, people now eat more, indeed much more than ever. Two recent studies, one published in the *Journal of the American Medical Association* and the other in the *American Journal of Public Health,* found that the size of meal portions Americans consume grew considerably during the past three decades. For example, hamburgers increased on average from 5.7 ounces to 7.0 ounces between 1977 and 1996, while soft drink portions increased from 13.1 to 19.9 ounces. As a result of such increased consumption, obesity in the United States is on the rise and becoming one of the nation's greatest public health problems. More than 50 percent of all Americans are now overweight and the incidence of obesity in adults has increased by more than 60 percent in the past ten years.[13]

Changing Conceptions of Time

Perhaps the most obvious shift in U.S. temporal perspectives during the late twentieth century related to environmental protection law was in Americans' view of nature. The perception of nature most widely embraced by the environmentalists in the late 1960s promoted the notion that nature was static and maintained an equilibrium or "balance." Pollution and excessive resource exploitation threatened the destruction of the fragile equilibrium underlying that balance, with potentially catastrophic consequences.[14] For many, Aldo Leopold's famous description of a "land ethic"—"A thing is right when it tends to preserve the integrity, stability, and beauty of the biotic community. It is wrong when it tends otherwise"—announced the guiding principle for modern environmental protection law.[15]

Many of the modern resource conservation and pollution control laws are, accordingly, premised on a theory of ecosystem equilibrium and seek to protect the natural environment from change. The Endangered Species Act is intended to safeguard the "balance of nature" and thereby prevent species extinction. The Clean Water Act's water quality standards seek to maintain "existing uses." The National Environmental Policy Act seeks to maintain natural harmonies between humankind and the environment. The Wild and Scenic Rivers Act and the Wilderness Act seek to "preserve" the natural environments within their respective statutory purviews.[16]

Ecologists today, however, have long since rejected the equilibrium view of nature. As described by Professor Dan Tarlock, the prevailing view is now that "the kinds of problems we face require a dynamic view of nature. . . . Ecosystems are patches or collections of conditions that exist for finite periods of time. Further, the accelerating interaction between humans and the natural environment makes it impossible to return to an ideal state of nature. At best, ecosystems can be managed, but not restored or preserved." In short, "[n]ature moves and changes and involves risks and uncertainties and . . . our own judgments of our actions must be made against this moving target."[17] Ecologists have largely abandoned their search for grand overarching theories of diversity and ecosystem stability in favor of simply trying to understand the workings of actual ecological communities and systems.[18]

Conceptions of time have also shifted in ways seemingly less directly relevant to environmental protection law, but no less profound in what they portend for environmental law's future. Most simply put, the pace of life today is faster than ever. People expect more, more quickly. Indeed, the pace has accelerated to such an extent that it presents fundamental challenges to the nation's ability to maintain environmental protection objectives and to make law for their future accomplishment.

The quickening of the pace of Americans' lives over the past thirty years is all the more striking because there was reason to expect that the opposite would occur. People live longer now than ever before. Technological advances allow people to do more with less. At least in the United States, people should be able to have more leisure time than at any other time in the nation's history. There is more reason for patience, more cause to be willing to invest in the future and postpone immediate gratification to ensure adequate resources in the future, and more reason to adopt a more relaxed, slower paced lifestyle.

However, almost every aspect of modern life in the United States reflects a quicker pace. Faster became better in all aspects of life. Fast food restaurants proliferated throughout the urban and rural landscape. In 1970, Americans spent about $6 billion on fast food; by the year 2000, the expenditures had risen to approximately $110 billion. McDonald's grew from about 2,000 restaurants in 1968 to about 28,000 restaurants around the globe and became the nation's largest purchaser of beef, pork, and potatoes, and the second largest purchaser of chicken. Commercial matchmaking responded to the ever busier lives of young, single professionals by reducing the time for initial meetings to a mere ten minutes or less—no time could be wasted, even in the pursuit of love. Societal obsessions with maximum productivity in the shortest possible time spilled over to the parents planning their children's "free" time as weeknights and weekends became overwhelmed by extracurricular activities ranging from sports to music.[19]

Technology no doubt played some transformative role in this quickening of pace. Centuries ago, the first mass production of clocks made the uniform keeping of time more possible and, consequently, more important. The rising use of time clocks, not coincidentally, emerged coincident with the United States' industrialization, carving time into smaller pieces and increasing productivity demands. More recent technological advances have magnified those effects. Time can now be measured with enormous accuracy, based on the vibrations of atoms that allow for precise measurements to the nanosecond—one-billionth of a second.[20]

Technology's impact on supply and demand has also been direct and immediate by vastly increasing the speed of commerce. In the mid-1980s, the notion of guarantying customers overnight deliveries impressed many business investors as a nonstarter. By the early 1990s, however, Federal Express was a multibillion-dollar business, offering its users a range of ever faster delivery options. As the 1990s progressed, what had once seemed extraordinarily fast—overnight delivery—itself became too slow for most people. First fax machines, then e-mail, and even "instant mail" dominated the field of communications and created even higher public expectations.[21]

Enhanced communications gave manufacturers and growers an increased capacity to produce more goods, a situation that quickly promoted corresponding increases in consumer demand. Absolute consumption rose significantly. Although energy consumed per dollar spent had gone consistently down since the 1960s, the number of consumption dollars (in constant dollars) overwhelmed those energy efficiency gains. Americans spent $4.132 trillion dollars on consumption in 1992; that number had risen to $4.913 trillion by 1997 (in 1992 dollars). Americans spent more each year on items such as shoes, jewelry, and watches ($80 billion) than they did on higher education ($65 billion).[22] In the mid-1980s, high schools still outnumbered shopping malls, but that is no longer so. Today, shopping malls outnumber high schools by a factor greater than two to one. As described by one commentator, so-called mega-malls and super malls have become the modern day equivalent of a Gothic cathedral in terms of the central role they play as "a symbol of cultural values."[23]

Another significant effect of fast-paced lifestyles was a pronounced shortening of time horizons. Americans became even less patient and demanded more immediate returns on their investments. This shift in attitudes was evident in the stock market. By the end of the 1990s, the average time that stocks were held prior to sale went from two years down to only eight months for sales in the New York Stock Exchange and down to five months for the NASDAQ. The long-standing common denominator for advance business planning had been five years, but that time period was often now only five months. For the Toyota Motor Corporation, what had been five-year business planning cycles were reduced to only one month.[24]

Similar reductions in investment time horizon were evident in many aspects of everyday life. College sports adopted freshmen eligibility rules that permitted, for the first time, first-year students to participate in varsity sports. At the same time, increasing numbers of the best athletes left college prior to graduation or even skipped college altogether in order to take advantage of lucrative professional salaries. Even the venerable American pastime—baseball—provides analogues that reflect the general shifts in societal attitudes. To reduce the time necessary for a complete game by six minutes, major league baseball reduced from twenty to twelve seconds the amount of time allowed between pitches.[25]

Consumer demand similarly reflected an increasing desire for immediate return and a diminishing attention span. Buyers turned over goods more quickly than ever. The average period of car ownership reduced from five years in the 1970s to approximately eighteen months in the 1990s. Even buyers of blue jeans were no longer so willing to wait for the jeans to fade naturally—by paying a premium, they could buy "pre-faded" pants. The fashion industry continued to encourage consumers to buy new clothes within increasingly shorter time periods. A cartoon on the editorial page of the *Washington Post* in January 2000 illustrated well the change in public attitudes. It juxtaposed a person from 1984 and a person from 2000, with the former echoing then-President Ronald Reagan's famous campaign inquiry "Are you better off than you were four years ago?" and the latter inquiring instead "Are you better off than you were four minutes ago?"[26]

Advertising and political sound bites emerged as the preferred, most effective, method of commercial and political communication. A three-minute segment of television news came to be considered "long." The national newspaper *USA Today,* not surprisingly, favored shorter articles for its readers, as did the *New Yorker* magazine, which had long been virtually a cultural icon with its unrelenting insistence on publishing lengthy, in-depth, reflective articles and essays, including Rachel Carson's *Silent Spring* in the 1960s before it was published as a book. During the 1990s, however, even the *New Yorker* began to respond to changing public attitudes by significantly shortening the length of the articles that it printed.[27]

Just as computer technology and the Internet had an impact on public conceptions of space, so too did they influence public conceptions of time. Personal computers, cellphones, and related communication devices, perhaps more than any other kind of consumer product, epitomized the increasing "turnover" nature of the nation's economy. They are not necessarily built to last or even to be repaired; or repair costs are set prohibitively high so as to encourage consumers to buy new products and throw away their old ones. A buyer of a black-and-white television in 1979 could be expected to retain that product for twelve years; a purchaser today of an expensive LCD screen television would likely replace it after five years because of technological improvements during the interim. Computer equipment, in particular, has become obsolete at an increasing pace as ever larger "memories" and ever faster communication devices became available and seemingly necessary. As predicted in the mid-1960s, the computer powering of silicon chips increased by twofold every eighteen to twenty-four months. Modems that a few years earlier had seemed extraordinarily fast were quickly replaced by even faster modems and finally by both hard-wire and wireless options that were themselves several orders of magnitude more rapid than their predecessors. For the public, the same few seconds of delay that had a few years earlier seemed virtually instantaneous now came to be viewed as an eternity of wasted time. According to the National Safety Council, more than 40 million computers became obsolete in the United States in 2001.[28]

Implications for Environmental Protection Law

These changing public attitudes and societal circumstances challenge the viability of current environmental protection law in both obvious and less obvious ways. The most obvious impact is the accelerating demand for resource consumption. By demanding more, and by demanding it more quickly, consumers are promoting even greater natural resource exploitation. Paper consumption is illustrative. Notwithstanding the emergence throughout the 1990s of technologies, such as e-mail, with obvious potential for reducing natural resource demand, paper consumption rose dramatically during that decade and continues to do so. When printers, copiers, scanners, and fax machines became capable of producing more drafts and copies more quickly, demand for that many more drafts and copies soon followed. Offices that add e-mail service find that their consumption of paper *increases* by 40 percent. Industry analysts currently project increases of office paper of another 50 percent in the next ten to fifteen years, mostly driven by the proliferation of laser printers.[29]

The second half of the twentieth century bore witness to an unprecedented explosion in consumption worldwide, reaching $24 trillion in expenditures by 1998, which was twice the level or expenditure in 1975. Worldwide, per capita consumption doubled for copper, energy, meat, steel, and timber; consumption of cement and plastic quadrupled and quintupled, respectively. Most of those increases, moreover, occurred in industrialized nations rather than in developing nations where such an increase might have indicated needed improvements in standards of living.[30]

For example, between 1990 and 2000 alone, personal consumption expenditures in the United States rose by over 74 percent, and clothing and shoe purchases rose by about 54 percent. Meeting such increased consumer demand requires accelerated resource exploitation, energy consumption, manufacturing, and transportation activities, all of which threaten to quickly overwhelm the gains that environmental protection and natural resource conservation laws might otherwise achieve. Not only does such overconsumption deplete the world's natural resource base more rapidly, but the associated industrial activity needed to meet consumer demand almost invariably raises absolute amounts of pollution. As the Chief Executive Office of Monsanto aptly put it, "The Earth can't withstand a systematic increase of material things. If we grow by using more stuff, we'd better start looking for a new planet."[31]

Overall environmental quality cannot be maintained even with a lowering of percentage emissions rates or increased energy efficiency when those achievements are more than offset by greater economic activity. Cars, for instance, may be constructed to be more efficient and to pollute less per vehicle mile traveled, but if such improvements are accompanied by a disproportionate increase in total number of vehicular miles traveled, the natural environment will nonetheless be degraded more than ever. Total vehicular miles traveled in the United States increased by almost 700 million miles, or 25 percent, during the 1990s, as Americans both increased their spatial horizons and sought to get there more quickly.[32]

Domestic energy consumption reveals the same tendency. Between the early 1970s and the late 1980s, the decreasing amount of energy consumption per dollar of gross domestic product (GDP) allowed overall domestic energy consumption to remain essentially the same while the GDP rose by 45 percent in constant dollars. During the 1990s, however, while there was still some decrease in energy consumption per dollar of GDP, it was more than offset by overall increases in GDP. Across the board, increased economic activity began to overwhelm the energy efficiency gains achieved from technological improvements during the late 1970s. Energy use, which fell by 18 percent between 1973 and 1983, had, by 1997, increased by 37 percent.[33]

The increased cognitive severance for consumers between environmental cause and effect exacerbates the potential environmental impact of such increased consumption. The celebrated ecologist Aldo Leopold long ago warned that "[t]here are two spiritual dangers in not owning a farm. One is the danger of supposing that breakfast comes from the grocery, and the other that heat comes from the furnace."[34] By the new millennium, technological advances and global markets had combined to sever almost completely any possible cognitive ties between the market decisions of both buyer and seller and the direct environmental consequences of those decisions. Nothing about consumer goods, including their market prices, necessarily reflect their environmental consequences, especially if related resource exploitation and manufacturing activities occur in jurisdictions lacking strict environmental laws. A simple home computer, which would seem to epitomize the upside potential for low-impact technology, gives no hint of the more than seven hundred different materials and hundreds of pounds of solid waste and thousands of gallons of wastewater required for its production.[35]

The impact of increased economic activity also has become more global in nature. Not only has the pace of economic activity increased—so too has its ecological reach. Decisions made by consumers in one nation have direct consequences on the state of the environment in other countries. For instance, China has become the dumping ground for millions of computers discarded in the United States each year because consumers want ever more powerful and faster computer processing. The heavy metals within the computer components leach out of the discarded electronic computer, contaminating local water supplies. Moreover, as scientific awareness has increased regarding the global and transboundary environmental impacts of activities nominally occurring outside U.S. borders, so too has it become more apparent that exporting resource exploitation and manufacturing does not preclude the subsequent "importation" back into the United States of related adverse environmental spillover effects. Accordingly, environmental protection law must either find some way to influence domestic consumer behavior or devise a means to promote meaningful environmental protection laws extraterritorially.[36]

The spatial and temporal dimensions of global climate change illustrate, perhaps all too well, the kinds of challenges now faced by environmental lawmaking. Scientific uncertainty is no longer the overriding threshold stumbling block to the development of laws addressing global climate change. Although wishful thinking no doubt persists in some quarters,[37] a broad scientific consensus now exists that human-induced global climate change presents a serious environmental and public health hazard that warrants global redress. The main impediments to any effective lawmaking arise not from remaining scientific uncertainty, but instead out of the enormous spatial and temporal dimensions to climate change and the correspondingly large distributional implications of competing international lawmaking strategies for redressing the causes of climate change.[38]

To address global climate change, it is not enough merely to ask people today to make sacrifices for benefits that might not be enjoyed for many years. It requires laws that effectively require significant economic sacrifices for environmental and human health benefits to be realized not just many decades, but more likely centuries from now. No matter what style of government is in place, that is quite a hard (if not well-nigh impossible) sell, but potentially especially so for a democracy in which voters often hold elected officials responsible for short-term consequences.

What makes the global climate change issue even more problematic for lawmakers, however, is that neither the costs nor the benefits of curtailing economic activity that contributes to climate change are evenly distributed around the globe. Some nations, such as the United States, have already benefited greatly from industrialization that has helped to load the atmosphere with carbon dioxide emissions and promoted the destruction of "carbon sinks" (such as rainforests) that otherwise would have naturally reduced atmospheric concentrations of greenhouse gases. For that reason, less-developed nations can forcefully argue that the more industrialized nations should take on the brunt of necessary reductions, which should also not preclude less-developed nations from becoming more industrialized.

There is simultaneously a mismatch in the benefits from preventing global climate change. The nature and degree of threats presented by global climate change naturally depend on location. Low-lying areas could literally be submerged by rising sea levels; even higher temperatures areas near the equator could be especially harmful; global warming would disrupt specific species and their ecosystems; relatively rapid changes in temperature could lead to increased cardiorespiratory mortality and to substantial spreading of infectious diseases (such as malaria, dengue, yellow fever, viral encephalitis, salmonellosis, and cholera) in unpredictable, yet discrete fashion. Even something as simple as differentials in species responses to climate change could have dramatic effects. For example, certain North American bird species are already shifting northward more quickly in response to rising temperatures, which could lead to destructively high populations of insects in those areas being abandoned.[39]

Consequently, nations around the globe harbor very different, and conflicting, views on what constitutes a fair basis of allocating the burden of curtailing greenhouse gas emissions. The 1997 Kyoto Protocol reflected the global community's initial effort to come up with at least a framework for sorting out these competing distributional concerns. The protocol's attempt to utilize an emissions trading program, roughly based on the Clean Air Act's program for sulfur dioxide emissions, sought to couple increased demands on industrialized nations with increased flexibility for achieving reductions in a less costly fashion. Under the protocol, a country like the United States could satisfy some of its emissions reduction requirements by, in effect, purchasing reductions achieved in other nations rather than by taking the more costly steps necessary to reduce carbon dioxide emissions within the United States. The subsequent withdrawal of the United States from the protocol, based on President Bush's concerns that the agreement asked too much of American citizens, simply underscores how difficult environmental lawmaking can become even as the environmental problems themselves become more pressing.[40]

Another direct implication for environmental protection law is that the environmental impact of accelerated economic activity may well increase exponentially rather than linearly. One reason, as described in chapter 1, is that exponentiality results from placing constant demands on an ever-shrinking natural resource base. A reduction of five hundred acres of wetlands may seem relatively small when there are tens of thousands of wetland acres available, but such a loss is not nearly so trivial when there are only five thousand total acres. Similarly, to the extent that chemical and biologic processes sometimes exhibit threshold effects, the addition of just a few more units of pollution can cause significantly greater adverse consequences.

A second reason for the tendency toward exponential impacts from increases in pace relates to the potential for a growing differential between the pace of human activity and that of nature itself. Nature, after all, has its own pace. Chemical and biologic processes necessary for sustaining plant and animal life or the creation of energy resources take a certain amount of time. The relevant time periods cannot be easily reduced to offset increases in human activity—indeed, such reductions can be impossible. For this reason, although there may not exist some absolute state of equilibrium in nature, the impact that a particular human activity has on the environment can depend on the relevant temporal dimension of natural processes. For instance, biologic processes can absorb and respond to impacts given sufficient time. Similarly, chemical reactions do not occur instantaneously. Intense human activities that do not allow the necessary time for natural cycles to occur can result in environmental consequences far greater than would otherwise result if the same amount of activity were to occur over a longer time period.

Moreover, there are several more subtle ways in which changing public attitudes about time and space may undermine the long-term maintenance of environmental protection law. If it is true that people now feel less attached to the natural world, then they are also likely to care less strongly about protecting natural ecosystems. For many, passion for environmental protection is rooted in personal ties and experiences with particular ecosystems, whether it be where they were born, where they lived for many years, or simply where they had especially meaningful life experiences. The term "grassroots" or "community" used to describe grassroots or community-based movements stresses the fundamental notion that such a movement is inextricably tied to a particular place where people live and work. Activists at the local level are motivated to protect their children and their homes. To the extent, therefore, that people feel less tied to specific places than ever before, either because they move so frequently or because they spend time with virtual natural environments, one can fairly anticipate less concern with environmental protection.

Environmental protection objectives are also likely to be undermined by the public's shortened time horizons and reduced willingness to wait for long-term returns. Much environmental protection depends on short-term sacrifices for what can be very speculative long-term gains. Environmental protection is the functional equivalent of a long-term investment (or, perhaps, betting on a sincere personal belief) in the future, perhaps never even to be realized during the lives of the present generation. Subscribing to an environmental protection regime may mean that in the present less groundwater can be extracted, fewer trees can be cut down, fewer fish can be harvested, or less carbon dioxide can be emitted so that the natural environment may still be sustainable for distant future generations.

For this reason, a significant reduction in attention span and long-term perspective is at odds with the kind of long-term planning that has proved so essential to environmental law's success during the past several decades. Because ecological cause and effect occurs over such great areas of space and such lengthy periods of time, meaningful environmental planning must be similarly expansive in perspective. Sound environmental decisionmaking cannot be accomplished, let alone implemented, impulsively or reflexively. Both public and private decisionmakers, however, currently possess the technological capacity to assimilate massive amounts of information, analyze that information, and make and communicate decisions in minutes, if not seconds. Technology simultaneously creates the potential for those decisions to have massive, distant, and irreversible consequences. What is missing, potentially removed from the decisionmaking equation, is the time necessary for prudential assessment, reflection, and contemplation prior to the exercise of judgment.

In his celebrated book *Bowling Alone—The Collapse and Revival of American Community,* Harvard Professor Robert Putnam provides detailed documentation and analysis of both the distintegration of community in the United States since the 1970s and its origins in both increased time pressures of daily life and urban sprawl. Putnam describes how current generations of Americans spend significantly less time than those who came of age after World War II in community activities, including those designed to promote long-term social aspirations; and they spend more time in pursuit of short-term ends, including simply spending increasing time in the car on errands. As Putnam himself points out, such a generational shift has potentially foreboding implications for many social programs dependent upon long-term, active public participation, including environmental protection.[41]

Finally, there are implications for environmental law of the changing attitudes within the scientific field of ecology: away from grand theories of ecological stability and balance in favor of more modest efforts simply to understand how specific complex ecosystems change and evolve over time. The assumptions of many lawmakers in the 1970s that there exists a discrete, discoverable, set of ecological principles akin to physics' laws of thermodynamics proved misplaced. Science will not supply the fixed standard for what constitutes the appropriate level of ecosystem protection for simple application by environmental lawmakers. Society must instead ultimately derive that standard from its own cultural, ethical, religious, and spiritual norms regarding the relationship between humankind and nature, and not from hard science. The inability of science to provide answers to basic ecological issues is likely one reason why there has been a resurgence in rethinking and rediscovering the relationship of the teachings of major religions—Christianity, Judaism, Islam, Hinduism, and Buddhism—and environmental protection. Tellingly, a television advertisement broadcast in 2002 in opposition to drilling in the Arctic National Wildlife Refuge invoked a Jewish prayer in which God declares: " 'This is a beautiful world I have given you. Take care of it; do not ruin it.' " The advertisement goes on to state that it was sponsored "by the Sierra Club and the National Council of Churches."[42]

In sum, apparent shifts in societal attitudes concerning time and space are relevant to environmental lawmaking in a surprising number of ways. These shifts, caused by growing scientific understandings of environmental injuries, developing technologies, and changing world circumstances, affect how ecological injuries must be addressed. They also suggest, however, the erosion of the very kind of public attitudes—attachment to place, commitment to the future, and practice of patience—that historically have proven so important to the initial development and subsequent maintenance of modern environmental protection law. Because, moreover, the public's passionate commitment to environmental protection has supplied much of the underlying political force necessary to defeat repeated efforts to reduce the stringency of the law's requirements, any such an erosion could have significant repercussions for environmental law's future evolution.

Reforming Environmental Law

Environmental law's future effectiveness will plainly turn on its ability to adapt to these developing ecological threats, evolving societal attitudes, and changing world circumstances. No wholly revolutionary reworking of the existing framework of environmental law should be required—the basic architecture can remain the same, but the precise focus and general mix of laws and lawmaking institutions involved must be reformed in order to achieve the necessary changes in industry and individual behavior.

The changing nature of both the domestic and world economies is one of the clearest examples of changed circumstances that warrant reforming aspects of environmental law. Each of these economies is quite different than they were in 1970 when modern environmental law was first fashioned in the United States. Many of these differences warrant shifts in regulatory regimes because of new challenges and new opportunities.

The U.S. economy, for example, has been marked by a relative rise in the service sector, including, of course, a substantial pollution control industry. The health of the nation's economy is no longer so predominantly focused on the manufacturing and industrial sectors. Much of the GDP is now driven by such service industries as retail sales, medicine, tourism, restaurants and hotels, business and financial consulting, and law. During the 1990s, the combined manufacturing, mining, and agricultural sectors constituted less than one-fourth of the U.S. GDP. By contrast, the combined financial, insurance, and real estate industries constituted 18 percent; wholesale and retail services constituted 17 percent; the combined transportation, commerce, and utilities sectors constituted 10 percent; and the health care industry constituted 6 percent. This shift in emphasis presents both new challenges and new opportunities.[43]

One challenge relates to the fact that service industries appear far more benign in their environmental impact than they actually are. Unlike a major industrial facility or a fossil fuel mining company, service industries do not generally directly emit pollutants or extract natural resources. People, accordingly, often view such activities as contributing to higher environmental quality, or, at worst, being environmentally neutral. But service industry impact on the environment can be far from benign. Service industries require, for instance, the production of huge amounts of energy, which in turn implicates the development, transportation, and exploitation of energy resources. Service industries also require the manufacture, transportation, and production of the myriad goods and equipment used in their daily operations. Each of those associated activities may have significant negative environmental impacts.

McDonald's restaurants, for example, serve more than 22 million meals per day. The activities associated with the provision of those meals, ranging from the growing of crops and the raising of cattle to the transportation and disposal of packaging, are truly extraordinary. The telephone industry is similarly illustrative. Even before merging with GTE to form Verizon, Bell Atlantic reportedly used 18,000 vehicles, 113,000 manholes, 2.5 million utility poles treated with chemical preservatives, and hundreds of millions of other poles across the country. Kinko's, the copying service company, purchases tens of thousands of tons of paper every year.[44]

Finally, service industries can often serve as indirect sources of substantial pollution. A shopping center, a baseball stadium, or a university campus can be a major indirect source of pollution simply because of the concentrated number of motor vehicles that each attracts. They also tend to be significant sources of water pollution due to the contaminants contained in the runoff from their buildings and parking lots. As far as the natural environment is concerned, the impact of these facilities is no different than that created by a large stack from a coal fire power plant emitting pollutants into the air or by a large pipe from a paper plant discharging directly into a major waterway.

To the extent that the production of necessary energy, goods, and equipment is accomplished by major industrial facilities otherwise subject to current environmental protection law, the challenge is simply one of degree:

to take into account the forces behind the increased pace of economic activity in order to guard against cumulative and aggregated environmental impacts. There are, however, several reasons to anticipate that many of the related environmental threats will not be so readily addressed by existing laws.

One reason relates to parallel changes in the world's economy. Although many of the associated manufacturing and industrial facilities remain in the United States, such facilities are increasingly built outside the United States. Their extraterritorial location does not, however, prevent their environmental impact from affecting Americans. Many Americans have close ties to other parts of the world, both to places they visit for professional and personal reasons and to places where their ancestors may have once lived or current relatives still live. Moreover, the environmental effects of extraterritorial activities do not necessarily remain extraterritorial. Goods produced elsewhere are often imported into the United States. If toxic chemicals are used in the production of food overseas, those chemicals may well "boomerang" home in consumer products.[45]

Activities in neighboring countries can also directly affect the air and water resources of the United States. A power plant in Canada that emits air pollutants or a manufacturing facility in Mexico that discharges waste into international waters has immediate impact on the United States. Transboundary pollution over much longer distances is also a significant phenomenon. What is emitted into the upper atmosphere on one side of the globe may well come down on the other side. To the extent, moreover, that all nations share certain global commons, including the ozone layer, fisheries, and the oceans, one can no longer safely presume that industrial activities exported to distant places have no serious consequences for domestic environmental quality.

A second reason that application of existing environmental law regimes may not be sufficient to address the increased demands placed on the ecosystem by the rising service industry in the United States is that many of those demands are created by domestic activities that are left largely unregulated by existing laws. As described in chapter 8, the brunt of much existing environmental law has been borne by the large industrial facilities; relatively less attention has been focused on small, more localized sources of resource exploitation and pollution or on industries that have otherwise persuaded legislatures to treat them more leniently. Over time, however, the pollution from these less regulated sources has naturally increased in relative importance. That has certainly been true, for instance, for "nonpoint" source water pollution, which the Clean Water Act defines as water pollution from sources such as runoff, which are less discrete than an industrial pipe but no less harmful in their aggregate impact. This is also true for air pollution: the influence of land use development patterns—for example, the construction of subdivisions, shopping centers, hospitals, or mass transit systems—on motor vehicle traffic is a major factor contributing to air quality.

The changing nature of the domestic and world economies is also important for environmental law because it changes the relative importance of possible regulatory touchstones, methods, and authorities. A "regulatory touchstone" in this context refers to the activities that are the most effective targets for regulation. The term "method" distinguishes between different types of regulatory regimes, including ambient standards, facility-specific emissions requirements or pollution control design standards, and tradeable emissions policies. Possible regulatory "authorities" include federal, state, and local government agencies or even, in light of the broader scope of current environmental concerns, international lawmaking entities. When environmental protection levels turned largely on domestic industry and manufacturing facilities, environmental protection laws could safely focus primarily on these economic activities. By directly regulating the amount of pollution emitted from a major industrial facility, lawmakers could seek to achieve established public health and environmental goals. When, however, the proportion of pollution originating from major domestic industrial sources decreases, a different regulatory focus becomes necessary.

Outlined below are several ways that reform of environmental law may be refocused to address the concerns described above. They range from the more obviously necessary to the more speculative and controversial.

Influencing Supply, Demand, and National Economic Policy through Better Information

The very same technologies that may render environmental protection more difficult may also be effectively enlisted in its promotion. The "information age," fueled by ever more powerful and faster computer technology, communication capability, and the Internet, creates enormous opportunities for environmental protection by redressing one of its biggest hurdles: uncertainty regarding ecological cause and effect and available pollution control technologies. By providing better information and substantially reducing transactions costs for its discovery, information technologies create new opportunities for effective and efficient environmental protection laws, ranging from more finely defined property rights to better focused regulations.[46]

With better scientific information, increased consumer demand for goods and services need not so singularly promote resource exploitation and environmental degradation. For instance, the proportionate rise of the service sector in the U.S. economy presents new regulatory opportunities to effectively marshal consumer demand to promote industry practices that are less ecologically destructive. In particular, governmental measures designed to reduce the cognitive severance between ecological cause and effect could make consumers aware of the environmental implications of their choices. In this respect, some of the same technological innovations that have increased the cognitive divide could be utilized to bridge it.

Consumers have already shown that they are willing to pay a premium for environmental protection in a variety of settings. Many will pay more for fruits and vegetables grown with the use of little or no pesticides, beef from cattle raised in a less environmentally destructive manner, wood from sources not contributing to the destruction of rainforests, and tuna caught with "dolphin friendly" techniques. They are willing to pay hundreds of millions of dollars each year for water that they do not have to fear is contaminated with dangerous chemicals.

So far, however, most of these consumer-driven effects have been ad hoc in origin. With the exception of California's Proposition 65, described in chapter 6, government has not undertaken a systematic effort to provide consumers with the kind of information that would be needed to generate a broader environmental effect by influencing consumer demand. The successes that have been achieved are isolated and limited in their reach and have largely resulted from the work of a few innovative individuals in governmental and nongovernmental organizations. For this reason, there remains a tremendous untapped potential for achievement of environmental gains simply by providing consumers with better information. The same advertising techniques that have all too successfully promoted increased consumption could be just as effectively used to educate American consumers about the true social costs and unduly wasteful character of what has sadly been mistaken for signs of economic progress. The potential to change consumer behavior is huge, just simply untapped.[47]

The other end of the market equation—supply—is similarly promising. Many environmental improvements can be accomplished by persuading major suppliers of consumer goods and services—such as Kinko's, McDonald's, and Home Depot—to take the initiative. For example, they can buy products that are manufactured with lower adverse environmental impacts or choose to operate their own businesses in environmentally conscious ways, by, for instance, adopting more effective recycling programs or using less-polluting vehicles. As large purchasers, their market leverage can also serve as the functional equivalent of a governmental requirement for stricter environmental standards in products but absent the political

controversies implicated by direct governmental intervention. Very large
gains in resource productivity are already technologically possible and even
greater gains can be made available, given the correct market incentives.[48]

Moreover, the same technologies that have partly promoted the cognitive severance between consumer choice and ecological impact could instead be effectively used to bridge that gap. Computer technology may
convert natural environments actually being destroyed into unblemished
"virtual" environments that may reduce public concern for the original,
but this technology also has the potential for making people aware of consequences occurring in distant places. Other technology has the potential to gather the kind of information necessary to influence consumer
choices, which, as California's Proposition 65 has shown, can have immediate, widespread effect on industry practices. Illustrative of the possibili-
ties presented by the Internet and information technology is the effort of
the environmental organization Environmental Defense to make housing
prices more responsive to the rates at which nearby facilities fail to comply
with applicable environmental laws. The EPA now administers several
on-line data bases that provide information on environmental quality and
contamination. The EPA's AIRData provides access to air pollution data,
including monitoring and emissions data, for sites across the nation; and
the agency's Cumulative Exposure Project provides data on the cumulative
exposure of Americans to toxics through food, air, and water, including demographic analysis. But, here, too, what is missing is any systematic effort
by government to unleash the potential for such supply- or demand-driven
regulatory initiatives by converting such raw data information into a form
more readily accessible to deliberately targeted audiences.[49]

In short, consumer preference for environmental protection offers a
potential, largely untapped, source for promoting environmental initiatives by focusing more on both the upstream (suppliers) or downstream
(consumers) of market transaction. Further, the rise of the service industry
provides the government with readily available targets for converting that
consumer preference into market incentives for businesses to "voluntarily"
reduce and otherwise mitigate their adverse environmental impacts. It is
environmental law's current challenge to convert these shifting economies
and technologies into new opportunities for more effective regulation.

More effective and widespread use of recent advances in information
technology can likewise be used to change business norms and, accordingly,
business behavior. Consumers are not the only ones who may change in response to greater awareness of ecological cause and effect. Business interests
may do so as well, either simply because of the societal pressure inevitably
created by public exposure of the impacts of business activities or because
the information reveals new opportunities for industrial efficiencies and

therefore for both being "green" and making a profit. Better and more rapidly available information can promote less wasteful industrial practices and more finely tuned pollution controls.[50]

Some commentators argue that the persistent and compelling need to change consumer and business norms portends the emergence of a new generation of environmental laws, dubbed "reflexive" environmental law, that eschews primary reliance on command-and-control approaches in favor of laws that seek instead to instill environmentally protective norms in public and private organizational actors. Under reflexive law, government does not directly regulate private behavior, including pollution emissions and natural resource exploitation. Government instead strives by laws such as information disclosure and alternative compliance options like Interior's habitat conservation plans or the EPA's Project XL "to coordinate the goals and activities of various elements of society. . . . Government's role, in a reflexive perspective, is to ensure that appropriate information is generated, conveyed and exchanged"[51] rather than to direct specific substantive outcomes. While there is considerable merit in many of these proposals, it seems plain that, like tradeable emission policies, their value in the foreseeable future remains as useful supplements rather than as substitutes for the command and control system, as even some of the latter's most longstanding critics readily acknowledge.[52]

Finally, analogous arguments support reform of national economic indicators, which currently fail to reflect the societal cost of much natural resource exploitation. Because conventional national accounting practices generally fail to account for the free goods and services provided by nature —such as air, water, forests, mountains—they similarly fail to provide any ready signal when those resources are rapidly depleted or degraded. Current accounting practices also perversely value environmental degradation and fail to consider the long-term economic implications, let alone their noneconomic consequences. As described by the EPA's Science Advisory Board, "[n]ational accounting schemes typically characterize revenue generated by activities that deplete or degrade environmental resources as 'income'"—such as the harvesting of invaluable redwood forests or scarce Atlantic Bluefin Tuna—"while failing to consider the resulting depletion of society's environmental capital asset."[53] Absent any formal expression in national economic accounts, government and private sector decisionmakers do not have the information they need to assess properly the true state of the nation's economy and formulate policy accordingly. For this reason, economists are increasingly arguing that just as the information that consumers face must be improved to promote sound environmental decisionmaking, so too must national economic indicators be reformed to promote sound governmental economic policymaking.[54]

Regulating Diffuse Sources

More directed efforts to influence both supply and demand must also be an important part of a package of reforms needed for more systematic regulation of diffuse sources of pollution. Environmentalists, government regulators, and industry have all long acknowledged that further improvements in environmental quality—if not the avoidance of further environmental degradation—will depend on the achievement of such an expansion of regulatory focus. Whether air pollution emissions from increased motor vehicular traffic and larger automobiles, water pollution from nonpoint source runoff, household disposal of hazardous substances in batteries, fertilizers, and pesticides, or individual private property owners destroying species' habitat, the need for more effective management of diffuse pollution sources is as widespread as it is fraught with political controversy. The U.S. public has long displayed a reluctance for self-regulation that is only matched by its zeal for the regulation of larger, industrial sources. Moreover, regulation of the more diffuse sources triggers heightened constitutional concerns because of implications for federalism, private property, and personal liberty.

Affecting the supply-and-demand interests of diffuse sources is one attractive option for many of the reasons previously described. Better informed consumers are more likely to change their purchasing decisions and, to some extent, even their lifestyles for improvements in environmental quality. This is an area of environmental law that is potentially ripe for the kind of economic incentive programs long touted by economists and resisted by some in the environmental community. Such incentive programs can be positive in nature, as seen with the provision of subsidies for the retirement of higher polluting motor vehicles. They can also be negative in character, as seen with the imposition of higher fees for the disposal of household waste, use of highways at specified times, driving motor vehicles with low fuel efficiency, or consumption of electricity during peak periods. Finally, these incentive programs can be seemingly neutral in their imposition, as seen with the traditional deposit-and-refund mechanisms used to promote recycling. They are roughly akin to dedicated taxes on purchases of tobacco or alcohol products, justified because of the social costs those products invariably impose on the community as a whole. None of these kinds of incentive programs is likely to generate the degree of environmental ire that occurs when environmental law appears to allow industry to simply "pay to pollute."

Moreover, if more stringent pollution control standards on industry are coupled with the possibility of industrial sources receiving "pollution control credit" based on the success of their efforts to decrease pollution by such diffuse sources, it is quite likely that industry itself will provide the necessary economic incentives. Many in industry have long complained that it is unfair and inefficient to make them reduce pollution when existing diffuse sources of pollution could achieve similar reductions at far lower costs. Allowing industry to capture pollution control credits based on their efforts to promote pollution reduction at diffuse sources would at least address these efficiency concerns. Any such scheme would, of course, have to take care to guard against the potential for phantom reductions to be used as credits to permit very real pollution emissions, but the need for such safeguards should not preclude such tradeable emissions programs when the political obstacles presented by direct regulation of diffuse sources seem otherwise insurmountable.

A regulatory program directed at smaller, diffuse sources would also need to phase-in controls over time. The more diffuse the sources, the greater the likelihood that the impact of regulation will be proportionately more disruptive. Diffuse sources tend to be small and poorly situated to quickly change their current practices and are therefore highly resistant to doing so.

For this reason, a phasing-in of controls over time can render politically palatable what might otherwise have been simply too controversial. Quite often, there are less-polluting practices available to diffuse sources, and, if given ample time, such sources can adapt relatively easily. The ardor of regulatory resistance is therefore likely to be considerably reduced by phased-in controls. Accordingly, controls may be achieved sooner under a phased-in approach than under an approach immediately applicable in full because of the delays that would inevitably result from the controversy and challenges likely to be triggered by the latter.

Illustrative of the potential for positive reform is former Interior Secretary Babbitt's effort to enhance endangered species protection. Secretary Babbitt sought to apply species protection measures directed to homeowners and owners of smaller parcels of land. He did so by providing for safe harbor provisions that offered landowners some guarantees against increased regulation as well as by providing other incentive and transitional devices to landowners. While sometimes of questionable legality under existing statutory programs, Babbitt's initiatives exemplified the potential for more finely tuning the regulation of diffuse sources in a manner more responsive to their particular needs and concerns.

Constructing International Environmental Lawmaking Institutions

The construction of an institutional framework at the international level for the development, implementation, and ultimately the enforcement of international environmental law is another pressing area for legal inno-vation. Effective implementation of existing international environmental law is dependent on the success of such institutional capacity building, and, even more fundamentally, the development of the kinds of complex multi-national arrangements and understandings necessary for the next genera-tion of international environmental law will be stymied without it.[55]

International environmental law currently suffers simultaneously from having too much and too little. On the one hand, there are approximately a thousand international legal instruments that include significant provi-sions addressing environmental protection concerns. The terms of these agreements are invariably overlapping in some respects and inconsistent in others. The system of environmental law formed by these combined agree-ments is also notoriously inefficient to the extent that "[n]ormally there are separate secretariats, monitoring processes, meetings of parties, sources of dispute resolution for each treaty."[56]

On the other hand, entirely missing from the cacophony of existing le-gal instruments are comprehensive agreements capable of effectively ad-dressing some of the world's most pressing and intractable environmental problems. Global climate change is plainly the most obvious, but problems exist in a host of other areas, such as deforestation and loss of biodiversity. But even apart from the areas lacking any substantive agreements, what is missing is any meaningful international capacity for implementation and enforcement of the agreements that do exist. As suggested by the U.S. ex-perience with domestic environmental law, no international agreement can anticipate and address with any great specificity the details of environmen-tal protection requirements. Some delegation to regulatory agencies of the details of lawmaking will be necessary because of the sheer complexity of the problems to be addressed and the changing nature of their scien-tific and technological parameters. So too, international environmental law, like domestic environmental law, will require some effective mechanisms for enforcement. Here too, as in the case of domestic U.S. environmen-tal law, much of that enforcement leverage will likely need to be exerted against host governments rather than against the actual sources of pollution themselves.[57]

Exacerbating both of these problems is the absence of the kind of in-ternational institution that could be capable of both coordinating the laws we already have and overcoming the barriers to the development of the kinds of laws that the world desperately needs. Several international enti-ties play leading roles in international environmental protection, including the United Nations (UN) Environment Programme; the UN Development Programme; the Food and Agriculture Organization of the UN; the UN Educational, Scientific and Cultural Organization; the World Bank and its affiliated Global Environment Facility; the World Meteorological Organization; the World Trade Organization (WTO); the UN Commission on Sustainable Development; and the numerous individual secretariats arising out of separate environmental treaties and conventions. The result of this hodgepodge of regulatory agreements is "[d]issipation of focus, competition for limited resources, bureaucratic infighting, and poor coordination among the core environmental bodies."[58]

Complicating the problem is the stark contrast between the international institutional disorganization surrounding environmental protection and the relatively sophisticated organization surrounding areas of international trade policy. Now administered by the WTO, the provisions of the General Agreement on Tariffs and Trades (GATT) have proved to be a powerful and effective source of international policy development and enforcement. While many in the environmental community frequently complain about the tendency of the WTO and, formerly, the GATT itself to trump competing social values, including environmental protection, in favor of free trade, environmental regulators and environmentalists cannot help but be jealous of the WTO's institutional authority. For this reason, some commentators have suggested a parallel international framework for environmental protection that would either roughly replicate, or at least be of sufficient capacity and stature to work in tandem with, the WTO and the terms of the GATT.[59]

Many different institutional arrangements are possible, with varying advantages and disadvantages. A World Environment Organization could be formed inside or outside the UN, separate from or embracing the UN Environment Programme, and have more or less lawmaking and enforcement authority than the WTO. Of course, the normal conundrum would be presented by any organizational effort: the more effective the proposed organization, the more effective the opposition to its creation. While the nature of the ecological problems to be addressed compels the construction of an international institutional framework for lawmaking and implementation, the distributional dimension of environmental protection law would generate substantial initiatives to undermine any such construction effort.

The best chance for overcoming this obstacle to innovation would lie in ensuring that any international governing body was responsive to the very different distributional perspectives toward environmental protection held by developing versus developed nations. Developing nations would have to be given a voice, including voting rights that ensured that their interests were not subordinated to those of the developed nations. Lawmaking would be made commensurately more difficult, but those laws that were enacted would have a correspondingly better chance of being meaningfully implemented and enforced by domestic governments. Moreover, once the institutional frameworks were in place, the increasingly compelling nature of the scientific facts regarding the need for coordinated global action (as witnessed in recent years with the amassed evidence of global climate change) would likely provide the needed impetus for lawmaking and law enforcement to occur.

No doubt, as suggested by the U.S. domestic experience with acid rain and the regulation of interstate air pollution, any international restrictions on economic activities because of their polluting effects would likely need to be coupled with distributional initiatives that eased or even offset the short-term economic impacts for developing nations. But until the existing fragmented and incomplete framework for international environmental lawmaking is replaced by an institutional framework capable of supporting the necessary international dialogue, global environmental problems will worsen and become even more entrenched, as underscored by the unfortunate withdrawal of the United States from the Kyoto Protocol.

CHAPTER TEN

Environmental Law's Second (and Quite Different) "Republican Moment"

As described in part 2, one explanation for environmental law's emergence in the early 1970s was that the nation was then undergoing a "republican moment"—an " 'outburst of democratic participation and ideological politics' "[1]—epitomized by Earth Day, which overcame the political obstacles that would otherwise have precluded the enactment of strong environmental protection laws. More than thirty years later, the nation is facing a new and different kind of "Republican moment" that includes many of the essential political ingredients for accomplishing the kind of major reform of environmental protection laws that many in the regulated community have long been seeking. If the past is prologue, this latest reform effort will, like similar such efforts in the 1970s, 1980s, and 1990s, not only fail but prompt a public backlash in favor of even more stringent laws. There is, however, more reason to believe that such a similar rebuff is not necessarily in the offing.

In writing of this new "Republican moment," the word "Republican" is deliberately capitalized. While the earlier use of "republican moment" was meant to invoke the political tradition referred to as "civic republicanism," the latter use of "Republican" refers instead to the current National Republican Party. The "moment" facing environmental law is the virtually unprecedented ascendancy in 2003 of the Republican Party in all three branches of the federal government. Although this is not the first time since 1970 that a single political party has been so dominant within the national government, it is the first time that a single political party has been both dominant and so relatively unified in its effort to reform environmental law in the kinds of way that the regulated community has long supported.

This chapter discusses, first, the extent to which the national Republican and Democratic Parties have become fundamentally opposed on matters of environmental policy and how that divide has now spread far beyond the most political branch, Congress, to the executive and judicial branches as well. Discussed next is what this development portends for environmental law.

The Partisan Divide in Environmental Law

As described in chapter 7, by the end of the 1990s, the 104th Congress and the Contract with America had largely dissipated any 1970s' vestige of environmental law's being a nonpartisan issue. A starkly partisan divide now exists in environmental law and is reflected in the workings not just of Congress, but in all three branches of the federal government. Notwithstanding the persistence of remarkably similar rhetoric by candidates for elected office from the two major political parties, the two dominant policy positions of the parties have so evolved as to represent very different views on the efficacy of existing environmental protection law and the need for its reformation. These differences are not matters of incidental emphasis or tone; they express starkly contrasting visions of both the substantive ends as well as the means of environmental law. The Republican Party generally favors less stringent environmental controls and increased resource exploitation, while the Democratic Party generally favors stronger environmental protection standards and resource conservation and preservation laws.[2]

Much of the substantive policy disputes derive from differing attitudes toward the use of discount rates in assessing the benefits of environmental controls as well as differing degrees of faith in the ability of future technological innovation to obviate the need for controls now. For instance, the higher one discounts the value of future benefits created by environmental protection laws, the less significant those benefits appear to be in determining today whether they are worth the more immediate and certain costs of pollution controls and resource conservation measures. So too, the more one is willing to discount as just another projected monetizable benefit the future human lives that will be saved from environmental controls today, the less necessary those present environmental controls become. Finally, the more optimistic one is about the ability of future technology to address environmental problems or to provide ready substitutes for some natural resources, the less worthwhile it seems to undertake economic sacrifices now. In 1970, there was no discernible divide between the two parties on these underlying assumptions. As described in more detail below, that today is no longer true.[3]

But the differences in viewpoint and outlook between the two major parties, in fact, currently extend even further and deeper. They are fundamentally opposed on matters of first lawmaking principles, including the extent to which private property rights to natural resources should be protected, the efficacy and neutrality of market forces, and the necessity of a strong national government on matters of public health and welfare. Contemporary leaders of the Republican Party, including both those holding elected office and those within the Party's professional staff, are far more persuaded of the inviolability of private property rights in natural resources than are their Democratic counterparts, who are more likely to be persuaded of the need for government regulation because of the spatial and temporal spillovers caused by unrestricted resource exploitation. Furthermore, those in the Republican Party are more accepting of the proposition that market forces provide an efficacious, neutral, and fair basis for the allocation and distribution of the nation's natural resources wealth; Democrats are more likely to perceive the limitations of the market in this respect and to question the market's alleged "neutrality" and its inherent fairness.[4]

Chapter 7 highlighted the extent to which these fundamental policy differences are revealed in Congress by the extraordinary chasm that has developed between the votes of Democrats and Republicans in both the Senate and the House on environmental issues. What were relatively small voting record differences in the 1970s have polarized into opposite ends of the voting spectrum. That partisan divide in environmental law is not, however, confined just to actions within the legislative branch, where partisan politics is often the norm, but has apparently intensified so as to reach both the executive and judicial branches, where such partisan behavior should be least anticipated. It is because, moreover, the Republican Party in 2004 controlled both the federal executive and legislative branches and, to that extent, appointments to the judicial branch as well that this second "Republican moment" may prove so significant for environmental law.

Executive Branch

The George W. Bush administration makes quite plain the depth and extent of the chasm growing between the two political parties on environmental protection policy. The administration sought to reverse almost all of the major environmental initiatives promoted by the Environmental Protection Agency (EPA) and the Departments of Agriculture and the Interior under the Clinton administration. Reminiscent of the 1980s, the new administration immediately undertook a series of widely publicized changes in the direction of national environmental policy that drew the condemnation of environmentalists, the protest of leaders in the opposing political party, and the critical attention of the national news media. President Bush appointed Gale Norton and Spencer Abraham, prominent supporters of the Federalist Society, to head respectively the Department of the Interior and the Department of Energy, two of the most important environmental policymaking positions in the federal government. Based on the advice of Secretary Abraham and others, the president quickly took the dramatic step of unilaterally withdrawing the United States from the Kyoto Protocol on Climate Change, publicly undermining his own newly installed EPA administrator, former New Jersey governor Christine Todd Whitman. After weeks of closed meetings with industry leaders, the vice president subsequently announced a new national energy policy that reflected the priorities and economic interests of White House allies in the energy industry. The policy favored more domestic oil production and less environmental protection, and paid little attention to conservation opportunities.[5]

Both the EPA and the Interior Department likewise pursued policy changes that provoked accusations of undue industry influence. The EPA withdrew (only to later reinstate in the face of widespread criticism) the Clinton administration's stricter arsenic standard for drinking water; promulgated changes in Clean Air Act rules that severely undermined the legal basis of a major enforcement initiative launched by the Department of Justice under President Clinton against major stationary sources of air pollution; suspended and then reversed new, very ambitious Clinton administration regulations to implement the Clean Water Act's water quality standards; announced its opposition to a reauthorization of the Superfund tax on industry for the cleanup of abandoned and inactive hazardous waste sites; relaxed rules barring the disposal in valleys and streams of thousands of tons of fill from "mountaintop mining"; and, overturning prior agency policy, determined that the nation's most significant greenhouse gas—carbon dioxide—is not an "air pollutant" subject to Clean Air Act regulation. Even the essential credibility of scientific information released by the agency became suspect, in light of accusations that political appointees at the agency and in the White House had, to minimize adverse political fallout, scrubbed out information in EPA reports on the toxic effects of dust pollution in New York City after the September 11th terrorist attacks, on the increases in pollution that would be allowed under the president's "Clear Skies" air pollution control initiative, and on the scientific consensus regarding the very real problem of global climate change. According to environmental enforcement data released by the EPA in early 2003, civil enforcement penalties decreased by 45 percent in 2002 and criminal penalties decreased by 34 percent. High-ranking career EPA officers, including the agency's inspector general and enforcement chief, resigned in protest of administration policies.[6]

Similarly, at the Department of the Interior, Secretary Gale Norton took a series of steps that abruptly changed Interior policy from that formulated under the prior Democratic administration and then-Secretary of the Interior Bruce Babbitt. Secretary Norton eliminated strict Clinton administration environmental regulations and bonding requirements applicable to mining on public lands; authorized oil drilling near national parks; barred the reintroduction of grizzly bears to the Northwest; reversed the Clinton administration policy to now reopen Yellowstone National Park to snowmobiling; and reduced a Clinton administration two-year mining moratorium on 1 million acres under consideration for national monument designation to a ban of new mining on only 117,000 acres of the land. Secretary Norton also spearheaded the administration's effort to open up the Alaska Arctic National Wildlife Refuge to oil exploration and development, which the previous administration had consistently opposed.[7]

The Forest Service likewise rejected two major environmental initiatives promoted by the Clinton presidency. The first called for increased environmental protection in Forest Service planning both by enhancing environmental review and by imposing greater substantive limits on the extent to which activities in the national forests could impinge on environmental values, especially species diversity. The Bush administration first postponed the effectiveness of those rules and more recently proposed new rules that significantly scale back on substantive and procedural forest planning requirements. The second major Clinton initiative from which the Bush administration's Forest Service apparently retreated concerns protection of roadless areas in national forests. The Forest Service promulgated highly protective rules at the very end of the Clinton presidency. The Forest Service has since stepped away from actively defending those rules from industry court challenge, which reportedly prompted the resignation of both the chief and deputy chief of the Forest Service. When, moreover, environmentalists intervened in the aftermath of the Forest Service's abandonment of any legal defense and successfully defended on appeal the legality of the Clinton roadless rules, the Forest Service began seeking to prevent any further interventions by environmentalists arguing in favor of the Clinton rules. Other high-ranking career employees similarly resigned from other federal environmental agencies because of their increased frustration with the new administration's policies.[8]

Finally, the administration of President George W. Bush reignited the controversy that had last been stoked in the final months of his father's administration by expanding the role of the Office of Management and Budget (OMB) in overseeing agency environmental protection, health, and safety rulemaking. The president nominated John D. Graham to head OMB's Office of Regulatory Analysis. Graham, while at Harvard University's Center for Risk Analysis, had long championed greater use of cost–benefit analysis and comparative risk analysis in the setting of environmental standards. Comparative risk analysis questions whether more stringent environmental protection standards necessarily promote greater public health, safety, and welfare by taking into account the potential for those standards to increase other risks—for instance, by encouraging other harmful activities or simply by decreasing wealth—which may positively correlate with better standards of living and human health. Many in the environmental community are highly critical of comparative risk analysis, based on their belief that its proponents tend to use it only to limit rather than to extend environmental protections and ignore its analytical limitations. Under Graham, OMB sought to apply risk analysis to EPA rulemaking more aggressively than ever, and in a manner strongly reminiscent of the regulatory reform efforts promoted by the OMB under David Stockman in the early 1980s in the Reagan administration.[9]

Judicial Branch

The impact on environmental issues of the increasing partisan chasm between the two major political parties is not, moreover, simply confined to the conduct of appointed policymakers in the executive branch or of elected officials in the legislature. There is reason to believe that such a partisan divide is similarly evident in their respective appointees to the judiciary, as reflected in the votes of judges in individual environmental cases as well as the substantive content of the resulting judicial opinions. To be sure, no one has yet undertaken a broad-based systematic empirical evaluation of the relationship, if any, between the political party affiliation of those who appoint judges and the decisions of those judges in environmental cases. But the handful of those scholars who have made some effort—some based on anecdotal evidence, some on rough sampling, and some on more rigorous empirical data—all agree that such a politically partisan dimension does exist.

Much of the academic inquiry has focused on the D.C. Circuit. That circuit is a natural subject of academic focus in considering the partisan nature, if any, of judicial treatment of environmental law issues because of the central role it has played in environmental law. The D.C. Circuit is unique in that respect because, by congressional design, it is the court that considers a disproportionate number of the many challenges to federal agency environmental decisionmaking. The court has jurisdiction, sometimes exclusive and sometimes concurrent with other courts of appeals, to review environmental agency rulemakings in the first instance on petition for review, and in other instances simply on appeal from lower court determinations.[10]

Four different analyses of the environmental rulings of the D.C. Circuit have reached similar conclusions: there is a significant correlation between the political party of the president who named a judge to the D.C. Circuit and that judge's votes in environmental cases. A study published in 1988 found that "[i]n cases with significant ideological implications—most major agency rulemakings—democratic D.C. Circuit judges are more likely to reverse agency policies at the behest of individuals, and republican D.C. Circuit judges are more likely to reverse agency policies challenged by business interests."[11] A second statistical inquiry, published in 1997, reached even starker conclusions. Examining the specific "allegation [that] judges appointed by Republican Presidents vote principally for laxer regulation and judges appointed by Democratic Presidents vote for more stringent regulation," the author concluded that "ideology significantly influences judicial decisionmaking on the D.C. Circuit especially in cases that rais[e] procedural challenges, that are less likely to be reviewed by the United States Supreme Court."[12]

A third study, also published in 1997, reached similar conclusions based upon an empirical examination of the tendency of D.C. Circuit panels to defer to federal agency administrative determinations pursuant to the Supreme Court's 1984 ruling in *Chevron U.S.A., Inc. v. Natural Resources Defense Council, Inc.,* 467 U.S. 837 (1984). The authors "found that panels controlled by Republicans were more likely to defer to conservative agency decisions (that is, to follow the *Chevron* doctrine) than were the panels controlled by Democrats. Similarly, Democrat-controlled panels were more likely to defer to liberal agency decisions than were those controlled by Republicans."[13] Finally, in 1999, the results of a fourth study concerning the likelihood of Democratic-versus Republican-appointed D.C. Circuit judges voting to deny an environmental plaintiff standing found that, during the 1990s, "Republican judges voted to deny standing to environmental plaintiffs in 79.2% of cases, while Democratic judges voted to deny standing to environmental plaintiffs in only 18.2% of cases."[14]

Nor is there any reason to suppose that this phenomenon, if true, is confined to the lower courts. One could certainly fairly posit that a Supreme Court justice appointed in current times by a Democratic president is more likely to vote in favor of results sought by environmentalists than would a justice appointed by a Republican president, notwithstanding obvious counterexamples such as Justices Stevens and Souter, and further posit that the environmental protection aspect of a case is likely to be wholly irrelevant to most justices. Republican appointees to the High Court, in the existing political climate, are far more likely to be sympathetic to enhancing constitutional protections of private property rights, restricting citizen standing to maintain environmental lawsuits, and limiting the national government's Commerce Clause authority to address environmental protection and resource conservation concerns, such as endangered species and wetlands protection. President Bush's repeated statements during his campaign that Justices Scalia and Thomas represent the kind of judicial philosophy he would like to promote on the Court makes that quite clear, as does the Republican Party's obvious disapproval of the voting record of Justice Souter.[15]

In contrast, the voting records of both Justices Ginsburg and Breyer, a Democratic president's most recent nominees to the Court, place those two justices on the opposite end of the environmental protection spectrum from Justices Scalia and Thomas on virtually all of the cross-cutting constitutional law issues of central and contemporary importance to environmental law. Justices Ginsburg and Breyer favor more relaxed approaches to standing requirements as applied to environmental citizen suit plaintiffs, a less aggressive role for the Takings Clause as applied to environmental restrictions on private property rights, and a more expansive view of congressional Commerce Clause authority to regulate activities affecting environmental quality. Justices Scalia and Thomas, by contrast, favor more demanding standing requirements, a more aggressive application of the Takings Clause, and a more limited view of congressional Commerce Clause authority. In the federal system, accordingly, the relevant philosophies of prospective judicial nominees, including on matters related to environmental law, have become routine fodder for partisan campaigning in national elections.[16]

Finally, the marked number of environmental law cases before the Supreme Court during its October 2003 term reflects at least the perception, if not the reality, that the current Court is disproportionately sympathetic to arguments that favor narrow readings of federal environmental protection requirements. In virtually unprecedented numbers, both industry and the federal government have been requesting and obtaining Supreme Court review of lower court decisions favorable to environmentalists. In the absence of any of the normal indicia of lower court conflicting authority necessary for an exercise of the Court's jurisdiction, the Court agreed to hear an industry challenge to the EPA's authority to veto a state permit under the Clean Air Act that the agency considered too lax; an industry contention that the federal courts of appeals have too broadly construed the scope of the Clean Water Act's prohibition on discharges of pollutants into navigable waters; and an industry claim that the Clean Air Act precludes a regional lawmaking authority in southern California from requiring operators of vehicle fleets to purchase low-emission vehicles. Also before the Court either on the merits or for consideration for plenary review are several cases brought by the solicitor general of the United States. These include the federal government's contention that lower federal courts erred in allowing environmentalists to challenge the lawfulness of the government's management of potential wilderness areas; the vice president's refusal to release to environmentalists documents that would reveal private meetings that he and others on his Task Force on Energy with whom he worked might have had with industry while developing the task force's highly influential 2001 report on national energy policy; and the president's legal position that neither the Clean Air Act nor NEPA applies to implementing actions taken by federal agencies pursuant to the president's decision to allow increased volume of trucks from Mexico into the United States.[17]

To be sure, because of the strength of the merits of their legal positions, environmentalists prevailed in some of these cases. Once the justices have the opportunity to study a case closely on the merits, they tend to center themselves. The Court's docket nonetheless presents a remarkably one-sided picture. These are all cases in which the court ruling on review is one that favored the more environmentally protective outcome. There are two different, but no less troubling, explanations. First, environmentalists and governmental agencies are unilaterally declining to seek High Court review when they suffer an adverse decision in the lower courts detrimental to environmental protection concerns, because of their assumption that the Court is unlikely to grant relief. Or, second, the Court is denying review in cases in which the lower courts ruled against positions favored by environmentalists and, absent a request from the Solicitor General, granting review only in cases in which the lower courts ruled against positions favored by industry. Whatever the explanation, the upshot is that the only major environmental cases before the Court these days tend to be opportunities to reverse rulings that broadly construe environmental protection requirements rather than the converse. The very highest level of the federal judicial branch, therefore, joins both the legislative and executive branches as an unlikely forum for relief from statutes, regulations, and judicial decisions that fail to provide sufficient environmental protection.

The Portent of Environmental Law's Second "Republican Moment"

Because of the partisan divide that now dominates environmental law in national politics, the emergence of environmental law's second "Republican moment," albeit the first one with a capital rather than a lowercase "R," may well prove enormously significant in the law's evolution. Most simply put, much of environmental law's evolution during the past thirty years, especially its successful resistance to deregulation efforts launched by President Nixon in the 1970s, President Reagan in the 1980s, and the

104th Congress in the 1990s, can be traced either to the bipartisan appeal of environmental issues or to the politically divided nature of the federal government. As recently as 2001, partly in response to the Bush administration's initial environmental policies, Senator James Jeffords of Vermont stunned the nation by leaving the Republican Party to become an independent aligned with the Democratic Party. Jeffords's switch allowed the Democrats to obtain majority status in the Senate and Jeffords to chair the Senate Committee on the Environment and Public Works.

But for that same reason, the emergence in 2003 of this new "Republican moment" in environmental law may have enormous implications. For the first time ever, since the beginning of the modern environmental law era, the political appointees and nominees to all three branches of the federal government are effectively controlled by one political party that seems largely united in its intent to question and fundamentally reform existing pollution control and resource conservation laws. In the 1970s, 1980s, and 1990s, divided government and bipartisan politics blocked major reform efforts. In the 1970s and 1980s, Democrats in Congress played a significant role in blocking the reforms efforts undertaken in the Nixon, Reagan, and Bush administrations. The only difference in the 1990s was that the Republicans controlled Congress and the Democrats controlled the executive branch; Republicans in Congress sought the same kind of reforms that Republicans in the executive branch had sought in the 1980s, but now the Democrats in the executive branch rather than those in Congress played the critical role in blocking major reforms.[18]

Moreover, in the 1970s and 1980s, the coalitions that opposed what they perceived to be an undermining of necessary protections included prominent Republicans as well as Democrats. Hence, even while President Ronald Reagan enjoyed a Republican Senate majority in the early 1980s, the Republican senator who chaired the Senate Committee on the Environment and Public Works, Vermont's Robert Stafford, was a classic Northeast Republican who did not share the views of those seeking to reduce the law's protections. Senator Stafford and his staff, accordingly, worked closely with the minority Democratic staff on the Environment Committee to block the efforts of his own party's administration to make major changes in the laws. In the 1990s, Speaker of the House Gingrich was similarly stymied by Northeast Republicans both in the House, including New York's Sherwood Boehlert, and in the Senate, including Rhode Island's John Chafee, who then chaired the Senate Committee on Environment and Public Works. Finally, as previously described, it was yet another Northeast Republican, James Jeffords, who stood as a barrier at the beginning of the current Bush administration's term in office.

Just two years later, the political dynamic dramatically shifted and in potentially historic fashion. The leadership of Republican Party became fairly united, including its chairs of the relevant legislative committees and cabinet officers. In the Senate, for example, Oklahoma Republican senator James Inhofe replaced the Independent senator James Jeffords as chair of the Senate Committee on the Environment and Public Works. New Mexico Republican senator Pete Domenici replaced the Democratic senator Jeff Bingaman (also from New Mexico) as chair of the Senate Committee on Energy and Natural Resources. Senator Inhofe has been a long-standing critic of EPA policies and Senator Domenici has long advocated increased resource development on public lands, including oil and gas exploration in the Arctic National Wildlife Refuge. The League of Conservation Voter (LCV) scores for Senators Inhofe and Domenici, based on their voting records on environmental legislation, for the first session of the 107th Congress were "0" and "8," respectively; the scores of Senators Bingaman and Jeffords were "64" and "76," respectively. An LCV score of "0" means that a member of Congress failed to support any of the environmental policy positions supported by the LCV, while a score of "100" reflects support for all LCV positions.[19]

Nor do the nation's environmental groups seem as able as they have been in the past to prevent the accomplishment of a major deregulatory initiative. The past successes of those organizations have largely depended on their ability to tap into public concerns and to lend their expertise to branches of government sympathetic to their concerns. In the current political environment, such a sympathetic government ear is increasingly hard, however, for environmentalists to discover, as it is difficult for environmentalists to attract the attention of the public, let alone financial contributors. In the early 1980s and then again in the mid-1990s, environmental activists quickly converted public concerns with the environmental policies of the Reagan administration and then with the 104th Congress into their own political muscle. The memberships of environmental organizations dramatically increased as did their fundraising.[20]

Today, no comparable massive infusion of funds and resources seems soon headed to national environmental organizations. Public support for strong environmental protection measures remains strong, but, apart from the obvious declining national economy, two developments have further reduced the ability of the national groups to rally public concern to bolster their resources.

First, the Republican Party has steadfastly avoided including a major reform of environmental laws as any part of its overt political agenda. Republicans have strategically sought to deemphasize their policy differences with Democrats on environmental issues. They have sought, in short, to avoid any repetition of the political mistakes they made with sweeping rhetoric during both the early Reagan years and the initial celebration of the Contract with America a decade later. They are, in effect, heeding Senator John McCain's advice that more regulatory reform can be achieved by using the "scalpel of reform" rather than the "meat ax of repeal."[21]

A document published for Republican elected officials and candidates by a Republican pollster is illustrative. It admonishes Republicans to "assure your audience that you are committed to 'preserving and protecting' the environment, but that 'it can be done more wisely and effectively.'" The document warns, "Absolutely do not raise economic arguments first," and instead "[t]ell them a personal story from your life." The document continues to advise that "[t]he three words Americans are looking for in an environmental policy . . . are 'safer,' 'cleaner,' and 'healthier'" and that Republicans should "[s]tay away from 'risk assessment,' 'cost–benefit analysis,' and the other traditional environmental terminology used by industry and corporations."[22]

The Republican Party seems to understand that the success of its legislative and executive branch efforts to reform environmental law will turn on whether they can avoid interfering with the public's aspiration for environmental protection. One obvious lesson of the past thirty years is that, although public aspirations for the strictest possible environmental protection laws have remained strong and seemingly uncompromising, a substantial divide remains between those aspirations and the public's actual commitment to change behavior and absorb short-term economic costs. Americans have shown increasing, not decreasing, appetites for resource consumption and less willingness to sacrifice the short term for the uncertainties of the long term, especially when resource preservation rather than human health protection is at stake.

The emerging Republican strategy reflects that divide between aspirations and commitment. Republican leaders seeking reform of existing environmental laws take care not to denounce the public's aspirations, but to embrace them, while reassuring the public those aspirations can be realized without the kind of immediate, substantial economic costs imposed by many existing environmental laws. The voters' elections of Presidents Ronald Reagan, George H. W. Bush, and George W. Bush to the White House and the emergence since the mid-1990s of Republican majorities in the House and, except for a brief interlude, in the Senate certainly provide strong empirical support for the effectiveness of that strategy.

Second, and perhaps even more fundamentally, post September 11th, 2001, the immediate threats created by the specter of a nation going to war, coupled with increasing economic hardship, redirected the public's focus away from the longer-term perspective of environmental law. Both the fundraising and political organizing abilities of environmental organizations have, accordingly, been substantially undercut. Ironically, while it was the hopelessness and social divisiveness of the Vietnam War that helped fuel the environmental movement in the late 1960s and early 1970s, it is the threat of domestic terrorism and prolonged war in the Middle East that appears to be sapping the movement of much of its political force more than three decades later.

There is, however, preliminary evidence that the states may increasingly step in to fill the political void in environmental lawmaking left by the absence of divided government at the federal level. Just a few years ago, the major voices heard from the states seemed primarily to be from those state officials complaining about the heavy-handedness of the federal government in compelling state acceptance and administration of strict pollution control laws. Heads of state environmental agencies complained that the EPA was interfering with state effectiveness, while insisting that "states are not branch offices of the Federal Government."[23] The agency, in turn, publicly expressed its skepticism of the effectiveness of some state efforts, concluding that many states lacked either the capacity or the will to enforce environmental requirements aggressively. The EPA threatened on several occasions to withdraw federal approval of state programs, but rarely carried out those threats.[24]

More recently, by contrast, the states are increasingly the ones either cajoling the federal government to do more or themselves initiating more demanding regulation. In the aftermath of the Bush administration's withdrawal from the Kyoto Protocol to the United Nations Framework Convention on Climate Change, many states passed their own laws designed to reduce emissions that might contribute to global warming. By late 2003, approximately half of the states had passed such legislation. Many states also brought formal legal challenges against the federal government. In late 2002 and early 2003, a group of (not coincidentally downwind) northeastern and western states publicly condemned the federal government's air pollution control policy and announced a series of court challenges. In December 2002, six northeastern states and the State of Washington challenged in court the EPA's newly issued New Source Review regulations under the Clean Air Act, on the ground that they unduly relaxed pollution control requirements applicable to existing major stationary sources of air pollution. In February 2003, three states in the Northeast gave formal notice of their intent to sue the EPA for failing to establish ambient air standards and regulations for carbon dioxide as a so-called criteria pollutant under the Clean Air Act, which would require nationwide regulations. Later that same month, ten northeastern states gave the EPA formal notice that they would sue the agency for failing to regulate carbon dioxide emissions from power plants under the Clean Air Act, as well as failing to update federal regulation of sulfur dioxide and particulate matter emissions from those plants. Finally, in November 2003, the attorneys general of New York and Connecticut announced they would bring new enforcement actions to fill the void left by the EPA's decision to drop lawsuits filed during the Clinton administration against old coal-fired power plants.[25]

Symbolic of the shift, California seems to be resurrecting the leadership role that it took in the 1960s. The state has sought to regulate carbon dioxide emissions, a greenhouse gas linked to global warming, stepping into an area of pollution control that the EPA has long declined to embrace and the Bush administration has shied away from.[26] California has also taken a leadership position in promoting so-called zero-emission motor vehicles. In the absence of an oppositional party in Congress capable of launching the kind of formal oversight hearings critical of administration policies, states like California appear to be taking on that role. Hence, in announcing its recent lawsuit against the EPA for relaxing air pollution control standards, California's attorney general declared that "[t]his is just one example of a much broader Bush plan to roll back existing environmental protections and encroach on California's authority to enforce its own laws. The Administration can try to make its policies more attractive by dressing them up as 'Healthy Forests' and 'Clean Skies.' We're not fooled. And we're not lying down."[27]

Of course, only time will tell whether environmental law's now-looming second "Republican moment" will be as significant for environmental law's evolution as was its first "republican moment." Perhaps the events of the early years of the new millennium will ultimately stand in parallel to the failed reform movements of the 1970s, 1980s, and 1990s, and even propel public demand for ever more stringent environmental protection laws. Or perhaps, history will tell a different story, in which the early efforts of the regulated community in the 1970s to develop an intellectual, scientific, and economic counterweight to environmentalism finally bore fruit in a second "Republican moment" decades later.

CONCLUSION

The Graying of the Green

Some conclusions about modern environmental law come easily. It defied most soothsayers of the 1970s, especially in the United States, who predicted that it would be a mere "fad" or "flash in the pan." The laws were neither systematically gutted by subsequent legislation nor were they the object of merely symbolic implementation. Pollution control and natural resource protection laws instead persisted, expanded, and settled into the legal landscape, changing legal norms throughout the nation's intersecting laws. By the end of the twentieth century, private economic expectations were more likely to depend on the existence of pollution control and natural resource conservation laws than they were to be surprised and frustrated by them.

Nor have the prophesies come true of those doomsayers who contended that strict environmental laws would lead to the collapse of the U.S. economy or that the laws were too late and too weak to avoid immediate environmental catastrophes. Not only has the U.S. economy generally thrived during the past several decades, but it has done so while making remarkable strides in many areas of environmental protection. The nation avoided many of the environmental disasters that such a rapidly increasing economy might well have otherwise caused, and did cause in other industrialized countries. The nation enjoyed decreased pollution and increased resource conservation in many significant respects, notwithstanding significant gaps in the coverage of existing laws. None of the extreme predictions of some environmentalists during the 1960s of water and food rationing or dramatically shortened life expectancies occurred in the 1970s or since, although the ongoing collapses of fisheries and accelerated rates of species extinction underscore that the environmental stakes of the past several decades have been quite real.

The actual costs of pollution controls have, moreover, almost always proved to be less than those industry projected in initially opposing their

251

imposition. Strict controls on automobile emissions were not "impossible," but were instead readily achievable. Industry estimated in 1990 that volatile organic compound controls applicable to stationary sources would cost $14.8 billion per year; the actual costs are now projected to be about $960 million. In 1989, the utility industry predicted that the Clean Air Act's acid rain program for the control of sulfur dioxide emissions would cost between $4.1 and $7.4 billion per year; actual costs are now estimated to be from $1 to $2 billion per year. Nor did the chemical industry prove correct in their exaggerated complaints that accelerating the phasing out of ozone-depleting chlorofluorocarbons would cause major economic disruption; industry quickly developed a ready chemical substitute for those chemical compounds being banned.[1]

By contrast, the benefits of pollution controls and natural resource management have often been much higher than initially anticipated, to the extent that they even lend themselves to monetization. Serious human health effects from particulate matter, for instance, turned out to be a larger problem than scientists first thought, which has prompted a further tightening of applicable air quality standards both in terms of the minimum size of particulate manner regulated and allowable concentrations in the ambient air. We also now better appreciate that the substantial benefits of environmental laws extend to the promotion of economically productive activities, including both those many large industries (e.g., fishing, tourism, computer technology) that depend upon a clean environment for producing their goods and services, as well as those new businesses that make up the burgeoning multibillion dollar environmental protection industry.

Likewise rebuffed have been those political scientists who contended that environmentalism is fundamentally incompatible with a democratic form of government. The experience of the last several decades suggests quite the opposite is true. Environmental protection law has generally fared much better under more democratic forms of government and has not promoted the ascendancy of fascist, totalitarian regimes. Less democratic governments have in fact fared more poorly than democratic polities. One reason for the difference likely has been the fundamental role that information disclosure has proven to play in environmental law, a basic policy that is promoted within democratic government and often viewed as antithetical to more totalitarian governed societies.

The decades since the early 1970s have not, however, been easy or quiet times for environmental law. They have been tumultuous, fraught with increasing social controversy and political conflict. This should not be a surprise. Nor is it necessarily unhealthy. As described at the outset of this book, there are deeply ingrained structural reasons for such controversy and conflict, ultimately rooted in a series of mismatches that exist between the kinds of laws necessarily promoted by environmental law and the demands and preferences of U.S. lawmaking institutions and processes. It is not easy to pass, implement, and enforce laws that impose costs on some and benefits on others, especially when the associated costs and benefits are potentially massive, riddled with uncertainty, and spread out over tremendous spatial and temporal dimensions. It is not easy to pass, implement, and enforce laws where the problems being addressed often promote centralized government decisionmaking, but where there are countervailing social values, embedded in the Constitution, that both limit such centralization and minimize government restrictions on individual activity. And, it is not easy to pass, implement, and enforce laws, when constantly changing technology and scientific information promote corresponding changes in complex legal rules, but the nation's lawmaking scheme prefers laws that are stable, settled, and clear.

The 1970s, 1980s, and 1990s, as well as events in more recent years, are simply illustrative of the resulting tensions. They explain why Nixon embraced environmentalism early on, but then concluded that it was a policy issue unlikely to provide short-term political awards; the consummate politician, Nixon quickly recognized that environmental protection was "not a good political issue, only a good defensive one."[2] These same tensions explain why the "regulatory taking issue" and "federalism" have been such persistent legal issues during more than three decades. They also explain why it is so intractably difficult to construct an effective set of legal institutions and laws to address global environmental issues, like global climate change, despite the increasing clarity of the scientific case for doing so.[3]

Notwithstanding the resulting debates and disagreements over its proper direction, environmental law has been remarkably successful, as it has evolved from a radical intruder into an essential element of a mature legal system in a democratic society. There has been slippage. There are the inevitable regulatory perversities: minor problems overregulated and major problems largely ignored. And there have been some serious and persistent socioeconomic and racial inequities, especially in the distribution of benefits of pollution controls. Some reform is justified. But a more careful, rigorously analytical approach in the first instance would likely have had far less success in terms of actual protections achieved than the more dramatic laws that the nation instead embraced over industry's objections. Sometimes, society is better off simply by hitting a problem with the legal equivalent of a two-by-four rather than taking the years necessary to determine the problem's precise dimensions and the optimum legal regime possible for its addressing.

Sheer human passion for human health and for the natural world supplied much of the necessary evolutionary force in environmental law's overcoming the hurdles impeding the enactment of such radically redistributive laws. Absent such passionate commitment to the goals of environmental law, including what must often seem to be the environmentalist's unreasonable refusal to compromise, it seems unlikely that environmental law would have achieved so much. It requires great stubbornness to overcome the strong political forces that are generated in opposition to laws that promise uncertain results only in the distant future at the expense of more discernible costs in the immediate present. Pragmatism is an essential element in effective lawmaking, but it is no substitute for passion and moral commitment.

However, neither modern environmental law in the United States nor those remarkable individuals who played such phenomenal and persistent roles in its promotion still possess the unbridled youthfulness and uncompromising focus they once enjoyed. In their own distinctive ways, they have each grayed. There is now greater appreciation of the pitfalls associated with perceiving policy disputes as always presenting starkly contrasting images of good versus evil. For many, there is also an inevitable sobering of aspirations and of their assessment of the American public's willingness to change individual behavior.

This aging of environmental law and environmentalism raises the larger issue of whether environmental law can maintain the passion and commitment needed to rebuff the never-ending efforts to make it more responsive to the concerns of the here and now at the expense of those in seemingly distant places and future times. The current winds of domestic political polarization, international instability, and armed conflict would seem to make it difficult to be optimistic that the nation and international community will soon be ready to work together to negotiate effective and equitable ways for addressing ever-looming global environmental problems. Perhaps, however, akin to the nation's experience with the Vietnam War in the late 1960s and early 1970s, the world and nation will emerge from current events more ready than ever to work together. The United States, needing to show the rest of the world its willingness to engage in multilateral cooperative efforts, could make environmental lawmaking emblematic of its renewed commitment. That the world's religions are beginning to develop a distinct spiritual environmentalist voice is suggestive of the possibility of such a future turn of events. The competing pathways that the nation and the world currently face are unsettlingly different. But, of course, that is a story for another teller and for another time.

Notes

Introduction

1. John Brooks Flippen, *Nixon and the Environment* 214 (2000).

2. North American Association of Environmental Education, www.naaee.org; U.S. Department of Commerce, Office of Environmental Technologies Exports of the Department of Commerce International Trade Administration (http://infoserv2.ita. doc.gov/ete/eteinfo.nsf/068f3801d047f26e85256883006ffa54/ 4878b7e2fc08ac6d85256883006c452c?OpenDocument) (data on domestic pollution control industry).

3. EPA, Draft Report on the Environment 2003, ii, xi (May 2003); EPA, Office of Air Quality Planning and Standards, Latest Findings on National Air Trends: 2000 Status and Trends, 5 (September 2001); Vice President Al Gore Clean Water Act Remarks, The Clean Water Act: A Snapshot of Progress in Protecting America's Waters (October 20, 1997) (25th anniversary of Clean Water Act), www.epa.gov/owow/cwa/25 report.html (visited May 14, 2002); Jonathan Rauch, "America Celebrates Earth Day— For the 31st Time," 32 *Nat'l J.* 1333 (April 29, 2000); Council on Environmental Quality, Twenty-fifth Anniversary Report (1997).

4. EPA, Office of Air Quality Planning and Standards, Latest Findings on National Air Quality, at 5–6; Council on Environmental Quality, Environmental Quality: The 1996 Report of the Council on Environmental Quality 42–44 (1997); "EPA: The First Twenty Years, Interview with William K. Reilly, EPA Administrator," 16 *EPA J.* 120 (Sept.–Oct. 1990).

Part One

1. See, e.g., R. A. Falk, *This Endangered Planet* (1972); H. J. McCloskey, *Ecological Ethics and Politics* 156 (1983); see generally R. J. Johnston, *Nature, State, and Economy* 139, 241–43 (1996); Michael Zimmerman, "The Threat of Ecofascism," 21 *Social Theory and Prac.* 207–38 (1995); William Ophuls, *Ecology and the Politics of Scarcity* (1977); Garrett Hardin, "The Tragedy of the Commons," 162 *Science* 1243, 1247–48 (1968);

Jonathan Porritt, *Seeing Green: The Politics of Ecology Explained* (1984); Robert Garner, *Environmental Politics* (1996).

Chapter One

1. Richard Grove, "The First Environmentalists," 15 *Wilson Q.* 66, 67 (Spring 1991).

2. George Perkins Marsh, *Man and Nature; Or Physical Geography as Modified by Human Action* 3 (1965 ed.).

3. Norman L. Christensen, Ann M. Bartuska, James H. Brown, Stephen Carpenter, Carla D'Antonio, Robert Francis, Jerry F. Franklin, James A. MacMahon, Reed F. Noss, David J. Parsons, Charles H. Peterson, Monica G. Turner, and Robert G. Woodmansee, "The Report of the Ecological Society of America Committee on the Scientific Basis for Ecosystem Management," 6 *Ecological Applications* 665–91 (August 1996).

4. See, e.g., R. A. Houghton and David L. Skole, "Carbon," in *The Earth as Transformed by Human Action: Global and Regional Changes in the Biosphere over the Past 300 Years* 393 (B. L. Turner ed., 1990); see also William K. Stevens, "Seas and Soils Emerge as Keys to Climate," *New York Times,* May 16, 2000, D1 ("[As] part of one of nature's grand and endlessly complicated global recycling networks[,] carbon is constantly exchanged among the air, the terrestrial biosphere, the oceans and the solid rock of the earth at varying rates on time scales ranging from hours to millions of years.").

5. Rudolf B. Husar and Janja Djukic Husar, "Sulfur," in *The Earth as Transformed by Human Action,* at 411.

6. Ibid., 411–14.

7. Boris G. Rozanov, Biktor Targulian, and D. S. Orlov, "Soils," in *The Earth as Transformed By Human Action,* at 203.

8. Ibid., 204.

9. Jill Jager and Robert G. Barry, "Climate," in *The Earth as Transformed by Human Action,* at 335.

10. See Andrew C. Revkin, "The Devil Is in the Details: Efforts to Predict Global Warming Hinge on Gaps in Climate Models," *New York Times,* July 3, 2001, D1, D2 (quoting Dr. Michael E Schlesinger, Director, Climate Research, University of Illinois).

11. Jager and Barry, "Climate," in *The Earth as Transformed by Human Action,* at 336–50; see William K. Stevens, "Seas and Soils Emerge as Keys to Climate," *New York Times,* May 16, 2000, D1.

12. Richard White, "Environmental History, Ecology, and Meaning," 76 *J. Am. Hist.* 1111, 1115 (1990), quoting Edward Goldsmith, "Ecological Succession Rehabilitated," 15 *Ecologist* 3 (1985).

13. Aldo Leopold, *A Sand County Almanac and Sketches Here and There* 225 (paperback ed. 1968).

14. First quotation from Turner, *The Earth as Transformed by Human Action,* at 1; second quotation from Peter M. Vitousek, Harold A. Mooney, Jane Lubchenco, and Jerry M. Melillo, "Human Domination of the Earth's Ecosystems," 277 *Science* 494, 494 (1997). See also J. R. McNeil, *Something New under the Sun: An Environmental History of the World* (2000).

15. Richard N. L. Andrews, *Managing the Environment, Managing Ourselves: A History of American Environmental Policy* 353 (1999); Vitousek et al., "Human Domination," at 494, 495; U.S. Department of Commerce National Marine Fisheries Services, *Our Living Oceans: The Economic Status of U.S. Fisheries* 1 (1996); Turner, *The Earth as Transformed by Human Action,* at 6.

16. Rozanov, Targulian, and Orlov, "Soils," at 213.

17. Andrew Goudie, *The Human Impact on the Natural Environment* 167 (4th ed. 1994); Howard W. French, "China's Growing Deserts Are Suffocating Korea," *New York Times,* April 14, 2002, sec. 1, p. 3, col. 1; McNeil, *Something New under the Sun,* at 48.

18. Husar and Husar, "Sulfur," at 410.

19. Vitousek et al., "Human Domination," at 496.

20. Halina Szejnwald Brown, Roger E. Kasperson, and Susan Swedis Raymond, "Trace Pollutants," in *The Earth as Transformed by Human Action,* at 437–53.

21. "Ecology: The New Great Chain of Being," 77(10) *Natural Hist.* 8–16, 60–69 (1968).

22. Lee Davis, *Environmental Disasters* 97 (1998); see also National Marine Fisheries Service, U.S. Department of Commerce, *Our Living Oceans: The Economic Status of U.S. Fisheries* 10–28 (1996); Thomas E. Dahl, *Wetlands Losses in the United States: 1780s to 1980s* (1990); Harry E. Schwarz, Jacque Emel, William J. Dickens, Peter Rogers, and John Thompson, "Water Quality and Flows," in *The Earth as Transformed by Human Action,* at 255; Goudie, *Human Impact,* at 177–226.

23. D. J. Rapport, H. A. Regier, and T. C. Hutchinson, "Ecosystem Behavior under Stress," 125 *Am. Naturalist* 617, 626, 635 (1985).

24. "Threats to Coral Reefs," *Seaweb,* www.seaweb.org/background/book/coral.html (visited February 26, 2003); U.S. Coral Reef Task Force, Working Group on Ecosystem Science and Conservation Research and Monitoring: Proposed Actions (March 1, 1999), http://coralreef.gov/research.cfm (visited February 26, 2003); National Oceanic & Atmospheric Administration News, *NOAA Scientists Are Working with Two Australian Groups to Improve Coral Reef Monitoring* (March 5, 1999), www.seaweb.org/background/book/coral.html (visited February 26, 2003).

25. Lester Brown, *The Twenty-ninth Day* (1978); Edwin Dale, "The Economics of Pollution," *New York Times Magazine,* April 19, 1970, *reprinted in* Louis L. Jaffee and Laurence H. Tribe, *Environmental Protection* 16–23 (1971).

26. Ibid.

27. Robert L. Peters and Thomas E. Lovejoy, "Terrestrial Fauna," in *The Earth as Transformed by Human Action,* at 353.

28. Turner, *The Earth as Transformed by Human Action,* at 13; Vitousek et al., "Human Domination," at 488; Mathis Wackernagel, Niels B. Schulz, Diana Deumling, Alejandro Callejas Linares, Martin Jenkins, Valerie Kapos, Chad Monfreda, Jonathan Loh, Norman Myers, Richard Norgaard, and Jorgen Randers, "Tracking the Ecological Overshoot of the Human Economy," 99(14) *Proc. Nat'l Acad. Sci. USA* 9266–71 (2002).

29. McNeil, *Something New under the Sun,* at 4; Brian C. O'Neill and Michael Oppenheimer, "Dangerous Climate Impacts and the Kyoto Protocol," 296 *Science* 1971–72 (2002).

Chapter Two

1. Dan Tarlock, "The Future of Environmental 'Rule of Law' Litigation," 17 *Pace Envtl. L. Rev.* 237, 257 (2000).

2. William H. Rodgers, *Environmental Law* § 1.2 (p. 24), § 3.2 (p. 146) (2d ed. 1994).

3. 40 C.F.R. § 50.7 (2000) (national ambient air quality standard for particulate matter); 62 Fed. Reg. 38,652 (July 18, 1997) (promulgation of final particulate matter standard).

4. 40 C.F.R. §§ 261.3, 261.21, 261.22, 261.23, 261.24 (2000) (definition of "hazardous waste").

5. United States v. Riverside Bayview Homes, 474 U.S. 121, 134 (1985); 33 C.F.R. § 323.2c (2000) (definition of "wetlands").

6. R. J. Johnston, *Nature, State, and Economy* 43 (1996); R. A. Houghton, and David L. Skole, "Carbon," in *The Earth as Transformed by Human Action: Global and Regional Changes in the Biosphere over the Past 300 Years* 393 (B. L. Turner ed., 1990).

7. See Mark Powell, "Introduction," *Science at EPA: Information in the Regulatory Process* 1–18 (1999); Thomas McGarity, "Substantive and Procedural Discretion in Administrative Resolution of Science Policy Questions: Regulating Carcinogens in EPA and OSHA," 67 *Geo. L.J.* 729 (1979); Samuel P. Hays, *Beauty, Health, and Permanence: Environmental Politics in the United States, 1955–1985,* 332–33, 342–43 (1987).

8. Dan Tarlock, "The Nonequilibrium Paradigm in Ecology and the Partial Unraveling of Environmental Law," 27 *Loy. L.A. L. Rev.* 1121, 1133 (1994).

9. Daniel A. Farber, "Environmental Protection as a Learning Experience," 7 *Loy. L.A. L. Rev.* 791, 791 (1994).

10. Philip M. Boffey, "The Debate over Dioxin," *New York Times,* June 25, 1983, A1:3, Keith Schneider, "New View Calls Environmental Policy Misguided," *New York Times,* March 21, 1993, A1:1; Gina Kolata, "Draft Report Raises Dioxin Risk, but Some Experts Contest It," *New York Times,* May 18, 2000, A27:1.

11. Stephen Budiansky, *Nature's Keepers: The New Science of Nature Management* (1995).

12. See, e.g., Amoco Prod. Co. v. Village of Gambell, 480 U.S. 531, 542 (1987) ("Environmental injury, by its nature, . . . is often permanent or at least of long duration, *i.e.,* irreparable. If such injury is sufficiently likely, therefore, the balance of harms will usually favor the issuance of an injunction to protect the environment."); Dolan v. City of Tigard, 512 U.S. 374, 411 (Stevens, J., dissenting) ("In our changing world one thing is certain; uncertainty will characterize predictions about the impact of new urban developments on the risks of floods, earthquakes, traffic congestion, or environmental harms. When there is doubt concerning the magnitude of those impacts, the public interest in averting them must outweigh the private interest of the commercial entrepreneur.").

13. See Howard A. Latin, "The 'Significance' of Toxic Health Risks: An Essay on Legal Decisionmaking under Uncertainty," 10 *Ecology L.Q.* 339 (1982).

14. See Office of Management and Budget, *Draft Report to Congress on the Costs and Benefits of Federal Regulations,* 67 Fed. Reg. 15014, 15037 (March 28, 2002) (table 11).

15. Joseph L. Sax, "Comment on Harte's Paper, 'Land Use, Biodiversity, and Ecosystem Integrity: The Challenge of Preserving Earth's Life Support System,'" 27 *Ecology L.Q.* 1003, 1007 (2001) ("difficulty . . . of linking specific conduct to the diffuse, sometimes remote-in-time, large-scale adverse impacts about which we are ultimately concerned").

16. Mary Evelyn Tucker and John A. Crim, eds., *Religion and Ecology: Can the Climate Change* 1–22, 23–31, symposium issue of *Daedalus* (Fall 2001).

17. Hays, *Beauty, Health, and Permanence,* at 363–65; Mark Sagoff, *The Economy of the Earth: Philosophy, Law, and the Environment* (1988); Steve Kelman, *What Price Incentives?: Economists and the Environment* (1981).

18. See, e.g., Bruce Yandle, "Escaping Environmental Feudalism," 15 *Harv. J.L. & Pub. Pol'y* 517 (1992); Roger Pilon, "Property Rights, Takings, and a Free Society," 6 *Harv. J.L. & Pub. Pol'y* 165 (1983).

Chapter Three

1. Reno v. Condon, 528 U.S. 141 (2000) (Tenth Amendment); College Sav. Bank v. Florida Prepaid Post-Secondary Educ. Expense Bd., 527 U.S. 666 (1999) (Eleventh Amendment).

2. United States v. Midwest Oil Co., 236 U.S. 459 (1915); Sanjay Ranchod, "The Clinton National Monuments: Protecting Ecosystems with the Antiquities Act," 25 *Harv. Envtl. L. Rev.* 535 (2001); 16 U.S.C. § 431 (2000).

3. John W. Bennett and Kenneth A. Dahlberg, "Institutions, Social Organization, and Cultural Values," in *The Earth as Transformed by Human Action: Global and Regional Changes in the Biosphere over the Past 300 Years* 73 (B. L. Turner ed., 1990).

4. See, e.g., International Paper Co. v. Ouellette, 479 U.S. 481 (1987) (manufacturing facility in New York with discharge pipe that released effluent in portion of lake just shy of Vermont border); Georgia v. Tennessee Copper, 206 U.S. 230 (1907) (copper plant in Tennessee that emitted sulfurous fumes that resulted in significant harm in Georgia); Commonwealth Edison Co. v. Montana, 453 U.S. 609 (1981) (90 percent of coal subject to state coal severance tax imposed on coal exported out of state).

5. See, e.g., Hodel v. Virginia Surface Mining Ass'n, 452 U.S. 264 (1981); Gibbs v. Babbitt, 214 F.3d. 483 (4th Cir. 2000) (upholding constitutionality of the Endangered Species Act); but see Solid Waste Agency of Northern Cook County v. U.S. Army Corps of Eng'rs, 531 U.S. 159 (2001) (narrowly construing jurisdictional scope of Clean Water Act to avoid constitutional issue).

6. As discussed in chapter 7, the Supreme Court embarked down just such a constitutional path in the 1990s, thereby unsettling the constitutional foundations of modern environmental law. See pages 132–37.

7. See, e.g., C & A Carbone Inc. v. Town of Clarkstown, 511 U.S. 383 (1994); Oregon Waste Sys. v. Environmental Dep't, 511 U.S. 93 (1994); Chemical Waste Management, Inc. v. Hunt, 504 U.S. 334 (1992); Fort Gratiot Landfill v. Michigan Dep't of Natural Resources, 504 U.S. 353 (1992); Philadelphia v. New Jersey, 437 U.S. 617 (1978).

8. Schneider v. State, 308 U.S. 147, 162 (1939)(First Amendment free speech); United States v. Ward, 448 U.S. 242 (1980) (Fourth Amendment); Lyng v. Northwest Indian Cemetery Protective Ass'n, 485 U.S. 49 (1988) (First Amendment free exercise clause).

9. Compare, e.g., William M. Treanor, "The Original Understanding of the Takings Clause and the Political Process," 95 *Colum. L. Rev.* 782 (1995) *with* Douglas W. Kmiec, "The Original Understanding of the Takings Clause Is Neither Weak nor Obtuse," 88 *Colum. L. Rev.* 1630 (1988).

10. Joseph Sax, "The Constitutional Dimensions of Property: A Debate," 26 *Loyola L. Rev.* 23, 33 (1992).

11. Lynda Butler, "The Pathology of Property's Norms: Living within Nature's Bounty," 73 *Cal. L. Rev.* 927, 953–67 (2000).

12. Joseph L. Sax, *Defending the Environment* 53–55 (1970).

13. Kirkpatrick Sale, *The Green Revolution* 95 (1993) (quoting José Lutzenberger).

Part Two

1. Daniel Farber, "Politics and Procedure in Environmental Law," 8 *J.L. Econ. & Organ.* 59, 66 (1992), quoting James G. Pope, "Republican Moments: The Role of Diverse Popular Power in the American Constitutional Order," 139 *U. Pa. L. Rev.* 287, 291 (1990).

2. Robert Gottlieb, *Forcing the Spring: The Transformation of the American Environmental Movement* 113 (1993); Richard N. L. Andrews, *Managing the Environment, Managing Ourselves: A History of American Environmental Policy* ix–x (1999).

Chapter Four

1. Daniel A. Farber, "Politics and Procedure in Environmental Law," 8 *J.L. Econ. & Org.* 59, 60 (1992). See Cass R. Sunstein, "Paradoxes of the Regulatory State," 57 *U. Chi. L. Rev.* 407, 414–18 (1990); Kenneth A. Manaster, "Ten Paradoxes of Environmental Law," 27 *Loy. L.A. L. Rev.* 917, 939 n. 51 (1994); David B. Spence, "Paradox Lost: Logic, Morality, and the Foundations of Environmental Law in the 21st Century," 20 *Colum. J. Envtl. L.* 145 (1995).

2. See David Sive, "The Functions and Features of Private Litigation in the Growth of Environmental Law," *Transcripts of Speeches: National Conference on Environmental Law* 3 (California Continuing Education of the Bar, Nov. 1970). The Conference on Law and the Environment was sponsored by the Conservation Foundation and held at Airlie House in Warrenton on September 11–12, 1969. See Philip H. Hoff and Rep. Paul N. McCloskey Jr., "Conclusion," in *Law and the Environment* (Malcolm F. Baldwin and James K. Page eds., 1970), 372–74. Although the Airlie House Conference well

marks the formal coining of the term "environmental law," the term was clearly in some contemporary usage before that date. Some infrequent use can be discovered in early discussions in law schools considering new course offerings and law review and other publications in the 1960s. See A. Dan Tarlock, "Current Trends in the Development of an Environmental Curriculum," in *Law and the Environment,* at 297, 303 and n. 25; Cheryl Prihoda and William Sitig, "Environmental Law Bibliography," *Law and the Environment,* at 375–412.

3. Malcolm F. Baldwin and James K. Page, "Introduction," in *Law and the Environment,* at ix, x; "Discussion," in *Law and the Environment,* at 338 (statement of George Lefcoe).

4. Wayne King, "Pollution Fight Pressed across the Nation," *New York Times,* February 24, 1970, A1:4.

5. See generally "Millions Join Earth Day Observances across the Nation," *New York Times,* April 23, 1970, A1:1; Nan Robertson, "Earth's Day, Like Mother's, Pulls Capital Together," *New York Times,* April 23, 1970, A30; Reorganization Plan No. 3 of 1970, 5 U.S.C. Reorganization Plan of 1970 No. 3, App. (2000) (creation of the EPA); Pub. L. No. 91-604, 84 Stat. 1676 (1970) (Clean Air Act); "Editorial Comments," 1 *Envtl. L.* iii (1970); Joseph L. Sax, *Defending the Environment: A Strategy for Citizen Action* (1970). For law school conferences, see *Transcripts of Speeches: National Conference on Environmental Law; Environmental Law* (Charles M. Hassert ed., Institute of Continuing Legal Education, 1971) (University of Michigan School of Law Conference). Some of the first environmental law casebooks include books by University of Maryland professor Oscar S. Gray, Columbia Law School professor Frank Grad, and Harvard Law School professors Louis L. Jaffe and Laurence H. Tribe. See Oscar S. Gray, *Cases and Materials on Environmental Law* (1970); Frank P. Grad, *Environmental Law* (1971); Louis L. Jaffe and Laurence H. Tribe, *Environmental Protection* (1971).

6. Robert Gottlieb, *Forcing the Spring: The Transformation of the American Environmental Movement* 113 (1993). See Federal Water Pollution Control Act Amendments of 1972, Pub. L. No. 92-500, 86 Stat. 816–903 (1972); Resource Conservation and Recovery Act, Pub. L. No. 94-580, 90 Stat. 2795–2841 (1976); Endangered Species Act of 1973, Pub. L. No. 93-205, 87 Stat. 884 (1973).

7. George C. Coggins and Robert L. Glicksman, 1 *Public Natural Resources Law* §§ 2.02–2.04 (1998).

8. Stewart L. Udall, "Plea for . . . A Green Legacy," *Christian Science Monitor,* September 11, 1961, 2–3. See also Stewart L. Udall, *The Quiet Crisis* (1963); Stewart L. Udall, *The Quiet Crisis and the Next Generation* (1988); Stewart L. Udall, "We Must Save the Beauty of Our Land," 84(4) *Carpenter* 2–5.

9. Paul W. Gates, *History of Public Land Law Development* ii (1968).

10. Gottlieb, *Forcing the Spring,* at 7–8; see Samuel P. Hays, *Beauty, Health, and Permanence: Environmental Politics in the United States, 1955–1985,* 53 (1987).

11. Robert J. Brulle, "Environmental Discourse and Social Movement Organizations: A Historical and Rhetorical Perspective on U.S. Environmental Organizations," 66(1) *Soc. Inquiry* 58, 70 (1996); Richard N. L. Andrews, *Managing the Environment,*

Managing Ourselves: A History of American Environmental Policy 117–26, 126–28, 129 (1999); Gottlieb, *Forcing the Spring,* at 55–59.

12. Andrews, *Managing the Environment,* at 129; see Benjamin McCready, *On the Influence of Trades, Professions and Occupations in the United States in the Production of Disease* (1837).

13. Quotation from Gottlieb, *Forcing the Spring,* at 47–51; see Alice Hamilton, *Exploring the Dangerous Trades: The Autobiography of Alice Hamilton, MD* (1943).

14. Gottlieb, *Forcing the Spring,* at 59–69.

15. N. William Hines, *"Nor Any Drop to Drink: Public Regulation of Water Quality"* (pts. 1–3), 52 *Iowa L. Rev.* 186, 432, 799, 803–13 (1966–67); Andrews, *Managing the Environment,* at 127–28, 204; Devra Davis, *When Smoke Ran Like Water* 15–30, 36–37 (2002); Gottlieb, *Forcing the Spring,* at 77–79; Philip Shabecoff, *A Fierce Green Fire* 94 (1993).

16. Hays, *Beauty, Health, and Permanence,* at 22–26, 91, 260–61; Andrews, *Managing the Environment,* at 207–8; Davis, *When Smoke Ran Like Water,* at 42–45.

17. James McEvoy, "The American Concern with the Environment," in *Social Behavior, Natural Resources, and the Environment* (William Burch et al. eds., 1972), at 214–36; David Vogel, *Fluctuating Fortunes: The Political Power of Business in America* 65 (1989).

18. Vogel, *Fluctuating Fortunes,* at 38.

19. Gladwin Hill, "Environment May Eclipse Vietnam as College Issue," *New York Times,* November 29, 1970, A1:2.

20. Raymond Tatalovich and Mark J. Wattier, "Opinion Leadership: Elections, Campaigns, Agenda Setting, and Environmentalism," in *The Environmental Presidency* (Dennis L. Soden ed., 1999), at 152–53; Wayne King, "Pollution Fight Pressed across the Nation," *New York Times,* February 24, 1970, A1:4; Andrews, *Managing the Environment,* at 209; John K. Smith, "Turning Silk Purses into Sow's Ears: Environmental History and the Chemical Industry," 1 *Enterprise & Soc.* 785, 808–9 (2000).

21. Stephen Kern, *The Culture of Time and Space: 1880–1918* (1983).

22. Ibid., 13–15, 19, 20–21, 29–30, 81, 105, 111, 212, 217, 287, 303.

23. Ibid., 164; see Frederick Jackson Turner, *The Significance of the Frontier in American History* (1893); Coggins and Glicksman, 1 *Public Natural Resources Law* §§ 2.03–2.04 (2000).

24. C. P. Snow, "The Moon Landing," *Look,* August 26, 1969, 68, 72. See also Michael Williams, *"Forests,"* in *The Earth as Transformed by Human Action: Global and Regional Changes in the Biosphere over the Past 300 Years* (B. L. Turner ed., 1990), at 190; Hays, *Beauty, Health, and Permanence,* at 209.

25. Andrews, *Managing the Environment,* at 212–13; Hays, *Beauty, Health, and Permanence,* at 28, 211–14.

26. Rachel Carson, *Silent Spring* 24 (1962).

27. Gottlieb, *Forcing the Spring,* at 81, 91, 171; Ralph Nader, *Unsafe at Any Speed: The Designed-in Dangers of the American Automobile* (1965); Phillip Shabecoff, *A Fierce Green Fire* 95 (1993).

28. "An Aroused Nation Seeks Billions to Dam the Rising Tide of Pollution," *New York Times,* January 6, 1969, C74; Hays, *Beauty, Health, and Permanence,* at 28, 55, 188;

Richard D. Lyons, "F.D.A. May Impose Swordfish Curbs: Mercury in Tests Reported to Exceed Guidelines," *New York Times,* December 23, 1970, A18; Richard D. Lysons, "Mercury Found in 89% of Swordfish Tested," *New York Times,* December 24, 1970, A1; Halina Szejnwald Brown, Roger E. Kasperson, and Susan Swedis Raymond, "Trace Pollutants," in *The Earth as Transformed by Human Action,* at 448–53; see Lisa Heinzerling, "Environmental Law and the Present Future," 87 *Geo. L.J.* 2025, 2065 (1999).

29. See "The Great Blob," *Newsweek,* February 17, 1969, 31–32.

30. Barry Commoner, *The Closing Circle: Nature, Man, and Technology* (1971).

31. Kern, *Culture of Time and Space,* at 12.

32. See Brenda Fowler, "Word for Word: The Doomsday Clock: How Many Minutes to Midnight 50 Years after the A-Bomb's Birth?" *New York Times,* December 3, 1995, sec. 4, 7:1.

33. Ibid.

34. Richard A. Posner, *Public Intellectuals: A Study of Decline* 131 (2001), quoting Paul R. Ehrlich, "Are There Too Many of Us," *McCalls,* July 1970, 46, 104.

35. See Joel Primack and Frank Von Hippel, "Scientists, Politics, and the SST: A Critical Review," 28(4) *Sci. & Pub. Affairs* 24, 30 (1972); William F. Baxter, "The SST: From Watts to Harlem in Two Hours," 21 *Stan. L. Rev.* 1, 32–37 (1968).

36. John Brooks Flippen, *Nixon and the Environment* 103–4 (2000).

37. Heinzerling, "Environmental Law," at 2029–31.

38. See, e.g., "Remarks of President Nixon on Signing Public Law 91–604, Dec. 31, 1970," 7 *Weekly Comp. Presid. Docs.* 11–12 (1971); 91 Cong. Rec. 32,918 (1970) (remarks of Senator Cooper); ibid., 42,392 (remarks of Senator Randolph).

39. 42 U.S.C. § 4321(b)(1) (1969).

40. 91 Cong. Rec. 29,069 (1969) (remarks of Senator Jackson).

41. 92 Cong. Rec. 38,801 (1972) (remarks of Senator Muskie).

42. Ibid., 10,241 (remarks of Representative Gray).

43. "Environmental Quality: The President's Message to the Congress Recommending a 37-Point Administrative and Legislative Program," 6 *Weekly Comp. Presid. Docs.* 160 (1970).

44. H.R. Rep. 91–378, 91st Cong., 1st Sess. 3 (1969).

45. 91 Cong. Rec. 26,576 (1969) (remarks of Rep. Rogers).

46. 92 Cong. Rec. 33,115 (1970). See also 91 Cong. Rec. 42,521 (1970) (remarks of Rep. Hechler).

47. 92 Cong. Rec. 38,801 (1972) (remarks of Senator Muskie).

48. Named Individual Members of the San Antonio Conservation Soc'y v. Texas Highway Dep't, 400 U.S. 968, 969–71 (1970) (Black, J., dissenting).

49. Ethyl Corp. v. EPA, 541 F.2d 1, 6 (D.C. Cir. 1976) (en banc).

50. Just v. Marinette County, 56 Wis. 2d 7, 16–17 (1972).

Chapter Five

1. 42 U.S.C. §§ 4331(a), 4344; Arthur W. Murphy, "The National Environmental Policy Act and the Licensing Process: Environmentalist Magna Carta or Agency Coup

de Grace," 72 *Colum. L. Rev.* 963 (1972); Daniel R. Mandelker, *NEPA Law & Litigation* § 1.01 (2d ed. 1992).

2. See Oliver A. Houck, " 'Is That All?' A Review of the National Environmental Policy Act, An Agenda for the Future, by Lynton Keith Caldwell," 11 *Duke Envtl. L. & Pol'y Rev.* 173, 173–74 (2000); Fred Anderson, *NEPA in the Courts: A Legal Analysis of the National Environmental Policy Act* (1973).

3. Richard S. Arnold, "The Substantive Right to Environmental Quality under the National Environmental Policy Act," 3 *Envtl. L. Rep.* 50,028 (1973); Vermont Yankee Nuclear Power Corp. v. Natural Resources Defense Council, Inc., 435 U.S. 519, 558 (1978); Stryker's Bay Neighborhood Council v. Karlen, 444 U.S. 223, 227–28 (1980).

4. Alfred A. Marcus, *Promise and Performance: Choosing and Implementing an Environmental Policy* 32–47 (1980); John C. Whitaker, *Striking a Balance* 54–60 (1976); John Brooks Flippen, *Nixon and the Environment* 85–87 (2000).

5. 120 Cong. Rec. 37594 (Nov. 26, 1974) (remarks of Sen. Cotton). These voting statistics are based on the last recorded roll call vote taken in each chamber for each of the major environmental pollution control bills ultimately passed by Congress in the 1970s. In most cases, the final votes were voice votes. These formal votes are not, of course, an accurate measure of congressional support for every aspect of the bills passed. Many parts of the bills were quite contentious and, if added by amendment during debate, might well have been adopted by the narrowest of margins.

6. Clean Air Act Amendments of 1970, Pub. L. No. 91-1604, §§ 109, 111, 112, 84 Stat. 1679–80, 1684–85 (1970).

7. Devra Davis, *When Smoke Ran Like Water* 106–7 (2002). See R. Shep Melnick, *Regulation and the Courts: The Case of the Clean Air Act* 305 (1983); Clean Air Act Amendments of 1990, Report of the House Comm. on Energy and Commerce, H.R. Rep. No. 101-490, 101st Cong., 2d Sess. 151–52 (1990).

8. See Clean Air Act Amendments of 1970, §§ 108, 109, 110, Pub. L. No. 91-604, 84 Stat. 1676, 1678–80 (1970).

9. See Federal Water Pollution Control Act Amendments of 1972, Pub. L. No. 92-500, §§ 101(a)(1), (2), 301(a), (b), 303(d), 304(a), 82 Stat. 816, 844, 846, 850 (1972).

10. United States v. Riverside Bayview Homes, 474 U.S. 121, 132–33 (1985), quoting S. Rep. No. 92-414, 92d Cong., 2d Sess. 77 (1972).

11. See EPA v. California, 426 U.S. 200, 202–8 (1976); Federal Water Pollution Control Act Amendments of 1972, Pub. L. No. 92-500, §§ 301(a), (b), 303, 401(a)(2), 402(b)(2)(B)(5), 404, 82 Stat. 844, 846, 877, 880, 884 (1972).

12. Roger C. Dower, "Hazardous Wastes," in *Public Policies for Environmental Protection* (Paul R. Portney ed., 1990), at 154–57.

13. Pub. L. No. 93-205, 87 Stat. 892–93 (1973).

14. David Markell, "States as Innovators: Its Time for a New Look to Our 'Laboraties of Democracy' in the Effort to Improve our Approach to Environmental Regulation," 58 *Alb. L. Rev.* 347 (1994); Daniel C. Esty, "Revitalizing Environmental Federalism," 95 *Mich. L. Rev.* 570 (1996).

15. Scott C. Whitney, "The Case for Creating a Special Environmental Court System: A Further Comment," 15 *Wm. & Mary L. Rev.* 33 (1973); Joel Yellin, "Science, Technology, and Administrative Government: Institutional Designs for Environmental Decisionmaking," 92 *Yale L.J.* 1300 (1983).

16. See Flippen, *Nixon and the Environment;* John Brooks Flippen, The Nixon Administration, Politics and the Environment (Ph.D. diss., University of Maryland, 1994).

17. Flippen, *Nixon and the Environment,* at 16–21.

18. Ibid., 28–30.

19. Robert F. Blomquist, " 'To Stir Up the Public Interest": Edmund S. Muskie and the U.S. Senate Special Subcommittee's Water Pollution Investigations and Legislative Activities, 1963–66: A Case Study in Early Congressional Environmental Policy Development," 22 *Colum. J. Envtl. L.* 1 (1997).

20. Flippen, *Nixon and the Environment,* at 52; see also ibid., 50–51, 110, 114, 134.

21. "Environmental Quality: The President's Message to the Congress Recommending a 37-Point Administrative and Legislative Program," 6 *Weekly Comp. Pres. Docs.* 160 (February 10, 1970). When President Nixon created the Environmental Quality Council by executive order in May 1969, Democrats accused him of doing so in an effort to forestall their efforts to secure federal legislation, including NEPA, which was then pending before Congress. See Walter Rugaber, "President Names Council to Guide Pollution Fight," *New York Times,* May 30, 1969, A1.

22. Flippen, *Nixon and the Environment,* at 52, 59, citing *New York Times,* January 4, 1970, sec. 4, p. 12; *New York Times,* January 23, 1970, 46; and *Washington Post,* January 22, 1970, 64, 67–73. See Reorganization Plan No. 3 of 1970, 5 U.S.C. Reorg. Plan of 1970 No. 3 App. (2000).

23. Flippen, *Nixon and the Environment,* at 88.

24. Ibid., 107–8; see also ibid., 115–16.

25. John C. Esposito and Larry J. Silverman, *Vanishing Air* 289 (1971) (Ralph Nader Study Group Report on Air Pollution) ("Senator Muskie has failed the nation in the field of air pollution control legislation."); E. Donald Elliott, Bruce Ackerman, and Bruce A. Millian, "Toward a Theory of Statutory Evolution: The Federalization of Environmental Law," 1 *J.L. Econ. & Org.* 313 (1985).

26. Flippen, *Nixon and the Environment,* at 38, 50–51, 133, 228.

27. Flippen, *Nixon Administration, Politics and the Environment,* at 287–88; see Flippen, *Nixon and the Environment,* at 133, 135, 136, 142.

28. Bruce J. Schulman, *The Seventies: The Great Shift in American Culture, Society, and Politics* 30 (2001), quoting Nixon Tapes, White House Conversation with Henry Ford II and Lee Iacocca, April 27, 1971, *quoted in* Tom Wicker, *One of Us* 515 (1991).

29. Flippen, *Nixon and the Environment,* at 143; see ibid., 145–48; Flippen, Nixon Administration, at 317.

30. "Project Cannikin and the National Environmental Policy Act," 1 *Envtl. L. Rep.* 10161 (1971).

31. *Flippen, Nixon and the Environment,* at 180; see ibid., 152–55, 187, 194.

32. 118 Cong. Rec. 36859 (October 17, 1972) (presidential veto); ibid., 36871 (Senate veto override); ibid., 37054 (October 18, 1972) (House veto override); Train v. City of New York, 420 U.S. 35 (1975); Train v. Campaign for Clean Water, Inc., 420 U.S. 136 (1975).

33. Flippen, *Nixon and the Environment,* at 199–200, 204–9; 119 Cong. Rec. 27649 (August 2, 1973); Russell E. Train, *Politics, Pollution, and Pandas* 156 (2003).

34. Flippen, *Nixon and the Environment,* at 214.

35. Ibid., 196, 217–19; Train, *Politics, Pollution, and Pandas,* at 171–75.

36. See note 27.

37. Richard J. Lazarus, "Congressional Oversight of EPA," 54 *Law & Contemp. Probs.* 205, 211, 212 n. 41 (1991).

38. Tom Turner, "Legal Eagles," in *Crossroads: Environmental Priorities for the Future* 49, 51–58 (P. Borrelli ed., 1988).

39. Calvert Cliffs Coordinating Comm. v. United States Atomic Energy Comm'n, 449 F.2d 1109, 1109 (D.C. Cir. 1971).

40. Scenic Hudson Preservation Conference v. FPC, 354 F.2d 608 (2d Cir. 1965).

41. Robert Rabin, "Federal Regulation in Historical Perspective," 38 *Stan. L. Rev.* 1189, 1298 (1986); EDF v. Ruckelshaus, 439 F.2d 584, 597 (D.C. Cir. 1974); Kennecott Copper Corp. v. EPA, 462 F.2d 846, 849 (D.C. Cir 1972).

42. *Calvert Cliffs,* 449 F.2d at 1109.

43. Weyerhauser Co. v. Costle, 590 F.2d 1011, 1043 (D.C. Cir. 1978).

44. EDF v. Ruckelshaus, 439 F.2d at 597. See generally Robert Glicksman and Christopher H. Schroeder, "EPA and the Courts: Twenty Years of Law and Politics," 54 *Law & Contemp. Probs.* 249, 273 (1991).

45. Robert J. Brulle, "Environmental Discourse and Social Movement Organizations: A Historical and Rhetorical Perspective on the Development of U.S. Environmental Organizations," 66 *Soc. Inquiry* 58 (1996); Marshall Robinson, "The Ford Foundation: Sowing the Seeds of Revolution," *Environment* 11 (April 1993); John B. Judis, *The Paradox of American Democracy: Elites, Special Interests, and the Betrayal of the Public Trust* 100 (2000).

46. Joseph L. Sax, "The Public Trust Doctrine in Natural Resources Law: Effective Judicial Intervention," 68 *Mich. L. Rev.* 471 (1970); Joseph L. Sax and Roger L. Conner, "Michigan's Environmental Protection Act of 1970: A Progress Report," 70 *Mich. L. Rev.* 1003 (1972); Joseph L. Sax and Joseph R. DiMento, "Environmental Citizen Suits: Three Years' Experience under the Michigan Environmental Protection Act," 4 *Ecology L.Q.* 1 (1974).

47. Sierra Club v. Morton, 405 U.S. 727, 734 (1972); United States v. Students Challenging Regulatory Agency Procedures, 412 U.S. 669, 686–88 (1973).

48. Kirkpatrick Sale, *The Green Revolution* 33 (1993).

49. Dick Kirschten, *"The Justice Department's Land Division Flies the Environmentalists' Banner,"* 11 *Nat'l J.* 2068 (1979).

50. Stryker's Bay Neighborhood Council v. Karlen, 444 U.S. 223, 227–28 (1980); Joseph L. Sax, "The (Unhappy) Truth about NEPA," 26 *Okla. L. Rev.* 239 (1973).

51. See *Strykers Bay;* Daniel R. Mandelker, *NEPA Law & Litigation* ch. 12 (2d ed. 1992).

52. Pub. L. No. 92-463, 86 Stat. 770 (1972); Note, "The Federal Advisory Committee Act," 10 *Harv. J. on Legis.* 217, 225 (1973); William H. Rodgers Jr., "The National Industrial Pollution Control Council: Advise or Collude?" 13 *B.C. Indus. & Com. L. Rev.* 719, 725 (1972).

53. See, e.g., *Implementation of the Clean Air Act Amendments of 1970: Part 1: Hearings before the Subcomm. on Air and Water Pollution of the Sen. Comm. on Public Works,* 92d Cong., 2d Sess. 236, 243, 324–28 (1972); Federal Regulation and Regulatory Reform, *Report by the Subcomm. on Oversight and Investigations of the House Comm. on Interstate and Foreign Commerce,* 94th Cong., 2d Sess. 121–25, 134, 148 (1976).

54. Department of Housing and Urban Development: Independent Agencies Appropriations for Fiscal Year 1973, *Hearings before the Subcomm. on HUD-Independent Agencies of the House Comm. on Appropriations,* 92d Cong., 2d Sess. 350 (1972) (statement of Rep. Whitten).

55. John P. Dwyer, "The Pathology of Symbolic Legislation," 17 *Ecology L.Q.* 233, 281 (1990).

56. R. Shep Melnick, *Regulation and the Courts: The Case of the Clean Air Act* 322 (1983).

57. Robert Gottlieb, *Forcing the Spring: The Transformation of the American Environmental Movement* 143–48 (1993).

58. See James E. Krier and Edmund Ursin, *Pollution and Policy* 135–95 (1977).

59. "President's Environmental Quality Message to Congress Recommending 37-Point Administrative and Legislative Program," 6 *Weekly Comp. Pres. Docs.* 160 (1970); H.R. Rep. No. 91-1146, 91st Cong., 2d Sess. 3 (1970); Richard B. Stewart, "Pyramids of Sacrifice? Problems of Federalism in Mandating State Implementation of National Environmental Policy," 86 *Yale L.J.* 1196, 1212 (1977).

60. 42 U.S.C. § 7409; Pub. L. No. 92-500, § 2, 86 Stat. 844 (1972); James E. Krier, "The Irrational National Air Quality Standards: Macro- and Micro-Mistakes," 22 *UCLA L. Rev.* 323, 324–35 (1974).

61. See, e.g., Burke Marshall, *Federalism and Civil Rights* (1964) (Gino Speranza Lectures).

62. Pub. L. No. 91-604, § 4(a), 84 Stat. 1680; Pub. L. No. 92-500, § 2, 86 Stat. 880 (1972).

63. Paul W. Gates, *History of Public Land Law Development* ii, 581 (1968); E. L. Peffer, *The Closing of the Public Domain* (1951); Bureau of Land Management, *Public Land Statistics* 5 (1990).

64. See, e.g., Nev. Rev. Stat. §§ 321.596–321.599 (1979); Wyo. Stat. § 36–12-109 (1980 Supp.); Bruce Babbitt, "Federalism and the Environment: An Intergovernmental Perspective of the Sagebrush Rebellion," 12 *Envtl. L.* 847 (1982).

65. William H. Rodgers, *Corporate Country: A State Shaped to Suit Technology* vii–xix, 111–13, 130 (1972); David Vogel, *Fluctuating Fortunes: The Political Power of Business in America* 59–61, 74–76 (1989).

66. Davis, *When Smoke Ran Like Water,* at 117–18, citing David Mastio, "Automakers Thrive under EPA Rules: Early Predictions of Economic Damage Never Materialized," *Detroit News,* May 8, 2000, 7A.

67. Judis, *Paradox of American Democracy,* at 160–63.

68. Vogel, *Fluctuating Fortunes,* at 220–21, quoting William Simon, *A Time for Truth* 233 (1978).

69. Vogel, *Fluctuating Fortunes,* at 220–26; Judis, *Paradox of American Democracy,* at 160–67; Francis J. Flaherty, "Right-Wing Firms Pick Up Steam; A Growing Force in Public Interest Work," 5 *Nat'l L.J.* 1 (May, 23, 1983); Iran Chinoy and Robert G. Kaiser, "Decades of Contributions to Conservatism," *Washington Post,* May 2, 1999, A25.

70. Judis, *Paradox of American Democracy,* at 162–63; see John H. Cushman Jr., "After 'Silent Spring,' Industry Put Spin on All It Brewed," *New York Times,* March 25, 2001, A14:1.

71. Vogel, *Fluctuating Fortunes,* at 221; see also ibid., 222–24.

72. Judis, *Paradox of American Democracy,* at 167.

73. Vogel, *Fluctuating Fortunes,* at 216–20.

74. Cushman, "After 'Silent Spring.' "

75. Ibid.

Chapter Six

1. "The Ecological Crisis: A Common Responsibility," Message of His Holiness Pope John Paul II for the Celebration of the World Day of Peace, January 1, 1990, available at http://conservation.catholic.org/ecologicalcrisis.htm.

2. Douglas E. Kneeland, "A Summary of Reagan's Positions on the Major Issues of this Year's Campaign," *New York Times,* July 16, 1980, A14:1.

3. "The Environment and the Stump," *New York Times,* October 22, 1980, A30:1; "Mr. Reagan v. Nature," *Washington Post,* October 10, 1980, A10.

4. Howell Raines, "States Rights' Move in West Influencing Reagan's Drive," *New York Times,* July 3, 1980, A7:1.

5. *The Environmental Presidency* 156–57 (Dennis L. Soden ed., 1999).

6. Quoted in David Vogel, *Fluctuating Fortunes: The Political Power of Business in America* 246–47 (1989). See generally *Mandate for Leadership: Policy Management in a Conservative Administration* (Charles L. Heatherly ed., 1981); Constance Holden, "The Reagan Years: Environmentalists Tremble," 210 *Science* 988 (1980).

7. "Presidential Task Force on Regulatory Relief," 17 *Weekly Comp. Presid. Docs.* 33 (January 22, 1981); *Role of OMB in Regulation, Hearing before the Subcomm. on Oversight and Investigations of the House Comm. on Energy and Commerce,* 97th Cong., 1st Sess. (1981); *Presidential Management of Rulemaking in Regulatory Agencies* (Nat'l Academy of Public Admin., 1987).

8. Executive Order 12,291, 17 *Weekly Comp. Presid. Docs.* 124 (February 17, 1981); Erik Olson, "The Quiet Shift of Power: Office of Management and Budget Supervision of Environmental Protection Agency Rulemaking under Executive Order 12291," 4 *Va. Nat. Res. L.J.* 1 (1984).

9. George C. Coggins and Doris K. Nagel, " 'Nothing Besides Remains': The Legal Legacy of James G. Watt's Tenure as Secretary of the Interior on Federal Land Law and Policy," 17 *B.C. Envtl. L. Rev.* 473, 489 (1990).

10. Seth S.King, "Watt Vows to Shun Conflict Cases," *New York Times,* January 8, 1981, A14:4; "Excerpts from News Conference with Reagan's Cabinet Choices," *New York Times,* December 23, 1980, A13:1; Joanne Omang, "Man with a Mission," *Washington Post,* March 9, 1981, A1; Executive Order No. 12,348, 47 Fed. Reg. 8547 (1982); see generally George C. Coggins, "The Public Interest in Public Land Law: A Commentary on the Policies of Secretary Watt," 4 *Pub. Land. L. Rev.* 1, 26–27 (1983).

11. Anne Burford, *Are You Tough Enough?* 84 (1986).

12. Lawrence Mosher, "Move Over Jim Watt, Anne Gorsuch is the Latest Target of Environmentalists," 13 *Nat'l J.* 1899 (1981); Phillip Shabecoff, "EPA Chief Draws Fire in Hard Job," *New York Times,* October 15, 1981, B15:1; Phillip Shabecoff. "Environmental Agency Chief Announces Reorganization," *New York Times,* June 13, 1981, sec. 1, p. 8, col. 1; Jonathan Lash, Katharine Gillman, and David Sheridan, *A Season of Spoils: The Story of the Reagan Administration's Attack on the Environment* 103–4, 119, 140–41 (1984).

13. David Hoffman, "Reagan Considers End to 3 Agencies," *Washington Post,* December 11, 1984), A1; Samuel P. Hays, *Beauty, Health, and Permanence: Environmental Politics in the United States, 1955–1985,* at 494.

14. H.R. Rep. No. 99-435, 99th Cong., 1st Sess. (1985) (legislative report on document controversy); Note, "The Conflict between Executive Privilege and Congressional Oversight: The Gorsuch Controversy," 1983 *Duke L.J.* 1333; Philip Shabecoff, "Rita Lavelle Gets 6-Month Prison Term and Is Fined $10,000 for Perjury," *New York Times,* January 10, 1984, A1:2.

15. Philip Shabecoff, "Many Are Divided on Watt's Legacy," *New York Times,* October 12, 1983, A20:1.

16. Steven R. Weisman, "Watts Quits Post; President Accepts with 'Reluctance,' " *New York Times,* October 10, 1983, A1:6. See Coggins and Nagel, " 'Nothing Besides Remains,' " at 520–21, 546–49.

17. Compare, e.g., 47 Fed. Reg. 8307 (1982) (lifting and proposing amendments to ban on disposal of containerized liquids in hazardous waste disposal facilities) with 47 Fed. Reg. 12,316 (1982) (reimposing interim controls on disposal of containerized liquids in hazardous waste disposal facilities); compare 47 Fed. Reg. 7841 (1982) (EPA suspension of hazardous waste reporting requirements) with 47 Fed. Reg. 44,938 (1982) (EPA lifting of suspension of reporting requirements). See, e.g., Natural Resources Defense Council, Inc. v. EPA, 683 F.2d 752 (3d Cir. 1982) (court orders EPA reinstatement of Clean Water Act regulations); Environmental Defense Fund v. EPA, 713 F.2d 802 (D.C. Cir. 1983) (court orders EPA reinstatement of Resource Conservation and Recovery Act hazardous waste permitting program); Sierra Club v. EPA, 719 F.2d 436 (D.C. Cir. 1983) (inclusion of plume impactation in the calculation of creditable stack height for electric power plants and other sources of air pollutants was an improper factor in regulations issued by the EPA.).

18. Chevron U.S.A., Inc. v. Natural Resources Defense Council, Inc., 467 U.S. 837 (1984); 47 Fed. Reg. 31,794 (1982); 49 Fed. Reg. 39,478 (1984); 51 Fed. Reg. 41,206 (1986).

19. William Drayton, "Economic Law Enforcement," 4 *Harv. Envtl. L. Rev.* 1 (1980); William Drayton, "Getting Smarter about Regulation," *Harv. Bus. Rev.* 38 (July–August 1981); Alfred A. Marcus, *Controversial Issues in Energy Policy* 94–95 (1992).

20. Murray Weidenbaum, "Regulatory Reform under the Reagan Administration," in *The Reagan Regulatory Strategy: An Assessment* (G. Eads and M. Fix eds., 1984), at 15, 38. See Philip Shabecoff, "Reagan and Environment: To Many a Stalemate," *New York Times,* January 2, 1989, A1:1.

21. See Murray Weidenbaum, *Regulatory Reform: A Report Card for the Reagan Administration* 17 (1983); Nolan Clark, "The Environmental Protection Agency," in *Mandate for Leadership II: Continuing the Conservative Revolution* 86 (1984).

22. Russell E. Train, "The Destruction of EPA," *Washington Post,* February 2, 1982, A15; Vogel, *Fluctuating Fortunes,* at 265–66.

23. Robert H. Nelson, "How to Reform Grazing Policy: Creating Forage Rights on Federal Rangelands," 8 *Fordham Envtl. L. Rev.* 645, 654–59 (1997).

24. Pub. L. No. 96-487, 94 Stat. 2374 (December 2, 1980).

25. "Alaska National Interest Lands Conservation Act, Remarks on Signing H.R. 39 into Law," 16 *Weekly Comp. Presid. Docs.* 2755–58 (1980).

26. 14 *Weekly Comp. Presid. Docs.* 2111–12 (1978) (presidential designation of national monuments in Alaska); *Notice of Proposed Withdrawal of Lands,* 43 Fed. Reg. 57,134 (1978).

27. 42 U.S.C. §§ 9601 *et seq.* (2000).

28. Donald G. McNeil Jr., "Upstate Waste Site May Endanger Lives," *New York Times,* August 1, 1978, A1:1 (Love Canal).

29. 42 U.S.C. §§ 9604, 9612 (2000).

30. See United States v. Chem-Dyne, 572 F. Supp. 802 (S.D. Ohio 1983). The author served as co-counsel to the United States in this case.

31. 42 U.S.C. § 9607(a)(1)&(2).

32. New York Shore Realty Corp. 759 F.2d 1032 (2d Cir. 1985) (landowner liability); United States v. Fleet Factors, 901 F.2d 1550 (11th Cir. 1990) (lender liability); Asset Conservation, Lender Liability, and Deposit Insurance Protection Act of 1996, Pub. L. No. 104-208, Div. A, title I, § 101(a), title II, § 2502(b), 110 Stat. 3009–41, 3009–464 (September 30, 1996) (limiting lender liability under CERCLA); Robert V. Percival, Christopher H. Schroeder, Alan S. Miller, and James P. Leape, *Environmental Regulation: Law, Science, and Policy* 236–40 (4th ed. 2003).

33. 42 U.S.C. § 9607(a)(3).

34. Sydney Shapiro and Robert Glicksman, "Congress, the Supreme Court, and the Quiet Revolution in Administrative Law," 1988 *Duke L.J.* 819, 829–30; William Ruckelshaus, "Environmental Protection: A Brief History of the Environmental Movement in America and the Implications Abroad," 15 *Envtl. L.* 455, 460–63.

35. Pub. L. No. 99-499, 100 Stat. 1613 (1986); see Timothy B. Atkeson, Seth Goldberg, Frederick E. Ellrod III, and Sandra L. Connors, "An Annotated Legislative

History of the Superfund Amendments and Reauthorization Act of 1986 (SARA)," 16 *Envtl. L. Reptr.* 10363 (1986); Philip Shabecoff, "House Votes Bill on Toxic Waste," *New York Times,* October 9, 1986, A27:1.

36. 42 U.S.C. §§ 6921–25, 6972.

37. James Rogers and Dorothy Darrah, "RCRA Amendments Indicate Hill Distrust of EPA," *Legal Times of Washington,* December 19, 1984, 28. See also Roger C. Dower, "Hazardous Wastes," in *Public Policies for Environmental Protection* (Paul Portney ed., 1990), at 165–67.

38. Mary Graham, *Democracy by Disclosure: The Rise of Technopopulism* 24–26 (2002).

39. Pub. L. No. 99-499, tit. III, § 301, 100 Stat. 1729 (1986), *codified at* 42 U.S.C. §§ 11,001–11,050.

40. "The Toxic 500," *USA Today,* August 2, 1989, 7A.

41. Graham, *Democracy by Disclosure,* at 31–36.

42. See, e.g., Casey Bukro, "Monsanto to Cut Back Emissions," *Chicago Tribune,* July 1, 1988, 4; Graham, *Democracy by Disclosure,* at 21–23; Sidney M. Wolf, "Fear and Loathing about the Public Right to Know: The Surprising Success of the Emergency Planning and Community Right-to-Know Act," 11 *J. Land Use & Envtl. L.* 217 (1996).

43. See, e.g., Elliot Diringer, "Prop. 65 Pushes Some Snacks Off Shelves: Firms Don't Want to Post Risk Warning," *San Francisco Chronicle,* February 23, 1988, A5; Elliot Diringer, "Prop. 65 begins to Affect Products, Buying Habits," *San Francisco Chronicle,* October 20, 1988, A1; John Howard, "How Voters Changed Industry: Prop. 65 Makes Businesses Own Up to Toxics," *San Francisco Examiner,* May 2, 1993, B1.

44. United States v. S.C.R.A.P., 412 U.S. 669 (1973); Sierra Club v. Morton, 405 U.S. 727 (1972); Citizens to Preserve Overton Park, Inc. v. Volpe, 401 U.S. 402, 411–13 (1971); Robert Glicksman and Christopher H. Schroeder, "EPA and the Courts: Twenty Years of Law and Politics," 54 *Law & Contemp. Probs.* 249, 257–76; Richard B. Stewart, "The Development of Administrative and Quasi-Constitutional Law in Judicial Review of Environmental Decisionmaking: Lessons from the Clean Air Act," 62 *Iowa L. Rev.* 713 (1977); Richard B. Stewart, "The Reformation of American Administrative Law," 88 *Harv. L. Rev.* 1669 (1975); Clean Air Act, 42 U.S.C. § 7607(d) (2001) (specifying procedural requirements for administrative proceedings and conditions before party is afforded judicial review).

45. Gerald W. Boston and M. Stuart Madden, *Law of Environmental and Toxic Torts: Cases, Materials, and Problems* (2d ed. 2001); Troyen A. Brennan, "Environmental Torts," 46 *Vand. L. Rev.* 1 (1993); Jeff L. Lewin, "Boomer and the American Law of Nuisance: Past, Present, and Future," 54 *Alb. L. Rev.* 189 (1990).

46. See, e.g., Lucas v. South Carolina Coastal Council, 505 U.S. 1003 (1992); Nollan v. California Coastal Comm'n, 483 U.S. 825 (1987); Agins v. City of Tiburon, 447 U.S. 255 (1980).

47. See, e.g., Gail Bingham, *Resolving Environmental Disputes: A Decade of Experience* 14 (1986); Kathryn R. Heidt, "The Automatic Stay in Environmental Bankruptcies," 67 *Am. Bankr. L.J.* 69 (1993); Lynda J. Oswald and Cindy A. Schipani, "CERCLA and the 'Erosion' of Traditional Corporate Law Doctrine," 86 *Nw. U. L. Rev.*

259 (1992); Richard J. Lazarus, "Meeting the Demands of Integration in the Evolution of Environmental Law: Reforming Environmental Criminal Law," 83 *Geo. L.J.* 2407 (1995); Kenneth S. Abraham, "Environmental Liability and the Limits of Insurance," 88 *Colum. L. Rev.* 942 (1988); Daniel A. Farber, "Equitable Discretion, Legal Duties, and Environmental Injunctions," 45 *U. Pitt. L. Rev.* 513 (1984); Cynthia A. Williams, "The Securities and Exchange Commission and Corporate Social Transparency," 112 *Harv. L. Rev.* 1197, 1246–73 (1999); *Joint Comm. on Taxation, Survey of Existing Tax Provisions Affecting the Environment* (1990).

48. Rorie Sherman, "The 'In' Speciality This Year: Big Business Seeks Environmental Lawyers," *Nat'l L.J.,* May 22, 1989, 1.

49. Michael B. Gerrard, "Trends in the Supply and Demand for Environmental Lawyers," 25 *Colum. J. Envtl. L.* 1, 8, 11 (2000); Richard J. Lazarus, "Fairness in Environmental Law," 27 *Envtl. L.* 705, 708 (1997); Richard J. Lazarus, "Environmental Scholarship and the Harvard Difference," 23 *Harv. Envtl. L. Rev.* 329, 336, 339 (1999).

50. "The Rise of Anti-Ecology," *Time,* August 3, 1970, 42; Anthony Downs, "Up and Down with Ecology: The Issue-Attention Cycle," 28 *Public Interest* 38 (1972); Bill Keller, "Environmental Movement Checks Its Pulse and Finds Obituaries Are Premature," 39 *Cong. Q.* 211 (January 31, 1981); Raymond Tatalovich and Mark, J. Wattier, "Opinion Leadership: Elections, Campaigns, Agenda Setting, and Environmentalism," in *The Environmental Presidency* (Dennis L. Soden ed., 1999), at 156–57.

51. Paul Ehrlich, *The Population Bomb* (1968); Donald G. McNeil, "Upstate Waste Site May Endanger Lives," *New York Times,* August 1, 1978, A1:1 (quoting Echkardt C. Beck, EPA regional director); Vogel, *Fluctuating Fortunes,* at 247.

52. John B. Judis, *The Paradox of American Democracy: Elites, Special Interests, and the Betrayal of the Public Trust* 199–201 (2000); Kirkpatrick Sale, *The Green Revolution* 80 (1993); Vogel, *Fluctuating Fortunes,* at 261–62.

53. See *Reauthorizations, Hearings before the Subcomm. on Toxic Substances and Environmental Oversight of the Senate Comm. on Environment and Public Works,* 97th Cong., 1st Sess. 1 (1981); *EPA Oversight, One-Year Review Joint Hearings before the Subcomm. on Environment, Energy, and Natural Resources of the House Comm. on Government Operations, Subcomms. on Health and the Environment and on Commerce, Transportation, and Tourism of the House Comm. on Energy and Commerce, and Subcomms. on Natural Resources, Agricultural Research, and Environment and on Investigations and Oversight of the House Comm. on Science and Technology,* 97th Cong., 2d Sess. 1 (1982); *EPA Enforcement and Administration of Superfund, Hearings before the Subcomm. on Oversight and Investigation of the House Comm. on Energy and Commerce,* 97th Cong., 2d Sess. 287–89 (1981–82).

54. *Briefing by the Secretary of the Interior, Oversight Hearings before the House Comm. on Interior and Insular Affairs,* 97th Cong., 1st Sess. (1981); *James G. Watt Nomination, Hearings before the Senate Comm. on Energy and Natural Resources,* 97th Cong., 1st Sess. pts. 1, 2, pp. 2, 8 (January 7–8, 1981).

55. *Offshore Leasing: Department of the Interior Oversight, Hearings before the Environment, Energy, and Natural Resources Subcomm. of the House Comm. on Government Operations,* 97th Cong., 1st Sess. 511, 527–35 (1981).

56. Crocker Coulson, "Federalist Pipers; Federalist Society," 198 *New Republic* 23 (1986); Neil A. Lewis, "Conservative 'Outsiders' Now at Hub of Power," *New York Times,* March 29, 1991, B16:3; Thomas P. Edsall, "Federalist Society Becomes a Force in Washington; Conservative Group's Members Take Key Roles in Bush White House and Help Shape Policy and Judicial Appointments," *Washington Post,* April 18, 2001, A4.

57. Stuart Taylor, "Attorney General Outlines Campaign to Rein in Courts," *New York Times,* October 30, 1981, A1:1; "Excerpts from Attorney General's Remarks on Plans of Justice Department," *New York Times,* October 30, 1981, A22:1.

58. Philip Abelson, "Toxic Terror, Phantom Risks," 261 *Science* 407 (1993); Bill McKibben, *The End of Nature* (1990); Sherry H. Olson, *The Depletion Myth* (1971).

59. Richard N. L. Andrews, *Managing the Environment, Managing Ourselves: A History of American Environmental Policy* 266–70 (1999); William Ruckelshaus, "Science, Risk, and Public Policy," 221 *Science* 1026, 1028 (1983); EPA, *Unfinished Business: A Comparative Assessment of Environmental Protection Priorities* (1987).

60. Vogel, *Fluctuating Fortunes,* at 221.

61. Seth Zuckerman, "Environmentalism Turns 16," *Nation,* October 18, 1986, 368–69; Robert Gottlieb, *Forcing the Spring: The Transformation of the American Environmental Movement* 117–61 (1993); Robert Percival, "The Political Origins of Modern Environmental Law: Environmental Legislation and the Problem of Collective Action," 9 *Duke Envtl. L. & Pol. F.* 9, 13, 15–20 (1998).

62. Gottlieb, *Forcing the Spring,* at 162–204, 207–34; Marc R. Poirer, "Environmental Justice/Racism/Equity: Can We Talk?" 96 *W. Va. L. Rev.* 1083, 1095 (1994).

63. See generally Luke W. Cole and Sheila R. Foster, *From the Ground Up: Environmental Racism and the Rise of the Environmental Justice Movement* 19–33 (2001); United Church of Christ Comm'n for Racial Justice, *Justice, Toxic Wastes and Race in the United States* (1987).

64. James N. Smith, "The Coming of Age of Environmentalism in American Society," in *Environmental Quality and Social Justice in Urban America* (James N. Smith ed., 1974), at 1.

65. Peter Marcuse, "Conservation for Whom?" in ibid., 17, 27.

66. Rev. Richard Neuhaus, "In Defense of People: A Thesis Revisited," in ibid., 59, 62.

Chapter Seven

1. Keith Schneider, "The 1992 Campaign: Bush on the Environment: A Record of Contradictions," *New York Times,* July 4, 1992, 1:1.

2. Steven Mufson, "Darmen Laments the Decline of the Romantic Spirit; Budget Director and Critic Warns against Hiding behind the Environmental Movement," *Washington Post,* May 2, 1990, A7.

3. See, e.g., *Interference with Implementation of the Clean Air Act by the White House Council on Competitiveness, Hearings before the House Comm. on Energy and Commerce,* 102d Cong., 1st Sess. (March 21, May 1, July 22, November 14, 1990, and December 10, 1991); Memorandum from the Office of the President to Certain Department and

Agency Heads, Reducing the Burden of Government Regulation (January 28, 1992); *EPA's Criminal Enforcement Program, Hearing before the Subcomm. on Oversight and Investigations of the House Committee on Energy and Commerce*, 102d Cong., 2d Sess. (1992).

4. Keith Schneider, "Bush Aide Assail Preparations for the Earth Summit," *New York Times,* August 1, 1992, 1:4; Steven Greenhouse, "Ecology, the Economy, and Bush," *New York Times,* June 14, 1992, sec. 4, 1:2.

5. See Thomas O. McGarity, "Deflecting the Assault: How EPA Survived a 'Disorganized Revolution' by 'Reinventing' Itself a Bit," 31 *Envtl. L. Reptr.* 11,249, 11,250–58 (2001).

6. H.R. 9, 104th Cong., tit. III (as introduced January 4, 1995); H.R. 1022, 104th Cong. (1995); Mark Sagoff, *Economy of the Earth: Philosophy, Law, and the Environment* (1988).

7. H.R. 9, 104th Cong., tit. VIII; S. 343, 104th Cong. (1995); compare John D. Graham and Jonathan B. Weiner, *Risk versus Risk: Risk Tradeoffs in Protecting Health and the Environment* (1995) with Donald T. Hornstein, "Reclaiming Environmental Law: A Normative Critique of Comparative Risk Analysis," 92 *Colum. L. Rev.* 562 (1992) and David C. Vladeck and Thomas O. McGarity, "Paralysis by Analysis: How Republicans Plan to Kill Popular Regulation," *American Prospect* 80 (Summer 1995).

8. See H.R. 2099, 104th Cong. (1995) (Veterans Administration, Housing and Urban Development and Independent Agencies Appropriation Bill); John H. Cushman Jr., "Congressional Republicans Take Aim at an Extensive List of Environmental Statutes," *New York Times,* February 21, 1995, A14:1; John H. Cushman Jr., "The 104th Congress: The Environment: House Approves Sweeping Changes on Regulations," *New York Times,* March 1, 1995, A1:6; "GOP's War on Nature," *New York Times,* May 31, 1995, A20; Jerry Gray, "In House, Spending Bills Open Way to Make Policy," *New York Times,* July 19, 1995, A16:5; John H. Cushman Jr., "Senate Backs Cuts in Environmental Spending," *New York Times,* December 15, 1995, A35:1; Philip Shabecoff, *A Fierce Green Fire* 120 (1993).

9. H.R. 9, 104th Cong., tit. IX (as introduced January 4, 1995); H.R. 925, 104th Cong. (1995); *The Right to Own Property, Hearings before the Senate Comm. on the Judiciary,* 104th Cong., 1st Sess. (1995); *Private Property and Environmental Laws, Hearings before the Senate Comm. on the Environment and Public Works,* 104th Cong., 1st Sess. (1995).

10. See The Omnibus Property Rights Act of 1995, S. 605, S. Rep. 104–239, 104th Cong., 2d Sess. (1996) (S. 605, § 204[f]).

11. Hugh Dellios, "Environmental Groups Now on the Endangered List," *Chicago Tribune,* April 16, 1995, C3; Christopher Boerner and Jennifer Chilton Kallery, *Restructuring Environmental Big Business,* Policy Study No. 124, Center for the Study of American Business, Washington University (January 1995).

12. See Gwen Ifill, "The 1992 Campaign; The Environment: Clinton Links Ecology Plans with Jobs," *New York Times,* April 23, 1992, A22:11.

13. See Jonathan Z. Cannon, "EPA and Congress (1994–2000): Who's Been Yanking Whose Chain?" 31 *Envtl. L. Rptr.* 10,942, 10,947–48 (2001), quoting Clinton's remarks at Rego Event, March 16, 1995.

14. Robert Glicksman and Christopher H. Schroeder, "EPA and the Courts: Twenty Years of Law and Politics," 54 *Law & Contemp. Probs.* 249 (1991).

15. Joseph L. Sax, "Property Rights and the Economy of Nature: Understanding Lucas v. South Carolina Coastal Council," 45 *Stan. L. Rev.* 1433 (1993). Please note that I served as co-counsel to South Carolina in the *Lucas* litigation in the Supreme Court.

16. See, e.g., Valley Forge Christian College v. Americans United for Separation of Church and State, Inc., 454 U.S. 464, 471–74 (1982).

17. Bennet v. Spear, 520 U.S. 154, 176–77 (1997). See also Lujan v. National Wildlife Fed'n, 497 U.S. 871 (1990); Lujan v. Defenders of Wildlife, 504 U.S. 555 (1992); Steel Co. v. Citizens for a Better Env't, 523 U.S. 83 (1998);

18. Lujan v. Defenders of Wildlife, 504 U.S. at 606 (Blackmun, J., dissenting).

19. Ibid., 566.

20. See Wickard v. Filburn, 317 U.S. 111 (1942).

21. See United States v. Lopez, 514 U.S. 549, 558–60 (1995); See Sara Sun Beale, "The Unintended Consequences of Enhancing Gun Penalties: Shooting Down the Commerce Clause and Arming Federal Prosecutors," 51 *Duke L.J.* 1641 (2002).

22. See United States v. Olin, 107 F.3d 1506 (11th Cir. 1997) (Superfund); National Ass'n of Home Builders v. Babbitt, 130 F.3d 1041 (D.C. Cir. 1997) (Endangered Species Act); Wilson v. United States, 133 F.3d 251 (4th Cir. 1997) (Clean Water Act).

23. See, e.g., Public Interest Research Group of New Jersey v. Magnesium Elektron, 123 F.3d 111 (3d Cir. 1997); Florida Audubon Soc'y v. Bentsen, 94 F.3d 658 (D.C. Cir. 1996); United States v. Alcan Aluminum Corp., 964 F.3d 252 (3d Cir. 1992); United States v. CDMG Realty, 96 F.3d 706 (3d Cir. 1996); Christopher H. Schroeder and Robert L. Glicksman, "*Chevron, State Farm,* and EPA in the Courts of Appeals during the 1990s," 31 *Envtl. L. Rptr.* 10,371 (2001).

24. Calvert Cliffs' Coordinating Comm., Inc. v. Atomic Energy Comm'n, 449 F.2d 1109, 1111 (D.C. Cir. 1971).

25. Antonin Scalia, "The Doctrine of Standing as an Essential Element of the Separation of Powers," 17 *Suffolk U. L. Rev.* 881, 884, 897 (1983).

26. See Philip Shabecoff, "Environmental Groups Told They Are Racist in Hiring," *New York Times,* February 1, 1990, A16.

27. Martin V. Melosi, "Environmental Justice, Political Agenda Setting, and the Myths of History," 12(1) *J. Pol'y Hist.* 43, 55 (2000); Robert Gottlieb, *Forcing the Spring: The Transformation of the American Environmental Movement* 7–8, 55–69 (1993); Robert J. Brulle, "Environmental Discourse and Social Movement Organizations: A Historical and Rhetorical Perspective on the Development of U.S. Environmental Organizations," 66(1) *Soc. Inquiry* 58, 70 (1996).

28. Quoted in Karl Grossman, "The People of Color Environmental Summit," in *Unequal Protection: Environmental Justice and Communities of Color* (Robert D. Bullard ed., 1994), at 273, 278.

29. Robert D. Bullard, *Dumping in Dixie: Race, Class, and Environmental Quality* (1990).

30. Bunyan I. Bryant and Paul Mohai, "The Michigan Conference: A Turning Point," 18 *EPA J.* 9 (1992).

31. See Keith Schneider, "Minorities Join to Fight Polluting Neighborhoods," *New York Times,* October 25, 1991, A20; *Disproportionate Impact of Lead Poisoning on Minority Communities: Hearings before the Subcomm. on Health and the Environment of the House Comm. on Energy and Commerce,* 102d Cong., 2d Sess. (1992); 138 Cong. Rec. S7489 (1992) (statement of Senator Albert Gore Jr., introducing the Environmental Justice Act, S. 2806, 102d Cong., 1st Sess. [1992]).

32. Executive Order 12,898, 59 Fed. Reg. 7629 (1994).

33. EPA, *Environmental Justice Initiatives 1993,* 5, 9–10 (1994); Sam Agpawa and Ray Ford, EPA Region IX Air Division, *Environmental Justice Strategy* (revised July 27, 1998) ("Action Plan : . . . Identify areas that have potential EJ concerns and take into consideration for EJ concerns when targeting inspections or enforcement."); EPA, Office of Environmental Justice, *Environmental Justice: Annual Report 1996,* 14 (August 1997) (describing CERCLA remedy relocating 338 African American families in Pensacolo, Florida); EPA, *Supplemental Environmental Projects Policy,* 63 Fed. Reg. 24,796 (1998) (encouraging settlement agreements in environmental justice communities that address local needs of those communities); 42 U.S. § 7412(k)(3) (federal regulation of "area sources" of hazardous air pollutants in urban areas); EPA, *Draft Integrated Urban Air Toxics Strategy to Comply with Section 112(k), 112(c)(3) and Section 202(1) of the Clean Air Act,* 63 Fed. Reg. 49,240, 49,242, 49,442–43 (1998); Richard J. Lazarus, "Highways and Bi-ways for Environmental Justice," 31 *Cumberland L. Rev.* 569, 594–96 (2001).

34. EPA, *Environmental Justice Initiatives 1993,* 6 (1994); Keith Harley, "The Chicago Cumulative Risk Initiative," 7(1) *DePaul Envtl. L. Dig.* 6–8 (1996) (describing EPA effort to develop model for assessment of cumulative environmental risks in Chicago area, especially those faced by children); The Chicago Cumulative Risk Initiative, vol. 1, no. 1 (March 1997 and June 1998 Update) (same).

35. See Craig Anthony Arnold, "Planning Milagros: Environmental Justice and Land Use Regulation," 76 *Denver U. L. Rev.* 1, 47–48 (1998); *In re* Louisiana Energy Servs., L.P., 47 N.R.C. 113 (1998); "Company Evades 'Environmental Racism' Test," *New York Times,* September 20, 1998, sec. 1, 42:1; Richard J. Lazarus and Stephanie Tai, "Integrating Environmental Justice into EPA Permitting Authority," 27 *Ecology L.Q.* 617 (1999); Lynn E. Blais, "Environmental Racism Reconsidered," 75 *N.C. L. Rev.* 75 (1996).

36. See Luke Cole and Sheila Foster, *From the Ground Up: Environmental Racism and the Rise of the Environmental Justice Movement* 167–83 (2001) (annotated bibliography of studies); Jay Hamilton and Kip Viscusi, *Calculating Risks* 159, 160, 233 (1999); Daniel L. Millimet and Danikel J. Slottje, "Environmental Compliance Costs and the Distribution of Emissions in the U.S.," 42 *J. Regional Sci.* 87–105 (2002).

37. Clean Air Act, 42 U.S.C. §§ 7410, 7413; see Richard L. Revesz, "Federalism and Environmental Regulation: A Public Choice Analysis," 115 *Harv. L. Rev.* 553, 578–83 (2001); Paul R. Portney, "Air Pollution Policy," in *Public Policies for Environmental Protection* (Paul R. Portney ed., 1990), at 50–51.

38. R. Stevens Brown, "The States Protect the Environment," *ECOStates Magazine,* Summer 1999; Clifford Rechtschaffen and David L. Markell, *Reinventing Environmental Enforcement and the State/Federal Relationship* 91–124 (2003).

39. John H. Cushman Jr., "E.P.A. and States Found to be Lax on Pollution Law," *New York Times,* June 7, 1998, sec. 1, 1:6.

40. *The Federal–State Relationship: A Look into EPA's Reinvention Efforts, Hearings before the Subcomm. on Oversight and Investigation of the House Comm. on Commerce,* 105th Cong., 1st Sess. (1997); Rena Steinzor, "Reinventing Environmental Regulation through the Government Performance and Results Act: Are the States Ready for the Devolution?" 29 *Envtl. L. Rptr.* 10074, 10082 (1999); "State Privilege-Immunity Laws for Audits Could Hurt Program Delegation, Official Says," 26 *BNA Envtl. Rep. Curr. Dev.* 2253 (1996); "Audit Law Changes Clear Way for State to Run Federal Enforcement," 28 *Envtl. Rep. Curr. Dev.* 388 (1997).

41. See Michael Herz, "United States v. United States: When Can the Federal Government Sue Itself?" 32 *Wm. & Mary L. Rev.* 893, 933–38 (1991); Michael W. Steinberg, "Can EPA Sue Other Federal Agencies?" 17 *Ecology L.Q.* 317, 331–41 (1990).

42. Department of Energy v. Ohio, 503 U.S. 607 (1992).

43. See 63 Fed. Reg. 57,356 (1998); for interstate cases, see e.g., Connecticut v. EPA, 696 F.2d 147, 169 (2d Cir. 1982); New York v. EPA, 852 F.2d 574 (D.C. Cir. 1988).

44. Worcester v. Georgia, 31 U.S. (6 Pet.) 515 (1832); Winters v. United States, 207 U.S. 564 (1908) (reserved water rights); Washington v. Washington State Commercial Passenger Fishing Vessel Ass'n, 443 U.S. 658 (1979) (fishing rights).

45. 33 U.S.C. § 1377(e) (Clean Water Act); 42 U.S.C. § 300j-11 (Safe Drinking Water Act); 42 U.S.C. §§ 7410(o), 7601(d) (Clean Air Act); Wisconsin v. EPA, 260 F.3d 741 (7th Cir. 2001) (Clean Water Act); Arizona Public Serv. Comm'n v. EPA, 211 F.3d 128 (D.C. Cir. 2000); David F. Coursen, "Tribes as States: Indian Tribal Authority to Regulate and Enforce Federal Environmental Laws and Regulations," 23 *Envtl. L. Rep.* 10,579, 10,585 (1993).

46. Phillipe Sand, *Greening International Law* (1994); Edith Brown Weiss, ed., *Environmental Change and International Law: New Challenges and Dimensions* (1992); Robert V. Percival, Christopher H. Schroeder, Alan S. Miller, and James P. Leape, *Environmental Regulation: Law, Science, and Policy* 1034–40 (4th ed. 2003); Edith Brown Weiss and John Jackson, *Reconciling Environment and Trade* 11 (2001).

47. See Edith Brown Weiss, "International Environmental Law: Contemporary Issues and the Emergence of a New World Order," 81 *Geo. L.J.* 675 (1993).

48. U.N. Doc. A, 21 *I.L.M.* 1261 (1982) (Law of the Sea); 31 *I.L.M.* 818 (1992) (Biodiversity Convention); 28 *I.L.M.* 657 (1989) (Basel Convention).

49. Weiss and Jackson, *Reconciling Environment and Trade,* at 3.

50. T.I.A.S. No. 1700, 55 *U.N.T.S.* 187 (GATT); 33 *I.L.M.* 1133 (1994) (WTO).

51. Weiss and Jackson, *Reconciling Environment and Trade,* at 3.

52. See Herman Daly, "From Adjustment to Sustainable Development: The Obstacle of Free Trade," 15 *Loy. L.A. Int'l & Comp. L.J.* 33 (1992).

53. GATT Article XX(b), (g).

54. WTO, "United States: Import Prohibition of Certain Shrimp and Shrimp Products," WT/DS58/AB/R (October 12, 1998).

55. Carmen G. Gonzalez, "Beyond Eco-Imperialism: An Environmental Justice Critique of Free Trade," 78 *Den. U. L. Rev.* 979, 987–92 (2001).

56. Thomas W. Lippman, "Christopher Puts Environment High on Diplomatic Agenda; Abuse of Natural Resources Imperils U.S. Interests, Secretary of State Says," *Washington Post,* April 15, 1996, A10.

57. Woodrow International Center for Scholars, *Environmental Change & Security Project Report, Issues* 1–9 (Summer 1995–Summer 2003); EPA, *Environmental Security, Environmental Security: Strengthening National Security through Environmental Protection* (September 1999).

58. David E. Sanger, "Talks and Turmoil: The Overview; President Chides World Trade Body in Stormy Seattle," *New York Times,* December 2, 1999, A1:6; Timothy Egan, "Talks and Turmoil: The Violence; Black Masks Lead to Pointed Fingers in Seattle," *New York Times,* December 2, 1999, A1:3; Sam Howe Verhovek, "Talks and Turmoil; the Hosts; Seattle Is Stung, Angry and Chagrined as Opportunity Turns to Chaos," *New York Times,* December 2, 1999, A16:1; Stephen Greenhouse and Joseph Kahn, "Talks and Turmoil; Workers Rights, US Efforts to Add Labor Standards Fails," *New York Times,* December 3, 1999, A1:1.

59. E.g., William H. Rodgers, *Environmental Law* § 1.2 (1994); Daniel A. Farber, "Environmental Protection as a Learning Experience," 27 *Loy. L.A. L. Rev.* 791, 791 (1994).

60. "Greening the Cabinet," *New York Times,* January 25, 1990, A22:1.

61. Nan Robertson, "Earth's Day, Like Mother's, Pulls Capital Together," *New York Times,* April 23, 1970, A30.

62. See generally Michael Gerhardt, *The Federal Appointments Process: A Constitutional and Historical Analysis* (2001).

63. See note 13.

64. Samuel P. Hays, *Beauty, Health, and Permanence: Environmental Politics in the United States, 1955–1985,* 463 (1987). I compiled the scores for all members of Congress, commencing with the League's first set of scores in 1971 through 2000.

65. See "Energy/Natural Resources: Long Term Contribution Trends." Web site of the Center for Responsive Politics, www.opensecrets.org/industries/indus.asp?Ind=E (visited January 5, 2002); "Coal Mining: Long Term Contribution Trends." Web site of the Center for Responsive Politics, www.opensecrets.org/industries/indus.asp?Ind= E1210 (visited January 5, 2002).

66. *A History of the U.S. Department of the Interior during the Clinton Administration 1993–2001,* 3–4 (prepared for the Clinton Administration History Project, Washington, D.C. 2000); Joseph L. Sax, "Environmental Law at the Turn of the Century: A Reportorial Fragment of Contemporary History," 88 *Cal. L. Rev.* 1, 5 (2000).

67. See *Joint Commitment to Reform Oversight and Create a National Environmental Performance Partnership System* (May 15, 1995).

68. EPA, *Reinventing Environmental Protection: 1998 Annual Report* (1999); Philip K. Howard, *The Death of Common Sense, How Law Is Suffocating America* (1994); Eric W. Orts, "Reflexive Environmental Law," 89 *Nw. U. L. Rev.* 1227 (1995).

69. See Regulatory Reinvention (XL) Pilot Projects, 60 Fed. Reg. 27,282 (1995); Common Sense Initiative, 59 Fed. Reg. 55,117 (1994); Environmental Leadership Program, 59 Fed. Reg. 32,062 (1994); EPA Supplemental Environmental Projects Policy, 63 Fed. Reg. 24,796, 24,796 (1998).

70. Charles Sabel, Archon Fung, and Bradley Karkkainen, *Beyond Backyard Environmentalism* 41–46 (2000); Holly Doremus, "Adaptive Management, the Endangered Species Act, and the Institutional Challenges of "New Age" Environmental Protection," 41 *Washburn L.J.* 50, 68–77 (2001); Rena I. Steinzor, "Devolution and the Public Health," 24 *Harv. Envtl. L. Rev.* 351 (2000).

71. See generally John D. Leshy, "The Babbitt Legacy at the Department of the Interior: A Preliminary View," 31 *Envtl. L.* 199, 218 (2001); *History of the U.S. Department of the Interior during the Clinton Administration,* at xxiv–xxx; Fundamentals of Rangeland Health and Standards and Guidelines for Grazing Administration, 60 Fed. Reg. 9894 (1995); Mining Claims under the General Mining Laws, 65 Fed. Reg. 69,998 (Nov. 21, 2000); Solicitor Op. M-37005, Whether Public Lands Withdrawn by Executive Orders 6910 and 6964 or Established as Grazing Districts are "Reservations" within the Meaning of Section 4(e) of the Federal Power Act (January 19, 2001); Solicitor Op. M-37004, Use of Mining Claims for Purposes Ancillary to Mineral Extraction (January 18, 2001); Solicitor Op. M-36994, Patenting of Mining Claims and Mill Sites in Wilderness Areas (May 22, 1998); Solicitor Op. M-36989, Managing Areas Eligible for Protection under the Wild and Scenic Rivers Act (November 12, 1997).

72. 62 Fed. Reg. 38,652, 38,762 (1997) (air quality standards); John H. Cushman Jr., "On Clean Air, Environmental Chief Fought Doggedly, and Won," *New York Times,* July 5, 1997, sec. 1, p. 8, col. 1; 63 Fed. Reg. 57,356 (1998) (interstate air provisions); 66 Fed. Reg. 5001 (2001) (diesel fuel regulations); David Stout, "Seven Utilities Sued by U.S. on Charge of Polluting Air," *New York Times,* November 4, 1999, A1:6; 65 Fed. Reg. 43,586 (2000) (water quality regulations).

73. Sandra Beth Zellmer, "Sacrificing Legislative Integrity at the Altar of Appropriations Riders: A Constitutional Crisis," 21 *Harv. Envtl. L. Rev.* 457 (1997).

74. Emergency Supplemental Appropriations for Additional Disaster Assistance, for Anti-Terrorism Initiatives, for Assistance in the Recovery from the Tragedy that Occurred at Oklahoma City, and Rescissions Act, Pub. L. No. 104-19, §§ 2001–2002, 109 Stat. 194, 240–47 (1995); Michael Axline, "Salvage Logging: Point & Counterpoint: Forest Health and the Politics of Expediency," 26 *Envtl. L.* 613 (1996).

75. Bruce Babbitt, "Road to Ruin," *New York Times,* June 25, 1998, A23:2 (op-ed); Tom Kenworthy and Judith Eilperin, "White House Backs W. Va. on Mining, Conservationists Say Action Undermines Vetoes, Conflicts with Environmental Stance," *Washington Post,* October 30, 1999, A2; "Mr. Clinton Wins on Riders," *New York Times,* November 21, 1999, 4:14, col. 1 (editorial).

76. See 65 Fed. Reg. 43,586–43,670 (2000); Matthew Wald and Stephen Greenhouse, "E.P.A. Institutes a Water Program before a Bill Blocking Them Becomes Law," *New York Times,* July 12, 2000, A17:1; Pub. L. No. 106-246, 114 Stat. 511 (July 13, 2000).

77. Murray Weidenbaum, *Rendezvous with Reality: The American Economy after Reagan* 222 (1988); see, e.g., Andrew C. Revkin and Neela Banerjee, "Energy Executives Urge Some Gas-Emission Limits on Bush," *New York Times,* August 1, 2001, C1:2 (" 'What business wants is policy certainty,' an environmental expert for a large international energy company said. 'Bush has injected only turbulence.' ").

78. David R. Berg and Grant Ferrier, *Meeting the Challenge: U.S. Industry Faces the 21st Century: The U.S. Environmental Industry* 10–14, 28 (U.S. Department of Commerce Office of Technology Policy, September 1988); Deborah Vaughn and Carl A. Pasurka, "The U.S. Environmental Protection Agency: A Proposed Framework for Assessment," in Office of Economic Community Development, *The Environment Industry* (1995), at 225 (proceedings of Workshop on the Global Environment Industry, Washington, D.C., October 13–14, 1994); U.S. Department of Commerce, Office of Environmental Technologies Industries (Web site information); U.S. Department of Commerce Bureau of the Census, *Statistical Abstract of the United States* 221 (2000) (chart 366); see generally Vaughn and Pasurka, "The U.S. Environmental Protection Agency"; R. Shep Melnick, *Regulation and the Courts: The Case of the Clean Air Act* 176–77 (1983).

79. Robert Constanza, Ralph D'Arge, Rudolf De Groot, Stephen Farber, Monica Grasso, Bruce Hannon, Karin Limburg, Shahid Naeem, Robert V. O'Neill, Jose Paruel, Robert G. Raskin, Paul Sutton, and Marjan van den Belt, "The Value of the World's Ecosystem Services and Natural Capital," 387 *Nature* 253, 259 (1997). See *Valuing the Earth: Economics, Ecology, and Ethics* (Herman E. Daly and Kenneth N. Townsend eds., 1993); James Salzman, Barton H. Thompson Jr., and Gretchen C. Daily, "Protecting Ecosystem Services: Science, Economics, and Law," 20 *Stan. Envtl. L.J.* 309, 315–16 (2001).

80. EPA, Office of Water, Liquid Assets, "The Business of Clean Water: How Water Quality Affects Major Economic Sectors 2000," www.epa.gov/ow/liquidassets/business.html (visited December 10, 2001).

81. Bruce Guile and Jared Cohen, "Sorting Out the Service Economy," in Marion Chertow and Daniel Esty, *Thinking Ecologically: The Next Generation of Environmental Protection* 76–77 (1997); James Salzman, "Beyond the Smokestack: Environmental Protection in the Service Economy," 47 *UCLA L. Rev.* 411, 413 (1999).

82. See, e.g., Garner M. Brown and Jason Shogren, "Economics of the Endangered Species Act," 12 *J. Econ. Persp.* 3, 12 (Summer 1998) (estimating annual whale watch industry in California of approximately $200 million and $90–200 billion ecotourism industry worldwide).

83. Jared Diamond, "The Greening of Corporate America," *New York Times,* January 8, 2000, A13:1.

Part Three

1. Richard MacLean and Frank Friedman, "Green Arthritis," 17 *Envtl. Forum* 36 (November–December 2000).

Chapter Eight

1. See Ronald Outen, "Environmental Pollution Laws and the Architecture of To-bacco Road," in National Research Council, *Multimedia Approaches to Pollution Control: Symposium Proceedings* 139 (1987).

2. See The Conservation Foundation, *An Issue Report: Controlling Cross-Media Pollutants* (1984); The Conservation Foundation, *The Environmental Protection Act, Second Draft* (1988); William K. Reilly, "The Turning Point: An Environmental Vision for the 1990s," 20 *BNA Envtl. Rep. Curr. Dev.* 1386 (1989) (Annual Marshall Lecture to NRDC); Lakshman Guruswamy, "Integrating Thoughtways: Re-Opening of the Environmental Mind?" 1989 *Wis. L. Rev.* 463 (1989).

3. See Clean Air Act, tit. I, §§ 108–110, as added Pub. L. No. 91-604, § 4(a), 84 Stat. 1678 (December 31, 1970).

4. Clean Air Act, tit. II, § 210, as amended Pub. L. No. 91-604, §§ 8(a), 10(b), 84 Stat. 1694, 1700 (December 31, 1970) (preemption provision); Clean Air Act, tit. I, § 111, as added Pub. L. No. 91-604, § 4(a), 84 Stat. 1683 (December 31, 1970) (new source performance standard).

5. Federal Water Pollution Control Act Amendments of 1972, tit. III, §§ 301(a)–(b), 304, 502(14), 502(16), Pub. L. No. 92-500, 86 Stat. 844, 850, 886 (October 18, 1972).

6. Federal Water Pollution Control Act, tit. IV, § 402, as added Pub. L. No. 92-500, § 2, 86 Stat. 880 (October 18, 1972).

7. Federal Water Pollution Control Act, tit., III, § 304(b), as added Pub. L. No. 92-500, § 2, 86 Stat. 850 (October 18, 1972); see E. I. duPont de Nemours & Co. v. Train, 430 U.S. 112 (1977); EPA v. National Crushed Stone Ass'n, 449 U.S. 64 (1980).

8. Federal Water Pollution Control Act, tit. III, §§ 303, 304, as added Pub. L. No. 92-500, § 2, 86 Stat. 846–50 (October 18, 1972).

9. See Oliver A. Houck, "Of Bats, Birds, and BAT: The Convergent Evolution of Environmental Law," 63 *Miss. L.J.* 403 (1994).

10. Clean Air Act Amendments of 1977, tit. I, §§ 160–169a (Prevention of Significant Deterioration), §§ 171–176 (Nonattainment), as added Pub. L. No. 95-95, tit. I, § 127(a), (b), 91 Stat. 731–42, 746–49 (November 16, 1977).

11. Clean Air Act Amendments of 1977, tit. I, §§ 165(a), 169a(b), 173(a), as added Pub. L. No. 95-95, tit. I, § 127(a), (b), 91 Stat. 731–42, 746–49 (November 16, 1977).

12. See American Mining Congress v. EPA, 824 F.2d 1177, 1189 (D.C. Cir. 1987) ("mind numbing").

13. See 42 U.S.C. §§ 7411(a)(2), (a)(4), 7479(2)(C), 7501(4); 40 C.F.R. §§ 51.165(a)(1)(v)(C), 51.166(b)(2)(iii), 52.21(b)(2)(iii); 43 Fed. Reg. 26,396 (June 19, 1978); David Stout, "Seven Utilities Sued by U.S. on Charge of Polluting Air," *New York Times,* November 4, 1999, A1:6. Because, however, the Bush administration has since promulgated both final and proposed air pollution control rules that would largely reinstate and expand the prior practice of grandfathering existing facilities from more stringent controls, the new/existing dichotomy appears, at least temporarily, to have been revived in the Clean Air Act. See 67 Fed. Reg. 80,186 (2002); 68 Fed. Reg. 61,248 (2003).

14. Barry Boyer and Errol Meidinger, "Privatizing Regulatory Enforcement: A

282 NOTES TO PAGES 176–182

Preliminary Assessment of Citizen Suits under Federal Environmental Laws," 34 *Buff. L. Rev.* 833, 868–69 n. 88 (1985); Lisa Jorgenson and Jeffrey J. Kimmel, *Environmental Citizen Suits: Confronting the Corporation* 19 (1988); Jeffrey G. Miller, *Citizen Suits: Private Enforcement of Federal Pollution Control Laws* 14 (1987) (citizen suits 90 percent under CWA).

15. Clean Air Act Amendments of 1990, Pub. L. No. 101-549, tit. V, §§ 501–507, 104 Stat. 2635–45 (November 15, 1990).

16. 33 U.S.C. § 1313(d)(1)(A), (D); Oliver A. Houck, "TMDLs: The Resurrection of Water Quality Standards-Based Regulation under the Clean Water Act," 27 *Envtl. L. Rep.* 10,329 (1997).

17. J. B. Ruhl, "Farms, Their Environmental Harms, and Environmental Law," 27 *Ecology L.Q.* 273 (2000).

18. 65 Fed. Reg. 43,585 (2000) (Browner regulations); Oliver A. Houck, "The Clean Water Act TMDL Program V: Aftershock and Prelude," 32 *Envtl. L. Rep.* 10,385 (2002); Eric Pianin, "EPA Jettisons Clinton Rule on Cleaning Up Waterways," *Washington Post,* December 21, 2002, A2.

19. See American Law Institute, *Restatement (Second) of Torts* §§ 821B, 821D.

20. See *Solid Waste Agency of Northern Cook County v. U.S. Army Corps of Eng'rs,* 531 U.S. 159 (2001) (Commerce Clause); Christopher H. Schroeder, "Environmental Law, Congress, and the Court's New Federalism Doctrine," 78 *Ind. L.J.* 413 (2003).

21. U.S. Const. art. IV, § 3, cl. 2 ("The Congress shall have Power to dispose of and make all needful Rules and Regulations respecting the Territory or other Property belonging to the United States"); see Kleppe v. New Mexico, 426 U.S. 529 (1976).

22. For scholarship questioning whether absolute private property rights in natural resources ever truly existed in the United States, see John Hart, "Land Use in the Early Republic and the Original Meaning of the Takings Clause," 94 *Nw. U. L. Rev.* 1099 (2000); William Treanor, "The Original Understanding of the Takings Clause and the Political Process," 95 *Colum. L. Rev.* 782, 792–94 (1995).

23. 43 U.S.C. §§161–284 (Homestead Act); 30 U.S.C. §§ 21–42 (General Mining Law); see Act of Sept. 20, 1850, 9 Stat. 466; Act of July 1, 1862, ch. 120, 12 Stat. 489 (various railroad laws); see generally Paul Gates, *History of Public Land Law Development* 341–86 (1968); Leo Sheep Co. v. United States, 440 U.S. 668, 670–77 (1979).

24. See Peter A. Appel, "The Power of Congress 'Without Limitation': The Property Clause and Federal Regulation of Private Property," 86 *Minn. L. Rev.* 1 (2001); Robert L. Glicksman, "Pollution on the Federal Lands I: Air Pollution Law," 12 *UCLA J. Envtl. L. & Pol'y* 1 (1993); Robert L. Glicksman, "Pollution on the Federal Lands II: Water Pollution Law," 12 *UCLA J. Envtl. L. & Pol'y* 61 (1993); Robert L. Glicksman, "Pollution on the Federal Lands III: Regulation of Solid and Hazardous Waste," 13 *Stan. Envtl. L.J.* 3 (1994).

25. See, e.g., National Forest Management Act, 16 U.S.C. § 1605; Federal Land and Policy Management Act, 43 U.S.C. §§ 1712, 1714, 1732(b); Federal Onshore Oil and Gas Leasing Reform Act, 30 U.S.C. §226; Outer Continental Shelf Lands Act, 43 U.S.C. § 1338; Livestock Grazing Regulations, 43 C.F.R. pts. 1780, 4100, 60 Fed.

Reg. 9814 (1995); Hardrock Mining Regulations, 43 C.F.R. pt. 3800, 66 Fed. Reg. 54,834 (superseding and amending regulations promulgated during Clinton administration at 65 Fed. Reg. 69,998 [2001]); George Pring, " 'Power to Spare': Conditioning Federal Resource Leases to Protect Social, Economic, and Environmental Values," 14 *Nat. Resources Law.* 305 (1981); Joseph W. Dellapenna, "The Importance of Getting Names Right: The Myth of Markets for Water," 25 *Wm. & Mary Envtl. L. & Pol'y Rev.* 317, 365–67 (2000).

26. Joseph L. Sax, "Environmental Law and Regulation," in American Bar Association, *Common Law Common Values Common Rights* (2000), at 229; Eric T. Freyfogle, "Context and Accommodation in Modern Property Law," 41 *Stan. L. Rev.* 1529, 1548–53 (1989); Eric T. Freyfogle, "The Owning and Taking of Sensitive Lands," 43 *UCLA L. Rev.* 77, 103–6 (1995).

27. See generally Robert N. Stavins, "Lessons from the American Experiment with Market-Based Environmental Policies," in *Harnessing the Hurricane: The Challenge of Market-Based Governance* (John Donahue and Joseph Nye eds., 2002); Steven Kelman, *What Price Incentives?: Economists and the Environment* (1981).

28. 42 U.S.C. §§ 7651–76510 (sulfur dioxide emissions program); 42 U.S.C. § 7503(c) (offsets); Maria L. La Ganga, "Firms Can Earn Pollution Credits by Buying Old Cars; Environment: AQMD Approves Groundbreaking Plan to Let Companies Delay Costly Smog-Reduction Efforts," *L.A. Times,* January 9, 1993, A1 (describing problem of credit for reductions that would otherwise occur).

29. See Ann Powers, "Reducing Nitrogen Pollution on Long Island Sound: Is There a Place for Pollutant Trading?" 23 *Colum. J. Envtl. L.* 137 (1998); EPA, Effluent Trading in Watersheds Policy Statement, 61 Fed. Reg. 4994 (1996); EPA, Proposed Water Quality Trading Policy, 67 Fed. Reg. 34,709 (May 15, 2002); Announcement of Final Safe Harbor Policy, 64 Fed. Reg. 32,717 (1999) (Interior program enhancing private property protection); Suitum v. Tahoe Regional Planning Agency, 520 U.S. 725 (1997) (Lake Tahoe transferable development rights).

30. See 40 C.F.R. §§ 1502.4 , 1502.9(c), 1508.8(b), 1508.27(b)(4).

31. 42 U.S.C. §§ 4331(b)(1), 4332(2)(C)(iv), (v).

32. Daniel R. Mandelker, *NEPA Law and Litigation* ch. 12, § 13.01 (2d ed. 1992) (Supp. August 2000).

33. 16 U.S.C. §§ 1600–1614 (forests); 42 U.S.C. §§ 1701–1784 (fisheries); 16 U.S.C. §§ 1801–1883 (public lands); 16 U.S.C. §§ 1451–1464 (coastal zone); 30 U.S.C. §§ 181–287 (coal); 33 U.S.C. § 1288 (clean water); 42 U.S.C. §§ 6941–6949a (solid waste).

34. See, e.g., Mary Graham, *The Morning after Earth Day: Practical Environmental Politics* 46, 116 (1999).

35. 42 U.S.C. §§ 6924–6927 (2003) (Energy Policy Act of 1992); Richard B. Stewart, "A New Generation of Environmental Regulation," 29 *Cap. U. L. Rev.* 21 136–39 (2001); *"Errol E. Meidinger, Environmental Certification Programs and U.S. Environmental Law: Closer Than You May Think,"* 31 *Envtl. L. Rep.* 10,162, 10,178 (2001) (reproducing Forest Stewardship Council Principles and Standards); Mary Graham, *Democracy by Disclosure: The Rise of Technopopulism* 58–59 (2002).

36. Notice of Adoption of Amendments to Registration and Report Forms to Require Disclosure with Respect to Compliance with Environmental Requirements and Other Matters, Sec. Act Rel. No. 5,386, Sec. Ex. Act Rel. No. 10,116, 1 SEC Dock. 1 (April 20, 1973); Robert Repetto and Duncan Austin, *Coming Clean: Corporate Disclosure of Financially Significant Environmental Risks* (2000) (World Resources Institute publication); Robert Repetto and Duncan Austin, *Pure Profits: The Financial Implications of Environmental Performance* (2000) (World Resources Institute); Cynthia A. Williams, "The Securities and Exchange Commission and Corporate Transparency," 112 *Harv. L. Rev.* 1197, 1246–63 (1999).

37. J. Clarence Davies and Jan Mazurek, *Pollution Control in the United States: Evaluating the System* 29–30, 269, 289 (1998); Bradley Karkkainen, "Information as Environmental Regulation: TRI and Performance Benchmarking, Precursor to a New Paradigm?" 89 *Geo. L.J.* 257, 263–70 (2001).

38. Donald T. Hornstein, *Reclaiming Environmental Law: A Normative Critique of Comparative Risk Analysis,* 92 *Colum. L. Rev.* 562, 614–15 (1992).

39. Richard B. Stewart, "The Reformation of American Administrative Law," 88 *Harv. L. Rev.* 1669, 1670 (1975).

40. See Joseph L. Sax, "New Direction in Law," in *Environmental Law* 1–20 (Charles M. Hassert ed., 1971).

41. Sax, "Environmental Law and Regulation," at 224 (collection of essays on common heritage by distinguished British and American authors). See also Paul Slovic, "Perceived Risk, Trust, and Democracy," 13 *Risk Analysis* 675–82 (1993).

42. American Trucking Ass'n v. Browner,175 F.3d 1027,1036–37 (D.C. Cir. 1999), *reh'g granted in part,* 195 F.3d 4 (D.C. Cir. 1999), *rev'd and vacated,* 531 U.S.457 (2001).

43. Id. at 475.

44. Pub. L. No. 98-616, 98 Stat. 3224–87 (November 18, 1984); see 42 U.S.C. § 6924.

45. 42 U.S.C. §§ 7412, 7475(c), 7503, 7661a.

46. *Environmental Crimes Act of 1992, Hearings before the Subcomm. on Crime and Criminal Justice of the House Comm. on the Judiciary,* 102d Cong., 2d Sess. 14 (1992) (statement of Rep. Schumer).

47. See *Profile of Organized Crime: Great Lakes Region, Hearings before the Senate Comm. on Gov't Affairs, Permanent Subcomm. on Investigations,* 98th Cong., 2d Sess. 248–58, 277–82, 426–46, 475–91 (1984); *Profile of Organized Crime: Mid-Atlantic Region, Hearings before the Senate Comm. on Gov't Affairs, Permanent Subcomm. on Investigation,* 98th Cong., 1st Sess. 232–53, 248–58 (1983); A. A. Block and F. R. Scarpitti, *Poisoning for Profit: The Mafia and Toxic Waste in America* (1985); Timothy Egan, "Mob Looks at Recycling and Sees Green," *New York Times,* November 28, 1990, B1–2.

48. For a fuller discussion, see Richard J. Lazarus, "Meeting the Demands of Integration in the Evolution of Environmental Law: Reforming Environmental Criminal Law," 83 *Geo. L.J.* 2407 (1995).

49. Robert N. Stavins, "Market-Based Environmental Policies," in *Public Policies for Environmental Protection* (Paul Portney ed., 2000), at 35–41; "Finding of Significant Contribution and Rulemaking for Certain States in the Ozone Transport Assessment

Group Region for Purposes of Reducing Regional Transport of Ozone," 63 Fed. Reg. 57,356, 57,456 (1998); Jennifer 8. Lee, "E.P.A. Drafts New Rules for Emissions from Power Plants," *New York Times,* December 2, 2003, A24:3; Proposed National Emission Standards for Hazardous Air Pollutants, 69 Fed. Reg. 4,652 (2004).

50. E. Donald Elliott, "Toward Ecological Law and Policy," in *Thinking Ecologically: The Next Generation of Environmental Policy* (Marion R. Chertow and Daniel C. Esty eds., 1997), at 183; see Stewart, "New Generation of Environmental Regulation" at 63–77.

51. Lisa Heinzerling, "Selling Pollution, Forcing Democracy," 14 *Stan. Envtl. L.J.* 300 (1995).

52. James Salzman and J. B. Ruhl, "Currencies and the Commodification of Environmental Law," 53 *Stan. L. Rev.* 607, 627–30, 662–64 (2000); Jonathan Remy Nash and Richard L. Revesz, "Markets and Geography: Designing Marketable Permit Schemes to Control Local and Regional Pollutants," 28 *Ecology L.Q.* 569, 576–82 (2001); Lily N. Chinn, "Can the Market Be Fair and Efficient? An Environmental Justice Critique of Emissions Trading," 26 *Ecology L.Q.* 80 (1999).

53. See William F. Pedersen, "The Limits of Market-Based Approaches to Environmental Protection," 24 *Envtl. L. Rep.* 10,173 (1994); Oliver A. Houck, "The Clean Water Act TMDL Program V: Aftershock and Prelude," 32 *Envtl. L. Rep.* 10,385, 10,399 (2002); Susan Bruninga, "Draft Trading Policy Contains Safeguards, EPA Official Says, but Some Still Skeptical," 33 *BNA Envir. Rep. Curr. Dev.* 1391, 1392 (June 21, 2002).

54. Houck, "Clean Water Act TMDL Program," at 10,407.

55. 531 U.S. 159 (2001).

56. Id. at 162–67.

57. Id. at 172–74.

58. 42 U.S.C. §§ 7410, 7661a (CAA); 33 U.S.C. §§ 1288, 1313, 1342(b) (CWA); 42 U.S.C. §§ 6926, 6941 (RCRA); 30 U.S.C. §§ 1252–1254 (SMCRA).

59. Robert L. Fischman and Jaelith Hall-Rivera, "A Lesson for Conservation from Pollution Control Law: Cooperative Federalism for Recovery under the Endangered Species Act," 27 *Colum. J. Envtl. L.* 45, 89–132 (2002); 33 U.S.C. § 1344 (Clean Water Act); 16 U.S.C. § 1538 (Endangered Species Act); 43 U.S.C. §§ 371–431 (Reclamation Act); 16 U.S.C. §§ 791–825 (Federal Power Act); David H. Getches, "The Metamorphosis of Western Water Policy: Have Federal Laws and Local Decisions Eclipsed the State's Role?" 20 *Stan. Envtl. L.J.* 3, 52–59 (2000).

Chapter Nine

1. Robert C. Cowen, "Concern Grows over Danger Posed by Orbiting Space Junk," *Christian Science Monitor,* January 23, 1998, 9; see generally National Research Council of the National Academy of Science, *Orbital Debris: A Technical Assessment* (1995).

2. Rebecca Bratspies, "Finessing King Neptune: Fisheries Management and the Limits of International Law," 25 *Harv. Envtl. L. Rev.* 213, 217 (2001); see generally National Marine Fisheries Service, *Our Living Oceans: The Economic Status of U.S. Fisheries"* 1–3, 17–19 (1996).

3. Worldwatch Institute, *State of the World 2003,* 5–6 (2003).

4. Theo Colburn, Dianne Dumanoski, and John Peterson Myers, *Our Stolen Future* 40, 87, 122, 172–79, 189–91, 198–209 (1997).

5. Stephen Kern, *The Culture of Time and Space: 1880–1918,* 186, 222 (1983).

6. Laurence H. Tribe, "Ways Not to Think about Plastic Trees: New Foundations for Environmental Law," 83 *Yale L.J.* 1315 (1974).

7. Gerald Frug, *City Making: Building Communities without Building Walls* 101 (1999); James Gorman, "Getting Away, On the Web and From It," *New York Times,* June 13, 2002, E1:4; Sarah Krakoff, "Mountains without Handrails . . . Wilderness without Cellphones," 27 *Harv. Envtl. L. Rev.* 417 (2003).

8. United Nations Human Development Program, *Human Development Report 1998: Overview* 3–5 (1998); Hilary French, *Vanishing Borders: Protecting the Planet in the Age of Globalization* 71–85 (2000).

9. Ulrich Beck, *Ecological Enlightenment* 22–23 (1992).

10. Michael Janofsky, "Small Cars Losing the Parking-Space War," *New York Times,* June 18, 2002, A12:3; "Fuel Economy below Late 80's Levels, E.P.A. Says," *New York Times,* October 30, 2002, C4:3; Keith Brandsher, *High and Mighty—SUVs: The World's Most Dangerous Vehicles and How They Got That Way* 241 (2001).

11. Peter T. Kilborn, "Census Shows Bigger Houses and Incomes, but Not for All," *New York Times,* May 15, 2002, A14:5; Robert H. Frank, *Luxury Fever* 21 (1999); F. Kaid Benfield, Matthew D. Raimi, and Donald D. T. Chen, *Once There Were Greenfields* 5–10 (1999).

12. Betsy Otto, Katherine Ransel, Jason Todd, Deron Lovaas, Hannah Stuntzman, and John Bailey, *Paving Our Way to Water Shortages: How Sprawl Aggravates the Effects of Drought* 11 (2002).

13. Samara Joy Nielsen and Barry M. Popkin, "Patterns and Trends in Food Portion Size 1977–1998," 289 *JAMA* 450–53 (2003); Lisa R. Young and Marion Nestle, "The Contribution of Expanding Portion Sizes to the U.S. Obesity Epidemic," 92 *Am. J. Pub. Health* 246–49 (2002); U.S. Department of Health and Human Services, Office of the Surgeon General, *The Surgeon General's Call to Action to Prevent and Decrease Overweight and Obesity* (2001); Note, "The Elephant in the Room: Evolution, Behavioralism and Counter Advertising in the Coming War against Obesity," 116 *Harv. L. Rev.* 1161, 1161 (2003).

14. See Dan Tarlock, "The Nonequilibrium Paradigm in Ecology and the Partial Unraveling of Environmental Law, 27 *Loy. L.A. L. Rev.* 1121, 1126–27 (1994), quoting Eugene P. Odum, *Fundamentals of Ecology* 25 (2d ed. 1959).

15. Aldo Leopold, *A Sand County Almanac and Sketches Here and There* 225 (paperback ed. 1968).

16. S. Rep. 307, 93d Cong., 1st Sess. 2 (1973) (Endangered Species Act); 40 C.F.R. § 131.12 (2003) (EPA Clean Water Act antidegradation regulation); 42 U.S.C § 4331 (NEPA); 16 U.S.C. §§ 1131 et seq. (Wilderness Act); 16 U.S.C. §§ 1271 et seq. (Wild and Scenic Rivers Act).

17. Tarlock, "Nonequilibrium Paradigm," at 1129, quoting Bill McKibben, *The End of Nature* 190 (1989).

18. Marc Sagoff, "Ethics, Ecology, and the Environment: Integrating Science and the Law," 56 *Tenn. L. Rev.* 77, 82, 84–88, 211 (1988); Jonathan Bart Wiener, "Law and the New Ecology: Evolution, Categories, and Consequences," 22 *Ecology L.Q.* 325, 326 (1995). See generally Daniel B. Botkin, *Discordant Harmonies: A New Ecology for the Twenty First Century* (1990).

19. James Gleick, *Faster: The Acceleration of Just About Everything* (1999); Eric Schlosser, *Fast Food Nation: The Dark Side of the All American Meal* 3–4 (2001); Monte Williams, "Who Says You Can't Hurry Love?: Eight Minutes in the Life of a Jewish Single: Not Attracted? Next!" *New York Times,* March 5, 2000, sec. 1, p. 27; "We Believe in Rushing Things. Only Lavalife Can Have You Meeting People in 10 Minutes," *Washington City Paper,* May 24, 2002, 139 (advertisement); Debra Nussbaum, "How a Speeded-Up Society Trickles Down to Children; from Infancy to Academics, the Race Is On," *New York Times,* October 31, 1999, sec. 14 N.J. 1:2.

20. Gleick, *Faster,* at 4, 6–7, 41.

21. Ibid., 85–86.

22. U.S. Department of Commerce, Bureau of Census, *Statistical Abstract of the United States* 465, 597 (119th ed. 1999) (charts 729, 954).

23. John De Graff, David Wann, and Thomas H. Naylor, *Affluenza: The All Consuming Epidemic* 13 (2001).

24. Gretchen Morgenson, "Investing Longtime Best Bet Is Being Trampled by the Bulls," *New York Times,* January 15, 2000, A1:1; Gleick, *Faster,* at 75.

25. Gleick, *Faster,* at 143.

26. *Washington Post,* January 22, 2000, A19.

27. Gleick, *Faster,* at 98, 99, 140; Bob Spichen, "Tina Brown's New New Yorker: Its More Than Vanity Fair," *L.A. Times,* October 1, 1992, E1:2.

28. Nancy Keates, "Can We Fix It?" *Wall St. J.,* September 27, 2002, W1; Jane Spencer, Guaranteed to Last a Whole 90 Days," *Wall St. J.,* July 16, 2002, D1 (television retention); James Salzman, "Beyond the Smokestack: Environmental Protection in the Service Economy," 47 *UCLA L. Rev.* 424 n. 26 (1999) (silicon chips); Peter S. Goodman, "China Serves as Dump Site for Computers," *Washington Post,* February 24, 2003, A1.

29. James Brooke, "That Secure Feeling of Printed Document: The Paperless Office? Not by a Long Shot," *New York Times,* April 21, 2001, C1:2.

30. Alan Durning, *How Much Is Enough?* 29, 43–61 (1992); Herman Daly and John Cobb, *For the Common Good: Redirecting the Economy toward Community, the Environment, and a Sustainable Future* 44–61, 361–81 (1994); United Nations Human Development Program, *Human Development Report 1998,* at 1–2.

31. Quoted in DeGraff, Wann, and Naylor, *Affluenza,* at 3. See Bureau of Economic Analysis, National Income and Product Accounts Tables, Table 8.7 Selected Per Capita Product & Income Series and Table 2.2 Personal Consumption Expenditures by Major Type of Product, www.bea.doc.gov/bea/dn/nipaweb/ TableViewFixed.asp#Mid (visited February 6, 2003).

32. Paul Erlich, Gary Wolff, Gretchen C. Daily, Jennifer B. Hughes, Scott Daily, Michael Dalton, and Lawrence Goulder, "Knowledge and the Environment," 30 *Eco-*

logical Econ. 267, 270–72, 274–77 (1999); U.S. Department of Transportation, Federal Highway Administration, Office of Highway Policy Information, *Gross Domestic Product (GDP) and Vehicle-Miles Travel (VMT) 1960–2000,* available at www.fhwa.dot. gov/onh00/table4.htm (visited May 6, 2002).

33. Richard N. L. Andrews, *Managing the Environment, Managing Ourselves: A History of American Environmental Policy* 229 (1999); Bureau of Census, *Statistical Abstract of the United States,* at 597 (chart 954); Allen R. Myerson, "Power Hungry: U.S. Splurging on Energy after Falling Off Its Diet," *New York Times,* October 22, 1998, A1:4; see U.S. Department of Energy, Energy Information Agency, *Annual Energy Review 2000,* 38 (2000) (table 2.1a).

34. Leopold, *Sand County Almanac,* at 6.

35. Durning, *How Much is Enough?* at 55 ("The ecological wakes of the blouse, car, and strawberry—like the production lines themselves—span the globe."); DeGraff, Wann, and Naylor, *Affluenza,* at 88 (waste in home computer).

36. United Nations Human Development Program, *Human Development Report 1998,* at 3–5 (1998); Goodman, "China Serves as Dump Site for Computers," at A1.

37. Barton H. Thompson, "Tragically Difficult, The Obstacles to Governing the Commons," 30 *Ecology L.Q.* 241, 258–59 (2000).

38. Intergovernmental Panel on Climate Change, *Climate Change 2001: The Scientific Basis* (United Nations Environment Program 2001); National Research Council of the National Academy of Sciences, *Climate Change Science: An Analysis of Some Key Questions* (December 2001); Katharine Q. Seelye and Andrew C. Revkin, "Panel Tells Bush Global Warming Is Getting Worse," *New York Times,* June 7, 2001, A1:5.

39. Intergovernmental Panel on Climate Change, *Climate Change 2001: Impacts, Adaptation, and Vulnerability* (United Nations Environment Program 2001); National Research Council of the National Academy of Sciences, Committee on Climate, Ecosystems, Infectious Diseases, and Human Health, Board on Atmospheric Sciences and Climate, *Under the Weather: Climate, Ecosystems, and Infectious Disease* (2001); Alison Mitchell, "Democrats See Gold in Environment," *New York Times,* April 22, 2001, sec. 1, p. 20, col. 1; T. L. Root et al., "Fingerprints of Global Warming on Wild Animals and Plants," 421 *Nature* 57–60 (2003); Andrew C. Revkin, "Global Warming Found to Displace Species," *New York Times,* January 2, 2003, A1:3.

40. Thompson, "Tragically Difficult," at 259–60, 277; Jonathan B. Wiener, "Responding to Global Warming Problem: Something Borrowed for Something Blue: Legal Transplants and the Evolution of Global Environmental Law," 27 *Ecology L.Q.* 1295 (2001).

41. Robert Putnam, *Bowling Alone: The Collapse and Revival of American Community* 19, 155–61, 191, 212–13, 255–75 (2000).

42. Gary Gardner, "Engaging Religion in the Quest for a Sustainable World," in *State of the World 2003* (Worldwatch Institute 2003), at 152, quoting National Council of Churches, available at www.webofcreation.org/ncc/anwr.html; Sagoff, "Ethics, Ecology, and the Environment," at 159–60, 197–204; Jim Motavelli, "The Growing Religious Mission to Protect the Environment: Stewards of the Earth," *XIII E—The Environmen-*

tal Magazine, November–December 2002, 24; Mary Evelyn Tucker and John A. Grim, eds., "Religion and Ecology: Can the Climate Change," 130 *Daedalus* 23–31, 99–242 (2001).

43. Bruce Guile and Jared Cohen, "Sorting Out a Service-Based Economy," in *Thinking Ecologically: The Next Generation of Environmental Protection* (Marion R. Chertow and Daniel C. Esty eds., 1997), at 76–77.

44. Ibid.; Salzman, "Beyond the Smokestack," at 449–500.

45. Ulricht Beck, *Risk Society: Toward a New Modernity* 37–38 (Mark Ritter trans., 1992).

46. Daniel C. Esty, "Environmental Protection in the Information Age," Yale Law School Public Law and Legal Theory Research Paper Series, Research Paper No. 58 (Draft July 2003), 44–50 (forthcoming 79 *N.Y.U. L. Rev.* [2004]).

47. Paul Hawken, Amory Lovins, and L. Hunter Lovins, *Natural Capitalism: Creating the Next Industrial Revolution* 9–21, 260–84 (1999); Redefining Progress, www.rprogress.org (Web site of nonprofit public policy organization "that creates policies and tools to encourage accurate market prices, to protect our common social and natural assets, and to foster social and economic sustainability").

48. Guile and Cohen, "Sorting Out a Service-Based Economy"; Salzman, "Beyond the Smokestack," at 454–59, 461–64, 468–69, 477–79; Hawken, Lovins, and Lovins, *Natural Capitalism,* at 11–20.

49. Clifford Rechtschaffen, "How to Reduce Lead Exposures with One Simple Statute: The Experience of Proposition 65," 29 *Envtl. L. Rep.* 10,581 (1999); EPA, *Air Data: Access to Air Pollution Data,* www.epa.gov/air/data/index.html (visited February 25, 2003); EPA, *Cumulative Exposure Project,* www.epa.gov/cumulativeexposure/index.htm (visited February 25, 2003).

50. Daniel C. Esty, "Next Generation Environmental Law: A Response to Richard Stewart," 29 *Cap. U. L. Rev.* 183, 202–3 (2001); E. Donald Elliott, "Environmental Markets and Beyond: Three Modest Proposals for the Future of Environmental Law," 29 *Cap. U. L. Rev.* 245, 251, 257–64 (2001).

51. Richard B. Stewart, "A New Generation of Environmental Regulation," 29 *Cap. U. L. Rev.* 21, 130–31, 151.

52. Eric W. Orts, "Reflexive Environmental Law," 89 *Nw. U. L. Rev.* 1227 (1995).

53. EPA Science Advisory Board, *Reducing Risk: Setting Priorities and Strategies for Environmental Protection* 15 (1990).

54. National Academy of Sciences, *Nature's Numbers: Expanding the National Economic Accounts to Include the Environment* (William D. Nordhaus and Edward C. Kokkelenberg, eds., 1999).

55. See Daniel C. Esty, "What is the Most Compelling Environmental Issue Facing the World on the Brink of the Twenty-first Century: Stepping Up to the Global Environmental Challenge," 8 *Fordham Envtl. L. Rev.* 103 (1996); Steve Charnovitz, "A World Environment Organization," 27 *Colum. J. Envtl. L.* 323 (2002); see generally *Institutions for the Earth: Sources of Effective International Environmental Protection* (Peter M. Haas, Roberts O. Keohane, and Marc A. Levy eds., 1993).

56. Edith Brown Weiss, "International Environmental Law: Contemporary Issues and the Emergence of a New World Order," 81 *Geo. L.J.* 675, 699–700 (1993); Daniel C. Esty, "The Value of Creating a Global Environmental Organization," *Environment Matters Annual Review* 13–14 (2000).

57. Ruth Greenspan Bell, "Developing a Culture of Compliance in the International Environmental Regime," 27 *Envtl. L. Rep.* 10,402 (1997).

58. Esty, "Value of Creating a Global Environmental Organization," at 14; see also Frank Bierman, "The Case for a World Environmental Organization," *Environment* 23 (November 2000).

59. C. Ford Runge, "A Global Environmental Organization (GEO) and the World Trading System," 35 *J. World Trade* 399 (2001); Daniel C. Esty, "GATTing the Greens: Not Just Greening the GATT," *Foreign Affairs,* November–December 1993, 32; Jeffrey L. Dunoff, "Resolving Trade-Environment Conflicts: The Case for Trading Institutions," 1994 *Cornell Int'l L.J.* 607 (1994).

Chapter Ten

1. Daniel Farber, "Politics and Procedure in Environmental Law," 8 *J.L. Econ. & Organ.* 59, 66 (1992), quoting James G. Pope, "Republican Moments: The Role of Diverse Popular Power in the American Constitutional Order," 139 *U. Pa. L. Rev.* 287, 291 (1990).

2. See Jonathan Z. Cannon and Jonathan Riehl, Presidential Greenspeak: How Presidents Talk about the Environment and What It Means (Working Paper Draft, December 2002) (describing common presidential rhetoric); compare "American Partners in Conservation and Preservation: Stewardship of Our Natural Resources," in Official Platform of the National Republican Party, available at www.rnc.org/GOPInfo/Platform/2000platform6.htm (visited January 7, 2003) with "Protecting Our Environment," in Official 2000 Platform of the National Democratic Party, available at www.democrats.org/about/2000platform.html (visited January 7, 2003).

3. See Daniel A. Farber and Paul A. Hemmersbaugh, "The Shadow of the Future: Discount Rates, Later Generations, and the Environment," 46 *Vand L. Rev.* 267, 279–87 (1993); Lisa Heinzerling, "Environmental Law and the Present Future," 87 *Geo. L.J.* 2025 (1999); compare Lisa Heinzerling, "Discounting Life," 108 *Yale L.J.* 1911 (1999) with John J. Donohue III, "Why We Should Discount the Views of Those Who Discount Discounting," 108 *Yale L.J.* 1901 (1999).

4. See, e.g., "Official Platform of the National Republican Party" ("We link the security of private property to our environmental agenda for the best of reasons: Environmental stewardship has best advanced where property is privately held."); ibid., ("Wherever it is environmentally responsible to do so, we will promote market-based programs that are voluntary, flexible, comprehensive, and cost-effective."); Official 2000 Platform of the National Democratic Party ("The Republicans have tried to sell off national parks; gut air, water, and endangered species protections; let polluters off the hook; and put the special interests ahead of the people's interest. . . . [W]e must dramatically reduce climate-disrupting and health-threatening pollution in this country,

while making sure that all nations of the world participate in this effort. Environmental standards should be raised throughout the world in order to preserve the Earth and to prevent a destructive race to the bottom.").

5. Rewriting the Rules, report prepared by the Majority Staff of the Senate Comm. on Governmental Affairs (October 24, 2002); Alison Mitchell, "Democrats See Gold in Environment," *New York Times,* April 22, 2001, sec. 1, p. 20, col. 1; "Clueless on Global Warming," *New York Times,* July 19, 2001, A24:1 (editorial); "No Greens Need Apply," *New York Times,* August 19, 2001, sec. 4, p.12, col. 1 (editorial); "More Environmental Rollbacks," *New York Times,* October 29, 2001, A10:1 (editorial); Katharine Q. Seelye, "Bush Team Is Reversing Environmental Policies," *New York Times,* November 18, 2001, A20:5; "Poor Marks on the Environment," *New York Times,* January 28, 2002, A14:1 (editorial); "Park Rangers with Respirators," *New York Times,* March 6, 2002, A20:1 (editorial); "Landscapes under Siege," *New York Times,* March 7, 2002, A30:1 (editorial); "Nature Overrun," *New York Times,* April 4, 2002, A22:1 (editorial); "Parks under Siege," *New York Times,* April 24, 2002, A26:1 (editorial); "Grizzlies at Risk," *New York Times,* May 19, 2002, sec. 4, p. 14, col. 1 (editorial); Thomas B. Edsall, "Federalist Society Becomes a Force in Washington; Conservative Group's Members Take Key Roles in Bush White House and Help Shape Policy and Judicial Appointments," *Washington Post,* April 18, 2001, A4; Douglas Jehl and Andrew C. Revkin, "Bush in Reversal, Won't Seek Cut in Emissions of Carbon Dioxide," *New York Times,* March 14, 2001, A1:4; David E. Sanger, "Bush Will Continue to Oppose Kyoto Pact on Global Warming," *New York Times,* June 12, 2001, A1:1; National Energy Policy Development Group, *National Energy Policy: Reliable, Affordable, and Environmentally Sound Energy for America's Future* (May 2001); David E. Sanger, "Energy Plan Urges New Drilling, Conservation and Nuclear Power Review," *New York Times,* May 17, 2001, A1:6; Don Van Natta Jr. and Neela Banerjee, "Bush Energy Plan Followed Industry Push," *New York Times,* March 27, 2002, A20:1; "One-Way Discussion of Energy," *New York Times,* March 28, 2002, A30:1 (editorial).

6. Douglas Jehl, "E.P.A. to Abandon New Arsenic Limits for Water Supply," *New York Times,* March 21, 2001, A1:4; Katharine Q. Seelye, "E.P.A. to Adopt Clinton Arsenic Standard," *New York Times,* November 1, 2001, A18:1; Katharine Q. Seelye, "Draft of Air Rule Is Said to Exempt Many Old Plants," *New York Times,* August 22, 2003, A1:1; Matthew L. Wald, "E.P.A. Says It Will Change Rules Governing Industrial Pollution," *New York Times,* November 23, 2002, A1:1; 67 Fed. Reg. 80,186 (2002) (EPA's new final "new source review" rules); 68 Fed. Reg. 58,172 (2003) (EPA's now final changes to the meaning of "routine maintenance"); Christopher Drew and Richard A. Oppel Jr., "Lawyers At E.P.A. Say It Will Drop Pollution Cases," *New York Times*, November 6, 2003, A1:6; Bruce Barcott, "Up in Smoke—The Bush Administration, the Big Power Companies and the Undoing of 30 Years of Clean Air Policy," *New York Times Magazine,* April 4, 2004, 38; Eric Pianin, "EPA Jettisons Clinton Rule on Cleaning Up Waterways," *Washington Post,* December 21, 2002, A2; 66 Fed. Reg. 53,044 (2001); Katharine Q. Seelye, "Bush Proposing Changes on Toxic Sites," *New York Times,* February 24, 2002, sec. 1, p. 1, col. 5; Katharine Q. Seelye, "Bush Slashing Aid for E.P.A. Cleanup at

33 Toxic Sites," *New York Times,* July 1, 2002, A1:6; "Shortchanging Superfund," *New York Times,* July 6, 2002, A12:1 (editorial); "Burying Valleys, Poisoning Streams," *New York Times,* May 4, 2002, A12:1 (editorial); Control of Emissions from New Highway Vehicles and Engines, 68 Fed. Reg. 52,922 (2003) (EPA denial of petition to regulate carbon dioxide and other greenhouse gases from motor vehicles under the Clean Air Act); Kirk Johnson and Jennifer 8. Lee, "When Breathing Is Believing, New Yorkers Doubt E.P.A. Credibility on Air Safety, but Truth Is Complex," *New York Times,* November 30, 2003, sec. 1, 37:3; Andrew C. Revkin and Katharine Q. Seelye, "Report By E.P.A. Leaves Out Data on Climate Change," *New York Times,* June 19, 2003, A1:1; Jennifer 8. Lee, "Critics Say E.P.A. Won't Analyze Clean Air Proposals Conflicting with President's Policies," *New York Times,* July 14, 2003, A9:1; Mike Ferullo, "EPA Figures Show Sharp Decreases in Criminal, Civil Penalties for Fiscal 2002," 34 *BNA Envtl. Rep. Curr. Dev.* 314 (2003); Katharine Q. Seelye, "E.P.A. Official Quits, Criticizing Bush's Policies," *New York Times,* March 1, 2002, A19:5; "EPA Official Quits after Move," *New York Times,* April 23, 2002, B2:6.

7. Mining Claims under the General Mining Laws, 66 Fed. Reg. 54,834 (2001); Katharine Q. Seelye, "Bush White House Reverses Clinton Decision on Mining," *New York Times,* October 26, 2001, A14:5; Timothy Egan, "Bush Administration Allows Oil Drilling Near Utah Parks," *New York Times,* February 8, 2002, A14:1; Katharine Q. Seelye, "Bush Team Is Reversing Environmental Policies," *New York Times,* November 18, 2001, A20:5; "Park Rangers with Respirators," *New York Times,* March 6, 2002, A20:1 (editorial); "Interior Ends Clinton Mining Moratorium on 1 Million Acres in Southwestern Oregon," 33 *BNA Envtl. Rep. Curr. Dev.* 1208 (2002); Michael Grunwald, "Interior Drilling Won't Violate Polar Bear Pac; Stance Contradicts Wildlife Agency's Drafts," *Washington Post,* January 18, 2002, A23; Michael Grunwald, "Warnings on Oil Drilling Reversed; US Quickly Revises Arctic Caribou Study," *Washington Post,* April 7, 2002, A1; Don Van Natta Jr., "Video Inspires New Dispute over Alaska Refuge Drilling," *New York Times,* April 12, 2002, A22:1.

8. The prior Clinton administration's national forest planning rules were published at 36 C.F.R. pt. 219 (2002). The new rules of the Forest Service under the Bush administration are set forth at 68 Fed. Reg. 33,814 (2003). See Robert Pear, "Bush Plan Gives More Discretion to Forest Managers on Logging," *New York Times,* November 28, 2002, A1:1. The Clinton administration's national forest roadless rules were published at 66 Fed. Reg. 3244 (2001), from which the Bush administration has since distanced itself. Elizabeth Shogren, "A Natural Split with Bush, and Many Quit; Environment: Longtime, Key Officials Who Favor Conservation Say They Are Frustrated by New Rules," *L.A. Times,* June 3, 2002, A1; Douglas Jehl, "Forest Service Chief Quits, and Asks Bush to Hold Firm," *New York Times,* March 28, 2001, A19:1; Kootenai Tribe of Idaho v. Veneman, 313 F.3d 1094 (9th Cir. 2002) (upholding Clinton administration's Forest Service rules); Mike Ferullo, "Administration Argues Appeal of Decision Striking Down Roadless Rules," 34 *BNA Envtl. Rep. Curr. Dev.* 2557 (2003).

9. See John D. Graham and Jonathan B. Weiner, *Risk versus Risk: Risk Tradeoffs in Protecting Health and the Environment* (1995); Cindy Skrzycki, "OMB Proposes Changes

in Federal Rulemaking; Agencies Would Be Required to Do More Analyses of Risks, Costs and Benefits," *Washington Post,* February 4, 2002, A7; Public Citizen, *Safeguards at Risk: John Graham and Corporate America's Back Door to the Bush White House* (2001).

10. See, e.g., 33 U.S.C. § 1369(b) (Clean Water Act judicial review provision); 42 U.S.C. § 6976(a)(1) (Resource Conservation and Recovery Act judicial review provision); 42 U.S.C. § 7607(b) (Clean Air Act judicial review provision).

11. Richard J. Pierce Jr., "Two Problems in Administrative Law: Political Polarity on the District of Columbia Circuit and Judicial Deference of Agency Rulemaking," 1988 *Duke L.J.* 300, 301.

12. Richard Revesz, "Environmental Regulation, Ideology, and the D.C. Circuit," 83 *Va. L. Rev.* 1717, 1717–18, 1719 (1997).

13. Frank B. Cross and Emerson H. Tiller, "Judicial Partisanship and Obedience to Legal Doctrine: Whistleblowing on the Federal Courts of Appeals," 107 *Yale L.J.* 2155, 2175 (1998).

14. Richard J. Pierce Jr., "Is Standing Law or Politics?" 77 *N.C. L. Rev.* 1741, 1760 (1999).

15. Neil A. Lewis, "The 2000 Campaign, The Judiciary: Presidential Candidates Differ Sharply on Judges They Would Appoint to the High Court," *New York Times,* October 8, 2000, sec.1, 28:1 ("the influential group of Republicans eagerly hoping to gain control of the White House and the nominating procedure has adopted 'No More Souters' as its private slogan").

16. Ibid.

17. See Alaska Dep't of Environmental Conservation, U.S. Sup. Ct. No. 02-658 (decided January 21, 2004); Engine Manufacturers Ass'n v. South Coast Air Quality, U.S. Sup. Ct. No. 02-1343 (decided April 28, 2004); South Florida Water Management Dist. v. Miccosukee Tribe, U.S. Sup. Ct. No. 02-626 (decided March 23, 2004); Norton v. Utah Wilderness Alliance, U.S. Sup. Ct. No. 03-101 (*cert. granted,* November 3, 2003); Cheney v. U.S. District Court for the District of Columbia, U.S. Sup. Ct. No. 03-475 (*cert. granted,* December 15, 2003); DOT v. Public Citizen, U.S. Sup. Ct. No. 03-358 (decided June 7, 2004).

18. Richard J. Lazarus, "The Greening of America and the Graying of United States Environmental Law: Reflections on Environmental Law's First Three Decades in the United States," 20 *Va. Envtl. L.* 75, 85–88, 90–95 (2001).

19. Eric Pianin and Helen Dewar, "Oil, Air, Energy Laws in Play: Environmentalists Fear New Senate," *Washington Post,* November 18, 2002, A1; Environmental Scorecard 2002, official Web site of the League of Conservation Voters, www.lcv.org/scorecard/index.asp (last visited January 8, 2003).

20. John B. Judis, *The Paradox of American Democracy: Elites, Special Interests, and the Betrayal of the Public Trust* 199–200 (2000).

21. Senator John McCain, "Nature Is Not a Liberal Plot," *New York Times,* November 22, 1996, A31:2.

22. The Environment: A Cleaner, Safer, Healthier America, The Luntz Research

Companies: Straight Talk, www.ewg.org/pdf/LuntzResearch_environment.pdf (site visited March 14, 2003).

23. John H. Cushman Jr., "E.P.A. and States Found to Be Lax on Pollution Law," *New York Times,* June 7, 1998, sec. 1, 1:6.

24. *The Federal–State Relationship: A Look into EPA's Reinvention Efforts, Hearings before the Subcomm. on Oversight and Investigation of the House Comm. on Commerce,* 105th Cong., 1st Sess. (1997); Rena Steinzor, "Reinventing Environmental Regulation through the Government Performance and Results Act: Are the States Ready for the Devolution?" 29 *Envtl. L. Rep.* 10,074, 10,082 (1999).

25. Jennifer 8. Lee, "The Warming Is Global but the Legislation in the U.S. Is All Local," *New York Times,* October 29, 2003, A20:1; Katharine Q. Seelye, "9 Northeast States File Suit over New Rules on Pollution," *New York Times,* January 1, 2003, A1:1; Eric Pianin, "New Pollution Standards Prompt Suit; 9 States Challenge U.S. Decision to Relax Rules," *Washington Post,* January 1, 2003, A1; Matthew L. Wald, "E.P.A. Says It Will Change Rules Governing Industrial Pollution," *New York Times,* November 23, 2002, A1:1; Jennifer 8. Lee, "7 States to Sue E.P.A. over Standards on Air Pollution," *New York Times,* February 21, 2003, A25:3; Richard A. Oppel Jr. and Christopher Drew, "States Planning Own Lawsuits over Pollution," *New York Times,* November 9, 2003, sec. 1, 1:5.

26. Danny Hakim, "At Front on Pollution," July 3, 2002, A1:5); "California Leads on Warming," *New York Times,* July 8, 2002, A18:1.

27. News release, California Department of Justice. "Attorney General Lockyer Files Challenge to Bush Administration Proposal to Relax Clean Air Requirements" (February 27, 2003); see Cal. Health & Safety Code §§ 43018(b), (c); 13 C.R.R. § 1962.

Conclusion

1. Devra L. Davis, *When Smoke Ran Like Water* 117–18 (2002), citing David Mastio, "Automakers Thrive under EPA Rules: Early Predictions of Economic Damage Never Materialized," *Detroit News,* May 8, 2000, 7A; Robert D. Brenner, "Clean Air Act: Progress and Challenges Ahead," 20 *St. Louis U. Pub. L. Rev.* 7, 8 (2001).

2. John Brooks Flippen, *Nixon and the Environment* 135 (2000).

3. John Brooks Flippen, The Nixon Administration, Politics and the Environment 287–88 (Ph.D. diss., University of Maryland, 1994).

Index

abandoned dump sites, x, 107, 108, 240
Abraham, Spencer, 239–40
Acid Deposition Program, 184, 200, 201
acid rain, 145, 200, 201, 236, 252
Adams, John, 84
adaptation to ecological change, 11
Addams, Jane, 52
administrative law, 48, 114, 190
adversarialism, 87, 90, 91
Advertising Council, 96
aerosol cans, 20
Agnew, Spiro, 78
agriculture: fertilizers, 210; runoff, 17, 159; as share of U.S. GDP, 226; suburbanization using prime farmland, 212. *See also* Department of Agriculture; pesticides
air: national accounting practices failing to account for, 231; as shared resource, 25–26. *See also* air pollution
AIRData, 230
Airlie House Conference (Conference on Law and the Environment) (1969), 47–48, 260n2
air pollution: air pollution "banks," 143; automobile industry promoting federal legislation on, 91; George H. W. Bush administration on, 106, 240; city and state laws on, 54; Clinton administration initiatives, ix, 158–59, 160; complexity of setting standards for, 17; decrease since 1970,

x; diffuse sources of, 232; federal legislation of 1950s and 1960s, 52–53; federal legislation of 1970s, 70; mid-twentieth-century concern about, 52; nineteenth- and early-twentieth-century concern about, 51; nonpoint sources of, 228; on-line data base on, 230; ozone emissions, 158, 160, 200; particulate matter, 17, 158, 160, 252; and political boundaries, 36, 71, 93, 143, 148, 159, 181–82, 236, 259n4; service industries as source of, 226; Wilson's 1859 paper on, 5. *See also* Clean Air Act
Air Pollution Control Act (1955), 52
Air Quality Act (1967), 52
air travel, 55, 62
Alaska: Arctic National Wildlife Refuge, 127, 225, 241, 247; federal land ownership in, 50, 93; nuclear weapons test planned for Amchitka Island, 77; oil pipeline in, 78
Alaska National Interest Lands Conservation Act (ANILCA) (1980), 98, 107
Amazon, 25
Amchitka Island, 77
American Antiquities Act (1906), 33, 49
American Bar Association, 115
American Council on Science and Health, 95
American Electric Power Company, 96

bicycles, 55, 56
Billings, Leon, 84
Bill of Rights, 28, 29, 38–39
Bingaman, Jeff, 247
biodegradability, 63
biodiversity: Biodiversity Convention, 127, 147; international legal instruments lacking for, 234
biosphere, 6
Black, Hugo, 65
Blackmun, Harry, 134, 275n18
Black Sea, 11
blue jeans, pre-faded, 218
Boehlert, Sherwood, 246
Bookchin, Murray, 58
Borneo, 11, 25
Boston Harbor, 105, 126
bounded domain, 39–40
BPT (best practicable control technology), 174, 197
Breyer, Stephen, 244
Brooke, Edward, III, 151
Brower, David, 83, 90
Browner, Carol, 131, 149, 157, 158–59, 160, 178
budgetary reductions, 130
Buffalo (New York), 108
Bullard, Robert, 138
Bulletin of Atomic Scientists, 61
Bureau of Land Management, 94, 102
Burford, Robert, 102
Bush, George H. W.: conservative judicial appointments of, 132; considered for administrator of Environmental Protection Agency, 76; cross-media approach of, 169; and Federalist Society, 120; opposition to environmental protection legislation, xii, 126–27; as presidential candidate in 1988, 105–6, 126, 151; on Task Force on Regulatory Relief, 100; as vice-presidential candidate in 1980, 98
Bush, George W.: California opposition to, 250; environmental policy of, xii–xiii, 239–42; and grandfathering existing facilities, 281n13; and Jeffords, xiii, 246; on Kyoto Protocol, xii, 222, 240, 249; on Scalia and

Thomas, 244; tradeable emissions program of, 184, 200
business (industry): and George H. W. Bush, 126–27; and Clinton administration policies, 157–58, 160; and Contract with America, 129, 130; on cost of pollution control, 92, 167; and demise of bipartisanship on environmental policy, 153, 156; environmental law opposed by, 94–97, 122; Environmental Protection Agency opposed by, 88; grassroots environmentalists opposing, 123; information technology for changing business norms, 230–31; "paying to pollute," 232; pollution control credits for, 232–33; pollution control industry, xiii, 162; public distrust of, 117; Reagan trying to make environmental policy more friendly to, 98, 99, 100, 102, 104; shift in attitudes in 1990s, 161–65

CAA. *See* Clean Air Act
cadmium, 10
Caldwell, Keith, 68
California: automobile emissions requirements of, 91–92; oil and gas drilling off shore of, 119, 126; Proposition 65, 112–13, 164, 187, 229, 230; relinquishes control over Yosemite National Park, 36; as resuming leadership role in new millennium, 250; whale watching industry of, 280n82
campaign donations, 40, 79, 156
cancer: carcinogens, 59, 108, 112; pollution linked to, 52
cap and trade programs, 200–201
carbon: accelerating rates of releases of, 13, 210; carbon tax, 198; cycle of, 6, 256n4; destruction of natural "sinks," 210, 221; hydrocarbons, 70; soil and, 7, 9
carbon dioxide: and Amazon rainforest destruction, 25; George W. Bush administration on, 240; climatic change resulting from emissions, 210; in greenhouse effect, 8, 20, 240; human effect on levels of, 9, 10; in

free market: constitutional preference for, 38, 39; market in tradeable emissions rights, 183–84, 200–202, 222, 233; partisan divide over, 239; preservation versus market value, 28
free riders, 41
free trade, 146–48, 149, 235
Friends of the Earth, 83, 90
frontier, closing of the, 56, 209
FWPCA. *See* Federal Water Pollution Control Act Amendments

gas, natural. *See* natural gas
gasoline, 200
General Agreement on Tariffs and Trade (GATT), 147–48, 235
General Mining Law (1872), 181
Geyelin, Philip, 96
Gingrich, Newt, viii, 246
Ginsburg, Ruth Bader, 244
glass windows, 212
Global Environment Facility, 235
globalization, economic, 146, 213, 220–21, 227
global warming: allocating burdens of addressing, 222; and Amazon rainforest destruction, 25; greenhouse effect, 8, 20, 222, 240; international negotiations over, 145, 149; state laws for reducing emissions, 249; threshold character of, 14; uncertainty about causality of, 20
Gore, Al, 128, 131, 139
Gorsuch, Anne Burford, 101; business community's shift in attitudes and, 162; congressional scrutiny of, 118–19; deregulatory agenda of, 101, 102; environmental laws as stronger despite, 116, 117; as Environmental Protection Agency administrator, 101; news reports hostile to, 117–18; as polarizing, 104; Ruckelshaus replaces, 105
Grad, Frank, 261n5
Graham, John D., 241–42
grandfathering of existing facilities, 175, 281n13
grassroots environmental organizations, 122–24, 137–40, 223

Gray, Oscar S., 261n5
greenhouse effect, 8, 20, 222, 240
Greenpeace, 83
Green Seal program, 188
grizzly bears, 241

habitat: conservation, 157, 206, 231; destruction, 13, 63, 232; wildlife refuges, 49, 107
Haldeman, Bob, 77
Hamilton, Alice, 51
Hardin, Garrett, 2
"hard look" doctrine, 48, 81, 114
Harris, Robert, 102
Harvard University Center for Risk Analysis, 241
Hatfield, Mark, 152
Hazardous Materials Transportation Act, 53
hazardous waste: Basel Convention on the Control of Transboundary Movement of Hazardous Waste, 147; clandestine dumping of, 195; complexity of defining, 18; Comprehensive Environmental Response Compensation and Liability Act on, 107–10; exportation of, 149; household, 232; Reagan administration court cases regarding, 269n17; Resource Conservation and Recovery Act on, 73. *See also* Resource Conservation and Recovery Act; toxic substances
health. *See* human health
health-based environmental performance standards, 197–99
Heritage Foundation, 95, 96, 100
high schools, shopping malls outnumbering, 217
highways, 212, 232
Hines, Bill, 48
Historic Sites, Buildings and Antiquities Act (1935), 49
Home Depot, 229
Homestead Act (1862), 181
Hoover Institute, 96
house size, 214
Hubble space telescope, 209
human genome project, 211